RESEARCH IN
COMMUNITY
AND
MENTAL HEALTH

Volume 1 • 1979

RESEARCH IN COMMUNITY AND MENTAL HEALTH

An Annual Compilation of Research

Editor: ROBERTA G. SIMMONS
 Department of Sociology
 University of Minnesota

VOLUME 1 • 1979

 JAI PRESS INC.
Greenwich, Connecticut

ISBN NUMBER: 0-89232-063-X

Manufactured in the United States of America

CONTENTS

RESEARCH IN COMMUNITY AND MENTAL HEALTH

Volume 1 • 1979

Part I

CHILDREN AND MENTAL
HEALTH

GROUP REJECTION AND SELF-REJECTION*

Morris Rosenberg, UNIVERSITY OF MARYLAND

The idea that rejection of one's group is conducive to rejection of one's self is rooted in a long theoretical and empirical tradition. One of the most important early statements of this position appeared in a series of articles by Kurt Lewin (1948) on the theme of "self-hatred among Jews," which has since strongly influenced social psychological thought on minority group membership.

In the period of the European ghetto, Lewin pointed out, Jews were confined to special sections of the city, were restricted in their freedom of occupational choice, and were easily recognized by their yellow badge, special garb, and other overt signs. Such stigmatization and restriction generated a good deal of stress and tension, but at least there was no

Research in Community and Mental Health, Vol. 1, pp 3–20.

problem of self-identification. The Jew accepted himself as a Jew and identified as a Jew. With the emancipation, however, Jews were able to expand into the broader society and were no longer easily distinguished from the general population. But social boundaries in the form of prejudice remained. Seeking to achieve acceptance into the higher-status group, the Jew's ties with his religious group weakened; at the same time, prejudice prevented the Jew from achieving complete acceptance by the outside group. Socially identified as a Jew, he experienced ambivalent self-identification and self-hatred.

Speaking of mid-twentieth century America, Lewin argued that the Jew "dislikes or hates his own group because it is nothing but a burden to him. . . . A Jew of this type will dislike everything specifically Jewish, for he will see in it that which keeps him away from the majority for which he is longing. He will show dislike for those Jews who are outspokenly so and will frequently indulge in self-hatred" (Lewin, 1948:164). In one way or another, numerous writers have returned to this theme (Cartwright, 1950; Kardiner and Ovesey, 1951; Silberman, 1964; Proshansky and Newton, 1968; Gordon, 1972; Grier and Cobbs, 1968; Trimble, 1974), although in recent years the focus has been on blacks, with increasing attention to other minority groups such as Puerto Ricans, Mexican-Americans, and American Indians.

When one examines the term "self-hatred" more carefully, it becomes apparent that two different meanings are involved. The first is hatred or rejection of one's *self* as a person, i.e., *individual* self-hatred or low self-esteem. Lewin's primary interest, on the other hand, was in what might be called "group self-hatred," i.e., rejection of, or disidentification with, one's *group* (e.g., religion, race, class, nationality). Most writers appear to assume that, since one's group is an important part of one's self, rejection or hatred of that group reflects rejection or hatred of oneself. According to Proshansky and Newton (1968): "The Negro who feels disdain or hatred for his own racial group is expressing—at some level of awareness—disdain or hatred for himself."

Erik Erikson (1966:155) echoes this view: "The individual belonging to an oppressed and exploited minority, which is aware of the dominant cultural ideals but prevented from emulating them, is apt to fuse the negative images held up to him by the dominant majority with his own negative identity. . . . There is ample evidence of 'inferiority' feelings and of morbid self-hate in all minority groups; . . ."

The implication of such observations is that group self-hatred either constitutes individual self-hatred or inevitably generates it. Yet a moment's reflection makes it evident that it is at least logically possible to reject one's group but respect oneself, and vice versa. The issue we thus wish to examine in this paper is the widely held assumption that rejection of one's group leads to rejection of oneself, i.e., low self-esteem.

Group Rejection

The present study is based on a sample of 1,988 school children in Baltimore City from grades 3–12, 63 percent of whom were black. In this investigation, children's attitudes toward both their race and their religion were studied, as well as their personal feelings of self-worth. (For sample details, see Rosenberg and Simmons, 1972.)

When writers speak of self-hatred among Jews, black self-hatred, group disidentification, negative reference groups, etc., they are essentially using different terms to express the idea of *group rejection*. There are, however, several aspects, elements, or dimensions of group rejection which should be distinguished.

One of these has been called *group self-hatred*. Although this term has numerous connotations, its central meaning usually refers to *lack of pride in one's group*. As a result of his socialization, it is contended, the minority group member comes to share the low regard toward his group held by the wider society. As a crude indicator of this concept, we asked our respondents: "How proud are you of being Negro?" "How proud are you of your religion?" "How proud are you of your school?"

A second dimension of group rejection is *disidentification*. This somewhat elusive idea refers to the degree to which the group is experienced as an integral and inseparable part of the self. In this sense, group identification is considered a form of introjection, defined by Webster as "The adoption of externals (persons or objects) into the self, so as to have a sense of oneness with them and to feel personally affected by what happens to them." For the person who identifies with the group, the distinction between *me* and *my group* is unclear; the fate of the group is experienced as the fate of the self. In this study, group identification was chiefly indexed by the question: "If someone said something bad about [the Negro or colored race; your religion; your school; etc.], would you feel almost as if they had said something bad about you?"

A third dimension of rejection is *group unimportance*. Although the individual may not be ashamed of his group nor deny that it is part of him, he may still consider it a peripheral part of the self. Members of third- or fourth-generation immigrant groups, nominal members of religious groups, graduates of certain high schools, residents of certain states or countries, might be examples. In this study, this aspect of group rejection was indexed by the question: "Is [being Negro or colored; your religion; your school; etc.] very important to you, pretty important, or not very important to you?"

These indicators of group pride, identification, and importance of "your religion" were combined to form a measure of *religious* group attachment and rejection. For black children, the same three indicators of "your race" were combined with three others[1] to form a score of *racial* group rejection.

Self-esteem was measured by means of a six-item Guttman scale (Reproducibility = 90.2 percent, Scalability = 67.6 percent). It contained such items as: (1) "Everybody has some things about him which are good and some things about him which are bad. Are more of the things about you good, bad, or are they both about the same?" (2) "A kid told me: 'There's a lot wrong with me.' Do you ever feel like this?" (3) "How happy are you with the kind of person you are?" These items, it should be noted, avoid all reference to race, religion, or any other group affiliation; they refer to an overall feeling of self-acceptance or self-rejection. The scale is intended to determine the extent to which the individual respects himself and considers himself a person of worth, not whether he considers himself superior to others. The validity of this measure is discussed in Rosenberg and Simmons (1972: Ch. 2).

Table 1A examines the relationship between the black child's attitudes toward his race and his personal self-esteem. It is apparent that the two are virtually unrelated. The self-esteem of those black respondents whose racial attachment is relatively weak differs little from that of those with strong race identification and pride.

Turning to religious group rejection (Table 1B), we find the results are virtually the same. Contrary to theoretical expectation, rejection of one's religious group does not appear to be associated with any propensity to reject oneself as a person.

In light of the widespread assumption that the minority group member who rejects his group is thereby rejecting himself—that the two are virtually *identical*—the empirical finding that they are scarcely even *related* can only be greeted with skepticism or astonishment. One reason it may be so difficult to find other research dealing with the relationship of group self-hatred to individual self-hatred may be that investigators have considered it pointless to examine what appeared to be a virtual tautology.

A modest amount of additional evidence is, however, available. One finding stems from a study of high school juniors and seniors in ten high schools in New York State conducted in 1960 (Rosenberg, 1965). The only indicator of group attachment available in that study was the question:

Table 1. Racial and Religious Group Attachment and Self-Esteem
(Baltimore Study)

A

Racial Group Attachment (Blacks)

Self-Esteem	Strong	Medium	Weak
Low	19%	16%	20%
Medium	35	39	34
High	46	45	46
N = 100%	(327)	(158)	(728)

X^2 = 2.307 df = 4 n.s.

- - - - - - - - - - - - - - - - - -

B

Religious Group Attachment

Self-Esteem	Strong	Medium	Weak
Low	25%	27%	29%
Medium	31	33	30
High	44	40	41
N = 100%	(613)	(414)	(245)

X^2 = 2.821 df = 4 n.s.

"How important is your religious group to you?" Table 2 indicates that the adolescent's global self-esteem bears only a slight relation to whether he considers his religious group important to him. Furthermore, whatever small relationship there is appears among Catholics and Protestants, not among Jews, the group to which the theory most appropriately applies.

The third study involves a sample of 1,637 seniors of whom 241 were black, enrolled in thirteen high schools in Connecticut's five major metropolitan areas in 1966. Cummings and Carrere (1973) were interested in examining the relationship between the black's tendency to identify him-

Table 2. Importance of Religious Group and Self-Esteem
(New York State Study)

Self-Esteem	Importance of Religious Group		
	Very	Fairly	Not
High	46%	48%	42%
Medium	26	24	24
Low	28	28	34
N = 100%	(1244)	(841)	(206)

$X^2 = 4.66$ df = 4   n.s.

self in racial terms and his self-esteem. Their assumption was that "when
a black person incorporates the words 'Negro' or 'colored' into his self-
image, he is also internalizing the negative connotations associated with
them" because these terms arouse negative associations in the minds of
white people. The procedure employed was Kuhn's Twenty Statements
Test, in which respondents were asked to respond to the question: "Who
Am I?" About one-third of the blacks identified themselves in racial
terms. The results showed no significant difference in the self-esteem of
those who did or did not identify themselves in racial terms. In fact, the
identifiers had slightly (not significantly) *higher* self-esteem, a result interpreted by Cummings and Carrere (1973) as contrary to the symbolic
interactionist hypothesis initially advanced.

In sum, although the data are limited, they squarely contradict the
widely held assumption that rejection of one's group either reflects or
generates low global self-esteem in the individual. A finding so offensive
to theoretical expectation demands explanation. The central question this
paper will address, then, is: Why, despite the strong reasons for expecting
it, do racial and religious identification appear to show so little empirical
association with self-esteem?

MULTIPLE CONTRIBUTORY FACTORS

In implying that attitudes toward one's group will give rise to corresponding attitudes toward oneself, investigators assume that the social identity
element is important to the individual. Our data, as we shall see, lend
support to this assumption. The point is that the self-concept is an extremely complex structure containing a very large number of elements or
components, each of which may be invested with pride or shame. In

focusing on a particular social identity element, it is easy to overlook the fact that to the black or Jew or Mexican-American, there is more to life than being black or Jewish or Mexican-American. A person is not only black but also good-looking or popular; not only Jewish, but also musically talented and athletically adept; not only Mexican-American, but also rich and respected.

The self-concept, in our view, is the sum total of the individual's thoughts and feelings with reference to himself as an object. The number of elements which may contribute to the global evaluation of this object is simply enormous (Kuhn and McPartland, 1954). Gordon (1968) finds no less than thirty broad categories into which answers to the "Who Am I?" question can be classified, each category containing a large number of items or elements. It is thus not that a particular social identity element, e.g., race or religion, is unimportant but that there are so many other self-concept components that are equally or more important. This fact, we suggest, may weaken and blur the relationship between attitudes toward one's group and toward oneself as a whole. To provide some hint of the range of elements that may compete with race or religion in influencing someone's global feeling of worth, we shall consider three factors: (1) ego-extensions, (2) dispositions, and (3) achievements.

Comparison with Ego-Extensions   As James (1890) long ago noted, the individual's self-feeling extends far beyond the bounds of his skin to incorporate all objects eliciting the distinctive feeling of "me" or "mine," e.g., mother, father, siblings, home, school, clothes, friends, etc. These are *ego-extensions*—elements technically external to the self which are nevertheless experienced as part of it. How do race and religion compare with these other elements in terms of the three dimensions of attachment or rejection mentioned above: identification, pride, and importance? In Table 3, Column A, the ego-extensions are ordered in terms of the frequency with which respondents averred that they would feel an attack on the ego-extension as an attack upon themselves; this is probably the surest indicator of "identification." With regard to "importance" and "pride," (Columns B and C), we were able to ask about only six ego-extensions each. While the ego-extensions in the three lists are not identical, they are comparable and their rank orders, computed by a Spearman Rank Order Correlation, are very similar. (Rhos are as follows: columns A and B = .90; columns A and C = .70; columns B and C = 1.00.)

The important point about Table 3 is that, while race and religion are widely felt to be an integral part of the self, mother, father, and siblings are even more generally accepted as ego-extensions, and other objects— such as clothes, schoolwork, friends, father's job, and school—are also chosen by more than half the sample. Furthermore, Columns B and C

Table 3. Identifications with Potential Ego-Extensions

Potential ego-extension	A Attack on ego-extension felt as attack on self	B Ego-extension "very important"	C "Very proud" of ego-extension
Mother	88.5%		
Father	82.6		
Family		86.2%	
Siblings	80.0		
Negroes (black children only)	77.6	67.0	79.2%
Religion	74.4	64.8	69.5
Home			65.2
Clothes	71.2		
School work	66.6		
Friends	61.9	34.3	39.5
Father's job	59.5		60.6
School	50.0	57.1	48.4
Toys	31.5		
Neighborhood		24.8	32.0
President of U.S.	27.2		
Governor of State	24.2		

show that, although it is true that their race and religion are considered "very important" by most children and that they are "very proud" of these group affiliations, a number of other ego-extensions also appear to involve the self deeply. Racial and religious identification may thus have an effect on the individual's self-esteem, but so may any of a large number of ego-extensions which also constitute a part of the self-concept. Race, religion, or nationality are important, but they are not of exclusive, and may not even be of central, importance compared to other groups, individuals, or objects with which the individual may identify.

Comparison with Dispositions   *Dispositions* generally refer to tendencies to respond in certain ways, and include the individual's skills, abilities, interests, attitudes, values, "personality characteristics," etc. These dispositions characteristically enter the self-concept as a language of adjectives. No one can say how many traits there are, although years ago Allport and Odbert (1936) constructed a list of over 17,000 adjectives, many of which are descriptive of individuals and may arouse feelings of pride or shame. Often these personal attributes are experienced as touching the very core, the innermost essence, of the self. In certain cases, our social identity elements are felt to be the external, superficial aspects of our selves while our traits or personal attributes may be felt to be more of what we truly are; if so, general feelings of worth might rest more centrally on the latter.

Consider the issue of pride. With regard to one of the aspects of group rejection or acceptance, namely, group pride, Table 4 shows that there is an association with individual self-esteem, although it is a modest one. The point is that a person may be proud of his social identity elements (race, religion, nationality, sex, occupation, etc.) and he may also be proud of his traits (honesty, wisdom, morality, generosity, etc.) One way to compare the importance of such self-concept components is to see whether the individual's pride or shame in certain traits (intelligence, appearance, social skill) are more or less closely related to his global self-esteem than his pride or shame in certain aspects of social identity (race or religion). Table 4 shows that they are; the relationship between self-estimates of personal attributes (how intelligent, good-looking, easy to get along with you are) to self-esteem is evidently much stronger than that of degree of pride in one's race or religion.

The relative importance of these different aspects of the self-concept to global self-esteem may be highlighted in another way. When an inves-

Table 4. Relationship of Self-Esteem to (A) Three Traits and (B) Two Social Identity Elements

	Gamma	N	X^2	df	P<
Relationship of self-esteem to . . .					
A Traits					
How smart are you?	.2564	(1,831)	44.78	6	.001
How good-looking are you?	.2629	(1,735)	67.43	6	.001
How easy are you to get along with?	.1868	(1,811)	31.66	6	.001
B Social Identity Elements					
How proud of your race (blacks)	.0823	(1,073)	4.28	6	.639
How proud of your religion?	.0872	(1,649)	8.53	6	.202

tigator focuses on race, religion, or nationality, he ignores all other characteristics of the individual. When another focuses on intelligence or attractiveness, he does the same. In reality, of course, some of the individual's characteristics will be sources of pride to him, others sources of shame. Hence, a simple way of assessing the relative importance of social identity elements and personal attributes is to compare the self-esteem of pupils who are proud of their race or religious group but have little respect for their intelligence with those who think they are smart but have less pride in their race or religious group.

Table 5 suggests that the pupils who consider themselves "very smart" but who are "pretty" or "not very proud" of their religious or racial group are more likely to have high self-esteem than those who see themselves as "pretty" or "not very smart" but are "very proud" of their religion or race. (The differences in low self-esteem are minor.) The pupil's pride in his intelligence thus appears to be somewhat more important than his pride in race or religion in influencing his global self-esteem.

We do not mean to imply that all traits are more central to the individual's feeling of personal worth than all social identity elements; certainly this is not the case. Our only point is that, given the enormous number of traits available and the centrality of some of these, it is unlikely that feelings about one's group will be of decisive influence in determining feelings of self-respect.

Table 5. Relative Importance of Self-Estimate of Intelligence
and of Pride in Race or Religion for Self-Esteem

	Intelligence and Religious Pride		Intelligence and Race Pride (Blacks)	
Self-Esteem	Very smart, somewhat proud of religion	Somewhat smart, very proud of religion	Very smart, somewhat proud of race	Somewhat smart, very proud of race
Low	18%	26%	21%	20%
Medium	23	33	24	34
High	59	41	55	46
N = 100%	(34)	(958)	(29)	(721)
	$X^2 = 4.287$	df = 2 n.s.	$X^2 = 1.311$	df = 2 n.s.

Comparison with Achievements In speaking of race and religion, it is important to observe that these are ascribed, not achieved, statuses. While the American value system strongly emphasizes that achievement should be the sole criterion of social worth and basis of social prestige, this teaching is so widely violated as to express little more than a pious hope. Yet it may not be totally without effect, if only because lower-status groups have such apparent incentive for accepting it.

If children were indoctrinated with the normative belief that the worth of a person is based on what he has actually achieved rather than on the accident of birth, then their ascribed statuses might have relatively little importance for their self-esteem; their true worth would rest on other, firmer foundations. Unfortunately, it is difficult to test this general reasoning with our sample of children, because children actually have so few achieved statuses. If we broaden our definition to encompass "areas of achievement," however, it may be possible to get some purchase on the problem. Two of these will be considered: (1) election as an officer in a school club (the relationship between such political success and self-esteem can only be assessed for high school students who are club members); (2) academic success. If a person's worth is seen to reside in what he personally has accomplished rather than in his ascribed statuses, then the former should be more closely associated with his global self-esteem than the latter.

Table 6 shows this to be the case: The relationship of the pupil's

Table 6. Relationships of Some Ascribed and Achieved Statuses to Self-Esteem, for Secondary School Pupils

	Relationship to Self-Esteem in Secondary Schools				
	Gamma	N	X^2	df	P<
Ascribed statuses					
Proud of race (blacks)	.0403	(437)	4.19	6	.651
Proud of religion	.0184	(784)	5.95	6	.429
Achieved statuses					
Marks in school	.1298	(743)	22.68	6	.001
President in club (for club members)	.1281	(247)	2.36	2	.307

achievements to his global self-esteem is stronger than that of these ascribed statuses. The former relationships are modest at the elementary school level but respectable in secondary school; caution is indicated in drawing conclusions, however, since the "club president" question may be due to statistical chance. While it is difficult to generalize from these limited data, they suggest that as children grow older, their ascribed statuses may decline in importance as a basis for assessing their worth and their achieved statuses tend to loom larger.

Evidence from some other studies also suggests that achievement may be more important than ascription in determining self-esteem. A number of studies have shown that the child's ascribed statuses—race (Rosenberg and Simmons, 1972), religion (Gordon, 1963; Anisfeld et al., 1962), nationality rank (Rosenberg, 1965), social class (Bachman, 1970)—either show no relationship to self-esteem or at most a moderate relationship. With regard to certain achievements, on the other hand—marks in school (Coopersmith, 1967; Purkey, 1970; Fitts, 1972), sociometric status, or election to class office (Rosenberg, 1965)—clear relationships to self-esteem often do appear.

In sum, the self-concept is a complex structure consisting of a multiplicity of elements. The individual's race and religion are important parts of the self-concept, but (1) they are matched or overshadowed in importance by a number of ego-extensions; (2) they are less important than at least certain personal attributes; and (3) they are ascribed rather than achieved, thus reducing their importance in an open-class system of stratification. Given the large number of self-concept components and their relative importance, one can understand how a given social identity element might explain relatively little variance in global self-esteem.

GROUP DISIDENTIFICATION AND GROUP SELF-HATRED

As noted earlier, the individual's rejection of his group may be expressed in disidentification, self-hatred, or unimportance. We believe that when Lewin (1948), Kardiner and Ovesey (1951), Proshansky and Newton (1968), etc., speak of group "self-hatred," they are essentially referring to a feeling of *lack of pride* in one's group; the individual is assumed to share the low regard in which his group is held in the wider society. It is essentially for this reason that a number of recent sociopolitical movements have focused on enhancing group pride (black pride, yellow pride, pride in *la raza,* etc.) as a means of raising the self-respect of its members. In the past, it is argued, minority group members internalized the derogatory and contemptuous attitudes of the majority toward their own groups, resulting in feelings of shame, embarrassment, and chagrin at the unworthiness of their groups and, as a consequence, of themselves as individuals. These recent group ideologies have attempted to reverse this trend by arousing pride in the group—in its history, its heroes, its achievements and social contributions, its standards of beauty (e.g., "black is beautiful"), its distinctive culture, etc.

Although obviously related, it is useful to highlight the distinction between group pride and group identification. As noted above, the alleged low group pride of minority group members receives little support in our data. Nearly four-fifths of the black children said that they were "very proud" of their race and almost 70 percent of all respondents claimed equal pride in their religion. Whether all these respondents did in fact feel such strong group pride is uncertain, but it seems reasonable to think that the small number who said they were "not proud" of their race or religion probably did hold such feelings. Presumably, it is this group which writers usually have in mind when they speak of "group self-hatred."

Group disidentification, on the other hand, refers to the feeling that the group is not an integral part of the self, that the fate of the group and of the self are separate and distinct; the group is not introjected. Though not referring to groups, the general idea has probably best been described in James' (1890) discussion of the "Empirical Self."

> The Empirical Self of each of us is all that he is tempted to call by the name of *me*. But it is clear that between what a man calls *me* and what he simply calls *mine* the line is difficult to draw. We feel and act about certain things that are ours very much as we feel and act about ourselves. Our fame, our children, the work of our hands, may be as dear to us as our bodies are. . . . If they wax and prosper, he feels triumphant; if they dwindle and die away, he feels cast down—not necessarily in the same degree for each thing, but in much the same way for all.

Given this distinction between low group pride and group disidentification, we would advance the following curious proposition: Among people with low group pride, disidentification, rather than injuring self-esteem, may actually protect it. The principle is not obscure. Take a student attending Community Junior College who knows that his school has low prestige and who, indeed, agrees that this poor reputation is justified; this attitude certainly expresses "group self-hatred" or low pride in group. But assume that his sense of personal worth is totally separated from the school's reputation ("I just go there"); in this case, his self-esteem would be unaffected. In other words, it would be group identification, not disidentification, that would damage self-esteem.

We attempted to test this reasoning in the Baltimore study. For example, consider those black children with "racial self-hatred," that is, the

Table 7. Self-Esteem and Group Identification Among Pupils
Expressing Low Group Pride

	Black Students with Low Pride in Race Who:		Students with Low Pride in Religion Who:	
	Identify	Disidentify	Identify	Disidentify
% Low Self Esteem	46%	23%	56%	30%
N = 100%	(11)	(22)	(18)	(23)
	$X^2 = 1.793$	df = 1 n.s.	$X^2 = 2.632$	df = 1 n.s.

small proportion who say they are "not proud" of their race. Table 7
indicates that if their racial identification is strong (attack on race experienced as attack on self), then 46 percent have low self-esteem; but if they
disidentify with their race, then only 23 percent have low self-esteem. For
those with racial self-hatred, racial disidentification appears to protect
individual self-esteem.

Similar results appear with respect to religious identification. Once
again we confine our attention to those with religious self-hatred ("not
proud" of their religion). Among those who identify with the group, 55
percent have low self-esteem, whereas among those who disidentify, only
30 percent have low self-esteem.

Because so few children actually manifest lack of racial and religious
pride, these findings are no more than suggestive, and the conclusions
cannot be accepted without further research. Nevertheless, they strongly
call into question the widespread assumption in the literature that the
individual who rejects his group is at some level rejecting himself. Under
conditions of group self-hatred—feelings of low pride in or respect for
one's group—such disidentification may protect one's feeling of self-
worth, while identification may harm it.

Some important causal implications inhere in these observations.
Theoretical reasoning suggests that if a group is derogated in the society,
members of that group will come to share the general disdain for it and for
themselves as group members; disidentification with one's group thus
eventuates in low personal self-esteem (Proshansky and Newton, 1968).
In light of the foregoing, however, it is possible that *group identification
and disidentification may be as much a consequence as a cause of self-
esteem.* If a fundamental human motive is the defense and enhancement
of the self (Murphy, 1947; McDougall, 1932; Combs and Snygg, 1959;
Schwartz and Stryker, 1970; Gordon and Gergen, 1968; Gergen, 1971),

then it is possible that identification and disidentification may be motivated by a desire to protect and enhance one's feeling of self-worth. In other words, if the individual feels pride in his group, then we would expect him to identify with it (consider it an integral part of himself), thus enhancing his self-esteem; but if he does not feel proud of his group (perhaps because he internalizes society's negative attitudes toward his group), then he would be motivated to disidentify with it, thereby also protecting his self-esteem. Attitudes toward one's group may be a cause of self-esteem, but the motive to protect self-esteem may be in part responsible for attitudes toward one's group.

The data in Table 8 are consistent with this interpretation. There we see that respondents tend to identify with groups of which they are proud, to disidentify with groups of which they are not. Both outcomes protect self-esteem. It is only those who identify with groups of which they are *not* proud who suffer blows to their self-worth. Such people probably represent the archetypes for the theoretical discussions of self-hatred among Jews, self-hatred among blacks, etc. According to our data, they are few in number, a finding consistent with Guttentag's (1970) literature review.

Table 8. Pride in Group and Introjection of Group

"If someone said something bad about [group], would you almost feel as if they had said something bad about you?"	"How proud are you of your [group]?"		
	Very proud	Pretty proud	Not very proud
Would you feel bad if <u>race</u> insulted	82%	72%	31%
N = 100%	(823)	(170)	(35)
	X^2 = 52.692	df = 2	p < .001
Would feel bad if <u>religion</u> insulted	83%	59%	44%
N = 100%	(941)	(374)	(41)
	X^2 = 104.31	df = 2	p < .001

The outcome for self-esteem is thus a happy one. We tend to consider as an integral part of ourselves those membership groups we admire but as separate from ourselves those membership groups we disdain. Even in a society characterized by widespread prejudice and unequal group evaluation, individuals can avail themselves of mechanisms to protect and enhance their self-regard.

SUMMARY AND DISCUSSION

The purpose of this paper has been to subject to empirical investigation an important theoretical assumption which has largely remained unquestioned, and hence unexamined, over the years, namely, that group rejection results in self-rejection. It has been reasoned that we live in a society strongly characterized by prejudice and discrimination; that certain groups—racial, religious, national—are derogated, disdained, and characterized as inferior by the larger society; that the minority group member internalizes the social definition of his group's worth; that he therefore disidentifies with his group, accepting the prestigious majority as his reference group; and that, in rejecting his membership group, he thereby rejects himself.

This argument, while plausible, fails to meet the empirical test. Not only are group self-hatred and individual self-hatred not identical, but their association is very weak, according to the limited data available.

Two of the reasons for this anomalous finding have been discussed. The first is to be found in the nature of the self-concept, here defined as the totality of the individual's thoughts and feelings with reference to himself as an object. The self-concept consists of a multiplicity of components, including dispositions and ego-extensions, having different priority, centrality, and weight in determining the individual's global self-evaluation. These components are perceived, evaluated, and ordered. Not only are race and religion but two of these, but they are apparently less likely to be central to the self than certain other ego-extensions and to contribute less to self-esteem than certain traits or areas of achievement.

The second reason is to be found in the nature of group rejection. Even if people do share society's low regard for their group, this attitude need not deleteriously affect their global self-esteem if the group is not introjected, i.e., experienced as an integral, inseparable part of the self. Needless to say, such group identification is not purely accidental. People are motivated to protect their self-esteem, and they consequently tend to introject only those groups of which they are proud. Hence, group self-hatred need not necessarily generate individual self-hatred.

This is not meant to suggest that group rejection may not have other noxious consequences for the individual. The pain and bitterness of isolation from one's group is a recurrent theme in fiction and in social science. The need for the feeling of belonging, the experience of mutual acceptance, and the sense of security that comes from unity with a group certainly stand as sociological dicta. In discussions of group disidentification or self-hatred, however, there is one point widely overlooked, namely, *that it is not the group which rejects the individual but the individual who rejects the group.* If, on the basis of personal choice, the individual refuses to identify with other members of his minority group, why should this make *him* feel inferior? He may, on the contrary, consider himself better than other members of his group. One can see why the individual's rejection of his group may contribute to insecurity by producing feelings of isolation but not why it should contribute to feelings of personal worthlessness.

FOOTNOTES

*The research reported here was funded by a grant from the National Institute of Mental Health (MH27747) whose support is gratefully acknowledged.

1. These additional items might be called a "negative reference group" type of disidentification, reflecting the individual's wish *not* to belong to the group. In the literature on black self-hatred, at least two psychiatrists have remarked on a powerful longing among blacks to be white. Brody (1963) has noted that black boys attending psychiatric clinics often preferred to play with white rather than black puppets. He contends that this response reflects "anxiety or guilt-laden wishes to be white rather than Negro." Similarly, Kardiner and Ovesey (1951:263) spoke at length about group self-hatred among blacks. They noted: "In its most regressive form, the ideal becomes the frantic wish to be reborn white."

Our study attempted to tap this feeling by asking the following: (1) "If you could be anything in the world when you grow up, would you want to be Negro, white, or something else?" (2) "If you could be born again, would you like to be born of a different race, not Negro or colored?" (3) "Do you think you would be happier if you were not Negro?"

Whatever may be the situation at the unconscious level, these data reveal little evidence of widespread black self-hatred. No more than 9 percent of the black children answered any of these questions affirmatively, although 23 percent answered "maybe" to the last question. Some black children did, however, agree with one or another of these statements, and such agreement might be considered indicative of group rejection.

REFERENCES

Allport, G., and H. S. Odbert (1936), "Trait-names: A psycho-lexical study," *Psychological Monographs* 47, No. 211:1–171.

Anisfeld, M., N. Bogo, and W. E. Lambert (1962), "Evaluational reactions to accented English speech," *Journal of Abnormal and Social Psychology* 65, 4:223–231.

Bachman, J. G. (1970), *Youth in Transition,* Volume II: *The Impact of Family Background and Intelligence on Tenth-Grade Boys.* Ann Arbor, Michigan: Survey Research Center, Institute for Social Research.

Brody, E. B. (1963), "Color and identity conflict in young boys: Observations on Negro mothers and sons in urban Baltimore," *Psychiatry* 26 (May): 188–201.

Cartwright, D. (1950), "Emotional dimensions of group life," pp. 439–447 in M. L. Reymert (Ed.), *International Symposium on Feelings and Emotions.* New York: McGraw-Hill.

Combs, Arthur, and Donald Snygg (1959), *Individual Behavior.* New York: Harper.

Coopersmith, Stanley (1967), *The Antecedents of Self-Esteem.* San Francisco: Freeman.

Cummings, Scott, and Robert Carrere (1973), "Black culture, Negroes, and colored people: Racial self-image and self-esteem among black adolescents." Unpublished.

Erikson, E. H. (1966), "The concept of identity in race relations: Notes and queries," *Daedalus* 95:145–171.

Fitts, William H. (1972), *The Self-Concept and Performance.* Nashville, Tennessee: Dede Wallace Center.

Gergen, K. (1971), *The Concept of Self.* New York: Holt, Rinehart and Winston.

Gordon, Chad (1963), *Self-Conception and Social Achievement.* Doctoral dissertation, University of California at Los Angeles. Ann Arbor: University Microfilms.

—— (1968), "Self-conceptions: Configurations of content," pp. 115–136 in C. Gordon and K. Gergen (Eds.), *The Self in Social Interaction.* New York: Wiley.

—— (1972), *Looking Ahead: Self-Conceptions, Race and Family as Determinants of Adolescent Orientation to Achievement.* Washington, D.C.: American Sociological Association.

Grier, William H., and Price M. Cobbs (1968), *Black Rage.* New York: Basic Books.

Guttentag, M. (1970), "Group cohesiveness, ethnic organization, and poverty," *Journal of Social Issues* 26 (2): 105–132.

James, William (1950), *The Principles of Psychology.* New York: Dover. (Copyright, 1890 by Henry Holt and Co.)

Kardiner, Abram, and Lionel Ovesey (1951), *The Mark of Oppression.* New York: Norton.

Kuhn, M. H., and T. S. McPartland (1954), "An empirical investigation of self-attitudes," *American Sociological Review* 19:68–76.

Lewin, Kurt (1948), *Resolving Social Conflicts.* New York: Harper.

Luck, P. W., and J. Heiss (1972), "Social determinants of self-esteem in adult males," *Sociology and Social Research* 57: 69–84.

McDougall, William (1932), *The Energies of Men.* London: Methuen.

Murphy, G. (1947), *Personality.* New York: Harper.

Proshansky, H., and P. Newton (1968), "The nature and meaning of Negro self-identity," pp. 178–218 in M. Deutsch, I. Katz, and A. R. Jensen (Eds.), *Social Class, Race, and Psychological Development.* New York: Holt, Rinehart and Winston.

Purkey, W. W. (1970), *Self-Concept and School Achievement.* Englewood Cliffs, New Jersey: Prentice-Hall.

Rosenberg, Morris (1965), *Society and the Adolescent Self-Image.* Princeton, New Jersey: Princeton University Press.

——, and R. G. Simmons (1972), *Black and White Self-esteem: The Urban School Child.* Washington, D.C.: American Sociological Association.

Schwartz, Michael, and Sheldon Stryker (1970), *Deviance, Selves and Others.* Washington, D.C.: American Sociological Association.

Silberman, Charles (1964), *Crisis in Black and White.* New York: Random House (Vintage Books).

Trimble, J. E. (1974), "Say goodbye to the Hollywood Indian: Results of a nationwide survey of the self-image of the American Indian." Paper presented at the Annual Meeting of the American Psychological Association. New Orleans, Louisiana, August 31.

CHRONIC DISEASE AND CHILDHOOD DEVELOPMENT: KIDNEY DISEASE AND TRANSPLANTATION*

Susan D. Klein, UNIVERSITY OF COLORADO MEDICAL CENTER

Roberta G. Simmons, UNIVERSITY OF MINNESOTA

Chronic illness in childhood might be expected to challenge the coping mechanisms of both the child and his family. Pain, fatigue, and other symptoms, the trauma of hospitalization and treatment procedures, uncertainty of prognosis, and changes in the child's treatment by family and peers all appear to provide sources of stress for the child (Mattsson, 1972). Some have suggested that disease poses more of a problem to the child than to the adult.

> In a child, physical illness and emotional disturbance threaten to, or actually do, interfere with the process of growth itself, and are expressed in distortions or blocks in development.
>
> (Murphy, 1961:218)

Research in Community and Mental Health, Vol 1, pp 21–59.
Copyright © 1979 byJAI Press, Inc.
All rights of reproduction in any form reserved.
ISBN 0-89232-063-X

21

The major task of this paper is to examine and measure the effects of chronic illness on the child's psychosocial development, particularly on multiple aspects of the self-picture. As part of a larger study on the impact of kidney transplantation (Simmons et al., 1977), this analysis focuses on chronic disease and kidney transplantation in children. Major kidney disease is one of the serious chronic illnesses in childhood, and at least 10–15 percent of all kidney transplants are being given to children (Bernstein, 1971). Kidney transplantation in children, although much rarer than chronic kidney disease, is such an expensive new technology that ethical questions have been raised about its psychological consequences and many centers have been reticent to transplant children (*American Journal of Public Health,* 1969). The goal of kidney transplantation is to remove the patient from the role of social invalid and thereby enhance his self-image, improve his general adjustment, and reduce tension in the family. It would make little sense to spend huge sums of money on a method of physical rehabilitation which produced psychologically crippled youngsters. One object of this paper, then, is to measure the extent of psychological rehabilitation required of the transplanted children in comparison to that of the chronically ill youth.

Although there is a sizable literature on the chronically ill child, most of it is based on case-study material and small samples and lacks standardized, quantitative measurement and normal controls (Richardson et al., 1961; Litman, 1974). With quantitative measures, the adjustment of the children with chronic kidney disease will be compared to that of *transplanted children* who have been "restored" to health, as well as to the adjustment of *normal children.* In particular, we will ask what dimensions of "adjustment" or quality of life are likely to suffer. What is the impact on the self-image in specific? Which types of children are particularly vulnerable?

There are a number of variables which might be expected to affect the vulnerability of the child: e.g., disease severity (Pless and Roghmann, 1971), visibility or invisiblity of the condition (Goldberg, 1974; McAnarney et al., 1974), the actual symptomatology of being sick (Eichhorn and Andersen, 1962), and the patient's perception and definition of the illness (Eichhorn and Andersen, 1962; Offord and Aponte, 1967). The effect of these and other characteristics of the child and of the disease will be explored.

Because of the interdependence of the child and his family, we have also sought to analyze the impact of the child's disease upon the family. Different aspects of the crisis will be distinguished, as well as factors associated with the family's vulnerability in the face of crisis. Patterns for coping with the disease will be explored, including strategies for managing the sick child and their consequences for his or her adjustment.

The general picture of the adjustment of the chronically ill child which emerges from the literature is unclear. While many case studies detail the disruptive impact on the child of long-term illness, the few quantitative studies are contradictory in their findings. On the one hand, some research shows little difference in adjustment between ill children and normal controls (Collier, 1969; Crain et al., 1966; Gates, 1946). On the other hand, behavioral and academic problems were reported by Pless and Roghmann (1971) and by Sultz (1972). High rates of hospitalization and school-related problems are frequent difficulties according to the parents of chronically ill children ($N = 390$) in Sultz's research (1972). The Rochester Child Health Survey is one of the most methodologically rigorous studies, consisting of a probability sample of 1,700 children of whom 350 were chronically ill (Pless and Roghmann, 1971). In reviewing the results from this survey and two similar British studies, Pless concludes that about one-third of all chronically ill children develop secondary social and psychological problems. Neither of these studies, however, explored the impact of chronic disease on self-esteem and other aspects of the self-image. (Also see Haggerty et al., 1975; and Pless in this volume).

Korsch et al. (1973) used the California Test of Personality to measure a group of *posttransplant* children in particular ($N = 51$) and found that the overall adjustment scores of the patients did not differ from normal standard scores, but their social adjustment was significantly lower. According to the Piers-Harris scale, there is some indication the patients may suffer low self-esteem, although the control group is too small ($N = 8$) to justify conclusions. Other research with regard to the child's post-transplant adjustment has been qualitative and psychiatric in nature (see Bernstein, 1970, 1971; Khan et al., 1971; Sampson, 1975).

It has been estimated that about one out of every ten children will have at least one chronic illness by the age of 15 (Pless and Roghmann, 1971) and thus it would appear important to have an understanding of the effects of illness upon the self-image and upon other dimensions of adjustment. The chronic kidney diseases under study here are similar to other non-crippling, nonvisible diseases like asthma and diabetes. Like these diseases, the symptomatology, severity, and prognosis of chronic kidney diseases may vary greatly. In many cases the child is unlikely to have severe problems, whereas in other instances the outcome is uncertain. Because of new medications and other medical innovations, most of these conditions are no longer fatal and will not result in complete kidney failure. In some cases, however, the disease is almost certain to progress to a terminal stage requiring treatment on the artificial kidney machine (hemodialysis) or transplantation.[1] Although the incidence of complete kidney failure resulting from chronic kidney disease is difficult to determine, it has been estimated at one per 1.5 million population a year for children between 1 and 14 years of age (Meadow et al., 1970; Scharer, 1971). It is, then, a small and very sick subgroup that goes on to transplantation.

Although generally our society finds the death of a child unacceptable, transplanting children has been controversial. For instance, a metropolitan newspaper recently reported the story of a rural family which lost three sons in turn to a rare kidney disease (*Minneapolis Tribune,* March 31, 1974:10B). The doctors at a major Midwestern clinic had told the parents that transplantation would but briefly delay death and recommended only that the parents help the children enjoy the remainder of life. Yet less than 100 miles away was the University of Minnesota with one of the largest pediatric transplant programs in the country. There is little doubt these children would have been accepted for transplantation at the university, where the probability of a child surviving after a kidney has been donated from a living relative has been 86 percent at one year and 77 percent at 10 years. (When the kidney has been donated from a cadaver, survival has been 82 percent at one year and 63 percent at ten years. See Bernstein, 1977). Factors which have been cited as contraindicating transplantation for children include: the possibility of only a short reprieve from death as balanced against the trauma of the procedure, the stressful side effects of the necessary medications, and the retardation in growth that frequently cannot be reversed by the transplant. The child's emotional vulnerability and the stress to the family are also regarded by some as too costly to recommend the procedure. Yet, these evaluations of the emotional effects of pediatric transplantation are not backed by empirical data.

In order to provide relevant empirical data and to explore the impact of kidney disease and transplantation upon children, then, two related studies have been conducted: Chronically ill patients and their families have been interviewed with survey questionnaires, and a group of children with long-term successful transplants have been similarly interviewed.

METHOD

Population
  Chronically Ill Children
A population of seventy-two chronically ill patients, ages 8 to 20, was selected from the University Pediatric Kidney Clinic. Many of the children attending this clinic have acute and nonserious conditions, whereas we wished to study only those whose disease was serious and chronic.

Thus a duration criterion of at least one year from time of diagnosis was used to help ascertain that the disease was chronic, and also to enable us to concentrate on children and families whose coping mechanisms were likely to have achieved some stability. The physicians were asked to classify every patient who had an appointment at the Kidney Clinic within the designated time period; their identification of seriously ill children was largely based on the existence of the following major diseases: chronic pyelonephritis, chronic glomerulonephritis, polycystic kidney disease, congenital interstitial nephritis, diabetic glomerulosclerosis, chronic end-stage renal disease (undetermined etiology), hypoplasia, or lupus erythematosus.

The mothers of all children who were designated by the phsycians as meeting these criteria were contacted by telephone to confirm that the child was of proper age (over 8 and still in the home) and that the child had been under treatment for a year. All children who met these criteria between May, 1972, and October, 1973, were interviewed, except one whose parents refused to cooperate. Hence, we interviewed the entire population rather than a sample of the more seriously ill patients attending this clinic. Only nine of these patients had reached the stage which required hemodialysis or transplantation; ten others had the very serious systemic disease of lupus erythematosus, three of whom classified themselves as severely ill at present.

In addition to the chronically ill patients themselves, forty-four *"normal siblings"* closest in age to the sick child were interviewed and served as a control group. Sixty-five *mothers* were interviewed as well, thus providing three separate perspectives on the meaning of the disease to the child and his family: patient, sibling, and mother. Although there were no actual refusals to be interviewed by the mothers whose children were studied, one out-of-town mother was unable to travel the long distance to the clinic; one family had no mother; and five mothers of soon-to-be transplanted children were already being extensively studied as part of the larger research project and we did not feel we could ask them to complete these questionnaires as well. Similarly, in sixteen families there were no siblings at home of eligible age to be interviewed, seven out-of-town families could not arrange to have the normal sibling travel the long distance to the clinic and three siblings of pretransplant children were being intensively studied as part of the larger study and were not asked to participate in this aspect of the study. Only two in-town eligible siblings could be counted as refusals, since they did not appear able to arrange the time for the interview.

Since normal siblings may themselves be affected socially and psychologically by the disease in the home, an additional control group was also used from a prior study by Rosenberg and Simmons (1972). In a two-stage random sample study of Baltimore school children, twenty-five schools had been sampled and 1,918 children from grades 3–12 had been interviewed, using many of the same measures to be used here. Since the Baltimore sample is 63 percent black, we have attempted to make the sample more comparable by using only the 621 white children aged 10–18.

Transplanted Children

Another group of pediatric patients was also interviewed. All children, aged 8 to 20, who had received a kidney transplant at the University before June, 1973, and had maintained it for at least a year, were interviewed with the same questionnaire as used on the chronically ill children and their siblings. This part of the study involves fifty-two children who were an average of two and a half years posttransplant. The transplanted child has been saved from death and continual sickness but must follow a regimen of daily medication and frequent check-ups. In addition, long-term prognosis is uncertain. Our study allows us to compare the adjustment of children saved by transplantation to the adjustment of those suffering chronic kidney disease as well as to that of normal controls.

Measures

The research instruments include both closed and open-ended items. The questionnaires for the children (the chronically ill patients and their siblings and the posttransplant children) are in two parts. Section one contains mainly closed-ended questions to measure multiple aspects of the self-image. Section two deals more specifically with the child's illness, how he feels when he is sick, and what kinds of limitations he has experienced. Other questions probe his role in the family as well as his school adjustment and other activities. The mothers of the chronically ill children completed a written questionnaire as well as an interview which provided further background data as well as information on the impact of the disease on the child and his family.

An important focus of this research has been to assess the effects of chronic disease and transplantation on the adjustment of individual family members. The measures of psychosocial adjustment have been adopted from previous research where they had been tested for reliability and validity, and reliability has been satisfactorily established for this population (Rosenberg and Simmons, 1972; Simmons et al., 1973; Klein, 1975). The relevant scales measure level of happiness (or at the other extreme the level of depressive affect) as well as the degree of anxiety and the disturbance along various dimensions of the self-image: self-esteem, stability of the self-concept, self-consciousness, estimate of popularity, and satisfaction with looks.

FINDINGS

I. Level of Adjustment of the Patient

In order to measure adjustment or quality of life of the ill child, it is necessary to specify the dimensions of quality of life. In the following analysis we focus on (1) physical well-being and ability to perform daily activities, (2) social or interpersonal adjustment, and (3) emotional well-being (see Figure 1).

Physical Well-Being, Daily Activities, and Social Adjustment

The Child with Chronic Kidney Disease

The child's sense of *physical well-being* is a most basic indicator of the effects of his disease and whether or not he defines himself as ill. In response to a general closed-ended question about how healthy they feel, only 21 percent of the children with chronic kidney disease, as compared to 57 percent of their siblings describe themselves as "very healthy." The chronically ill child, his sibling, and mother all agree that this child is sick more often than other children (see Table 1).

In addition, the chronically ill patients report they tire more easily ($p < .001$). They are also more likely than their siblings to worry about their health and to report their mothers worry about how they feel. In comparing the child to his peers, the mother feels he is less active and at a disadvantage when competing *physically* with other children. More than half of the chronically ill children were reported by their mothers to have experienced limitations in their school *activities*. Only 68 percent of the children report they go to gym classes, and of those only about two-thirds engage in all the regular activities.

School is an important focus of much of the child's activity, and other researchers have found *academic difficulties* associated with chronic illness (Pless and Roghmann, 1971; Sultz, 1972). In terms of absenteeism, a global measure of interference with academic life, these chronically ill children are at a disadvantage. Thirty-seven percent of the mothers answered that absenteeism had been a problem. Mothers were asked separately about days of school missed on the average by the sick and normal child. In comparison, the sick children missed more days—with 18 percent missing over five days a month whereas none of the siblings missed so many days.

In terms of quality of academic performance 25 percent of the children were reported to have stayed back at least one year in school, and one-fourth of those repeats were specifically attributed by the mother to sickness. In addition, 52 percent of these children have needed a tutor. While

Figure 1

Dimensions of Adjustments for Adults and Children

Physical Well-Being

    Global Feelings of Well-Being and Symptomatology
    Ability to Perform Daily Activities

Emotional Well-Being

    Happiness Level
    Self-Image Level

        Self-Esteem
        Self-Consciousness
        Stability of the Self-Picture
        Sense of Distinctiveness
        Satisfaction with Body-Image
        Perceived Opinion of Significant Others (Perceived Popularity)

    Anxiety Level
    Gross Psychopathology and Suicidal Behavior

Social Well-Being: In Major Life Roles

    Social Life

        Satisfaction
        Participation

    Vocational or School Adjustment

        Satisfaction
        Participation

    Adjustment of Other Family Members

        Family Disruption
        Individual Adjustment

rates for normal children are unavailable, the levels of absenteeism and below-grade performance for this group seem high.

Other information was gathered about outside-school activities. Open-ended questions were asked of all three family members regarding clubs, hobbies, interests and what the child did after school. Because of the

Table 1

Responses to question: "Compared to other kids, do you think you (your child, your sister) is sick more often than other kids, sick about the same, or sick less often?"

	Chronically ill child regarding self	Normal control sibling regarding chronically ill child	Mother regarding chronically ill child	Normal control sibling regarding self	Transplanted child regarding self
More often	29%	32%	22%	0%	11%
About the same	49	39	44	32	49
Less often	22	29	34	68	40
	(N=72)	(N=44)	(N=64)	(N=44)	(N=37)

$p < .001$

qualitative nature of these data, differences were considered significant only if they were verified by more than one source and if they persisted when sex of the child was controlled. A variety of evidence suggests that the normal sibling is more physically active; he more often reports working outside, a significant fact for rural families. The most important differentiation in activities seems to be between team sports and social interaction groups (e.g., Girl Scouts). Consistently, according to all three respondents, the normal siblings are more often *physically active* by participating in team sports, whereas the sick child is more involved in *social activities*. The difference in physical activity was expected whereas the latter difference was not. Are these sick children really more socially competent?

If anything, these chronically ill children seem to have some obvious social liabilities—like a lack of energy. In addition, 42 percent of the mothers admit they make a special effort to keep the child away from others who are sick. Despite these obstacles, however, a series of questions about numbers of friends, frequency and type of social contacts revealed virtually no difference between the sick and normal children. There is limited evidence, in fact, that the sick girls may be more socially competent: The mothers report that these girls get along somewhat better with other children than do their female siblings (83 percent vs. 62 percent), although there is little difference between the sick boys and their brothers.

Thus, in terms of physical and academic performance, but not social activity, these children with chronic disease seem to be at somewhat of a disadvantage in comparison to their siblings. A small number of these children, the most disadvantaged, go on to transplantation. How do transplanted children compare on the same indicators of well-being?

The Transplanted Child

The transplanted children fall between the chronically ill and normal siblings in *perceiving themselves as healthy*. Thirty-five percent of the posttransplant patients rate themselves as "very healthy," as compared to 21 percent of the chronically ill and 57 percent of the normal siblings. Only 21 percent of the posttransplant children report they are sick "very often" or "pretty often" compared to 40 percent of the chronically ill children and 9 percent of the normal controls. Comparing themselves to other children (see Table 1) the transplanted children are more similar to the normal controls in terms of reported frequency of feeling sick, although they still report tiring more easily.

How does the posttransplant child fare in *school?* The number of days he reports to be absent is not significantly smaller than that reported for the chronically ill child; 16 percent miss five or more days a month as compared to 18 percent of the chronically ill children. Only 19 percent of the posttransplant patients say their condition keeps them from participating in regular school *activities,* whereas 31 percent of the chronically ill children report such limitations. They are also somewhat more likely to go to gym (75 percent vs. 68 percent). Only 8 percent of these patients report they currently need a tutor. However, the average grades reported by these children were lower than those reported by the mothers of the chronically ill children: only 16 percent of the transplant children received a grade average of B or better in contrast to 77 percent of the chronically ill children. With regard to activities, the posttransplant children are more likely than the sick children to report they engage in physically active endeavors with their friends and that they work outside the home after school.

In general, although these patients demonstrate greater activity and feelings of well-being, they still define their health as a larger problem than do normal youngsters. Because of the danger of immunological rejection and destruction of the new kidney, these children seem more fearful of getting sick (56 percent of them vs. 39 percent of the chronically ill children report they feel frightened when they get sick). The transplanted youngsters are also more likely than the chronically ill children to feel their kidney disease has kept them "from being good at lots of things" (40 percent vs. 26 percent). Transplantation returns the child to life and activity but leaves him with an awareness of his vulnerability. What then is the impact on his emotional well-being?

Disease and Emotional Well-Being

One of the major foci of this research has been to explore the impact of chronic illness and transplantation on several dimensions of the child's emotional well-being, particularly on multiple aspects of the self-image. As a general indicator of mental health and adjustment, there are probably few factors as important to the individual as his picture of himself (see Rosenberg, 1965; Wylie, 1974).

In a large study of 1,918 normal school children in Baltimore, Simmons et al. (1973) showed that several dimensions of the self-image were particularly vulnerable to the stress of adolescence. Thus, it was hypothesized that the combination of illness and adolescence would be especially stressful. We predicted that preadolescent and adolescent children who were chronically ill would indicate even greater disturbance in self-image than their healthier age-peers.

First of all, *global self-esteem,* that is, the child's overall positive or negative evaluation of himself, might be adversely affected by being physically impaired and different. Secondly, an increase in *self-consciousness* may accompany illness as it does normal adolescence. The self, which is different because of illness, may become so salient in interaction with others that the interaction becomes embarrassing for the individual. Third, the question arises whether the *stability of the self-picture,* the sense of identity, is shaken by the uncertainties related to changed health status, just as it is with the changes of early adolescence (see Lecky, 1945; Erikson, 1956). The *body-image,* or the child's satisfaction with his looks, may also be affected, since chronic kidney disease often retards growth and since the steroid medication given to the transplant patients frequently produces acne, a moon-face, and rotund figure, at least temporarily. Finally, the *accorded self,* the opinions he believes others hold of him, his estimates of his own *popularity,* which take a negative turn in normal adolescence, might also respond unfavorably to the stress of being ill and different from one's peers.

Other dimensions of the self-image were explored—including the extent to which the ill child reveals his *true feelings* about himself to others, and his sense of being *distinctive,* or different. Aside from the self-image, the ill and transplanted children were compared to others in terms of their overall level of depressive affect and anxiety.

Adjustment of Sick and Normal Children

How do the children with chronic disease and the transplanted child fare in terms of socioemotional adjustment? The major differences between the ill and healthy children involve their body-image or satisfaction with their looks (see Table 2). Only along this dimension do the ill children appear to suffer. The greatest degree of dissatisfaction with looks is dem-

Table 2

Social-Emotional Adjustment for Sick Children and Normal Controls

	Baltimore controls*	Sick children	Normal siblings	Post-transplant children
	(N=621)	(N=72)	(N=44)	(N=52)
Happiness				
Low	42%	35%	40%	34%
Medium	46	51	44	43
High	12	14	16	23
	100%	100%	100%	100%
Self-Image				
Self-Esteem				
Low	37	31	41	40
Medium	29	37	25	34
High	33	32	34	26
	100%	100%	100%	100%
Self-Consciousnes				
Low	19	44	41	50
Medium	44	42	46	33
High	37	15	14	17
	100%	100%	100%	100%

p < .001

	Baltimore controls*	Sick children	Normal siblings	Post-transplant children
Stability of Self–Picture				
Low	33	35	46	47
Medium	22	28	20	16
High	45	37	33	38
	100%	100%	100%	100%
Sense of Distinctiveness				
Not different	11	16	5	22
Little different	26	33	27	22
Very different	63	51	68	56
	100%	100%	100%	100%

Table 2 (continued)

	Baltimore controls* (N=621)	Sick children (N=72)	Normal siblings (N=44)	Post-transplant children (N=52)
Body-Image, Satisfied With Looks				
Not satisfied	22%	39%	28%	55%
A little satisfied	42	36	40	36
Very satisfied	35	25	32	8
	100%	100%	100%	100%
				p < .001
Relationship To Others Show True Feelings				
Not show	30	26	29	22
Show little	51	44	41	47
Show lot	20	29	29	31
	100%	100%	100%	100%
Estimate of Popularity				
Not popular	8	7	7	14
Little popular	23	28	20	23
Very popular	69	65	72	63
	100%	100%	100%	100%
Anxiety				
High	11	12	14	12
Medium	54	53	54	54
Low	34	34	32	33
	100%	100%	100%	100%

*Using only white children ages 10–18.

onstrated by posttransplant children: 55 percent of them and 39 percent of the chronically ill are classified as "not satisfied," compared to only 28 percent of the siblings and 22 percent of the Baltimore controls ($p < .001$). The transplanted children are undoubtedly distressed by the side effects of steroid medication they must take to prevent immunological rejection of the new kidney. These side effects often involve a "Cushingoid" moon-face and rotund figure. Sometimes the chronically ill and transplanted children's growth pattern is disturbed.

Apart from dissatisfaction with looks, other dimensions of the self-image appear *surprisingly undamaged* in the total sample of ill children and among the transplanted youths. Self-esteem, self-consciousness, self-image stability, a sense of distinctiveness, felt ability to reveal true feelings, and estimates of popularity are all unhurt.[2]

For the bulk of the chronically ill children, the level of happiness also appears no lower than that of the controls. Yet there are a few patients who show severe evidence of depression, according to their mothers or physicians. Four chronically ill adolescents made suicidal attempts or threats. Among the four chronically ill suicidal patients were two youngsters heading for kidney transplantation, each of whom had watched a relative die after an unsuccessful transplant. The other two suicidal patients were among the ten patients who had lupus erythematosus, a particularly severe disease affecting the kidney as well as other body systems. We have reported elsewhere the susceptibility of five transplanted adolescents to suicidal thinking when there was a threat that the new kidney might not work (see Bernstein, 1977).[3]

II. Factors Affecting the Child's Adjustment to Illness

Other than for a few extreme cases, then, is the emotional stress of chronic illness exaggerated? It would be premature to reach this conclusion before investigating whether there are subgroups of the population

Figure 2

Children at Greater Risk

Those with more severe illness
Adolescents
(Females)
Children from rural, lower class, large families
Children dissatisfied with their appearance
Children who take less responsibility for their own care
Children whose mothers are confused by the sick role

which are more severely affected than others by the disease experience. Figure 2 identifies those types of children who are more vulnerable to the stress of illness, and the following discussion focuses on factors that might be expected to increase vulnerability.

Effects of Disease Severity on Adjustment of the Chronically Ill Child
The first set of factors explored were those which involve various definitions of the severity of the *chronically ill* child's disease. The initial hypothesis is that children who are more seriously ill will show greater disturbance of the self-picture and a lower level of happiness. Two objective and one subjective measure of severity have been correlated with the nine indicators of the child's adjustment (see Table 3). The two external judgments are those of the physician and the child's mother, one a medi-

Table 3

Effect on Chronically Ill Child of Objective and Subjective Severity
of the Disease — Pearson's Correlations and Canonical Correlations

	Objective Definitions		Subjective
	Physician's	Mother's	Child's own
	rating of	rating of	rating of
Child's emotional state:	severity	severity	severity
Happiness	$-.18^\phi$	-.15	-.22†
Self-esteem	-.01	$-.18^\phi$	-.34+
Self-consciousness	.02	.13	.38*
Stability of the self-picture	.11	-.14	$-.18^\phi$
Sense of being distinctive, different	$-.19^\phi$	$.20^\phi$	.19†
Satisfaction with one's looks	-.03	-.12	.01
Showing true feelings to others	-.23†	-.26†	-.31+
Estimate of Popularity	.08	-.32+	-.38*
Anxiety	.08	$.18^\phi$	.43*
Canonical Correlation	.37	.43	.59+
Common Variance	14%	19%	35%

* p $\leq$ .001
+ p $\leq$ .01
† p $\leq$ .05
ϕ p $\leq$ .10

cal and the other a family expert. The third measure of severity involves the child's own subjective perception of his disease.

Severity as defined by the physician was found to correlate significantly and negatively with three aspects of the child's adjustment (see Table 3). Severity as judged by the mother is associated at statistically significant levels with five measures of adjustment. Although the objective severity of the child's condition does affect the child, several aspects of the self are unaffected.

The child's own definition of the severity of his disease, however, correlates more highly and significantly with almost all of the measures of adjustment in a negative direction (Table 3). Although there is a high correlation between the three definitions of severity, the highest correlation is between that of the mother and that of the child, and it is these two family definitions which seem to have wider ramifications for the child.[4] In comparing the canonical correlations between each of the three definitions of severity and the nine adjustment measures, the child's subjective definition is found to account for more of the variance in the child's adjustment (35 percent) than the two objective definitions (14 percent explained by physician's definition and 19 percent by that of the mother). The fact that the child's *own* perception of his disease correlates most highly with his other self-assessments probably cannot be dismissed as simply a function of measurement consistency; i.e., that responses from the same individual are always likely to correlate more highly than responses from different individuals. In fact, this pattern of a higher correlation among answers collected from *one* person does not always occur for these variables. For example, the *child's* definition of the severity of the disease is more important for the *mother's* self-reported adjustment than is her own definition of the severity of the child's disease. Since the true seriousness of the disease is frequently hidden from the child, it would appear that his own interpretation becomes more important than the reality, both for his own and his mother's psychological health.

However, with a one-point-in-time study (a cross-sectional design), it is impossible to be certain of this causal direction. Perhaps, as posited, those children who perceive the disease to be a great problem react to this perception with a less favorable self-image and level of happiness. If the above is the major causal direction, then we *could* conclude that the child's own subjective experience has more extensive and pervasive effects than the objective severity of his disease. However, it is also possible that those children who previously suffered from low esteem and a low level of happiness are the ones who are least able to cope with the disease and are most likely to perceive it as a major problem.

Effect of Age and Sex on Adjustment of the Chronically Ill and Transplanted Child

Other than differences due to disease severity, is the adjustment of these children related to background or status factors? In the Baltimore study, Simmons et al. (1973) found that disturbance in the self-image of normal children was related to their *age*. *Early adolescents* (age 12 to 14 or 15) showed a negative drop in many scales, followed by a leveling or positive turn, especially for self-esteem, during late adolescence.

In this study of chronically ill children, we found that age significantly affects three indicators of adjustment: depression, self-consciousness, and global self-esteem.[5] As in the Baltimore sample, depression and self-consciousness increase among the chronically ill children in adolescence, with the big increase occurring in the early teen-age years. The normal siblings also show greater depression and self-consciousness at this time, although the role of the early teen years in the transition from childhood is less clear. The posttransplant children show, similarly, increased self-consciousness and depression with age.

Both the sick children and their siblings reveal a steady increase in self-esteem with age. In the Baltimore sample the transition year into puberty when youngsters moved into junior high school (age 12) was accompanied by a sudden, short-lived drop in self-esteem. Because of the small numbers of children at any particular age among the chronically ill population, it was impossible to test for this decrease in self-esteem found for the 12-year-olds in the Baltimore study. In any case, like the Baltimore children, the older adolescents demonstrate higher self-esteem than any other age child. Thus, age-related changes appear to be similar for the chronically ill children as for normal groups of youth.

The findings with regard to the self-esteem of the *transplanted* children are clearer in identifying early adolescence as stressful and late adolescence as less so. Although the number of cases is too few to have firm confidence in the results ($N = 35$ for this analysis), the early adolescents appear to demonstrate considerably lower self-esteem than their older or younger counterparts. Only 27 percent of the transplanted youngsters, ages 8–12, score low in self-esteem as compared to 58 percent of the early adolescents (ages 13–15) and 33 percent of the older children (ages 16–20). The psychiatric difficulties of adolescent transplanted children has also been discussed by Bernstein (1977).

The sex of the child might also be expected to have a general impact upon his or her self-image that is independent of the illness. Among *adults,* females have been found to adjust better to illness and to transplantation than males (Simmons et al., 1977, Chapter 3). Yet the explanations for these results seemed to lie in the adult roles of men and women. The male had to attain successful job-rehabilitation to be self-content, while the woman could define herself as rehabilitated without leaving the home. Within the home, the female's activity was so necessary for family order that she was presumed to be highly motivated to leave the sick-role. However, these sex-role considerations are not relevant for adolescents and children. That is, the female child or adolescent should have no easier time than the male at defining herself as rehabilitated, and her full participation within the family should be no more important than that of the male. Thus, if these sex-role explanations have any validity, female children should not demonstrate higher adjustment than the males, even though the adult females did cope better.

In fact, the Baltimore study of normal children indicates that in certain respects, females are less well off than males in adolescence (F. Rosenberg and Simmons, 1975; Simmons and Rosenberg, 1975). The ill children seem to react the same way as do the normal youth. For both the sick children and their siblings, once again females are generally less well off than male children in terms of stability of self-concept and satisfaction with their looks, but are better off in terms of happiness. For the transplanted children, females also were more unhappy with their appearance, although no other sex differences were found. It is not surprising that females are less satisfied with their appearance. In our culture good looks is more important for the female than the male; and in adolescence, at a time when appearance changes rapidly, females are more likely to react negatively to these changes, whether ill or healthy.

In general, the effects of age and sex upon the self-image appear to be reflective of general developmental differences, rather than a consequence of chronic illness in particular.

Effect of Family Background on the Adjustment of the Chronically Ill Child[6]
Family background factors also appear to have general consequences for children's self-images rather than specific effects for the ill child. In general, the urban middle-class family appears more beneficial for the self-image of both the ill children and their siblings than does the rural lower-class family. Even controlling for socioeconomic status[7] and religion, rural youngsters (particularly the ill children but also their siblings) score lower in self-esteem than their urban counterparts and also more negatively along other dimensions of the self-picture (although the findings are not totally consistent). For example, the partial correlation between rural-urban residence and self-esteem is .32 ($p = .008$) for the ill children and .21 for their siblings (see Klein, 1975, for more detail).[8]

Several studies conducted in the 1930's and 40's hypothesized that rural life would be *more* beneficial than urban for the adjustment of the child

(Mangus, 1949). Yet these studies did not show rural children scoring higher than big-city children in the California Test of Personality (Mangus, p. 14); and our research also fails to show an advantage of rural life. In fact, at least in this population, a rural background is a disadvantage for the child. But why should rural residence be associated with lower self-esteem? We could hypothesize that it is due to the fact that rural families tend to be larger (our data do show the farm families to be larger). Perhaps in small families, which are more common in the city, children receive more parental attention, to the benefit of their self-esteem.

Large family size does appear to be associated with detrimental self-image effects, although not totally consistently. Both sick children and their siblings are much less likely to reveal their true feelings if they live in a large family ($r = -.23$[9] and $-.33$[9]). Likewise, children from large families, especially if sick, are more likely to be highly self-conscious ($r = -.23$[9]). The *self-esteem* of the siblings is also negatively affected by being in a large family: 46 percent of siblings from large families have low self-esteem in contrast to only 33 percent from small families. However, the self-esteem of the ill children is unaffected by family size, and therefore the rural-urban differences in their self-esteem could not be due to family size differentials.

Thus, in this population both the ill and healthy children from small, urban families appear better adjusted on several, though not all, dimensions. These families seem to act as positive resources for all children in handling stress. Whether these findings will be replicated in other studies is an open question. In the Baltimore study, there are no rural children to test (see Rosenberg and Simmons, 1972). It appears unlikely but not impossible that our findings are specific to children in families containing a chronically ill member.

Satisfaction with Body-Image: The Adjustment of the Chronically Ill and Transplanted Child

Apart from the severity of the illness, and the background statuses of the child and his family, the child's appearance would also be expected to affect his adjustment, particularly in the case of the transplanted child. As the illness becomes visible, we would expect its effects to be greater. As indicated above, the most significant difference between the *chronically ill* and *transplanted* children relates to their satisfaction with body-image. Thirty-six percent of the ill children and 65 percent of the transplanted children say the disease has affected their appearance. Over half (55 percent) of the transplanted children report they are not satisfied with their body-image, compared to 22 percent of the Baltimore controls, 28 percent of the normal siblings, and 39 percent of the children with chronic kidney disease. Eighty percent of the transplanted youngsters perceive they are "too short" in comparison to 39 percent of the ill children and 23 percent of the siblings. These subjective perceptions are generally validated by the interviewer's rating of the transplanted child's appearance: 41 percent of the posttransplanted children were rated as obviously Cushingoid (moon-faced) to the interviewer with 29 percent rated as full-faced but not obviously abnormal, and 31 percent classified as lacking Cushingoid features. Almost half of the transplanted youngsters were categorized by the interviewer as being very small for their ages.

The appearance of some posttransplant youngsters has been one of the main arguments against transplantation for children. While both adults and children may become Cushingoid in response to the steroid medication, particularly when threatened kidney rejection requires high steroid doses, the adolescents tend to look more abnormal even at lower dosage levels. In particular, the growth retardation associated with their previous kidney diseases, plus the protuberant abdomen and prominent jowls associated with the Cushingoid state make them look more bizarre. Girls who are developing figures but not growing as tall as normal, appear most abnormal when their faces and waists are swollen. In most patients with successful kidney transplants, these problems abate with time; and most adolescents, though still short, appear increasingly normal four to five years after transplantation.

The growth retardation of severe kidney disease is somewhat reversed by the transplant,[10] but in many cases growth during the adolescent years is suboptimal. Some children grow rapidly immediately after the transplant, some grow poorly. Some who grow poorly during their first few posttransplant years may spurt up later. In fact, some children who do not grow for the first few years after the transplant may grow several inches in their early twenties. In general, however, girls grow less well than do boys. This is particularly striking for girls in early adolescence.

In a series reviewed in 1974 of all adolescents who were transplanted before age 19, who currently were age 15 or older, and who had reached ten months or more posttransplant, 20 percent of the boys (three out of fifteen) had not yet attained 5 feet in height and 53 percent were below 5½ feet. Four girls or 21 percent (four out of nineteen) were 4½ feet or less in height and 53 percent were below 5 feet.

In short, growth is variable and frequently disappointing. Failure to grow is related not only to preexisting kidney disease, and dose of steroids, but also appears to be related to the degree of imperfection in kidney function. A degree of kidney compromise which would allow for apparent perfect health in an adult does not support the continued normal growth of the adolescent (Najarian et al., 1971; DeShazo et al., 1974).

How significant for the child's adjustment is the dissatisfaction with appearance associated with transplantation? In general, dissatisfaction with one's looks is detrimental to the psychosocial adjustment of the transplanted child. Posttransplant children who are *satisfied* with their appearance are found to be at least as well adjusted and more often better adjusted than the normal controls on the nine scales administered. The satisfied children fare so well that they statistically balance the dissatisfied, allowing us to conclude that transplanted children as a whole are not psychologically harmed.

Those transplanted children who are dissatisfied with their appearance are vulnerable. They tend to exhibit lower self-esteem than those who are satisfied ($r = .43, p = .05$); they rate themselves as less popular ($r = .27$); they feel more distinctive ($r = -.22$) and self-conscious ($r = -.34, p = .03$). In contrast to children who were satisfied with their appearance, the dissatisfied show higher anxiety ($r = -.33, p = .03$), lower levels of happiness ($r = .28, p = .05$), and more instability of the self-concept ($r = .30, p = .05$). Similar signs of negative adjustment were found to be associated with external ratings of the transplanted child's appearance.

The correlations between satisfaction with looks and the scales of adjustment for the *chronically ill* children are in the same direction but are smaller; the chronically ill children who are dissatisfied with their looks demonstrate greater instability of the self-picture ($r = .15$), and lower self-esteem ($r = .10$).

As noted earlier, there were no differences found between the chronically ill children and their siblings in terms of numbers and kinds of friends. Among the transplanted and chronically ill children, differences in social activities are related to body-image problems. Compared to children who are more satisfied with their appearance, transplanted children who are dissatisfied have fewer friends of the same and opposite sexes; for instance, 50 percent of those who are satisfied with their appearance report having a friend of the opposite sex in contrast to 25 percent of those who are dissatisfied, although this difference does not hold for the chronically ill children. In describing their after-school activities both the chronically ill and transplanted children[11] are more likely to mention socializing with peers if they are satisfied with their appearance than if they are dissatisfied (47 percent vs. 26 percent of the transplanted children; 77 percent vs. 52 percent of the chronically ill). In terms of the transplanted children, the objective rating of Cushingoid appearance was related similarly to the child's sociability. Most of the chronically ill and transplanted children, whether satisfied or dissatisfied, however, do report they have a "best friend" (78–94 percent, depending on which type of child).

Generally, the evidence suggests that dissatisfaction with one's appearance provides a measure of the child's vulnerability. Unfortunately, causal directions are difficult to establish without longitudinal data. It is possible that children who have self-image problems before becoming diseased are those who become critical of their looks and sensitive post-transplant to steroid-induced changes. However, because the interviewer's objective rating of the child's appearance correlates with the child's subjective opinion, it appears that "dissatisfaction with looks" is more than just a reflection of the child's overall response set.

III. Impact of the Chronically Ill Child on the Family as a Whole
In our society the family is the social unit most directly responsible for the care of its sick members. The effects of illness on the child cannot be understood without exploring the impact of the disease on his family, and the amount of protection and support which the family offers the sick child.

It is often a "crisis" for the family when a child is diagnosed as having a chronic disease. The impact of the disease upon the family was probed in the interviews with the children chronically ill with kidney disease, their mothers and siblings. Since we secured these three viewpoints only for the chronically ill children and not for the transplanted youngsters, the bulk of the family analysis will focus on chronic illness.

The immediate responses reported by the mothers to the diagnosis (of kidney disease) were characterized by pessimism, a felt lack of understanding, and a fear that the child might die. Over time, the mothers reported their understanding and acceptance increased and their worry decreased. Although the disease was still perceived as a significant problem, it could be cognitively assimilated into the family's ongoing life.

A series of questions was asked to explore what the child's disease actually meant to the family. These items were placed in a factor analysis which yielded three general factors. The first factor describes the *general* practical disruption caused the family, the second the *emotional* stress, and the third the *financial* burden of the disease. The general impact factor deals with the level of disruption in the family—for instance, how much time and energy the child's illness has consumed or how much it has interfered with the family routine.

The stressor event in each family is similar—the diagnosis of a serious and chronic childhood disease. The stressor does, however, vary in its seriousness; and severity should, hypothetically, be related to impact on the family. The data show that the more serious the child's disease (as defined by mother, child, and physician) the greater the general, emotional, and financial hardships for the family (see Klein, 1975).

Furthermore, although the stressor event was similar in each of the families studied, the way in which the family defined the event and the impact the event had on the family varied. The family carries with it certain recuperative resources, indexed by socioeconomic status, religous affiliation, family composition, and modes of family functioning, upon which it draws during a crisis. Some of these background factors are positive resources, whereas others may increase the family's vulnerability. Furthermore, background factors may act positively or negatively depending on which of the three hardship dimensions described above is considered. Several factors which have been found (Hansen and Hill, 1964) to affect the family's response were examined in relation to perceived hardship.

Effect of Family Size, Structure, and Residence on Family Responses to Chronic Childhood Illness

Overall family size does not appear to be either an advantage or handicap in meeting this crisis. Whether or not there is an older sibling at home is a related aspect of family structure. Although no differences are shown in terms of general disruption, there is some evidence that having older children in the home is a resource in alleviating the emotional hardship of having a child with chronic kidney disease. Where there is an older sibling in the house, fully 53 percent of the families report a low emotional impact, in contrast to only 37 percent of those without an older sibling. Thus, it is not the family size *per se* that is important, but the sibling structure.

Rural families are more likely to show a high level of general disruption than urban families (33 percent vs. 16 percent), although there are no differences between rural and urban families in regard to emotional or financial impact. Just as the ill children and their siblings fared less well in a rural environment, the rural family appeared to find illness a greater stress. Further analyses, controlling for religion and family size, failed to destroy the relationship between rural residence and general disruptive impact. This difference may be explained in part by the demands of farm life, which cannot yield easily to the needs of a disabled member. Greater distance from the medical center may also contribute to the difficulty.

Effect of Socioeconomic Status and Religion on Family Responses to Chronic Childhood Illness

If differences in family size do not explain the greater disruption for the rural family, socioeconomic status (SES) may, given the fact that rural families tend to be poorer. However, high or middle socioeconomic status, not lower, is associated with family difficulty along all three dimensions. For example, only 21 percent of those with high SES report a low level of general disruption in contrast to half of the lower-class families. This relationship holds when controlled for residence and religion. In terms of *financial* impact, the middle-class family is more likely to report a greater impact. This disadvantage for the middle-class family may in part be attributed to the fact that they did not qualify for medical assistance and had to bear almost all the medical costs themselves. In addition, the middle–class, in contrast to the lower classes, defines illness as more of an emotional or tragic crisis (Farber, 1960). Thus, socioeconomic differences cannot explain the greater problems for rural families.

As indicated above, religious differences do not explain the rural-urban findings either. Although Farber (1959) and Zuk (1959) found that the Catholic religion was a supportive factor in dealing with mental retardation, no significant differences in family impact in this study were found between Catholics and Protestants.

Effect of Family's Solidarity and Prior Experience on Family Response to Chronic Illness
Quality of the family's functioning is expected to be related to the family's level of solidarity. The following questions asked of the mother were used to measure family solidarity:

Do you think that the child's disease in any way
brought the family closer together or in any way
drew the family apart?
    yes, together
    neither
    no, apart

All families are different; some are very close
and others are not. Would you say the people in
your immediate family are
    very close
    pretty close
    a little close, or
    not at all close to each other?

How well do the people in your family get along
together at home? Does your family get along
    very well
    pretty well
    a little well, or
    not at all well?

When a problem comes up with the family, how willing
are the people in your immediate family to help out?
Are they
    very willing to help out
    somewhat willing

a little willing, or
not at all willing to help out?

Compared to most families you know, do you think
your family is
more happy
less happy, or
about the same as other families?

(Reliability and validity were satisfactory for this scale. See Klein, 1975). Families low in solidarity are more likely to report that the disease had a great general disruptive impact than families very high in solidarity (50 percent vs. 17 percent). *Highly* unified families are, however, more emotionally disrupted by the child's disease, perhaps because of the emotional interdependence of its members (36 percent vs. 50 percent show a low degree of emotional impact). No consistent relationship between family solidarity and financial hardship was found.

Another aspect of the family's functioning expected to help in problem solving is previous experience with similar problems (Hill, 1949). Our data suggest that previous experience is a resource in meeting the general and emotional aspects of the hardship. Of those mothers who reported that their families had experience with other serious diseases, 57 percent indicated a low level of general disruption this time (in comparison to 42 percent of the inexperienced) and 59 percent (vs. 39 percent) reported a low degree of emotional hardship associated with the child's disease. Experience is, however, a handicap with regard to the financial impact of the

Figure 3

Characteristics of Family at Risk for Hardship
During Chronic Childhood Illness

General disruptive impact	Emotional impact	Financial impact
Rural residence	– – –	– – –
Highest social class	Middle social class	Middle social class
– – –	No older children in home	No older children
Low family solidarity	High family solidarity	– – –
Lack of experience with similar crises	Lack of experience	Experience with similar crises

disease; those with previous illness reported greater hardship, suggesting the family's practical resources may already have been depleted. (See Bernstein, 1977, for a somewhat different picture of families with two transplanted children.)

In summary, characteristics of families at particular risk are shown in Figure 3. Few generalizations can be made about the family at risk for all three aspects of the crisis. A factor that seems to intensify one type of hardship—financial, emotional, or general disruption—may have no effect or may even mitigate another aspect of the stress.

IV. The Family and Its Relation to Individual Member's Adjustment

Effects of the Disease on the Adjustment of Other Family Members

Chronic illness would be expected to affect the adjustment of individual family members as well as the family as a whole. In fact, maternal adjustment was found to be affected by the child's disease. These mothers were administered the adult versions of some of the scales used with the children—i.e., we measured happiness, anxiety, and self-esteem. These measures, particularly the Rosenberg self-esteem scale, have been widely used elsewhere and have satisfactory reliability and validity (see Rosenberg, 1965; Wylie, 1974; Wells and Marwell, 1976; Robinson and Shaver, 1969; Simmons et al., 1977: Chs. 3, 6). In terms of findings, the greater the severity of the disease as perceived by the *child,* the lower the mother's happiness ($r = -.20$, $p = .06$) and the greater her anxiety ($r = .15$) and guilt ($r = .31$, $p = .004$).

Severity of the child's disease as estimated by the mother was also found to be related to the adjustment of the normal sibling, although not totally consistently. Greater severity was especially related to lower self-esteem of the siblings ($r = -.23$, $p = .08$), a tendency to conceal true feelings ($r = .34$, $p = .02$), and a higher level of anxiety ($r = .33$). Furthermore, controlling for the severity of the disease, we find that if the sibling reports he is very disturbed and unhappy about the disease, his overall level of happiness is likely to be low ($r = -.38, p = .02$). Either the specific anxiety over the disease renders the sibling generally unhappy, or the less happy child interprets the illness in an especially negative light. In either case, the child in a home where a brother or sister is suffering from a more severe chronic disease is likely to show an impaired self-image. The fact that a severe disease has emotional costs for the sibling as well as the ill patient helps to explain why there is not a greater difference between the self-images of the sick children and their normal sisters and brothers. However, the lack of difference between the ill children and the Baltimore "controls" still remains to be explained (see Conclusion).

Sharing or Focusing the Burden of Childhood Illness

In addition to overall emotional adjustment, we can investigate the specific reaction to the burden of the illness on the part of family members. Many studies have indicated that of all the family members, the mother bears the greatest impact when one member is chronically ill (Litman, 1974). Is this pattern true in this population as well? We asked family members how upset and unhappy various family members had been by the disease (the "emotional" impact), how much each member had to give up, and how much the daily life of each had been disturbed by the disease (more "practical" hardships). According to the mother *and the normal sibling,* the mother is more likely to bear the brunt of the *emotional* impact. (Only one-third of the mothers see themselves as relatively undisturbed emotionally, in comparison to their perception that 42 percent of the fathers, 53 percent of ill children, and 60 percent of the normal siblings are undisturbed.) *Both* parents are seen as worrying more than their children, including the ill child.

Some interesting findings emerge when the practical and emotional aspects of the impact are differentiated. According to the mother, it is the ill child himself whose daily life is most disturbed on the practical level, and who has had to sacrifice the most: 54 percent of the children are seen as significantly affected by the disease in this way compared to 40 percent of the mothers, 33 percent of the fathers, and 25 percent of the normal siblings. In terms of nursing care for the sick child, however, mothers assume the greatest burden, followed by the child himself. While other family members help with the housework, they appear to participate little in the care of the ill child, at least according to our data. (For more detail see Klein, 1975.)

Unfortunately, however, in this and most studies of chronic illness in children, the father's perception has not been measured and therefore we are relying for this information on the view of the mother, the sick child, and the normal sibling. It is possible they underestimate the father's input.

It was initially hypothesized that a family member upon whom the burdens of disease were focused would be maladjusted. That is, if one individual assumed the hardship himself or herself without family sharing or support, there would be a mental health cost for that individual. There were few families (14 out of 72) in which the mother alone seemed to bear the burdens of care, however, and the effects on her adjustment seemed minimal.

To test the relationship between sharing of the burden and the ill child's adjustment, families were divided into three groups *according to the mother's perception:*

1. Those in which the ill child does not share in the burden of care.
2. Those in which the burden is shared by all members, including the child.
3. Those in which the burden of care is absorbed primarily by the sick child.

Correlations with the nine scales of the child's adjustment show that the way the family manages the burden is somewhat important for the child, but for several scales in the direction *opposite* to the way predicted. Children upon whom the burden of care is *focused,* in contrast to those who do not assume a major burden of self-care demonstrate *higher* stability of the self-concept ($r^{12} = .15$),lower anxiety ($r^{12} = -.19$, $p = .08$), are able to show their feelings more ($r^{12} = .36$, $p = .002$), tend to be more satisfied with their appearance ($r^{12} = .41$, $p = .001$), and are less likely to see themselves as different ($r^{12} = -.14$) even when severity of the disease and age are controlled. Thus, a strategy of giving the child sole responsibility for his own care seems positive for the child's adjustment along several self-image dimensions.

Further evidence that it is beneficial for the child to assume responsibility for his own care is obtained from the child himself. If the child indicated in answer to several questions that he took care of himself when he was sick, he was more likely to demonstrate high self-esteem ($r = .29$, $p = .02$).[13] The way the family manages the burdens of the disease is important then not only for the family members but to the child himself.

Tension in Managing the Sick Child's Role and Adjustment
The parent's management of the disease not only involves the extent to which the burden is shared, but also the level of emotional confusion or calm with which the sick-role is approached. Qualitative information from parents of ill and transplanted children suggest that certain dilemmas face the mothers, and mothers respond with varying levels of confusion. A major dilemma for the mother is whether to treat the child as "normal" or whether to make certain he receives special treatment. The danger of giving him special treatment is that of creating a psychological invalid. The above discussion indicates that the independent child who assumes responsibility for his own care is an emotionally healthier youngster. On the other hand, if the child is treated as "normal" in all situations, the danger is that his physical health may be placed at serious risk, as in the following case:

A 10-year-old girl received her father's kidney and was successfully transplanted. When she returned home, she did well and was able with some parental help to administer her own medications. A year later her parents decided to send her to camp, like other "normal" children. The medications at camp had to be administered through the camp nurse, and the nurse was sent these with instructions. When the child returned home, however, her blood tests indicated that she had started to reject the kidney. Upon questioning, the child indicated that when she went to the camp infirmary for her medications she could not find the nurse and did not receive her medicines for a week or more. The insidious chronic rejection of the kidney could not be halted and after a very stressful time period, the kidney had to be removed. The mother then donated her kidney to maintain the child's life.

This case is complicated by the fact that the "normal" child is not expected to handle medications and is frequently dependent upon busy adults who fail to comprehend special needs. To escape the dependency of illness is difficult for the maturing child, since he cannot evade the expected dependency of childhood. The parent feels compelled, therefore, to give him special protection in order to maintain his physical health. Yet some parents are very confused as to the proper course of action in this and other situations.

In order to investigate the consequences of maternal confusion in managing the child's sick role, we asked her:

Do you generally feel you have been able to handle your child's illness well enough or do you feel it's been a problem for you?

Parents sometimes feel confused about whether a child with this disease should be treated differently or whether (he, she) should be treated the same as other children. Has this been a problem for you—deciding how to treat your child? Has it been a great problem, somewhat of a problem, a little problem, or no problem for you?

How much of a bother is the child's regular treatment? Is it a big bother, a little bother, or no bother at all?

How hard is it for your child to follow the doctor's orders? Very hard, a little hard, or not at all hard?

This index of tension in managing the sick child's role, or the mother's difficulty in handling the child, does not correlate significantly with measures of maternal adjustment. It is more important in understanding the child's adjustment, however. Controlling for the severity of the disease, on seven of the nine scales, the mother's perceived tension in managing the sick child's role is associated with *negative* adjustment for the child. (On the two other scales there is no difference.) The child's sense of being different and distinct ($r^{14} = .20$, $p = .08$), his level of anxiety ($r = .26$, $p = .03$), the stability of his self-picture ($r^{14} = -.11$), and the child's ability to reveal his true feelings to others ($r = -.30$, $p = .01$) are affected by the mother's tension in managing the sick role. Although the correlations are

not large, the importance of these findings is increased by the independence of the measures—the indicators of the mother's role-tension are
derived from her own reports while the measures of the ill child's adjustment are obtained from the child. And according to these measures, if the
mother is confused in her handling of the ill child, the child himself is at
risk psychologically. The mother's conflict in handling the child thus provides a link between the coping of the family and that of the child.

SUMMARY AND DISCUSSION

The Chronically Ill Children

In *summary,* chronically ill children as a group appear to be quite
healthy in terms of their self-image and socioemotional adjustment. Although they are more dissatisfied with their physical appearance, these
children on the average are not more disturbed than normal controls in
regard to their level of self-esteem, self-consciousness, self-image stability, sense of distinctiveness, ability to reveal true feelings to others, or
perceived level of happiness. These findings suggest a puzzle: Why don't
the chronically ill youngsters demonstrate a more damaged self-picture?
This question is especially puzzling since adult patients with terminal
kidney disease on hemodialysis show significant *damage* along these
same dimensions. (See Simmons et al., 1977, Ch. 3.)

We can offer several hypotheses. First, the majority of these children
were considerably less ill and less symptomatic than the above pretransplant adults on hemodialysis. Only nine of them were ready for
hemodialysis or transplantation, for example. And those children who are
suffering from more serious diseases do show greater socioemotional disturbance.[15]

Secondly, the child's functional role is not as vulnerable to illness as
that of an adult. For the most part, a chronically ill child continues with
school, whereas the adult may be unable to maintain a job or perform his
family responsibilities. In fact, the role of the normal child and the classic
definition of the "sick role" (Gordon, 1966) are very similar, since both
the child and the ill person are generally exempt from social responsibility
and not expected to take care of themselves. Thus, the deviations caused
by disease are not so disrupting to the child as to the adult.

Third, parents can protect a child in ways in which the adult cannot be
protected. The parents can help the child *deny* the seriousness of his
condition (Salk et al., 1972; Mattsson and Gross, 1966a,b). For instance,
in comparing the way in which the ill child describes the personal costs of
his disease with the descriptions given by his normal sibling and mother,

some interesting discrepancies emerge. Most often the sibling reports that the illness has caused considerable sacrifices for the ill child, whereas the sick child himself minimizes these costs. The mothers' perceptions fall in between: For example, 30 percent of the siblings and 18 percent of the mothers but only 3 percent of the ill children report that the ill child has had to give up "very much" ($p = .005$). For the child, the use of denial seems functional, allowing him to maintain a high level of adjustment.[16]

Along with this denial the parents abide by a philosophy, endorsed by physicians, to treat the child "normally" (Collier, 1969; Mattsson and Gross, 1966a,b; Minde, 1972; Davis, 1963).

I felt it was important for him to lead as normal a life as possible.

We managed to put it (the disease) as part of family life. I tried to keep life on an even keel . . . I preferred to have it as something as normal as possible—Michael's going to the hospital and Bobby's going to school. It was just something he did. It was accepted as something normal. (Mother of adolescent boy with chronic kidney disease.)

The comments of this mother are characteristic of the attitude of most of the mothers interviewed. The mothers were asked: "Do you feel this child should be treated completely the same as other children, that (he, she) should be treated with some special consideration, or that (he, she) should be treated with a great amount of special consideration?" Eighty-two percent of the mothers responded with the ideology that the children should be treated the *same* as other children, and only 18 percent suggested some special consideration was appropriate. Yet, as indicated above, these children are at times very sick and require special care. The actual treatment of the child often conflicted with the labeling being given to behavior, as the children were given extra attention to maintain their normalcy.

In addition to the ability of the parents to label the ill child as "normal," they can also protect him or her with extra love and attention. Rosenberg (1965) and Rosenberg and Simmons (1972) have shown that the most powerful variables affecting children's self-images are the perceived opinions of significant others. If children believe that others rate them highly, they rate themselves highly. We have seen that the sick children do not perceive themselves to be less popular with peers than do the normal controls. In addition they are somewhat *more* likely than their siblings to report their mothers rate them highly. In answer to the multiple choice question, "Would you say your mother thinks you are a wonderful person, a pretty nice person, a little bit of a nice person, or not such a nice person?" 43 percent of the sick children selected "a wonderful person," versus 36 percent of their siblings and 26 percent of the Baltimore controls. This favorable opinion of the mothers is undoubtedly protective for the child's self-image: Our data indicate that those children who report their mothers think they are "wonderful persons" score more favorably on scales of self-esteem, self-consciousness, stability of the self-picture, satisfaction with looks, and ability to reveal their true feelings to others.

Furthermore, when asked to which family member they are closest, 29 percent of the sick children in contrast to 18 percent of the siblings chose their mother. They are also somewhat more likely than their own siblings to see themselves as the mother's favorite (14 percent vs. 7 percent), whereas the siblings are more likely to choose the father as the closest (7 percent vs. 20 percent). This evidence suggests the interaction pattern in the family may be altered, with the ill children perceiving a special alliance to their mothers. At any rate, the sick children do not appear disadvantaged within the context of the family.

Crain et al. (1966) did a similar study of the sociopsychological functioning of 19 diabetic children and 16 of their siblings. They too found that the functioning of the sick children did not differ significantly from that of their siblings. Furthermore, in trying to explain the lack of difference they showed that (1) the diabetic children were closer than their siblings to the mother, and (2) the mother's behavior was significantly related to the ill child's performance. Crain's study as well as our own suggests that there are costs for siblings in a family with a sick child, and that closeness with the mother helps the ill child to compensate for the potential stress of chronic ill health. That the sibling loses some maternal attention also helps to explain why the differences between siblings and ill children are not greater, or always in the predicted direction.

We propose that the family of the ill adult does not protect him and his self-image in the way demonstrated by the mother of the ill child. Classic studies of the unemployed male during the Depression indicate that even though the state of the economy was well-known, the male without a job lost considerable prestige within his own family (Angell, 1936). When the adult cannot perform his or her role and exposes the family to considerable stress, feelings of rejection seem more likely to occur than in the case of the child.

The effects of chronic illness on the child must be understood within the structure and functioning of the family. In this paper, the family's own coping as a unit has been examined also. Three aspects of the crisis for the *family* have been differentiated: general disruption, emotional stress, and financial burden. Those factors have, in turn, been related to variables in the family's background which may be resources or liabilities in meeting the demands of a child's disease. The disease was found to have an impact on the adjustment and self-image of the child's mother and siblings. The more severe the disease, the more negative the impact. The presence of an older sibling in the home, however, appears to reduce the emotional impact of the disease in the family.

One strategy for handling the sick child is to increase his' or her responsibility for self-care. Where this occurs, regardless of the severity of the disease, the ill child shows a higher level of self-esteem. These data suggest that the ill child himself should share with the mother in assuming the burden of daily care. Of course, with a one-point-in-time study we cannot be certain of the causal sequence: It is possible that children who have higher self-esteem prior to the disease are the ones who will assume more responsibility for their own care, rather than that independence in handling their illness produces higher self-esteem. In either case, there appears to be no psychological evidence to contraindicate giving the child a high degree of responsibility.

Physicians involved in the treatment of these families should be aware that if the mother is confused as to how to handle the sick role of the child, the child is likely to be at risk psychologically.

Despite these guidelines, the exact best balance for handling the child may be difficult to establish. The following two cases help describe attempts to achieve the balance, first in an unsuccessful case where the child is at risk, and second, in a case where the adjustment level is high.

The first mother has a ten-year-old boy with chronic kidney disease. She reports, "We show no difference between him and the other kids." When the child is hospitalized at the university two hundred miles from home, he is sometimes visited by his family on weekends. Although the mother acknowledges the boy is lonely, she expects the child to be very "mature." "He's very kind—he understands I can't be there (when he's in the hospital)." The patient himself voiced loneliness as his biggest problem in being sick. He was given *no special consideration* and was expected to understand that the family's needs outweighed his own need for support. Extreme denial of the seriousness of the boy's condition and complete responsibility by the child for his own care resulted, in this case, not only in psychological stress but also in poor disease control. Thus, in some cases balancing of attention for the ill child against other family needs is difficult to achieve. This case suggests that problems can emerge when the child is given extreme responsibility, unaccompanied by special emotional attention.

The second mother has a sixteen-year-old son who has had chronic kidney disease from age 2.

I've tried to keep it as normal as possible, so it didn't seem like the attention was given because he was sick. He's had a lot of special attention but I don't want it to be something out of the ordinary. It's better to make it part of the daily routine. He may have to live with it all his life . . . . It (the disease) might have had a maturing effect—

he's quite mature for his age. He's able to accept responsibility. . . . He organizes, carries through, he's very adult. He's had a lot of responsibilities from taking the medication; a lot depends on it—his life. It's serious business; we never really talked about it, but we knew.

In this mother's account, a need for special attention was recognized along with an effort to establish normalcy and responsibility. She alludes also to a positive personality gain or increased maturity attributed to the disease experience.

This increased maturity among the ill children was mentioned in several cases and should not be ignored as a possible outcome of crisis. We asked the chronically ill children and their mothers and siblings what changes the disease had affected in the child. Although fourteen siblings (32 percent) and nineteen mothers (29 percent) mention negative personality changes (touchiness, irritability, withdrawal) in the ill child, twenty-one mothers (33 percent) commented on positive personality changes, including increased maturity and appreciation of life. Among the children themselves, eight (11 percent) mention similar gains, although the more salient changes attributed to the disease were negative body changes, decreased energy, and activity restrictions. In terms of *personality* impact, however, the child and his mother tend to perceive the effects as more positive than negative. These feelings of greater maturity and a more fundamental appreciation of life due to the health crisis were also mentioned by adult posttransplant patients (see Simmons et al., 1977, Chapter 3).

In sum, the general low visibility of kidney diseases, the fact that many children lack extensive symptomatology, the continuing high opinions of significant others, the special closeness to the mother, and the tendency toward denial all mediate to protect these chronically ill children. In spite of the stresses of disease, the children as a group appear to cope well with illness and emerge healthy psychologically.

The Transplanted Children
As a group, the children who have had kidney transplants also seem to exhibit healthy self-images and favorable levels of emotional adjustment, showing almost no differences from the normal controls on the quantitative self-image measures. In terms of physical well-being and school activity, however, some negative effects are still evident, with the transplanted children falling between the normal and chronically ill youngsters in their self-assessments. On one hand, the transplanted children participate more in school activities than the chronically ill youngsters and perceive themselves as physically healthier; while on the other hand, they are more fearful of future illness and earn considerably lower marks in school.

With both the transplanted and ill children, the major point of vulnerability lies in satisfaction with the body-image. The children with kidney transplants are considerably more likely to be dissatisfied with their looks than either normal youngsters or chronically ill children. According to an observer, two-fifths of the transplanted children are rated as obviously abnormal in terms of their moon-faced appearance; and one-fifth of the older adolescents are still extraordinarily short. That subgroup of youngsters who are dissatisfied with their physical appearance also indicate a lower level of sociability, as well as damage along a variety of dimensions of the self-image.

When the physical appearance is not affected, however, children react remarkably well to the stress both of disease and of transplantation. While the parents' role in protecting the *transplanted* children has not been measured specifically as it was in the case of the chronically ill youngsters, it is likely that many of the same family dynamics are operative.

In conclusion, these results point to a surprising resiliency on the part of children faced with chronic illness and kidney transplantation. It is proposed that this resiliency is due to some extent to extra protection and emotional support of the children by their families, a protection that is not afforded to chronically ill adults. Other factors leading to the relatively high adjustment of these children appear to be (1) the low visibility of chronic kidney disease (those for whom the disease is more visible, whose physical appearance suffers, do show negative self-image damage); (2) the fact that many patients lack extensive symptomatology; (3) the continuing high opinion of significant others; and (4) a tendency toward denial fostered by the family. Evidence indicates that regardless of the severity of the disease, children who cope better are those (1) who are allowed to assume more responsibility for their own medical care, (2) whose mothers are not confused and overwhelmed by the necessary medical regime, and (3) whose mothers are perceived as holding an extremely high opinion of them.

FOOTNOTES

*Roberta G. Simmons wishes to acknowledge grant support for this project. These are grants from the National Institute of Mental Health MH AM 18135; 2R01 MH 18135; and two NIMH Research Scientists Development Awards #5 K1 MH 41688 and #2 KO2 MH 41688.

[1]When a patient's kidneys no longer function, he is said to have end-stage renal disease and life cannot be maintained without either kidney transplantation or recourse to dialysis (the artificial kidney machine). A patient on dialysis is connected through a tube attached to an artery and vein in his wrist or leg to a machine through which his blood flows and is cleansed

before being returned to his body. The process takes 6–8 hours two to three times a week and many patients feel ill a high proportion of the time in between treatments. Kidney transplantation aims to remove the patient from the sick-role. A kidney either from a relative or a newly brain-dead cadaver is surgically placed within the patient where it ideally assumes necessary functions. The body is less likely to immunologically destroy the kidney of a relative because of genetic similarities—that is, the kidney is less likely to be immunologically "rejected." At the end of two years 74 percent of kidneys from siblings as compared to only 43 percent of kidneys from cadavers are still functioning (Twelfth Transplant Registry, 1975). Thus, siblings, parents, and children are considered prime candidates for donation. Although we all have two kidneys, only one is necessary. The risk to the donor is 1/2000 of not surviving the operation and a similar long-term risk.

2. Table 2 does show that the Baltimore children are significantly *more* likely than any of the Minnesota groups to score high in self-consciousness. If a Chi Square test is performed on the other three groups, eliminating the Baltimore sample, there is no significant difference.

3. Bernstein's (1977) series is not identical to that reported here, since it includes all youngsters ever transplanted here, while this paper focuses on those in whom the new kidney is still functioning.

4. Correlations of three definitions of severity: physician with mother, .32; physician with child, .28; mother with child, .57. It should be noted that whereas the mother's and child's definitions correlate negatively with almost all dimensions of the child's emotional adjustment, the physician's definition is less consistent in direction.

5. In general, throughout this paper, if one of the nine scales is not mentioned there is no relationship in either direction between it and the relevant factor being considered.

6. Since much of this background information was collected from the mothers, we do not have it for the posttransplant children in this cohort. For the effects of such factors on adult and adolescent patients transplanted from 1970–1973, see Simmons et al., 1977, Ch. 3.

7. As measured by the Hollingshead Two-Factor Scale (Bonjean et al., 1967).

8. On the other hand, when rural-urban residence is controlled, neither the children's social class background nor their family's religious orientation have consistent effects upon their self-esteem in particular, nor self-image in general.

9. $p \leq .05$

10. Our sample of chronically ill children contains many youngsters whose type of kidney disease is not severe enough to retard growth.

11. This indicator of sociability is not as good for the transplanted children as for the chronically ill, since in the latter case there are two other family members to verify the child's report and since there is a high level of missing data for this question among the transplanted children. Thus, these findings for the transplanted children must be regarded somewhat tentatively. The parallel direction of the findings for both groups is of interest, however.

12. These are partial correlations controlling for the severity of the disease and the child's age.

13. This is a partial correlation controlling for the child's age and the severity of the disease.

14. These are partial correlations, controlling for the severity of the disease.

15. In their study of chronic illness, Haggerty et al., 1975 also find that on key adjustment measures, differences occur primarily between severely ill children and other children, rather than between the moderately ill and normal youngsters.

16. The discrepancy between the ill child and the sibling may be due not only to denial on the part of the patient, but also because the normal sibling projects and exaggerates the plight of the sick youngster. The illness in imagination may be worse than in reality.

REFERENCES

"Should we transplant organs or efforts?" (editorial) *American Journal of Public Health,* 59(9), 1567–1568 (1969).

Angell, R. C. (1936), *The Family Encounters the Depression.* New York: Scribners.

Bernstein, Dorothy M. (1970), "Emotional reactions of children and adolescents to renal transplantation," *Child Psychiatry and Human Development,* 1(2), 102–111.

—— (1971), "After transplantation—the child's emotional reactions," *American Journal of Psychiatry,* 127(9), 1189–1193.

—— (1977), "Psychiatric assessment of the adjustment of transplanted children," Chapter 5 in Simmons, R. G., S. D. Klein, and R. L. Simmons, *Gift of Life: The Social and Psychological Impact of Organ Transplantation.* New York: Wiley Interscience.

Bonjean, Charles, Richard J. Hill, and S. Dale McLemore (1967), *Sociological Measurement.* San Francisco: Chandler.

Collier, B. N., Jr. (1969), "Comparisons between adolescents with and without diabetes," *Personnel and Guidance Journal,* 47(7), 679–684.

Crain, Alan J., Marvin B. Sussman, and William B. Weil, Jr. (1966), "Family interaction, diabetes and sibling relationships," *International Journal of Social Psychiatry,* 12(1), 35–43.

Davis, Fred (1963), *Passage Through Crisis.* Indianapolis: Bobbs-Merrill.

DeShazo, Claude V., Richard L. Simmons, Dorothy M. Bernstein, Maureen M. DeShazo, Justine Willmert, Carl M. Kjellstrand, and John S. Najarian (1974), "Results of renal transplantation in 100 children," *Surgery,* 76(3), 461–468.

Eichhorn, Robert L., and Ronald M. Andersen (1962), "Changes in personal adjustment to perceived and medically established heart disease: A panel study," *Journal of Health and Human Behavior,* 3(3), 242–249.

Erikson, E. H. (1956), "The problem of ego-identity," *Journal of American Psychoanalytic Association,* 4(1), 53–121.

Farber, Bernard (1959), "Effects of a severely mentally retarded child on family integration," *Monographs for the Society for Research in Child Development,* 24(2).

—— (1960), "Family organization and crisis: Maintenance of integration in families with a severely mentally retarded child," *Monographs for the Society for Research in Child Development,* 25(1).

Gates, M. (1946), "A comparative study of some problems of social and emotional adjustment of crippled and non-crippled girls and boys," *Journal of Genetic Psychology,* 68 (Second Half), 219–244.

Goldberg, Richard (1974), "Adjustment of children with invisible and visible handicaps," *Journal of Counselling Psychology,* 21(5), 428–432.

Gordon, Gerald (1966), *Role Theory and Illness: A Sociological Perspective.* New Haven: College andUniversity Press.

Haggerty, Robert J., Klaus J. Roghmann, and Ivan B. Pless (1975), *Child Health and the Community.* New York: Wiley.

Hansen, Donald, and Reuben Hill (1964), "Families under stress," pp. 782–822 in Harold T. Christensen (Ed.), *Handbook of Marriage and the Family.* Chicago: Rand McNally.

Hill, Reuben (1949), in collaboration with Elise Boulding, assisted by Lowell Dunigan and Rachel Ann Elder, *Families Under Stress: Adjustment to the Crisis of War Separation and Reunion.* New York: Harper.

Khan, Aman, M. A. Herndone, S. Y. Ahmadian (1971), "Social and emotional adaptations of children with transplanted kidneys and chronic hemodialysis," *American Journal of Psychiatry,* 127(9), 1194–1198.

Klein, Susan D. (1975), "Chronic kidney disease: Impact on the child and family and strategies for coping." Unpublished doctoral dissertation. University of Minnesota.

Korsch, Barbara, Vida Negrete, James E. Gardner, Carol L. Weinstock, Ann S. Mercer, Carl M. Grushkin, and Richard N. Fine (1973), "Kidney transplantation in children: Psychosocial follow-up study on child and family," *The Journal of Pediatrics*, 83(3), 399–408.

Lecky, P. (1945), *Self-Consistency*. New York: Island.

Litman, Theodor (1974), "The family as a basic unit in health and medical care: A social-behavioral overview," *Social Science and Medicine*, 8(9/10), 495–519.

Mangus, A. R. (1949), "Mental health of rural children in Ohio," *Ohio Agricultural Experiment Station Research Bulletin*, 682.

Mattsson, Ake (1972), "Long term physical illness in childhood—challenge of psycho-social adaptation," *Pediatrics*, 50(5), 801–811.

———, and Samuel Gross (1966a), "Adaptational and defensive behavior in young hemophiliacs and their parents," *American Journal of Psychiatry*, 122, 1349–1356.

——— (1966b), "Social and behavioral studies on hemophiliac children and their families," *Journal of Pediatrics*, 68(6), 952–964.

McAnarney, Elizabeth R., I. Barry Pless, Betty Satterwhite, and Stanford B. Friedman (1974), "Psychological problems of children with chronic juvenile arthritis," *Pediatrics*, 53(4), 523–528.

Meadow, Roy, J. Stewart Cameron, and Chisholm Ogg (1970), "Regional service for acute and chronic dialysis of children," *The Lancet*, 2(7675), 707–709.

Minde, Klaus K., G. D. Hackett, D. Killou, and S. Silver (1972), "How they group up: 41 physically handicapped children and their families," *American Journal of Psychiatry*, 128(2), 1554–1560.

"Rare kidney disease claims 3 sons," *Minneapolis Tribune*, March 31, p. 10B (1974).

Murphy, Lois (1961), "Preventive implications of development in the preschool years," pp. 218–248 in Gerald Caplan, (Ed.), *Prevention of Mental Disorders in Children*. New York: Basic Books.

Najarian, J. S., R. L. Simmons, M. B. Talent, C. M. Kjellstrand, T. J. Buselmeier, R. L. Vernier, and A. F. Michael (1971), "Renal transplantation in infants and children," *Annals of Surgery*, 174(4), 583–601.

Offord, D. R., and J. F. Aponte (1967), "Distortion of disability and effects on family life," *Journal of the American Academy of Child Psychiatry*, 6, 499–511.

Pless, Ivan, and Klaus Roghmann (1971), "Chronic illness and its consequences: Observations based on three epidemiologic surveys," *Journal of Pediatrics*, 79(3), 351–359.

Richardson, Stephen A., Albert H. Hastorf, Norman Goodman, and Sanford M. Dornbusch (1961), "Cultural uniformity in reaction to physical disabilities," *American Sociological Review*, 26(2), 241–247.

Robinson, John P., and Phillip R. Shaver (1969), "Measures of social psychological attitudes." (Appendix B to *Measures of Political Attitudes*). Survey Research Center, Institute for Social Research, August.

Rosenberg, Florence R., and Roberta G. Simmons (1975), "Sex differences in the self-concept in adolescence," *Sex Roles: A Journal of Research*, 1(2), 147–159.

Rosenberg, Morris (1965), *Society and the Adolescent Self-Image*. Princeton, N. J.: Princeton University Press.

———, and Roberta G. Simmons (1972), *Black and White Self-Esteem: The Urban School Child*. Washington, D. C.: American Sociological Association, Arnold and Caroline Rose Monograph Series.

Salk, Lee, Margaret Hilgartner, and Belle Granick (1972), "Psycho-social impact of hemophilia on the patient and his family," *Social Science and Medicine*, 6(4), 491–505.

Sampson, Tom F. (1975), "The child in renal failure," *Journal of the American Academy of Child Psychiatry,* 14(3), 462–476.

Scharer, K. (1971), "Incidence and causes of chronic renal failure in childhood," *Proceedings of the European Dialysis and Transplant Association;* 8, 211–217.

Simmons, Roberta G., Susan D. Klein, and Richard L. Simmons (1977), *Gift of Life: The Social and Psychological Impact of Organ Transplantation.* New York: Wiley Interscience.

———, Florence Rosenberg, and Morris Rosenberg (1973), "Disturbance in the self-image at adolescence," *American Sociological Review,* 38(5), 553–568.

———, Florence Rosenberg, and Morris Rosenberg (1973), "Distance in the self-image at adolescence," *American Sociological Review,* 38(5), 553–568.

Sultz, Harry A., Edward R. Schlessinger, William E. Mosher, and Joseph G. Feldman (1972), *Long Term Childhood Illness.* Pittsburgh: University of Pittsburgh Press.

"Twelfth Report of the Human Renal Transplant Registry," *Journal of American Medical Association,* 233(7), 787–796 (1975).

Wells, L. E., and G. Marwell (1976), *Self-Esteem: Its Conceptualization and Measurement.* Beverly Hills, Calif.: Sage Publications, Inc.

Wylie, Ruth C. (1974), *The Self-Concept* (Revised Edition). Lincoln, Neb.: University of Nebraska Press.

Zuk, G. H. (1959), "The religious factor and the role of guilt in parental acceptance of the retarded child," *American Journal of Mental Deficiency,* 64(1), 139–147.

ADJUSTMENT OF THE YOUNG CHRONICALLY ILL

I. B. Pless, McGILL UNIVERSITY

INTRODUCTION

About fifteen years ago I had an unusual experience which led to the formation of a hypothesis. An on-again, off-again, love-hate relationship with this hypothesis has governed much of my thinking since that time. Unlike many of my colleagues who merely diagnose and treat children, I had the opportunity to live with a group of "sick" children for four successive summers. This came about as a result of my serving as a physician at a camp for diabetic children. Each summer a cross-section of children with this disease come to this camp from all parts of the province. They came primarily for recreation, but also because at that time and even now, summer camping was unavailable to children with diabetes as well as many others with a chronic disorder requiring medical supervision. More

Research in Community and Mental Health, Vol. 1, pp 61–85.

positively, however, it is generally assumed that the camp experience is a good opportunity to teach the child how to "live with" the disease more effectively. During the course of the four summers the equivalent of 10,000 person-days was spent in close contact with these youngsters. Clearly the perspective such exposure provides is infinitely different from that which usually pertains in a doctor-patient relationship. Osler has suggested that a doctor does not truly understand a disease unless he experiences it himself. But surely the next best thing is to have daily contact with those with an illness or, better still, from an epidemiological perspective, to obtain such impressions from a large number of patients.

The result of this experience was a "clinical observation." Most such observations are little more than hunches based on impressions and instincts. They are often important and useful in diagnosis and treatment, but occasionally they also serve to generate hypotheses that warrant further investigation. In the case of this experience the impression gained was simply that these children had many more problems of a psychological and social nature than is generally appreciated.

At the time this idea was taking shape I was in the process of completing a residency in pediatrics. The observation was a revelation for which I was quite unprepared as a result of my earlier training, which, it should be stated, was no better or worse than most.

However, it will come as no surprise to anyone familiar with medical education that that training had remarkably little to say about what it is like to have a disease, to live with it, to cope with it, or to experience its consequences in the social sphere. The focus was almost exclusively on the biological manifestations. Yet in purely medical terms, diabetes is relatively straightforward. From the point of view of care, it is one of the few chronic diseases which can be controlled quite successfully by a specific form of therapy; so much so in fact that some people regard insulin treatment as tantamount to cure.

In spite of this optimism, an awareness of diabetes is present constantly in the lives of these children. There are constant reminders: Most children are required to test their urine at regular intervals, usually four times a day, and to adjust the dose of insulin which must be given as an injection each day.[1] Moreover, many children are required to follow a rather strict diet, which, although flexibility is possible through the exchange of one food for another, is nevertheless another daily reminder of the disease.

The clinical impression referred to previously was quite simply that many of these children with whom I had extended contact were often "maladjusted." In fact, my original impression was that the majority were disturbed in some significant way, either with respect to internalized feelings or to externalized symptoms or behaviors. It did not take long to realize, however, that this observation implied several assumptions which required closer scrutiny. Was it the case that *all* juvenile diabetics, or a majority of them, were maladjusted? Was it to be assumed that this was a problem unique to diabetes, or one which was shared by other illnesses? More broadly, was it a problem common to most chronic physical disorders?

This paper attempts to synthesize the development of my thoughts in response to these questions. It represents the distillation of fifteen years of studies and a reasonably comprehensive familiarity with the work of others, including those in disciplines other than pediatrics. At the risk of destroying the suspense, it can be stated from the outset that part of the answer to each of these questions is in the negative: Neither the proportion of children with chronic illnesses who are affected nor the severity of their problems was as great as it seemed it might be in 1962. At that time investigators in this field were able to begin with the thorough review Roger Barker and his colleagues had written in the early 50's (Barker et al., 1953).[2] This report must certainly stand as a watershed in the evolution of work dealing with the social psychology of illness. Interestingly, it is also the major contribution to our understanding of the significance of normal variations in physical development. And, while interest in the latter area of investigation appears to have diminished, the reverse is true in the case of chronic illness. Nevertheless, the clues provided by the studies of physical variations in children and adults are important and need to be considered by investigators who wish to view the problem from its broadest perspective.

Barker et al. provided ample evidence, as good as was available with the research methods of the day, which demonstrates the salience of variations in physical characteristics ranging from attractiveness to height and weight. The results pertaining to chronic illness were, however, largely inconclusive due to defects in the research design of most studies. Notwithstanding, the theoretical basis for a wide range of disorders was clear and the social psychology of disability was well launched by this effort.

The maiden voyage was marvelously fueled by the clear, perceptive work of Beatrice Wright, a colleague of Barker's, which followed several years later. In her seminal contribution, "Physical Disability—A Psychological Approach" (1960), Wright provides additional support for the theoretical background so well formulated by Lewin's disciples. Her evidence is drawn principally from conventional "scientific" sources, but she also included persuasive autobiographical accounts of experiences with disability.[3]

The questions answered in the negative led, as inevitably they must, to other more sophisticated questions. If it is not the case that *most* children or adults with a chronic illness are demonstrably maladjusted in one way or other, why is it that some are while others are not? More importantly, how early and how accurately can we identify those most likely to experience this additional misfortune? And, above all, what can be done to prevent this from coming about? This paper is accordingly divided into two parts: The first summarizes basic conceptual and methodological considerations; the second examines the evidence that suggests that only a minority, albeit a "significant" minority, of those with chronic disabilities are, in fact, maladjusted and attempts to describe characteristics which may distinguish one group from the other.

CONCEPTUAL AND METHODOLOGICAL CONSIDERATIONS

What does maladjustment mean? How can it be measured? Humpty Dumpty's testy answer to Alice,[4] so often quoted, is obviously unsatisfactory, but possibly closer to the truth than many might wish to admit. Regrettably it is the case that too many investigations are based on the premise that maladjustment can be measured in whatever way the author wishes; that defining it in a particular way makes it so. But if the concept is to have any meaning at all it can only be in relation to some epidemiologic or clinical perspective. In the former, there is an implicit statistical suggestion that adjustment is something which is normally distributed in the population; that those who deviate to some degree from the mean are, *ipso facto,* maladjusted. The practical application of this perspective is straightforward: It only requires that the measurement criterion, whether it be a psychological test or some other observable manifestation, be applied to a population and the scores or characteristics of outlying responses be identified. One can then apply the same procedure to a population of the chronically ill and determine in a fairly simple manner whether maladjustment is excessive, i.e., greater than the "expected" rate in this subgroup.

Coming at the same question from a clinical perspective, one is confronted with the apparently more difficult task of deciding whether, based on certain criteria (whether they be those agreed upon by others or not), the "expert" assessor (in this case physician, psychiatrist, psychologist, or social worker) judges an individual to be "maladjusted." Although it may be reasonable to assume that clinicians base such decisions on observations which are objective and verifiable, this is only likely to be so in isolated circumstances. In other words, there is nothing which, in theory, prevents a physician or psychiatrist from diagnosing *any* patient as emotionally disturbed, neurotic, or psychotic. The relationship of the functioning of these "cases" to that of other members of society may be of little or no relevance in this operation of labeling.[5]

Both are tenable approaches and, in fact, may be less incompatible than they might appear at first glance. The bulk of epidemiologic evidence comes from studies using some form of objective (or projective) assessments which, whether standardized on "normal" populations or not, attempt to compare those with chronic illnesses with others who are, in this respect at least, judged to be "healthy." Taken together, the results usually point to an excess in frequency of problems, regardless of the specific measures or definitions used. In spite of this, as will be described, the actual prevalence of these problems is much less than one might anticipate.

One reasonable explanation that comes immediately to mind is that in referring to children with a chronic illness, an extremely heterogeneous group of disorders is being considered. Not only do the broad types of disorder differ, with potentially different implications for adjustment, but within a diagnostic category other important features such as severity, duration, and age of onset also range widely. Nevertheless, it is reasonable to assume that living with a disease, however mild and whatever its other characteristics, has the potential of creating some form of stress. Current thinking suggests that this stress precipitates a response in the form of behaviors which are usually grouped within the construct of "coping" or "adaptive reactions." Thus, the basic question can be reformulated to ask why some forms of coping are apparently more successful than others or, alternately, why the level of stress generated by the same illness may differ so widely.

One simple answer is that the response to stress may be modified by one or more of three principal factors: personal assets, other environmental supports, or therapeutic intervention. Thus, if a child with a chronic illness had one or more of these to draw upon, his ability to cope successfully with the stress associated with the disease would be enhanced accordingly.

But it still remains to be established to what extent children with chronic illnesses are more likely to be maladjusted than those who are healthy, or if there are some children or some illnesses more likely to "cause" (or be associated with) maladjustment than others. The answer is of very great importance, certainly for the children themselves, and for their families, for whom the problem of maladjustment may be more important in the long run than many of the issues associated with the medical care of the underlying disease. Put in the simplest, humanistic terms, it is bad enough that a child is fated to live for the rest of his life with the anxiety, limitations, inconvenience, or danger posed by diseases like diabetes, epilepsy, cerebral palsy, or arthritis—little can be done to prevent the occurrence of most illness of this kind. But at the very least our understanding of this issue must be extended to ensure that the child with a chronic physical disability does not also have to live with the added burden of emotional maladjustment.

When viewed in these terms, the questions seem deceptively simple: But when we stop to think again about what is meant by maladjustment, and furthermore how it can be assessed objectively, a host of problems immediately appear. To begin with it is clear, as was stated, that not everyone using the term does so in the same way. (Perhaps even more worrisome, not everyone who talks about "maladjustment" is clear in their own mind what it is they are trying to convey.) As is the case with so many other relatively abstract concepts that are used in everyday life, as well as in the scientific world, coming to grips with their meaning and, more importantly, developing operational definitions is not easy.

Choices also have to be made between trying to decide whether adjustment will be defined in relation to the *child alone,* independent of his peers, or whether to use standards which reflect the frequency of presumably adjustive behaviors or symptoms among the peer group. If we choose the latter, the question then arises what is the reference group against which the child should be judged—other children with the same illness or healthy children?

A further choice has to do with whether we should try to define adjustment independent of existing measures and attempt to develop appropriate measures, or alternately, whether to be pragmatic, proceed to examine available measures and select from among them those which most closely approximate what we have in mind.

In the case of the handicapped child, we face yet another dilemma, since most measures which have normative standards are based on items developed in nondisabled populations. Many such items may be meaningless or require special interpretation when applied to children with particular types of disability. To what extent are we free to take liberties with standardized measures of this kind and make such allowances as may be appropriate for the group we are trying to assess?

Those who choose the first option of developing new measures to better reflect the concept are confronted with the difficult task of establishing the test's reliability and validity, and assessing its feasibility in clinical or research settings. If the choice is to select an established measure, we not only run into the problems listed but, in addition, must accept that we may be examining something quite different from the original concept. Clearly there is no ideal solution and in most instances the choice made must be to reach the best possible compromise.

Before proceeding with specific examples of the available types of measures, several terms need to be clarified: "disease," "disability," and "handicap." *Disease* (or any of its synonyms) is best used simply to describe the basic biological impairment or pathological process. Both *disability* and *handicap* are consequences of this impairment in the personal and social spheres, respectively. *Disability* is used to describe immediate direct manifestations of disease as it affects behavior. Examples may be a limp, the presence of pain or swelling, or shortness of breath. *Handicap,* on the other hand, is the effect of disability in the performance of specific activities and should only be thought of in a social context. It refers to the extent to which patients, because of their disabilities, are disadvantaged in the performance of some specific action. When the term is used in a generalized sense, e.g., to refer to "a handicapped child," it has unfortunate connotations which relate to the phenomenon of "spread." Beatrice Wright has described this as "a generalized devaluation of body function and perhaps even a devaluation of the self as a person" (1964).

The idea of adjustment is similar in many respects to the various interpretations applied in common usage to the terms "normality" or "health." We may think of a person being normal or well adjusted in four different ways: (1) First, adjustment may be regarded as the absence of disease; i.e., a reasonable rather than an ideal state of functioning. Implicit in this is the notion that some degree of dysfunctioning or ill health is permissible within the concept of normality. (2) The second is a view of adjustment (or normality) which is an "ideal" or utopian state. As Rogers has put it, a "fully functioning person is a platonic idea, a goal not to be obtained, only to be approximated" (1951). (3) The third view equates normality with the average, the middle range in a distribution of functional characteristics in which either extreme may be regarded as deviant or abnormal. Thus, one can be too tall or too short and the "normal" is the person who is just in between. (4) Finally, there is a view of normality or adjustment as a process, the end-result of a system of interaction which changes over time. The question is not where has he got to, but by what means is he getting there?

Each of these ideas when applied to the concept of adjustment is complicated by factors peculiar to the situation of disablement. The first is whether it is realistic (or fair) to apply to the disabled standards applicable to a nondisabled population; e.g., if we use scholastic progress, what allowances should we make for school loss directly due to the illness? The second is the need to distinguish between the process of adjusting *to* the disability and a more general view (in which disability may or may not play a part) of the process of "global adjustment."

There are two principal lines of thinking which seem useful in trying to formulate models for relating adjustment to chronic illness. The first is the self-concept model based on social psychology. In essence, this theory holds that bodily illness contributes to the formation of self-concept, which in turn affects behavior that may or may not be assessed as adjustment.

When the child with a chronic illness develops an emotional disturbance, certain important events are assumed to have taken place. Common sense (and some data) suggests that a process of self-devaluation or changes in self-concept in a negative direction may lie at the heart of the adjustment riddle. Although the idea of self-concept change is deeply rooted in the literature and is supported by empirical evidence from studies of adults, it is very difficult to measure in children, particularly those under ages 10 or 11 years. Measures tapping related dimensions, e.g., those dealing with self-evaluation, self-ideal discrepancy, self-esteem, or self-derogation, are also difficult to apply over the entire age range of childhood. Thus, at one end of the spectrum, we have measures that deal with what might be regarded as a first step in the process of maladjustment.

A critical point in the social psychology model arises when the child enters new situations. It is in these that the reactions of the disabled are often equated with adjustment. Essentially, three reaction patterns are commonly described: withdrawal, rejection or denial, and acceptance. It is generally assumed that the first two are unhealthy, or evidence of maladjustment, while the third is the most desirable. But is it? The dilemma is partly resolved by the suggestion of Dembo (1956), who distinguishes between patients who accept the status quo and those who accept the realities of their condition. Thus, while a disease may be greatly inconveniencing or limit particular activities, it does not spread to affect unrelated areas, and hence does not devalue the individual in a global way.

A second major school of thought that is useful in considering adjustment and physical illness is that which tries to define the methods used for coping with the stress imposed by the illness or its treatment. A distinction may be made between coping style and coping strategies. The former refers to "an enduring disposition" to deal with the challenges of illness, whereas strategy involves those techniques actually employed. Coping strategies represent an expression of both coping style as well as any attempts made to find new approaches to deal with stressful situations.[6]

With regard to childhood disability, Mattsson has expanded this formulation (1972). He includes under coping behavior "any adaptational technique used by the individual to master a major (psychological) threat and its attendant negative feelings in order to allow him to achieve personal and social goals." Thus, successful coping is in turn equated with the adaptation that results from "effective functioning" in the home, school, or in relations with peers. While this is a helpful definition, a difficulty remains in discovering appropriate measures of "effective functioning" for each area.

Several criteria are suggested by Mattsson. They include: (1) age appropriate dependence on the family, (2) little need for secondary gain from the illness, (3) acceptance of both the limitations and responsibilities imposed by the illness, and (4) the ability to find satisfaction in a variety of compensatory activities, e.g., intellectual pursuits. In addition, he suggests that cognitive flexibility, the appropriate release and control of emotions, and the adaptive use of psychological defenses such as denial, isolation, and identification are components in successful adaptation.

Pinkerton and I (1975) have attempted to integrate these two major streams of thought into a model of adjustment in which both coping and self-concept are linked in a temporal sequence. This integrated model suggests that a number of feedback loops are involved in the process of adjustment. These in turn lead sequentially to psychological functioning (or maladjustment) at a particular point in childhood, which is related subsequently to adjustment during adulthood (Figure 1).

At this point it is important to introduce a word of caution. When we talk about relationships between adjustment and illness, we often imply that in any such association the maladjustment is a reflection or consequence of the disorder. But it is obviously possible, however, for the reverse to be the case. Indeed, the assumption that psychosomatic illnesses exist is based on this belief. Proof of causality depends on satisfying several scientific criteria simultaneously. One must not only show a significant relationship between two events but also that their relationship in time is causally acceptable, and, further, that nothing else can explain their association. To meet all these criteria usually requires an experimental design virtually impossible in this instance. Unfortunately, most studies depend on various quasi-experimental or cross-sectional analyses. Thus, the best evidence may come from intervention studies based on assumptions about the direction of the relationship in question. Attempts at prevention of consequences by therapeutic intervention not only provide convincing evidence (if they're successful) but they are also of greatest interest to the clinician and, of course, of greatest benefit to the patient.[7]

Among the methods available for the assessment of adjustment, the situation is very little different at present than when we noted that "little unanimity has emerged in the choice of method adopted in assessment studies" (Pless and Pinkerton, 1975, p. 34). This observation prompted two conferences on the Measurement of Outcome in the Care of Children with Chronic Illnesses. The results, published recently by the Fogarty International Centre (Grave and Pless, 1976), were intended to be the last word—the product of the thinking of many experts in this subject. It was hoped that some agreement could be reached on the best mea-

Figure 1

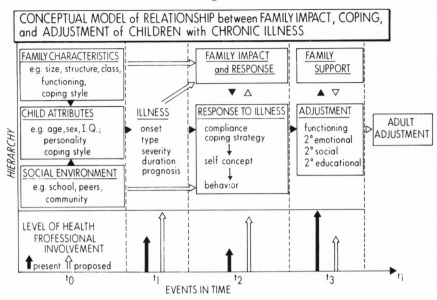

sure(s) for each of five parameters which, together, seemed reasonable goals in the care of these children. These parameters involved in addition to psychosocial functioning (i.e., adjustment), reduction in morbidity, physical functioning, school performance, and impact on the family. Unfortunately, there was again little if any agreement. Although each of the principal areas was examined thoroughly and several new procedures and approaches introduced, each met with criticism from some of those present. The reservations dealt largely with the issues already discussed, reflecting the basic semantic and conceptual confusion alluded to. In addition, the problem was compounded by the need to consider simultaneously all five parameters and hence the possibility (indeed the likelihood) that "trade-offs" might frequently exist, i.e., in order to improve the outcome in one area another might be worsened. Although there was general agreement that some method of applying values or weights to each outcome area might be desirable, there was also considerable reluctance to work toward the development of some form of index.[8]

Nevertheless, many methods have been employed to assess adjustment. The fact that so many procedures are available reflects both practical and theoretical considerations: Those who believe that *only* overt behavior is pertinent place little value on "paper and pencil" or subjective measures. Conversely, those who are interested exclusively in the underlying determinants of behavior prefer techniques designed to probe beneath the conscious. Although for some the ideal approach may be to have an expert psychiatrist interview patients in order to assess their adjustment, this is rarely done in research because it is costly and impractical. Thus, over the past fifty years, the balance remains equally tilted between objective, subjective, and projective measures. Whereas several specific projective approaches (e.g., figure drawings, the Rorschach, and the CAT) have stood the test of time, on the subjective side, new rating scales, inventories, and tests are constantly being introduced, suggesting that most are deficient in some way.

Generally speaking, adjustment measures can be divided into two broad categories, direct and indirect. Indirect procedures are not measures in the true sense of the word. They are rough indicators, usually based on social performance, through which we infer the operation of maladjustment. For most of these indicators to be useful, however, it is necessary to know the rates in a comparable healthy population and these are frequently difficult, often impossible, to obtain. Direct measures may be divided into objective, subjective, and projective categories. The only truly objective measures are those based on actual observations of behavior, a difficult task in a research situation. As a substitute, behavior ratings by parents, teachers, peers, or other observers are frequently used.[9]

Subjective measures include personality inventories, anxiety scales, self-concept scales, and a group of miscellaneous procedures not easily classifiable. The projective measures can be divided into figure drawings of various kinds, sentence completion tests, and the traditional clinical tests, e.g., the Rorschach, TAT and CAT, and ink blots.

Finally, although not a "measure" in the usual sense of the term, the importance of psychiatric, psychological, or social work interviews as a tool for assessing adjustment must be emphasized. These interviews, if they can be standardized, may yield the most relevant and valid information. In the Isle of Wight Survey, two psychiatrists interviewed each child following a procedure which had been shown to yield the same results when administered independently. This is difficult to do, but, if costs allow, it undoubtedly produces the maximum amount of information, processed by the best of all computers—the human mind.

The "medical model" focuses on the diagnosis and treatment of disease. It is not surprising, therefore, that those approaching the question of adjustment to chronic illness from a background in medical care should focus likewise on the side of maladjustment. Indeed, most of the research to date, from both behavioral and medically oriented investigators, has done so. The object has been to try to determine the frequency of maladjustment among this population, and more recently, a refinement of this objective has been to identify those at greatest "risk" in order to allow them to be the focus of preventive efforts. Unfortunately, the assumption that maladjustment can be prevented in any group is by no means established. It must be appreciated, however, that maladjustment among those with chronic illnesses comprises two somewhat distinct groups.

The first consists of those whose maladjustment may be regarded as purely, or predominantly, secondary to the presence of the underlying physical disease. Indeed, this is the main subject of discussion in this chapter. However, a second group must also be considered, since our current knowledge does not enable us to readily distinguish one from the other. This second group consists of those whose maladjustment arises from other causes, presumably the same causes which result in the "expected" rate among the normal population. To emphasize this point further, the reader must be reminded that various studies suggest that somewhere between 5 and 12 percent of a population of otherwise normal children (that is normal with respect to their physical health) experience significant problems of a behavioral nature requiring some form of therapy. (Rutter et al. 1970, p. 178). The differences in these rates depend largely on the procedure used for their identification.[10]

The development of child psychiatry at present offers relatively few techniques for the identification of high-risk situations among normal populations which lead to maladjustment, nor are there generally accepted procedures for the early detection of such problems analogous to presymptomatic screening.[11] Accordingly, opportunities for prevention are essentially limited to the exceptions to these statements. In spite of this somewhat gloomy appraisal, if the basic assumptions and hypotheses about the mechanism by which maladjustment follows hold in *some* cases of chronic illness, there is, in theory, reason for somewhat greater optimism about the possibilities for primary prevention in this particular subgroup. In addition, there is also some evidence of success at what might be regarded as the secondary or tertiary level of prevention. In a randomized clinical trial in which nonprofessional family counselors were used, it has been shown that the frequency of maladjustment was substantially decreased following one year of intervention during which the counselors provided support, counseling, and other forms of nonspecific therapy and assistance (Pless and Satterwhite, 1975).

The success of this "experiment" can be explained in a number of ways. Major emphasis was placed by the investigators on identifying and securing the services of people with characteristics that were assumed to be related to their effectiveness (Truax and Carkhauf, 1967). At another level, the work may be seen as fitting into the theoretical constructs formulated by Cassel during the last years of his career. Cassel postulated that the existence of generalized stress is related to various types of physical and mental illness (Kaplan and Cassel, 1975). The control measure proposed for this generalized stress model is a comparable form of generalized nonspecific support, e.g., that represented by the community-based counselors. Cassel elaborates on this theory, supported by considerable empirical evidence, in the following manner: "In the most general terms, the theory that has guided these studies has been that susceptibility to a wide variety of diseases and disorders (including somatic as well as emotional and behavioral disorders) is influenced by a combination of exposure to psychosocial stressful situations and the protection afforded against these situations by adequate social supports."

PATTERNS OF MALADJUSTMENT

Clearly there are, in summary, sound theoretical arguments, and some empirical support, for the proposition that the maladjustment associated with chronic illness may indeed be preventable, thereby supporting the assumption that the relationship is a causal one. A broader question still stands, however: Can such programs be justified if the actual rate of maladjustment among this group is not sufficiently high to use illness alone as an identifying risk factor? It is here that the evidence becomes confusing and contradictory. Although the bulk of the early literature argued strongly in favor of this viewpoint, more recent and better designed studies offer less and less support for the proposition. Not only does the evidence indicate that the frequency of maladjustment among chronically ill children is much less than had previously been assumed, there is even evidence that in some families the stress of such an illness may serve as a positive developmental stimulus promoting more positive adjustment.[12]

To illustrate the complexities of the picture at present, Rutter's recent review of the association between psychopathology and "brain damage" is pertinent (1977). Surely among the chronic disorders of childhood there can be no better example of an organic substrate in which emotional dysfunctioning is likely to be associated. Yet, as Rutter points out, it is by no means as simple as it would appear.

Drawing upon data from the Isle of Wight Survey, Rutter (1970) notes that among those with clear-cut neurological conditions the rate of psychiatric disorder was 34.3 percent compared with 6.6 percent in the general population of 10- and 11-year-old children and 11.5 percent among those with other physical disorders not involving the brain. Additional analyses effectively ruled out rater bias, the effect of low IQ, and age differences. However, it is clear that there is no specific type of behavior disturbance, no stereotype, seen in this group, and that psychosocial as well as biological influences are important, probably in an additive fashion. Unfortunately, the measure of "psychosocial disadvantage" used in this study is a crude (but reliable) one, whereas with a more sensitive measure of family function (e.g., Pless and Satterwhite, 1973), it may have been possible to demonstrate an interactive effect.

As was pointed out earlier, part of the confusion and apparent contradictions must surely stem from semantic difficulties. The problem of defining adjustment both operationally and conceptually in terms which are widely acceptable and meaningful is by no means resolved. Moreover, in the case of the so-called "brain damaged" child, many of the behaviors which directly reflect cerebral damage would certainly be interpreted among normal children as evidence of emotional dysfunctioning. However, it is clear that in this group of children, as in many others, certain forms of behavior are largely biological in origin and may have little emotional significance.

Findings
Two sets of studies undertaken by colleagues and myself are intended to shed some light on the confusion that surrounds this question. In addition to the important insights provided elsewhere in this volume by Klein and Simmons, a series of studies has taken place in Rochester, New York (see Pless and Satterwhite, 1975) and in London, England (see Pless and Douglas, 1971) which vary in design and therefore in the type of answers provided.

The British studies are based on a sample of a total cohort of all children born in Britain during one week in March, 1946. This cohort has been studied intensively under the aegis of the National Survey of Health and Development, the first of four such longitudinal studies conducted in Britain since the war years. In the 1946 cohort there were 4,724 children about whom medical, educational, and psychosocial information was available at age 15. It was at this point that I became interested in examining what had happened to those who at some time during their childhood, had experienced any chronic disorder. Through a systematic review of all records, more than 528 children were identified who met criteria established. Sufficient information was available to permit them to be categorized into three major groups according to type, duration, and severity of disability. These groups and their size are shown in Table 1, which includes the rates found on several measures of psychosocial functioning based on three criteria of adjustment when they were age 15. The table includes comparable figures for a group from the remainder of the cohort who, although similar in most other major characteristics, had not experienced any chronic disorder.

Although some significant differences are noted, no clear patterns are evident in relation to type of disability or other characteristics of the

Table 1

Psychological Correlates of Chronic Illness
(National Survey, 1946 cohort)
(percentages)

	Chronic disorder (N = 537)	Healthy controls (N = 4,112)
A. Two or more behavioral symptoms		
Severity of disability		
No disability or mild	23*	
Moderate or severe	27+	17
Duration of disability		
Temporary	22+	
Permanent	24*	17
Type of disability		
Cosmetic	22†	
Sensory	31+	17
All others	23+	

B. Other indicators	Boys (N = 256)	Girls (N = 191)	Boys (N = 1,664)	Girls (N = 1,537)
Teachers assessment				
Nervous	10.6	29.1+	11.9	18.3
Aggressive	20.7†	17.9	16.2	14.0
Self-assessment [1]				
Neurotic	31.0	33.0	32.2	30.7
Neurotic introvert	14.9	16.8	12.4	12.3
Trouble at school	20+		14	
Social isolation	21*		17	
School absences	27+		18	

According to a Chi Square analysis the differences between the ill and control groups are significant at the following levels:

† p < .10 > .05
* p < .05 > .01
+ p < .01

[1] Eysenck's Maudsley Personality Inventory.

disorder and any measure of maladjustment. Nor, for that matter, do the results fit clearly with any other hypothesized relationships. A preliminary examination of the rates of psychiatric illness found during early adulthood show few significant differences between those who had chronic illnesses during childhood and those who did not. There was, however, a suggestion that some subgroups within the total population may be more vulnerable for this event than others.

Additional analysis of this population by Douglas showed significant relationships between various aspects of psychosocial dysfunctioning during adolescence and the experience of early hospitalization (see Douglas, 1975). Although it was logical to assume this might be explained by the more frequent hospitalizations due to chronic illness, this was rejected. Instead it appears that the disturbances of behavior and learning are related to the stress imposed by hospitalization of *young* children, particularly those in vulnerable families. Essentially the same finding was confirmed by Rutter and his colleagues on a different population. Together they stand as potentially important clues which suggest that it may not be chronic illness as such, but other factors associated with it, that form the truly salient factors accounting for the relationship with maladjustment.

The series of studies conducted in Rochester over the period from 1967 to 1975 form another major body of evidence pertinent to this question. They began with essentially the same hypothesis—that there was an association between chronic illness and maladjustment that would be significantly in excess of that found among healthy children. The conceptual basis for this hypothesis was drawn originally from some of the literature in social psychology and subsequently from findings relating to stress and coping. These studies also introduced a provocative new idea, namely that the system of health services for these children may also play an etiological role in the occurrence of secondary maladjustment or at least a contributory one in the failure of its prevention. The Rochester studies are also unusual in that they are based upon a representative sample of the population and not one which may be biased due to selection process.[13] (In this sense they are similar to the British longitudinal studies but differ in that they are cross-sectional in nature.)

In 1967 the Rochester Child Health Studies drew a 1 percent random-sample of all households in Monroe County, New York. This sample was then examined to establish the presence of children in the home and, from among those present, two were randomly selected to be the focus of additional interview questions. Among the questions asked in an interview with the parent were a set dealing with symptoms of chronic illness. Based on responses to these, a group of those presumed to have a chronic illness were selected for additional study the following year. As well as those presumed to have a chronic illness, a matched group of those judged to be healthy was selected, controlling for age, race, sex, and socioeconomic status. More detailed household interviews, as well as information obtained from physicians and other sources, confirmed the presence of a chronic illness in 209 children from the original sample (11 percent). Comparable information was available from seventy-seven healthy controls. Both groups were then tested with a battery of psychological measures which included responses from the child, his parents, teachers, and peers. Because it was also hypothesized that family functioning might play a role in identifying groups with high-risk for maladjustment, a separate set of questions was included in the interview tapping this dimension of family life. These have subsequently been further developed into an index whose reliability and validity as well as stability over time have been established (Pless and Satterwhite, 1973; Satterwhite, Zweig, Iker, and Pless, 1976).

In view of our uncertainty about the most appropriate measure of adjustment, the results obtained from the psychological measures were combined into an overall adjustment index. This was done by examining the distribution of scores for the entire population, both healthy and chronically ill, and selecting those scores which were in the lowest 3 percentiles for each measure. Children with deviant scores on several measures were judged to be the most severely maladjusted, while those with no deviant scores were rated as well adjusted.

In many respects this approach is a compromise which essentially avoids the issue of deciding upon a more precise and meaningful definition of adjustment along the lines discussed previously. It does, however, serve to identify those who by other criteria appeared to be having difficulties in coping with day-to-day aspects of functioning, apart from their ability to cope with the basic biological consequences of their illness.

A detailed analysis of the patterns of adjustment obtained by this approach revealed the pattern of scores shown in Table 2. The rate of excessive maladjustment among the chronically ill group overall, when compared with their healthy peers, was much lower than anticipated. It was only when various data-dredging procedures were applied that subgroups were identified which appeared to be at significantly greater risk.[14] The one new factor that consistently emerged in all analyses, apart from the presence of illness, was the level of family functioning.[15] Nevertheless, most of the detailed analyses of the patterns of adjustment within this group fail to reveal many striking differences, although in view of the relatively small numbers and possibly insensitive measures it is conceivable that more "true" differences are present (Type II or beta error).

It was assumed that the severity of the disability would be related to the

Table 2

Psychological Maladjustment
by Clinical and Family Characteristics
% with Low Scores on Adjustment Scale

	Chronic disorders (N = 209)	Healthy controls (N = 166)
Clinical characteristics		
Severity		
No disability	28	
Mild disability	33	28
Moderate or severe	46+	
Duration		
Less than 1/3 life	36	
1/3 to 2/3 life	33	28
More than 2/3 life	37	
Type of disability		
Cosmetic	46+	
Sensory	46*	28
All others	31	
Family characteristics		
Family functioning		
Low (poor)	44*	35
Middle	39*	25
High (good)	28	18
Social status		
Low	52*	33
Middle	28	37
High	38	19
Education of mother		
Less than high school	42	37
High school only	33	28
Beyond high school	36*	17

According to a Chi Square analysis the differences between the ill and control groups
are significant at the following levels: $+ p < .10 > .05$ $* p < .05 > .01$

frequency of maladjustment. Although there was some mild evidence in support of this hypothesis, the relationship was not nearly as strong as had been anticipated. There are two possible explanations for this finding: The first is that it is not the level of severity as determined by objective criteria that is important, but rather the level as perceived by the parent which, accordingly, influences the parents' behavior toward the child. This phenomenon was well demonstrated by Bergman and Stamm (1967) in the case of cardiac "nondisease" in schoolchildren. In this study 40 percent of children with "innocent" heart murmurs had their activities restricted. Clearly the level of day-to-day functioning can be determined chiefly by the parents' perception of the disease and not by the biological realities. A second possible explanation derives from the observation made by others that the relationship between severity and psychosocial functioning may be curvilinear. Thus, those least affected emotionally are those with minimal or no disability secondary to the illness *and* those for whom the disease is severely disabling. Rutter (1977) suggests that the repeated finding that psychiatric disorder is more likely in the child with mild or moderate physical disabilities than in the severely crippled child "may be because the severely crippled child has adjusted to the fact that he obviously cannot compete in the ordinary world, whereas the mildly handicapped child has not. He can compete, but not very well, and paradoxically this makes it more difficult for him than if he were not able to compete at all." McAnarney et al. (1974) showed this to be the case with children with arthritis (JRA) and others have demonstrated it among those with sensory disorders, hemophilia, and heart disease.

In summary, the Rochester data are provocative but inconclusive. They fail to provide much support for the notion that maladjustment is widespread among children with chronic illnesses. At best they offer some clues about those who are most likely to be affected in this manner.

To test these clues while at the same time attempting to provide answers to the equally challenging question of whether such maladjustment as may be present during childhood is of long-term significance, e.g., whether it is also manifested during adolescence in a measureable fashion, we initiated a follow-up study in 1975 (see Orr et al., 1977). The purpose of this study was to determine which of the original group of Rochester children studied in 1967 (both those with and without chronic illnesses) were having difficulties during later adolescence. Fifty-six percent of those in the desired age group previously diagnosed as having a chronic illness and an approximately equal percentage of those in the healthy "control" group were located for purpose of follow-up.

The method of assessment involved a detailed personal questionnaire and the completion of the California Personality Inventory. The latter was selected after much deliberation, since although it provides scores based

Table 3

Follow-up of Chronic Illness and Adjustment
(Mean number of abnormal CPI scores)

	Chronic disorders (N = 91)	Healthy controls (N = 34)
A. Clinical characteristics		
Non-disabled	3.9*	
Disabled	4.1*	3.2
B. Family functioning	Both groups	
Low (poor)	4.7+	
High (good)	2.7	

* According to a t-test, the mean differences between the chronically ill and healthy groups do not reach statistical significance.

+ According to a t-test of the mean differences between high and low functioning families, $p < .01$.

on well standardized norms in a number of dimensions of interest, it has several limitations, not least of which is the fact that it is not a measure of "adjustment" as such.

The results point again to the primary importance of the level of family functioning at the time the original studies were carried out. The index score for 1968 appears to be a better predictor of the number of deviant results obtained from the CPI in 1975 than any of the measures of chronic illness (Table 3). Although further analyses of these data are still being carried out the conclusion for the moment must be to confirm the growing suspicion that chronic illness alone is less salient in influencing their immediate or subsequent adjustment than other factors, especially the quality of family life.[16] This may come as little surprise for many, particularly those who do not accept the assumptions upon which the theories of the social psychologists were originally based. Regardless, it should stimulate further efforts to develop and test these and other models around the issue of chronic illness and adjustment.

CONCLUSION

Is the choice between searching for factors relating to vulnerability, e.g., the identification of "risk factors" as opposed to those which relate to successful adjustment a hollow question? Do these simply reflect opposite sides of the same coin? Is this nothing more than another way of saying that health is, in fact, best defined as the absence of disease? In one respect the analogy is useful. Apart from those with exclusively theoretical interests in this subject, practical questions about adjustment must be directed toward determining, in advance, those who will step over the border of "making it," those who succeed in coping, however, marginal this success may be, rather than focusing on determinants in the relative few for whom the stress of major illness has disastrous psychological consequences. There are, of course, numerous examples in history and in literature of such unusual cases where apparently striking adult achievements appear to have been influenced by a childhood experience with illness (Illingworth, 1966). These may provide useful clues about the antecedents of such developments, but they are too few to be of real value to the clinician. Rather our task is to discover the common denominators of those who manage to cope at a level where day-to-day life is not overly disrupted, those for whom the chronic illness does not create new psychological burdens.

To return to the question, then, we need to know if the factors involved in success are simply the reverse of those which render those who fail to cope more vulnerable? The present state of the art does not permit a straightforward answer to this question. If we accept as "proven" the very fact that a chronic illness in itself requires adjustive processes, that it does require coping to deal with inevitable stress, that it requires the utilization of social and emotional resources, then we have a somewhat clearer statement of the paradigm which needs to be examined further. If, however, we wish to entertain an alternative hypothesis that for many children the presence of a chronic illness does not constitute any significant stress and, therefore, few, if any, adjustment processes are involved, this is quite another matter.

The evidence provides few clues as to which is the more accurate reflection of the true situation. All it tells us is that contrary to earlier impressions maladjustment is a relatively infrequent occurrence among children with chronic illnesses—that is to say "overt" maladjustment measureable with the instruments currently available. It has not yet been established whether or not the process involves an element of latency. In many physical diseases there is a long period during which the process of disease has begun but during which no evidence of actual pathology is evident, i.e., there are no clinical manifestations. During this latent or hidden period the seeds which have been planted begin to grow but only burst to the surface many years later. In a similar fashion, there may be reason to believe that chronic illness in childhood may also plant the seeds for future maladjustment, but it is only by examining the psychological functioning of adults that this could be established. Unfortunately, as yet, too few studies have attempted to do so in a systematic fashion or in large enough groups for whom the details of the earlier illnesses are well known.

In summary, our knowledge of the consequences in childhood has only reached the stage of early puberty. The work of pioneers in this field of somatopsychology, beginning in the 50's, has been advanced using the newer tools of the epidemiologist and those with skills in related quantitative fields in the social sciences to provide a rich body of data from which new theories can be tested. Since, however, at best only quasi-experimental approaches can be used, each step further will only provide a part of the answer and only when enough of the pieces of the puzzle are on the table can we assemble it to find "the answer."

In a brilliant essay, Lewis Thomas, drawing upon observations of the behavior of ants, termites, and bees who collectively join up to form a new or different "organism," notes that "the system of communications used in science should provide a neat, workable model for studying mechanisms of information-building in human society." He quotes Ziman, who suggested that "the invention of a mechanism for the systematic publication of fragments of scientific work may well have been the key event in the history of modern science. A regular journal carried from one research worker to another the various . . . observations which are of common interest . . . A typical scientific paper has never pretended to be more than another little piece in a large jigsaw—not significant in itself but as an element in a grander scheme."

A comforting thought to young investigators in this challenging field who, today, like the intrigued young pediatrician seventeen years ago, first confront, question, and seek to answer, only to discover that the ultimate "answers" do not clearly emerge after the completion of the first or even the fiftieth investigation!

FOOTNOTES

1. Juvenile diabetes is probably one of the earliest and best examples of a disorder for which "self-care" is readily accepted by most physicians. As a result of usually thorough instructions at the time of the diagnosis most children or their families acquire sufficient knowledge of the actual metabolism of the disease to permit them to, in effect, "write their own prescriptions," i.e., to adjust the dose of insulin in relation to urine test results. Furthermore, such injections are often self-administered as early as age 8 or 9 years. In spite of this dramatic example of the ability of even poorly educated families to become responsible for their own care, there are very few other instances where the profession has relinquished control to the same extent.

2. Their monograph summarized and assessed most of the earlier literature dealing with the following: differences in physical size, strength, and attractiveness; crippling; tuberculosis; impaired hearing and vision; and acute illness. Later works in a similar vein, e.g.,

Safflios-Rothschild (1970), Dinnage (1972), or Pilling (1973), do not attempt an equally comprehensive review. That of Pless and Pinkerton (1975), while it updates much of the literature over the subsequent two decades, has a much broader but less detailed perspective.

3. Our sophistication today is perhaps such that we risk losing sight of the value of historical sources and the profound insights they may add. In our quest for scientific truth, for provable associations which link cause and effect, we are too readily inclined to turn our backs on well documented "clinical" accounts of every-day life.

4. "I don't know what you mean by 'glory,'" Alice said.

Humpty Dumpty smiles contemptuously.

"Of course you don't—till I tell you. I meant 'There's a nice knock-down argument for you!'"

"But 'glory' doesn't mean 'a nice knock-down argument,'" Alice objected.

"When *I* use a word," Humpty Dumpty said in a rather scornful tone, "it means just what I choose it to mean—neither more nor less."

5. The description of the "clinical perspective" by which patients are "diagnosed" as maladjusted is deliberately exaggerated to make the point that in the sphere of mental health, unlike that of biological medicine, in the absence of solid criteria the assessor is free to make whatever judgments he or she may wish—and all too often does so!

6. Coping strategies presumably can be taught and hence form the basis for some of the more psychologically oriented rehabilitation techniques. Remarkably few of these techniques are employed with children, since they are not part of the repertoire of skills of either the primary physician or the disease specialist and very few disabled children are involved in rehabilitation programs as such. The emphasis in most formal programs is almost exclusively on physical therapy and related disciplines.

7. A modest example of an intervention aimed at prevention of maladjustment among children with chronic disorders, one which was tested using a randomized clinical trial design, is the family counselor program (Pless and Satterwhite, 1972). The results provide considerable support for postulated causal relationship.

8. Surprisingly perhaps the issue of trade-offs is rarely considered in the medical literature. One likely explanation is that the medical model assumes that the only reasonable or desired outcome is the reduction in morbidity—regardless of the price that may be incurred in other areas.

9. Since the publication of *Education, Health and Behavior,* the monumental Isle of Wight Survey, the so-called Rutter A & B scales have been increasingly popular. (Rutter et al., 1970) These are parallel measures of behavioral symptoms designed for completion by parents and teachers respectively. It should be noted, however, that in the original work (and in many of the subsequent applications) striking differences are obtained from parent and teacher rating the same child. Taken together this is a useful screening approach, but this finding emphasizes that the interpretation of behavior is affected by the setting, or that behavior itself differs in the home and the school. Thus, even parallel measures may not be assessing the same dimension.

10. These differences depend largely on the procedures used for the identification of behavioral disorders, but also on the setting. Thus, Rutter and his colleagues have shown differences in prevalence between children in an urban setting (London) and those in a mixed urban-rural area (Isle of Wight) using the same measures (Rutter et al., 1975).

11. A possible exception is found in the work of Cowen and his colleagues (1973), who, on the basis of parent interviews and child observations, successfully "predicted" children who were later to have behavioral problems in school. Moreover, they found that intervention in the school setting using nonprofessional aides was highly successful and the prgram has been widely emulated (Cowen et al., 1963).

12. Illingworth and Illingworth (1966) provide an impressive array of biographies (450 to

be exact) of famous men and women many of whom had a chronic disability during childhood. Not all are "success stories" by any means, but for those which do represent
"triumph in the face of adversity" they conclude that the experience with illness may have
played an important role. On epidemiological and other grounds this conclusion can be
questioned—I had the temerity to do so in a review of this book to which the authors
objected vigorously.

13. It is amazing to note how many studies are based on hospital or clinic populations, or
other highly selected subgroups, which cannot be considered representative of the "universe" in question. Nonetheless, few authors qualify the generalizations they are prepared
to draw from their findings; indeed, few appear to be aware that a potentially important
problem of bias exists.

14. The Rochester data show a linear trend with increasing severity of the disorder, no
systematic relations to duration of the disorder, and only somewhat higher risks for those
with cosmetic or sensory disorders. The latter category (type of disorder) and the "severe"
group have a simple risk ratio of 1.6—an excess of maladjustment of 18 percent. The family
characteristics most related to maladjustment involve indicators of lower social class, but
the association is not linear with either class or mother's education although it is with these
that the highest relative risks are associated.

15. This finding is consistent with the suggestion made by Cassel and his co-workers
reported above.

16. Significant differences between those with low and high family functioning index
scores were found for the following CPI traits: capacity for status, social presence, sense of
well-being, tolerance, good impression, achievement via independence, intellectual efficiency, and psychological mindedness—all in a direction favoring those with higher FFI
scores.

REFERENCES

Barker, R. G., B. A. Wright, L. Myerson, and M. R. Gonick. (1953), *Adjustment to Physical
    Handicap and Illness: A Survey of the Social Psychology of Physique and Disability*.
    New York: Social Science Research Council (Revised).
Bergman, A. B., and S. J. Stamm. (1967), "The morbidity of cardiac nondisease in school-
    children," *New England Journal of Medicine* 276:1008.
Coddington, R. D. (1972), "The significance of life events as etiologic factors in the diseases
    of children—II. A study of a normal population," *Journal of Psychosomatic Research*
    16:205.
Cowen, E., L. Izzo, H. Miles, E. Telschow, M. Trost, and M. Zax (1963), "A preventive
    mental health program in the school setting: Description and evaluation," *Journal of
    Psychology* 54:307.
Dembo, T., G. L. Leviton, and B. A. Wright (1956), "Adjustment to misfortune—A prob-
    lem of social psychological rehabilitation," *Artificial Limbs* 3:4.
Dinnage, R. (1972), *The Handicapped Child. Studies in Child Development Research Re-
    view*, Vol. 11. London: Longman.
Grave, G. D., and I. B. Pless (1976), *Chronic Childhood Illness–Assessment of Outcome*.
    Fogarty International Center and National Institute of Child Health Human Develop-
    ment, Maryland.
Illingworth, R. S., and C. M. Illingworth (1966), *Lessons from Childhood—Some Aspects of
    the Early Life of Unusual Men and Women*. London: E. & S. Livingstone.
Kaplan, B. H., and J. Cassel (Eds.) (1975), *Family and Health: An Epidemiological Ap-*

proach. No. 1. Institute for Research in Social Science, University of North Carolina, Chapel Hill.

Mattsson, A. (1972), "Long-term physical illness in childhood: A challenge to psychosocial adaptation," *Pediatrics* 50:801.

McAnarney, E., I. B. Pless, B. Satterwhite, and S. Friedman (1974), "Psychological problems of children with chronic juvenile arthritis," *Pediatrics* 53:523.

Orr, D. P., B. Satterwhite, and I. B. Pless (1977), "The relationship between family functioning and adolescent personality traits—A follow-up study." Plenary Session, Ambulatory Pediatric Association.

Pilling, D. (1973), *The Child with a Chronic Medical Problem—Cardiac Disorders, Diabetes, Hemophilia.* Slough: National Children's Bureau Report, NFER Publishing Co. Ltd.

Pless, I. B., and J. W. B. Douglas (1971), "Chronic illness in childhood: I. Epidemiological and clinical characteristics," *Pediatrics* 47:405.

———, and P. Pinkerton (1975), *Chronic Childhood Disorder—Promoting Patterns of Adjustment.* London: Henry Kimpton Publishers.

———, and B. Satterwhite (1972), "Chronic illness in childhood: Selection, activities, and evaluation of non-professional family counselors," *Clinical Pediatrics* 11:403.

——— (1975), "Chronic illness" (Chapter 3, p. 78), in *Child Health and the Community.* New York: Wiley.

——— (1975), "The Family Counselor" (Chapter 11, p. 288), in *Child Health and the Community.* New York: Wiley.

Rogers, C. R. (1951), *Client-Centered Therapy.* Boston: Houghton-Mifflin.

Rutter, M. (1977), "Brain damage syndromes in childhood: Concepts and findings," *Journal of Child Psychology and Psychiatry* 18: 1.

———, J. Tizard, and K. Whitmore (Eds.) (1970), *Education, Health and Behavior.* London: Longman.

———, A. Cox, C. Tupling, M. Berger, and W. Yule (1975), "Attainment and adjustment in two geographical areas—I. The prevalence of psychiatric disorder," *British Journal of Psychiatry* 126:483.

PSYCHOLOGICAL ANTECEDENTS OF TEEN-AGE DRUG USE*

Gene M. Smith, HARVARD MEDICAL SCHOOL AND THE
MASSACHUSETTS GENERAL HOSPITAL

Charles P. Fogg, THE COLLEGE OF BASIC STUDIES OF
BOSTON UNIVERSITY

The need to obtain a better understanding of the psychodynamics of teen-age drug use raises many questions: What influences cause students to use illicit drugs? Why do some marijuana users progress to "hard" drugs while others do not? How do differences in drug use relate to differences in attitudes, personality, and school performance? Do scores on such psychosocial measures vary with degree of drug involvement? Is future drug use predictable from psychosocial characteristics measured before drug use begins? Such questions have been addressed in numerous investigations; e.g., Block et al., 1973; Gergen et al., 1972; Goode, 1972; Groves, 1974; Hogan et al., 1970; Jessor et al., 1973; Johnson, 1972;

Research in Community and Mental Health, Vol. 1, pp 87–102.
Copyright © 1979 by JAI Press, Inc.
All rights of reproduction in any form reserved.
ISBN 0-89232-063-X

Johnston, 1973; Josephson et al., 1972; Kandel, 1975; McGlothlin et al., 1970; Mellinger et al., 1975; Naditch, 1975; Robins et al., 1970; Sadava, 1972; Segal, 1974; Smart et al., 1970; Whitehead et al., 1972.

Much of the presently available information concerning the reasons students take drugs has been obtained by direct questioning of students. Curiosity, search for "kicks," and peer pressure are frequently listed by students as reasons for taking drugs. But easily elicited responses to direct inquiries do not go deep enough. All students have curiosity; all like kicks; and all are exposed to peer pressure. Yet, not all experiment with drugs, and only some proceed to heavy drug involvement. The relevant question is not: "Why do students use drugs?" Rather, it is: "What influences cause some students to experiment with illicit drugs only occasionally, cause others to become deeply and detrimentally involved, and cause still others to avoid such substances altogether?" Our own approach is to seek information concerning that question by early assessment of personality, attitude, and behavior variables that might be predictive of later drug use. We recognize that decisions regarding drug use can be influenced by social, economic, and environmental variables. Our emphasis on psychological variables reflects one strategy designed to study a limited aspect of a complex problem from a particular vantage point.

The study that generated the results presented here concerns consequences as well as antecedents of teen-age drug use, but this report focuses on antecedents. Specifically, the analysis examines the relations between drug use, measured in 1971, and five psychosocial variables measured two years earlier. Two of the predictor variables measure rebelliousness, one by self-report and one by peer ratings. The other three are grade point average, cigarette smoking, and attitudes toward cigarette smoking. The predictive utility of each of the five psychosocial variables is considered alone and also as part of a multivariate composite. Details concerning the measurement of these five predictors are given below.

In the present analysis, 2,249 students are classified into five groups on the basis of drug use reported at Time 2 (1971).[1] These students were in grades 9 to 12 when drug-use status was determined (Time 2) and were in grades 7 to 10 when the five predictors were measured (Time 1). Group 1 reported that they had never used illicit drugs. Groups 2–4 reported that they were not users at Time 1, but had become users by Time 2. Group 5 reported that they were already drug users at Time 1. Groups 2–4 differ regarding type and amount of drug use. Specifically, Group 2 contains infrequent (1–10 times) users of marijuana who never used hard drugs (heroin, hallucinogens, stimulants, or sedatives); Group 3 consists of frequent (11 or more times) users of marijuana who never used hard drugs; Group 4 contains users of hard drugs. Differences among Groups 1, 2, 3, and 4 at Time 1 are of special interest because all students in those four groups were nonusers when the Time 1 predictors were measured.

The information analyzed here was obtained in a large five-year longitudinal study of nine cohorts from each of six participating school systems. Because of the size and complexity of our data base, we have decided to prepare a series of narrowly focused reports rather than a single, more comprehensive one. Other reports will concern different components of the total sample or will focus on different issues. For example, a concurrently published report (Smith and Fogg, 1978) predicts time of onset of drug use rather than type and amount of drug use. The analysis presented here is based on information collected from 2,249 students in four of the nine cohorts studied in three of the six participating school systems. Before proceeding with that analysis, however, we shall give a brief overview of the larger study.

GENERAL OVERVIEW OF THE STUDY

Approximately 12,000 to 14,000 students in grades 4 to 12 were studied each year for five years between 1969 and 1973 in six suburban school systems in the greater Boston area. Students were mostly from white, middle-income families. Each year, the participants were recruited on a school-wide basis and were asked to identify their questionnaires to permit longitudinal linkage. Each year we lost the preceding year's 12th graders and gained a new group of 4th graders. Participation in the study was of course voluntary; and, each year, some sample attrition resulted from absences, noncooperation, and scheduling problems. Typically, for cohorts of the age range used in the present analysis, about 90 to 95 percent of the enrolled students were present on the day of testing and approximately 75 to 85 percent of those completed questionnaires that were identified and were acceptable for analysis.

In 1969, information was collected regarding personality, grade point average, cigarette smoking, and attitudes toward cigarette smoking. Personality traits were measured both by self-report and by peer rating procedures. Information concerning grade point average was obtained from school records. Cigarette smoking and attitudes toward cigarette smoking were measured with self-report questionnaires. In 1970, the same information, except for the peer ratings, was collected again. In the 1971, 1972, and 1973 testings, the cigarette attitude questionnaire was deleted and drug questionnaires were added. Information concerning drug use was sought for the first time in the third year of the five-year study. For each of nine classes of drugs, we asked: How many times have you used this type of drug in your lifetime (never, only once, 2–5 times, 6–10 times, 11–25 times, more than 25 times)? As of one year ago, how many times had you used it? As of two years ago, how many times had you used it? The nine classes of drugs were identified for the respondents as follows:

1. Booze: gin, vodka, wine, beer, whiskey, brandy, etc.
2. Downs: reds, red devils, yellow jackets, barbs, nembutal, seconal, phenobarbital, sleeping pills, sedatives, goof balls, tranquilizers, lib (Librium), Valium, etc.
3. Grass, pot, marijuana, hash (hashish).
4. Heroin, opium, morphine, methadone, dilaudid, etc.
5. Nonprescription drugstore products: cough syrup, Dristan, Midol, Sinutabs, NoDoz, Sominex, Nytol, etc.
6. Sniffing stuff: glue, minimist, gasoline, hair spray, etc.
7. Special drug combinations: ups and downs together, purple hearts, dexamyl, bombers, alcohol and grass, treated grass, etc.
8. Tripping stuff: acid, LSD, mesc (mescaline), peyote, psilocybin, etc.
9. Ups: pep pills, cocaine, speed, dexies, dexedrine, benzedrine, bennies, uppers, meth (methedrine), amphetamine, etc.

Self-Report Measure of Rebelliousness

In 1969, a 400-item questionnaire was administered. All items were intended to measure personal characteristics considered relevant to school behavior and performance, or relevant to the more general concept of "socialization." Our concurrently published report dealing with time of onset of marijuana use (Smith and Fogg, 1978) provides information concerning other scales derived from this questionnaire. The present analysis uses only the self-report measure of rebelliousness, which is based on answers to the following twenty-four items:

8. Sometimes I enjoy doing things I shouldn't—just for the fun of it.
78. When I make a decision, I usually go by what my parents have taught me.
98. I obey my parents more than most people my age.
109. If my parents tell me to do something I don't want to do, I usually fight back for my rights.
118. I feel guilty when I break a rule.
133. My teachers think I am very cooperative.
140. When rules and regulations get in my way, I sometimes ignore them.
165. When I break the rules, it doesn't really bother me.
172. I never get into bad trouble at school.
179. If I don't like a teacher very much, I don't mind showing it.
190. If I don't like an order I have been given, I may not do it, or I may do only part of it.
195. When my parents tell me to do something, I usually obey quickly.

210. My teachers probably think I don't cooperate enough.

222. If I don't feel like doing something I'm told to do, I often put it off or just don't do it at all.

231. If I'm told to do something by my parents, I usually do it right away without arguing.

248. I sometimes get myself into trouble at school.

259. Some of my friends think I am too willing to follow the school rules.

294. Anyone who does what parents or teachers say just because they're parents or teachers, doesn't have much courage.

313. Sometimes I enjoy seeing how much I can get away with.

320. I feel that obeying your parents is a very important thing.

345. When I'm told to do something by a teacher, I do it.

371. I try to cooperate with my teachers.

380. Sometimes I don't follow a teacher's directions if they seem foolish to me.

391. I follow the rules even when I feel like breaking them.

The student was asked to give one of four responses to each item on the self-report questionnaire: definitely true; mostly true, usually true, or probably true; mostly false, usually false, or probably false; definitely false. In the case of items 8, 109, 140, 165, 179, 190, 210, 222, 248, 294, 313, and 380, the four responses just listed were scored 4, 3, 2, and 1, respectively. The remaining twelve items in the rebelliousness scale were scored 1, 2, 3, and 4, respectively. The score for "Rebellious" was the mean of the twenty-four scores for individual items. Thus, a high score indicates a high degree of self-attributed rebelliousness. The split-half reliability (corrected with the Brown-Spearman formula) for this twenty-four-item scale is typically between 0.80 and 0.85. Test-retest correlation coefficients over a two-year interval usually range between 0.50 and 0.65.

Peer Rating Measure of Rebelliousness

Peer rating data were obtained by use of procedures described previously (Smith, 1967). Each student in a homeroom of 20–30 students was asked to rate each of the other students on each of twenty bipolar traits. A rater was asked to examine each trait and select the four members of his or her peer group most like the left-hand pole and the four most like its opposite on the right. Selections on the left are considered positive nominations and those on the right are considered negative. The positive and negative nominations a ratee receives are scored + 1 and − 1, respectively. Failure to be nominated is scored zero. Thus, in a peer group of 25, a ratee's score on any trait can range from + 24 to − 24.

The peer rating measure of rebelliousness, referred to hereafter as "Obedient," was obtained from ratings made on the following bipolar trait.

OBEDIENT: obeys and	vs.	DISOBEDIENT: doesn't

OBEDIENT: obeys and cooperates with parents and teachers without arguing; feels it is important to obey rules.

vs.

DISOBEDIENT: doesn't always obey parents and teachers, especially if he thinks they are wrong; does not cooperate; doesn't mind breaking rules.

Evaluated as described above, a low score on "Obedient" indicates that a high degree of rebelliousness is attributed to the student by his or her peers. As reported earlier (Smith, 1967), reliability of peer ratings increases with the number of raters in a peer group. For groups of the size used in this analysis (20 to 30), the split-half reliability (corrected with the Brown-Spearman formula) for the trait "Obedient" typically ranges from 0.80 to 0.90.

Grade Point Average

To provide comparability across age levels and across different school systems, all grade point averages were standardized. Thus, the mean of each sample for each school is zero and the standard deviation is unity.

Cigarette Smoking

Cigarette smoking status was scored in terms of response to this question: "About how often do you smoke cigarettes?" The scoring procedure used was: never = 0; only a few in my whole lifetime = 1; one or two a week = 2; one or two each day = 3; several each day but less than half a pack each day = 4; about half a pack each day = 5; about a pack each day = 6; more than a pack each day = 7; more than two packs each day = 8.

Attitudes toward Cigarette Smoking

A 182-item questionnaire was used to measure attitudes toward cigarette smoking. Illustrative items are:

3. In school, girls who smoke are generally show-offs.

6. When a smoker gets down-hearted and blue, a cigarette usually helps lift him out of the bad mood.

7. Quitting smoking helps a person to live longer.

9. Among the boys, the class leaders here at school are more often smokers than nonsmokers.

20. I spend more time with smokers than with nonsmokers.

21. In school, boys who smoke are crude.

22. Boys who start smoking young are usually those who mature early.

25. Girls who smoke are less attractive than girls who don't smoke.

The same four response options used with the self-report personality questionnaire were used for the cigarette attitude questionnaire. The direction of scoring is such that a high score indicates unfavorability of attitudes toward cigarette smoking. Thus, an answer of "definitely true" for items 3, 7, 21, or 25 was scored "4" and an answer of "definitely false" for items 6, 9, 20, or 22 was scored "4." Seven smoking attitude scales, involving 115 of the 182 items, have each been found to be predictive of drug use (Smith and Fogg, 1975). The cigarette attitude score used in the present analysis is simply the mean of the 115 item scores that contribute to those seven scales.

RESULTS

Of 3,230 drug use questionnaires collected in 1971 from the samples used in the present analysis, fifty-two were rejected for inconsistent, frivolous, or questionable responses;[2] 381 of the questionnaires were unsigned and therefore could not be linked with the Time 1 data. An additional group of 236 questionnaires were signed and they indicated use of illicit drugs; but they did not provide sufficient retrospective information to establish whether the respondent was a nonuser at Time 1. Of the remaining 2,561 students, 2,249 were among those for whom Time 1 information was collected in 1969. Those 2,249 comprise the sample analyzed here.

Table 1 reports means, standard deviations, and sample sizes for each of the five predictor variables for each of the five comparison groups. As seen in the upper portion of Table 1, Group 1 and Group 5 occupy the most extreme positions on all five predictor variables. Members of Group 1 (the nonusers who remained nonusers) score highest on "Obedient," grade point average, and negative attitudes toward cigarette smoking; and they score lowest on "Rebellious" and cigarette smoking. Members of Group 5 (already drug users at Time 1) score lowest on "Obedient," grade point average, and negative attitudes toward cigarette smoking; and they score highest on "Rebellious" and cigarette smoking. Group 2 falls between Group 1 and Group 3 on all five predictors. Groups 3 and 4 are not significantly different from each other on any of the predictors, and both of those groups fall between Group 2 and Group 5 on each of the five predictors. If Group 3 and Group 4 are combined, each of the five predictor variables produces a monotonic progression. Rebelliousness and cigarette smoking increase from Group 1 to Group 5. Grade point average and negative attitudes toward cigarette smoking decrease.

Since Group 5 (already users at Time 1) is not relevant to predicting use from psychosocial data collected prior to onset of drug use, Group 5 does

Table 1

Means, Standard Deviations, and Sample
Sizes for Each Group on Each Predictor Variable

		Means			
Group:	1	2	3	4	5
Rebellious	1.93	2.17	2.37	2.41	2.59
Obedient	+2.85	+0.88	-1.00	-1.12	-2.69
Grade point average	+0.16	+0.02	-0.40	-0.16	-0.47
Cigarette smoking	0.75	1.50	2.08	1.90	2.71
Negative cigarette attitudes	2.89	2.67	2.58	2.54	2.51

		Standard Deviations			
Group:	1	2	3	4	5
Rebellious	0.48	0.52	0.48	0.58	0.61
Obedient	5.35	5.84	7.28	7.14	7.27
Grade point average	0.96	1.05	1.01	1.02	0.92
Cigarette smoking	1.17	1.58	1.83	1.69	2.15
Negative cigarette attitudes	0.39	0.41	0.35	0.41	0.38

		Samples Sizes			
Group:	1	2	3	4	5
Rebellious	1,402	235	84	202	120
Obedient	1,336	214	76	197	102
Grade point average	1,519	254	90	224	139
Cigarette smoking	1,457	248	84	214	130
Negative cigarette attitudes	1,407	244	77	201	119

not appear in the analyses reported in Tables 2–4; and since Group 3 (nonusers who became frequent, exclusive marijuana users) and Group 4 (nonusers who became users of hard drugs) are not significantly different on any of the five predictors, those two groups are combined and are referred to hereafter either as Group 3 + 4 or as "heavy users." The term "heavy users" is chosen with some misgivings, because the amount of heroin, stimulants, amphetamines, and hallucinogens used by our subjects is small compared with typical adult street usage. After all, our subjects are functioning students who still attend high school or junior high school. The requirement for inclusion in Group 4 is simply the report of *ever* having used any of the four "hard" drugs just mentioned. Moreover, any subject who reported having used marijuana more than ten times in his or her lifetime qualifies as a frequent user (Group 3) by the definition we employed. Thus, we use the term "heavy users" in a relative sense in referring to Group 3 + 4 and we emphasize the operations by which we define that term.

Some analyses in this report compare the three groups of primary interest (nonusers, infrequent marijuana users, and heavy users) by considering all three groups simultaneously; others evaluate them two at a time. We also compare nonusers (Group 1) *vs.* users (Groups 2, 3, and 4 combined) without differentiating levels of use.

The upper portion of Table 2 assesses differences among the three groups by analysis of variance. As shown there, the probability associated with the three-group differences is less than 0.001 for each of the five predictor variables.[3]

Table 2

Three-Group and Two-Group Univariate Comparisons
on Five Predictor Variables

Comparison of Nonusers,
Infrequent Marijuana Users, and Heavy
Users by Analysis of Variance

	Rebellious	Obedient	Grade point Average	Cigarette smoking	Cigarette attitudes
F-Value	117.13	58.57	20.29	120.13	104.75
Degrees of freedom	2, 1920	2, 1820	2, 2084	**2, 2000**	2, 1926
Probability	<.001	<.001	<.001	<.001	<.001

Two-group Comparisons: t-test Values

	Rebellious	Obedient	Grade point average	Cigarette smoking	Cigarette attitudes
Group 1 vs. Group 2*	-6.86†	4.94†	**2.02****	-8.76†	8.02†
Group 1 vs. Group 3+4	-14.73†	10.39†	6.36†	-14.73†	13.24†
Group 2 vs. Group 3+4	-4.94†	3.24+	**2.85 +**	-3.19+	3.43†
Group 1 vs. Group 2+3+4	-14.22†	10.11†	5.60†	-14.91†	14.00†

* Group 1 = nonusers; Group 2 = infrequent marijuana users; Group 3 + 4 = heavy users
    probability values for t-tests: ** = .05,   + = .01,   † = .001

The lower portion of Table 2 carries the three-group univariate analysis further by evaluating all fifteen pairs of group differences with the t-test. As shown, each of those results is significant at or beyond the 0.05 level. In addition, the bottom line in Table 2 shows that when level of use is ignored, users and nonusers are significantly ($p < .001$) different on each of the five predictor variables.

The main questions addressed by the analyses reported in Table 2 are: (1) Can users and nonusers be discriminated significantly by using psychosocial information collected prior to initiation of use by users? (2) Can depth of drug involvement be predicted with statistically significant accuracy from psychosocial information collected when all subjects were still nonusers? Clearly, when studied in predominantly white middle-class high school and junior high school students evaluated under the conditions described here, the answer to both of those questions is affirmative; and both answers can be given with a high degree of confidence.

A related question concerns the *accuracy* with which future decisions regarding drug use can be predicted when the contribution of the five psychosocial predictor variables is accumulated. To answer that question, multiple discriminant analyses were performed.[4] In comparing Group 1 *vs.* Group 2 *vs.* Group 3 + 4, only the first discriminant function reached statistical significance, and all predictors except grade point average contributed significantly to that function. To produce a model involving only the significantly contributing predictors, an additional discriminant analysis was run eliminating grade point average from the prediction battery. Again, only the first function was significant. Both analyses demonstrate that the discriminative information can be summarized by a single formula. The upper portion of Table 3 shows the standardized discriminant function coefficients, group centroids, and percent accuracy of group assignment produced by the first discriminant function in the five-variable analysis. The lower portion shows the corresponding results for the four-variable analysis. As expected, the results of those two analyses are essentially identical. Accuracy of group classification was 63.5 percent in the five-variable problem and was 63.2 percent in the four-variable problem. Both analyses were performed with a computer program that statistically equalizes the three sample sizes by appropriate weighting of each observation. The effect of this is to allow the three groups to contribute equally to determination of multivariate structure of the prediction equation.

To assess accuracy of group classification from a somewhat different perspective, the multivariate model derived from the three-group analysis involving four predictor variables was used to produce a composite score for further analysis. That composite variable was computed by applying to all raw scores the unstandardized coefficients associated with the stan-

Table 3

Results of Multiple Discriminant Analyses
of Three Groups Using Five Predictors and Using Four Predictors*

	Standardized coefficients		Centroids	Percent accuracy
Five predictors:	Rebellious	+.385	Group 1 =-.253	63.5
	Obedient	-.368	Group 2 = +.412	
	Cigarette smoking	+.344	Group 3+4 = +.882	
	Negative cigarette attitudes	-.281		
	Grade point average	+.064		
Four Predictors:	Rebellious	+.383	Group 1 = -.252	63.2
	Obedient	-.350	Group 2 = +.407	
	Cigarette smoking	+.335	Group 3+4 = +.883	
	Negative cigarette attitudes	-.279		

*   Group 1 = nonusers; Group 2 = infrequent marijuana users; Group 3 + 4 = heavy users.

dardized coefficients for the three-group analysis. The coefficients for "Rebellious" and cigarette smoking were positive; those for "Obedient" and negative attitudes toward cigarette smoking were negative. The composite means produced by that procedure are −.25, +.40, and +.88 for nonusers, infrequent marijuana users, and heavy users, respectively. The standard deviations associated with those three means are 0.85, 1.02, and 1.08, respectively. The composite mean scores have the same value as the group centroids shown in Table 3 (within the limits of rounding error), but we constructed the composite scores and examined their distributions to give the multivariate results an added degree of concreteness and clarity of meaning. We used the composite scores to assess the accuracy of classification when the three groups were compared two at a time, as well as when all three were considered simultaneously. We also compared the distribution of composite scores of nonusers (Group 1) with that of users (Group 2 + 3 + 4). Table 4 presents detailed results concerning correct and incorrect classification in the three-group problem and in each of four two-group problems.

For the three-group comparison, we plotted the three distributions of composite scores and established two lines of demarcation. The line between Group 1 and Group 2 was drawn at the mean of those two distribu-

tion means. The line between Group 2 and Group 3 + 4 was placed at the
mean of those two distribution means. Then we counted the number of
subjects classified correctly, the number misclassified into nonadjacent
groups (more serious errors), and the number misclassified into adjacent
groups (less serious errors). The three-group analysis misclassified 13.4
percent of the subjects into nonadjacent groups, misclassified 23.8 percent into adjacent groups, and correctly classified 62.8 percent of the
subjects. (See Table 4.)

We also used the lines of demarcation just mentioned to assess accuracy of classification when pairs of adjacent groups were considered and
the third group was not taken into account. Accuracy for classifying

Table 4

Accuracy of Status Assignment Using Composite Scores

Actual Status*

		1	2	3+4
	1	1067	109	73
Predicted Status	2	228	59	68
	3+4	204	86	168

accuracy = 63%

Actual

		1	2
	1	1067	109
Predicted	2	432	145

accuracy = 69%

Actual

		2	3+4
	2	168	141
Predicted	3+4	86	168

accuracy = 60%

Actual

		1	3+4
	1	1175	101
Predicted	3+4	324	208

accuracy = 76%

Actual

		1	2+3+4
	1	1132	210
Predicted	2+3+4	367	353

accuracy = 72%

* Status groups: 1 = nonusers; 2 = infrequent marijuana users; 3 + 4 = heavy users.

nonusers *vs.* infrequent marijuana users was 69 percent. For infrequent marijuana users *vs.* heavy users, accuracy was 60 percent.

For comparing the two nonadjacent groups (1 *vs.* 3 + 4), the discriminant line was the mean of the means of those two distributions; accuracy of classification was 76 percent. For comparing nonusers *vs.* users (1 *vs.* 2 + 3 + 4), the discriminant line was the mean of those two distribution means; accuracy of classification was 72 percent. (See Table 4.)

Of course, accuracy of group classification and degree of group separation concern the same basic issue, but we found it informative to consider the matter both ways. The mean composite score for nonusers (− .25) is separated from that of infrequent marijuana users (+ .40) by approximately two-thirds of a standard deviation; the mean for infrequent marijuana users is separated from that of heavy users (+ .88) by approximately one-half of a standard deviation; and the mean for nonusers is separated from that of heavy users by more than a full standard deviation. Whether considered in terms of group separation or accuracy of group classification, it is clear that psychosocial variables can predict subsequent teen-age use/nonuse and levels of use, and can do so with considerable accuracy.

COMMENTS

Our sample deals with a restricted subpopulation of American youth: mostly white, middle-class students from suburban neighborhoods. That fact has advantages as well as disadvantages. Sample homogeneity regarding economic, social, and racial variables does limit the generality of applicability of our findings; but such homogeneity also controls the otherwise disturbing effects of those potentially important variables and thereby permits a more penetrating analysis of the individual and personal determinants of decisions regarding drug use. Individuals from the same socioeconomic and racial background do differ regarding decisions to use or not use drugs. Indeed, individuals from the same family sometimes make quite divergent decisions.

The five predictor variables examined in this analysis were not selected for the specific purpose of measuring aspects of socialization, but it is our belief that all five are relevant to that process. We interpret our results as supporting the hypothesis that deeper drug involvement is associated with lower predrug compliance with desires and expectations of parents who hold traditional middle-class values.

Most presently available information concerning the relations between drug use and psychosocial characteristics is based on analyses of data collected at a single point in time. Few longitudinal studies of antecedents and sequelae of drug use have been reported (Kandel, 1976). Reproducible results found in cross-sectional studies serve an important orienting function by highlighting possible causes and effects of drug use, but they provide little clarification regarding the dynamics underlying the observed relationships. For example, what interpretation should be placed on the finding that users are more rebellious than nonusers? Does it mean that rebelliousness predisposes subjects to use illicit drugs, or that use of drugs produces rebelliousness, or that both causal sequences occur, or that neither occurs? Both sequences might be operative if existing preuse differences were exacerbated by drug use, or if the causal direction were population-dependent (e.g., in one population, rebelliousness causes drug use; but in another, it results from drug use). Neither might apply if a third unidentified influence were causing both the rebelliousness and the drug use.

The analysis reported here does not eliminate the uncertainty just mentioned, but it does help to reduce the interpretational alternatives. Clearly, for example, in the population we sampled, a cross-sectional association between rebelliousness and drug use is not due entirely to increased rebelliousness following upon initiation of drug use. Rebelliousness, poor academic performance, cigarette smoking, and favorable attitudes toward cigarette smoking are psychosocial characteristics that predate initiation of drug use. We do not yet know whether there is further divergence between users and nonusers on those variables after initiation. That question is being addressed in other analyses that are still in process.

CONCLUSIONS

Three conclusions regarding white middle-class American youth are drawn from the results presented here: (1) Rebelliousness, poor academic performance, cigarette smoking, and favorable attitudes toward cigarette smoking are associated with increased likelihood of illicit drug use among students who have not yet begun to use. (2) Those same characteristics predict subsequent degree of drug involvment. (3) The level of predictive accuracy found in the analyses reported here is sufficient to warrant further investigation of the theoretical and practical implications of these and related longitudinal relationships.

FOOTNOTES

*This work was supported by grant #DA00065 from the National Institute on Drug Abuse. We are pleased to acknowledge the assistance of Frederick T. Schwerin in preparing the data for analysis and the advice of our statistical consultants, William G. Cochran and Richard A. Labrie. We also wish to thank Ira H. Cisin for reading the report and for making numerous helpful suggestions.

1. An earlier analysis, reported at the 35th meeting of the Committee on Problems of Drug Dependence on May 22, 1973, used a different definition of Time 2. In that analysis, Time 2 was 1971 for some students and 1972 for others. In the present analysis, Time 2 is 1971 for all students.

2. Twenty-six of the rejected questionnaires gave unmistakable evidence of careless or noncooperative responding. These subjects were permanently eliminated from the data base. The remaining twenty-six subjects were deleted from the present analysis because of more subtle evidence of possible error in responding; however, those subjects remain in the data base and their data will be examined in further detail in later analyses.

3. The results are not tabularized in this report, but five-group comparisons (Groups 1 *vs.* 2 *vs.* 3 *vs.* 4 *vs.* 5) and four-group comparisons (Groups 1 *vs.* 2 *vs.* 3 *vs.* 4) were also performed; and in each case, the F-value was significant beyond the 0.001 level for each of the five predictor variables.

4. Our discriminant program requires each subject to have scores on all variables. Subjects with blanks on three or more predictors were deleted. Missing values for subjects retained in the analysis were replaced with the mean of the subject's drug status group on the missing predictor. The univariate results in Tables 1 and 2 involve no such imputations.

REFERENCES

Block, J. R., N. Goodman, F. Ambellan, and J. Reverson (1973), "A self-administered high school study of drugs." Hempstead, N.Y.: Institute for Research and Evaluation.

Gergen, M. K., K. J. Gergen, and S. J. Morse (1972), "Correlates of marijuana use among college students," *Journal of Applied Social Psychology* 2(1):1–16.

Goode, E. (1972), *Drugs in American Society.* New York: Knopf.

Groves, W. E. (1974), "Patterns of student drug use and lifestyles," pp. 241–278 in E. Josephson and E. E. Carroll (Eds.), *Drug Use: Epidemiological and Sociological Approaches.* New York: Wiley.

Hogan, R., D. Mankin, J. Conway, and S. Fox (1970), "Personality correlates of undergraduate marijuana use," *Journal of Counseling and Clinical Psychology* 32(1):58–63.

Jessor, R., S. L. Jessor, and J. Finney (1973), "A social psychology of marijuana use: Longitudinal studies of high school and college youth," *Journal of Personality and Social Psychology* 26:1–15.

Johnson, B. D. (1972), *Social Determinants of the Use of Dangerous Drugs by College Students.* New York: Wiley.

Johnston, L. (1973), *Drugs and American Youth.* Ann Arbor: University of Michigan.

Josephson, E. P., A. Z. Haberman, and J. Elinson (1972), "Adolescent marijuana use: Report on a national survey," pp. 1–8 in S. Einstein and S. Allen (Eds.), *Student Drug Surveys.* Farmingdale, New York: Baywood.

Kandel, D. B. (1975), "Stages in adolescent involvement in drug use," *Science* 190:912–914.

—— (1976), "Convergences in prospective longitudinal surveys of drug use in normal populations." Presented at the Society for Life History Research in Psychopathology, Fort Worth, Texas.

McGlothlin, W. H., K. Jamison, and S. Rosenblatt (1970), "Marijuana and the use of other drugs," *Nature* 228:1227–1229.

Mellinger, G. D., R. H. Somers, D. I. Manheimer (1975), "Drug use research items pertaining to personality and interpersonal relations: A working paper for research investigators," pp. 299–342 in D. Lettieri (Ed.), *Predicting Adolescent Drug Abuse: A Review of Issues, Methods and Correlates.* Rockville, Maryland: National Institute on Drug Abuse.

Naditch, M. P. (1975), "Ego mechanisms and marijuana usage," pp. 207–222 in D. Lettieri (Ed.) *Predicting Adolescent Drug Abuse: A Review of Issues, Methods and Correlates.* Rockville, Maryland: National Institute on Drug Abuse.

Robins, L., H. Darvish, and G. Murphy (1970), "The long-term outcome for adolescent drug users: A follow-up study of 76 users and 146 nonusers," pp. 159–178 in J. Zubin and A. Freedman (Eds.), *The Psychopathology of Adolescence.* New York: Grune and Stratton.

Sadava, S. W. (1972), "Becoming a marijuana user: A longitudinal social learning study." Paper presented at the annual meeting of the Canadian Psychological Association, Montreal.

Segal, B. (1974), "Drug use and fantasy process: Criterion for prediction of potential users," *International Journal of the Addictions*, 9:475–480.

Smart, R. G., D. Fejer, and J. White (1970), "The extent of drug use in metropolitan Toronto schools: A study of changes from 1968 to 1970." The Addiction Research Foundation, Toronto, Ontario.

Smith, G. M. (1967), "Usefulness of peer ratings of personality in educational research," *Educational and Psychological Measurements* 27(4):967–984.

———, and C. P. Fogg (1975), "Teenage drug use: A search for causes and consequences," pp. 227–282 in D. Lettieri (Ed.), *Predicting Adolescent Drug Abuse: A Review of Issues, Methods and Correlates.* Rockville, Maryland: National Institute on Drug Abuse.

——— (1978), "Psychological predictors of early use, late use, and nonuse of marijuana among teenage students," in D. Kandel (Ed.), *Longitudinal Studies in Drug Use: Substantive and Methodological Issues.* Washington, D.C.: Hemisphere Press—Wiley (forthcoming).

Whitehead, P. C., R. Smart, and L. Laforest (1972), "Multiple drug use among marijuana smokers in eastern Canada," *International Journal of the Addictions* 7:179–190.

PATTERNS OF SEXUAL IDENTITY DEVELOPMENT: A PRELIMINARY REPORT ON THE "TOMBOY"*

Katherine Williams, M.A. STATE UNIVERSITY OF NEW YORK AT STONY BROOK

Richard Green, M.D. STATE UNIVERSITY OF NEW YORK AT STONY BROOK

Marilyn Goodman, M.S. STATE UNIVERSITY OF NEW YORK AT STONY BROOK

COMPONENTS OF SEXUAL IDENTITY

Sexual identity is a basic and enduring personality trait permeating most areas of interpersonal interaction. It is difficult to conceive of another characteristic with such a profound and fundamental influence on shaping development and behavior. At first glance, the distinction between female/male, girl/boy, woman/man may seem obvious, based primarily on anatomy. However, sexual identity is a subtle and complex phenomenon. There are both physiological and psychosocial components which are crucial to its development and variations within each appear to modify its course of development.

Research in Community and Mental Health, Vol. 1, pp 103–123.
Copyright © 1979 by JAI Press, Inc.
All rights of reproduction in any form reserved.
ISBN 0-89232-063-X

One component is the physiological aspects of the individual. These are based on chromosomal make-up, hormonal levels, internal and external genitalia, and secondary sex characteristics. Generally, at birth, those individuals with female genitalia (and forty-six XX chromosomes) are assigned as females and those who have male genitalia (and forty-six XY chromosomes) are assigned as males. There are, however, instances when the chromosomal make-up and the appearance of the external genitalia are at variance, as in cases of hermaphrodism. Confusion of biological sex at birth can cause special problems in developing a coherent sexual identity (Money and Ehrhardt, 1972).

Physiological aspects impact on the development of sexual identity in at least two ways. First, the prenatal hormonal differences between males and females may have some postnatal effect on behaviors (Ehrhardt and Baker, 1974). Secondly, the physical appearance (external genitalia) of the child may have an impact on the way in which other individuals interact with the child (Money and Ehrhardt, 1972).

The psychosexual components of sexual identity evolve in three stages. The first is the development of core-morphologic identity. This is the basic awareness by the young child that "I am a girl" or "I am a boy." This awareness evolves early in life and appears to be fixed by age three years (Money, Hampson and Hampson, 1955; Stoller, 1968, Green, 1974). Studies of anatomically intersexed children indicate that individuals are extremely resistant to sex reassignment after this age. The second stage is the learning of gender roles (gender-role behavior), those cultural definitions of typical "masculine" and "feminine" behaviors. The third stage is the development of sexual object choice or sexual orientation, i.e., the awareness of sexual partner preference for other, same, or either sex partners.

For the most part, these components are consonant. If a child is born an anatomical female, she will develop the identity "I am a girl," will behave in a culturally typical feminine manner, and will develop an erotic interest in males. Similarly, a child born an anatomic male will develop the identity "I am a boy," will do the things the culture defines as "appropriate" for boys, and later will develop an erotic interest in females. However, often the various components of sexual identity are dissonant. Transvestites, for example, are anatomical males, have a core-morphologic identity as male, and are most often heterosexual. However, by dressing in feminine clothing, they are engaging in behavior that is seen as culturally appropriate for females. Homosexuals present a more complex picture. A homosexual's core-morphologic identity is in accordance with her or his anatomy, but the choice of a same-sex sexual partner is atypical. Gender-role behavior is usually consistent with core-morphologic identity. Transsexuals present the most complex organization of sexual identity components. For the transsexual, core-morphologic identity is in disagreement with anatomical sex. Female-to-male transsexuals, for example, have female anatomy but a core identity as male—"I am a man trapped inside a woman's body" (Benjamin, 1966). Gender-role behaviors and later sexual partner preference are usually in accordance with the core identity but in conflict with physical anatomy (Green and Money, 1969).

These variations in sexual identity accentuate the complexity of the development of this part of personality. The processes which are active during this development are only beginning to be more fully understood. Much research of atypical adults has been retrospective. Problems in such research have been addressed by Green (1974). The research described below is an attempt to follow a group of culturally atypical prepubertal boys and girls and a culturally typical matched group through adolescence and into adulthood to better understand the unfolding of these developmental processes.

THEORIES OF PSYCHOSEXUAL DEVELOPMENT

Infant Studies   Some researchers point to early sex differences as evidence of innate differentiation and to differential ways in which mothers treat male and female infants as early social conditioners of sex-typing. Infant males have been shown to excel in lifting their head from a prone position (Bell and Darling, 1965). Mothers of three-week-old boys have been observed to stretch boys' limbs more than those of the same-age girls. They were also observed to more often vocally imitate the sounds of girls (Moss, 1967). These findings have been seen as setting the stage for the greater verbal fluency of girls (Gari and Scheinfeld, 1968).

Somewhat later, 13-month-old boys have been found to separate further from their mothers than girls and to play differently with toys. Boys were observed to throw toys about, rather than gathering them. Boys were also found to react differently to a barrier placed between themselves and the toys; boys crawled to the end of the barrier, ostensibly trying to get past it, girls tended to sit where placed and cry (Goldberg and Lewis, 1969). The latter study, however, was not replicated (Maccoby and Jacklin, 1974).

The case for innate differences in these 13-month-old children is not without flaws. These same children had also been observed with their mothers at five months. Then, mothers held female infants more than male infants. Thus, the 13-month-old females' greater reluctance to move away from the mother may be confounded, and an argument can be made for either differences in innate autonomy or social conditioning.

Psychoanalytic Model   Psychoanalytic theories of gender identity development derive from the writings of Freud (1935). Freud's knowledge that before birth all mammals have both male and female anatomic structures led him to postulate a similar psychic bisexuality. The ultimate dominance of either a masculine or feminine identity depended upon the child's drives and experiences with parents during the first five to six years. Male and female children are seen as developing similarly for the first three years, through postulated oral and anal stages and up to the onset of the phallic stage. By the end of the third year significant differences in male-female development were considered to be unfolding.

During this period, the formation of love attachments to cross-sex parents and jealousy toward same-sex parents was seen as essential to normal sexual development. Males during this stage experience what Freud called the Oedipal complex. Love for the mother causes jealousy of the father, who is also an object of fear and admiration. In the child's mind, the father might retaliate for the son's love of the mother by a punishment which would result in the loss of the boy's penis. The son's resolution to this anxiety-producing situation is to identify with his father and later seek out another female partner. The analogous situation for the young girl is called the Electra complex. Here the girl, angered at her mother for a similar lack of a penis, turns to her father as a love object but, realizing the impossibility of replacing her mother, identifies with her and later seeks out another male partner.

More contemporary analysts have criticized Freud's formulation for his insistence that the age of onset of gender identity development and differentiation between girls and boys began only *after* the child was two to three years old. Recent work indicates that children begin developing a gender identity much earlier and that this may be fixed by age three (Stoller, 1968; Kleeman, 1971a, b).

Social Learning   This point of view, as noted by Gagnon (1977), suggests that once the child comes to label itself as a "boy" or "girl," it uses this information as a guide to organizing the environment. "Since there is no 'natural' relationship between gender identity and gender role performances, the child possesses a label with very little content. The label has a forward function, that is, it is used to organize the new things that happen. This is done by observing who works to earn the principal income, who is in charge of the housework, and who plays with cars or dolls. All of these activities are more or less gender typed, mostly by frequency than dramatic differences, and by verbal exhortations of what boys do and what girls do" (Gagnon, 1977:68). Appropriate masculine or feminine behaviors are learned, then, in much the same manner as are other behaviors, through identification with or imitation of live or symbolic role models.

Early role models and social reinforcement of appropriate gender behaviors come largely from parents. Identification with the "appropriate" role model is critical. The model must be perceived as nurturant to the child; it must be in command of goals desired by the child, especially power, love, and competence in areas the child regards as important; and the child must perceive some objective basis of similarity between itself and the model (Kagan, 1958). It is through observing and imitating parents that the child first begins to flesh out the behavior categories outlined by a gender identity.

Not only do the parents provide the model from which boys and girls can learn masculinity and femininity, they are also instrumental in this learning process through their reinforcement of the child's behaviors. Children seek approval from these significant others. The parents prefer the children to adopt socially appropriate gender-typed behavior and thus will more often positively reinforce gender-typical behavior and negatively reinforce gender-atypical behavior. In this manner, children usually learn rapidly to behave in the desired masculine or feminine ways (Mischel, 1966).

Not all writers stress the importance of both parents, or the availability of a male model, for masculine gender-role development. Colley (1959), for example, notes that the absence of one parent may not disrupt the formation of the child's gender-identity development as long as there is one appropriately identified parent with whom the child experiences close interaction. The parent, by differentially responding to the child, may offset the absence of the other parent. Thus, if a mother behaves toward her son "as if" he were a boy, she may counteract the absence of a male father figure.

As the child grows older and begins to move out from the family into the world of school and peers, the influence of parental identification and imitation is joined by the growing influence of peers and the mass media in the shaping of gender behaviors. Approval of peers becomes increasingly important. Movies, books, and especially television also provide plentiful and stereotypical models of "masculinity" and "femininity" which children can and do imitate in their role playing.

ATYPICAL DEVELOPMENTAL OUTCOMES

During the years in which most males and females develop a culturally typical sexual identity, a smaller number of children show atypical development. In popular terms, these children are "sissies" and "tomboys." They show a preference for the company, clothes, toys, and activities of other-sex children. How this early cross-gender behavior affects later sexual identity and behaviors is uncertain. However, that these early atypical gender-role behaviors are potentially enduring can be inferred from retrospective accounts of adults who have adopted atypical sexual lifestyles.

Green (1974), for example, in evaluating a group of adult male-to-female transsexuals ($N = 30$), found that they invariably gave retrospective childhood histories of wanting to be female and to participate in culturally traditional feminine behaviors. Very few (13 percent) preferred boys' toys or boys as playmates. Less than half preferred boys' clothes. Less than half had a clear concept of themselves as male. As children they were considered "sissies."

In their study of male and female homosexuals, Saghir and Robins (1973) found that 67 percent of the male homosexuals ($N = 89$) exhibited a similar "girl-like" syndrome in childhood as opposed to 3 percent of the male heterosexuals ($N = 35$). This syndrome was characterized as a persistent aversion to playing with other boys and being involved in boys' games and activities. As boys, these men preferred the companionship of girls, doing housework, and playing with girl-type dolls. They were often teased by other boys and siblings about their girl-type behavior. As a result they became isolated children, not comfortable in either the company of boys or girls. These behaviors began in early childhood and continued throughout the preadolescent and often the adolescent years.

Adult transvestites typically recall engaging in one specific type of cross-gender-role behavior—cross-dressing. This pattern may also begin in childhood. In their survey of 504 adult transvestites, Prince and Bentler (1972) found that 14 percent recalled their first cross-dressing experience at age 5, 40 percent between ages 5 and 10, and 37 percent reported their first cross-dressing between ages 10 and 18. There was no evidence presented, however, that these men engaged in other childhood "feminine" behaviors.

In discussing female transsexuals, Stoller (1972) describes an ideal-type female-to-male transsexual as a biologically normal and properly assigned infant girl who "begins to show masculine behavior and interests as early as age 3 or 4 (and in a few cases earlier). The progress of the development of gender identity (masculinity and femininity) then proceeds in a masculine direction, so that by the time the child is 7 or 8, she has invented a boy's name, plays only with toys boys usually prefer, walks and talks like a boy, has developed unusual physical skills (as in athletics), and is stating openly to family and friends that she is going to have the body changes (e.g., a penis) necessary to permit sex reassignment and life from then on as a man."

Green's (1974) evaluation of eleven female-to-male transsexuals indicates that these women were "tomboys," roughhoused, enjoyed sports, wanted to dress in boys' clothes, and remembered wanting to be boys. One hundred percent preferred boys' toys, and 45 percent preferred boys as playmates, while the remaining 55 percent preferred boys and girls equally as playmates. Seventy-three percent recalled preferring to dress in boys' clothes. Less than half (45 percent) recalled a clear self-concept as female.

Female homosexuals also often recall engaging in cross-gender behavior as children. Saghir and Robins (1973) reported that 70 percent of their female homosexuals ($N = 57$) recalled engaging in "tomboyish" behaviors during childhood and adolescence as opposed to 16 percent of the female heterosexuals ($N = 43$). They avoided typical feminine-oriented behaviors such as cooking, sewing, and playing house and were uninterested in being around mother. They preferred the companionship of boys and participating in their games. They chose to play with masculine-oriented toys such as guns, trucks, and sports equipment. As with the males discussed earlier, this was a pattern which started early in childhood and continued at least into adolescence.

From these accounts we can piece together a picture of childhood gender-role behaviors which differ markedly from the norm. We see boys who consistently prefer to dress in girls' clothes, play girls' games, associate with girls, fantasize themselves as girls, and want to be girls. We see girls who consistently prefer boys' dress, boys' games, boys as playmates, call themselves by boys' names, and want to be boys. Because these descriptions come from adults who have atypical sexual life-styles, it is tempting to conclude that these early cross-gender behaviors are indicative of later atypical adult sexual life-styles.

Unfortunately, however, most of the above accounts are based on the recollection of events which often took place decades before. While they offer tantalizing possible insights, recollections as a source of data should be used with the utmost caution. Memory of early childhood events can be faulty and often the past is reorganized to suit present purposes. For instance, the descriptions of the early histories of transsexuals are based on interviews with people motivated to undergo sex-reassignment procedures. It is to their benefit to recall (at least to the evaluators) a history of atypical gender-role behavior dating from as early in childhood as possible. Even without such specific goals, memory is continuously being reorganized to take into account the way the person thinks things should have been in the light of new personal experiences or information. People forget specific details, remembering, selectively, impressions of the past. When asked to recall, they may reconstruct their pasts in accordance with what they can patch together from bits and pieces of memory to form a coherent (albeit fictionalized) whole.

One strategy of research pointed to by these previous studies of adults, however, is to generate samples of male and female children whose behavior is similar to the childhood recollections of the atypical adults. These children can then be matched with children who share the same social and family-type background but who behave in a culturally typical manner. Four groups are possible: traditionally "masculine" boys, "feminine" boys, "tomboy" girls, and traditionally "feminine" girls. The children and their families can then be reevaluated periodically into and during adolescence and on to early adulthood. By so doing, a more valid record of childhood behaviors and interpersonal experiences associated with later typical and atypical patterns of adult sexuality may be provided.

For several reasons, the research project described below began with samples of boys. First, "feminine" boys ("sissies") experience social conflict and may be referred to a clinical setting. "Masculine" girls ("tomboys") do not and are not. The social connotations of the two popularized terms for cross-gender-role behavior by young males and females exemplify the disparate societal views toward these behavioral patterns.

Second, "feminine" boys appear to have a higher probability than "masculine" girls of maturing into sexually atypical adults. Although the incidence of "tomboyism" appears to be more common than "sissiness," more adult males are homosexually oriented (2:1), seek sex-change surgery (3:1), or are transvestites (there are essentially no female transvestites)—(Kinsey et al., 1948, 1953; Benjamin, 1966; Green and Money, 1969; Stoller, 1968).

Because of these considerations, the initial project stage was to generate a sample of prepubertal boys considered "feminine." These were boys who showed a preference for the toys, activities, clothes, and companionship of girls and typically role-played as females. These boys were located by professional referrals. A pilot study of eleven boys was generated in collaboration with Money (Green and Money, 1960, 1961). The larger study summarized here was initiated in 1969, in collaboration with Stoller. A group of sixty "feminine" boys was paired with an age-and-family-constellation-matched group of boys with typically masculine behaviors. The two groups of boys and their parents were evaluated by semistructured interviews, psychological tests, and systematic behavioral observations (Green, 1974).

The second project stage has been to generate a group of prepubertal girls labeled "tomboys" by their families who meet specific behavioral criteria, and a corresponding group of typically "feminine" girls. Since "tomboyism" is rarely seen as a problem for psychiatric referral, initial contacts with both groups of girls were made via newspaper advertisements for paid volunteers. At present, a group of forty-five "tomboy" girls and their families has been evaluated. The age-and-family-constellation-matched group of typically "feminine" girls is being generated. Criteria for "tomboyism" will be given below.

Five areas of behavior appear crucial for discriminating between typical and atypical gender-role development in children: clothing preference, toy preference, sports and rough-and-tumble play, choice of companions, and role playing. We have, at present, descriptive information on three groups of children: boys with typically feminine interests in these areas, boys with typically masculine interests in these areas, and girls with typically masculine interests.

TYPICAL AND ATYPICAL BOYS

The following overview describes two disparate groups of grade school boys. From the first two to three years of life the referred group was markedly different from the contrast group. The latter, generated by advertising for families with specific socioeconomic features to participate in a psychological study, is unremarkable behaviorally. The former contains boys whose behavior is similar to same-age typical girls. Because these groups have been described in detail elsewhere (Green, 1974; 1976), the following descriptions will be brief.

Clothing   The "feminine" boys' interest in dressing in girl's clothes far exceeded the occasional dress-up experiences of the "masculine" boys. Ninety-eight percent of the "feminine" boys had had experiences wearing women's or girls' clothes compared to 19 percent of the "masculine" boys. Articles of clothing worn included high-heeled shoes, outer garments, undergarments, and accessories. When genuine articles were unavailable, they were improvised from other materials. Cross-dressing behavior began early and was a frequent behavior for 69 percent of the "feminine" boys. None of the "masculine" boys wore cross-sex clothes frequently, 18 percent did so rarely, and 81 percent had no such experience. The "feminine" boys also showed a marked interest in their mother's clothing, frequently voicing approval or disapproval of her choice of outfits or accessories.

Toys and Doll Play   Interest in playing with feminine dress-up type dolls such as "Barbie" was very strong in the "feminine" boys. These dolls were the favorite toy of 17 percent of this group and a frequently played with toy for another 41 percent. The "masculine" boy group showed little interest in this activity: 55 percent never played with female-type dolls, the other 45 percent did so only occasionally. Doll play, like cross-dressing, began early for the referred group: 52 percent had begun by age three, 95 percent by age five.

Sports and Rough-and-Tumble Play   Rough-and-tumble physical activity and agressive play are stereotypically masculine boyhood behaviors. There is a strong difference between these two groups on this dimension. The referred group of boys is seen by their parents as being below average in their interest in sports and in participation in rough-and-tumble activities. These boys often decline to play with other boys because other boys play "too rough." "Masculine" boys, on the other hand, are seen by their parents as being average or above average in their interest in sports and participation in rough, aggressive activities.

Companions   In interpersonal relationships, "feminine" boys were seen by their parents as relating best with same-age or older girls. "Masculine" boys preferred the company of same-age or older boys. The male peer group was not unaware of the atypical behavior of the referred group, and this in turn influenced their social interactions. Rejected by boys, and in some cases, rejecting boys as playmates because of their rough play patterns, the "feminine" boys related far better to girls. The "masculine" boys were most often seen as good mixers in their interactions with the male peer group.

Role Playing   Interest in play-acting and role-taking also varies between the groups. Seventy-three percent of the "feminine" boys took a considerable interest in play-acting compared to the "masculine" boys, most of whom never engaged in this behavior or did so only occasionally. This difference in participation extended to house playing activities: only 7 percent of the referred group reportedly did not play house games, compared with 29 percent of the contrast group. The roles played were even more divergent: three times as many of the contrast group typically played father (39 percent vs. 13 percent) and 38 percent of the referred group typically played mother, compared with 0 percent in the contrast group. Finally, a female role, other than mother, was usually taken by 20 percent of the referred group, again compared with 0 percent in the "masculine" boy group.

ATYPICAL GIRLS

Announcements were placed in local newspapers asking for "tomboys" to participate in a psychological study. Thus, the initial criterion for inclusion in the study was a parental and/or self-label as "tomboy." This is important, because those girls who perceive themselves as "tomboys" are more likely to behave in ways which they feel are appropriate for this social category. Likewise, parents who perceive their daughters as "tomboys" are more likely to interact with them differently because of this ascription.

Due to the wide variation of behaviors assocated with "tomboyism," during the initial telephone contact parents of potential subjects were given a behavioral checklist concerning their daughter. This was used as a second screening criterion. Operationally, a "tomboy" was defined as a girl who is labeled a "tomboy" by her family and who has at least an equal division of male and female playmates if not a majority of male, who rarely or never plays with female-type dolls, who more often imitates a male in "make-believe" games, who participates in sports more with boys than girls, who prefers dressing in boy-type clothes, and who has said on occasion that she would like to be a boy.

Forty-five girls who met these criteria have been evaluated. They range in age from 4 to 12 years. Educational level, especially of the fathers, indicates that this group is biased toward the upper end of the socioeconomic spectrum. Four percent of the fathers had not completed high school, 39 percent completed high school, 30 percent completed college, and another 20 percent held graduate degrees. Forty-seven percent of the mothers completed high school, 29 percent completed two years of college, and 16 percent completed four years of college. Ninety-five percent of the families are Caucasian. Two-fifths of the parents are Catholic (fathers—42 percent, mothers—44 percent), almost one-third are Jewish (fathers—32 percent, mothers—31 percent), and one-fifth are Protestant (fathers—24 percent, mothers 20 percent). Eighty-four percent of the families were intact at the time of evaluation, 16 percent were broken by separation or divorce.

Information about the "tomboy" girls and their families is gathered in several ways. After the initial telephone screening, both parents are sent a detailed questionnaire dealing with demographic characteristics, family composition, marital interaction, parent-child relationships, and the child's behavior. Each parent also completes a series of attitude scales covering their attitudes toward this particular child and toward various aspects of child rearing in general. The parents participate both singly and together in a semistructured interview dealing with several areas of the parents' earlier life experiences, current marital relationship, relationship to their daughter, and descriptions of their daughter's behavior. The "tomboy" girls participate in a series of psychological tests which have been shown to reveal sex differences. They are also given the appropriate level Wechsler Intelligence Scale. Additional information about girls' interactions in school is provided by a schoolteacher rating form. Families are paid for their participation.

The following behavioral descriptions come primarily from the parental questionnaires concerning the girl's developmental history and current activities. The percentages quoted generally come from the mother's questionnaire even though both parents completed identical question-naires. The decision to use the mother's answers for the descriptive purposes here was made for two reasons. Mothers typically spend more time interacting with the children, observing them during many diverse situations. Therefore, they should be better able to judge the consistency of a child's behavior over time and across situations. Also, we have mothers' questionnaires for all subjects while four of the fathers were unavailable for participation in the research because of separation or di-vorce.

Cross-Sex Wish   It is not unusual for a person to express a wish to be a member of the other sex at certain times or for certain specific reasons. Mothers of the "tomboy" girls report that their daughters often express the desire to be a boy. Thirty-nine percent report this as "frequent" and another 42 percent report this as "once in a while." Few of the girls call themselves by boys' names. Sixty-three percent never do so, or do so only rarely. Another 27 percent call themselves by boys' names once in a while.

Clothing   Clothing preferences were a consistent factor in discriminat-ing the "feminine" and "masculine" boys (Green, 1976). Likewise, the desire to dress in masculine clothing is strong for many of the "tomboy" girls. Sixty-two percent of the mothers report that their daughters fre-quently wear boys' clothes. Thirty-six percent of the girls who wear boys' clothes wear both boys' shoes and boys' outer garments, 33 percent wear only outer garments and 11 percent wear only boys' shoes. In this respect, the "tomboy" girls resemble the cross-dressing behavior of the "feminine" boys. Forty-nine percent of these boys dressed in women's high-heeled shoes and outer garments, and another 16 percent wore wom-en's or girls' outer garments. Forty-nine percent of the mothers report seeing or hearing about their daughter's dressing in boys' clothes twenty or more times. This behavior began early: 31.5 percent by age four. This rose to 81.5 percent by age six. For 73 percent of these girls, the behavior

Table 1

Interest in Mother's Clothing

"My child comments on her/his mother's clothing styles."

	"Feminine" boys (N = 59)	"Tomboy" girls (N = 45)	"Masculine" boys (N = 48)
Never	2%	20%	19%
Occasionally	25	60	60
Frequently	73	20	21

Total: Chi Square 41.468, p $<$ .001
"Feminine" boys vs. "Tomboy" girls: Chi Square 30.799, p $<$ .001
"Tomboy" girls vs. "Masculine" boys: Chi Square 0.027, p $>$ .98

continued at the time of evaluation. It should be noted that with respect to clothing preferences the "tomboy" girls do not represent a wide variation from the cultural norm. Masculine style, tailored clothing for females is acceptable and encouraged in our society. Perhaps because of this availability of clothing made specifically for girls but modeled after boys' styles, only 29 percent of the mothers report ever seeing their daughters improvising masculine clothing.

Cross-dressing by male children is often alarming to parents, many of whom see this behavior as an early manifestation of later abnormal sexual behavior. For the parents of "tomboy" girls, however, this behavior is not viewed as a precursor of later problems. The vast majority see their daughter's desire to dress in boys' clothing as a passing phase and ignore it.

Few of these girls indicate an interest in feminine styles. Twenty percent never comment on their mother's clothing choices and another 60 percent do so only occasionally. In this respect they closely resemble the "masculine" boys' "interest" in their mother's clothing (Table 1).

Toys and Doll Play   One of the typical activities of young girls is playing with feminine, dress-up type dolls such as "Barbie." However, for the "tomboy" girls this type of play is of little interest. Seventy-five percent of the mothers report that their daughters rarely or never play with this kind of doll. They also do not show a strong interest in playing with the masculine "action" type of doll such as "G.I. Joe." Seventy-two percent never play with these male-type dolls or do so very rarely.

The "tomboy" girls do, however, show interest in playing with two stereotypically masculine toys—trucks and guns. Forty-seven percent of the mothers of the "tomboy" girls report that their daughters play with trucks frequently, and another 42 percent play with trucks occasionally. For those girls who play with trucks, the interest developed early—88 percent had begun by their fourth year. Ninety-one percent of the mothers see their daughter's interest in playing with trucks as a passing phase and most (76 percent) ignore it. There are a few mothers (9 percent) who, perhaps in the interest of breaking down certain sex-role stereotypes, encourage truck play. This pattern of reaction is true of the fathers also: 85 percent ignore the behavior and a few (8 percent) encourage it. Only a small percentage of the mothers (4 percent) discourage their daughters from playing with trucks and none of the fathers do so.

Guns seem to be less popular toys than trucks among the "tomboy" girls. Only 22 percent are reported as frequently playing with guns, another 50 percent do so occasionally. Nineteen percent never play with guns. For those girls who do play with guns, the age at which gun play began was bimodal, with 35 percent beginning between years two and three and 39 percent beginning between four and five. Like truck play, gun play is seen as a passing phase by most mothers (96 percent) and fathers (91 percent). However, unlike truck play, gun play is more often discouraged (23 percent of mothers, 19 percent of fathers) and never encouraged by either parent. Most often no action is taken vis-à-vis the behavior.

Sports and Rough-and-Tumble Play   The "tomboys" are described by their mothers as being very interested in sports and rough-and-tumble play. Sixty-four pecent of the mothers feel that their daughters participate in sports more than the average girl of that age. Another 33 percent feel they engage in an average amount of sports. The girls are also seen as more rough-and-tumble than other girls by 76 percent of the mothers. Not only are these girls interested in sports, but they appear to be specifically interested in participating with boys in their play. For 80 percent, playing sports with boys as opposed to girls is a favorite activity.

Companions   Peer groups among school-aged children tend mainly to be of the same sex. For example, 89 percent of the typically "masculine" boys were seen by their mothers as relating best to same age or older boys. However, this typical pattern does not seem to hold for atypical boys and girls. Eighty percent of the mothers of the "tomboy" girls report that their daughters relate best to males. Sixty-eight percent of these relate best to same age or older boys, a pattern similar to that reported for the typically "masculine" boys. Only 18 percent of these girls are seen as relating well to same age or older girls. In contrast, 73 percent of the

Table 2

Comparative Social Relationships

"My child relates best to:"

	"Feminine" boys (N = 51)	"Tomboy" girls (N = 43)	"Masculine" boys (N = 45)
Adult Men	0%	5%	4%
Boys	18	75	93
Younger	4	7	2
Same age	12	35	58
Older	2	33	31
Total Males	18	80	97
Adult women	12	0	0
Girls	71	20	2
Younger	8	2	0
Same age	41	9	2
Older	22	9	0
Total females	83	20	2

Total: Chi Square 72.866, p < .001
"Feminine" boys vs. "Tomboy" girls: Chi Square 35.329, p < .001
"Tomboy" girls vs. "Masculine" boys: Chi Square 7.583, p < .01

"feminine" boys relate best to same age or older girls, and only 14 percent relate best to same age or older boys (Table 2).

Atypical behavior on the part of male children can result in peer group ostracism for the child. This does not appear to be the case for the "tomboy" girls. In their social relations with other girls, 49 percent are seen by the mothers as good mixers. Twenty-nine percent are seen as leaders when they interact with other girls. Only 22 percent are loners and none of the mothers report that their daughters have been rejected by their female peer group. Thus, it appears that while these girls prefer the company of boys for many activities, they do not have difficulties relating to female peers.

The "tomboy" girls differ significantly from both the "feminine" boys and the "masculine" boys in their relationships to same-sex peers (Table 3). "Masculine" boys are more often seen as good mixers with same-sex

Table 3

Comparative Peer Group Relations

"My child, in her/his social relations to other girls/boys, is best
described as:"

	"Feminine" boys (N = 55)	"Tomboy" girls (N = 45)	"Masculine" boys (N = 45)
Leader	14%	29%	19%
Good mixer	29	49	70
Voluntary loner	38	22	3
Rejected	18	0	8

Total: Chi Square 34.027, p $<$.001
"Feminine" boys vs. "Tomboy" girls: Chi Square 15.414, p $<$.01
"Tomboy" girls vs. "Masculine" boys: Chi Square 13.620, p $<$.01

peers (70 percent) than are "tomboy" girls (49 percent) or the "feminine"
boys (29 percent). They are somewhat less likely than "tomboy" girls to
be seen as leaders (19 percent vs. 29 percent). The "femininine" boys are
more frequently seen as loners (38 percent) than are the "tomboy" girls
(22 percent) or the "masculine" boys (3 percent). They are also more
often rejected by their peers (18 percent vs. 0 percent vs. 8 percent).

Regarding their relationship to parents, 52 percent of the mothers report
that their daughters prefer both parents equally, 30 prefer their fathers,
and the remaining 18 percent prefer their mothers. Few of the girls frequently express a wish to grow up to be like mother. Forty-two percent
have never expressed this wish and another 48 percent do so only occasionally. Even fewer "tomboy" girls express a wish to grow up to be like
father—93 percent never do so or do so only occasionally. This is different from the pattern found among "masculine" boys (Table 4). Ninety-
three percent of the "masculine" boys never expressed the wish to grow
up to be like mother and 31 percent frequently express the wish to grow
up to be like father. On this dimension the "tomboy" girls more closely
resemble the "feminine" boys.

Role Playing and Imitative Behavior   One way that children develop
competence in adult behaviors is by imitation and practice through role
modeling. It is often thought that this type of fantasy behavior is more
frequent among girls. However, for these girls, play-acting or role-taking
does not appear to be a major interest. Sixty percent of the mothers report

Table 4

Child's Wish to Be Like Parent

"My child has stated her/his wish to grow up to be like her/his mother:"

	"Feminine" boys (N = 59)	"Tomboy" girls (N = 45)	"Masculine" boys (N = 45)
Never	58%	42%	93%
Occasionally	32	48	7
Frequently	10	11	0

Total: Chi Square 27.584, p < .001
"Feminine" boys vs. "Tomboy" girls: Chi Square 2.688, p > .6
"Tomboy" girls vs. "Masculine" boys: Chi Square 27.172, p < .001

"My child has stated her/his wish to grow up to be like her/his father:"

	"Feminine" boys (N = 59)	"Tomboy" girls (N = 44)	"Masculine" boys (N = 45)
Never	64%	59%	20%
Occasionally	34	34	49
Frequently	2	7	31

Total: Chi Square 32.808, p < .001
"Feminine" boys vs. "Tomboy" girls: Chi Square 1.938 p > .3
"Tomboy" girls vs. "Masculine" boys: Chi Square 16.690, p < .001

that their daughters have either no interest or only a slight interest in play-acting. The extent of interest in play-acting and role-taking for the "tomboys" closely resembles the level of interest of the "masculine" boys in contrast to the "feminine" boys. (Table 5).

Some of the girls do, however, engage in these activities upon occasion and their pattern of imitation is of interest. As noted earlier, the media has been playing an increasingly important role in providing behavioral examples for children. Eighty-four percent of the "tomboy" girls rarely or never imitate female characters they have seen on television or in movies. Another 9 percent do so only once in a while. Most of the imitation of television and movie characters is of males. Imitating male roles from television or movies is a favorite activity of 47 percent of the "tomboys" and another 24 percent do so once in a while.

Traditionally one of the ways in which children prepare themselves for

Table 5

Comparative Interest in Play-Acting and Role-Taking

"My child's interest in play-acting or role-taking."

	"Feminine" boys (N = 59)	"Tomboy" girls (N = 45)	"Masculine" boys (N = 47)
Absent	2%	11%	19%
Slight	25	49	60
Considerable	73	40	21

Total: Chi Square 31.136, p < .001
"Feminine" boys vs. "Tomboy" girls: Chi Square 12.585, p. < .01
"Tomboy" girls vs. "Masculine" boys: Chi Square 4.227, p > .10

assuming adult roles associated with the family is to play "mother-father" or "house" games. Comparatively, the "tomboy" girls are more similar to the "masculine" boys on this dimension. Ninety-three percent of the "feminine" boys, 77 percent of the "tomboy" girls, and 71 percent of the "masculine" boys play house.

While most of the "tomboy" girls occasionally play house, as with television and movie role imitating, many take male roles. Forty-seven percent of the mothers report that their daughters play a male role of some type, either father, brother, or another male. Of these, 47 percent take male roles frequently or always, and another 44 percent do so occasionally. Only 21 percent of the mothers report that their daughters take a

Table 6

Comparative Participation in "Mother-Father" or "House" Games

	"Feminine" boys (N = 55)	"Tomboy" girls (N = 44)	"Masculine" boys (N = 44)
Yes	93%	77%	71%
No	7	23	29

Total: Chi Square 8.564, p < .02
"Feminine" boys vs. "Tomboy" girls: Chi Square 4.868, p < .05
"Tomboy" girls vs. "Masculine" boys: Chi Square .53, p > .9

Table 7

Role Taken in "House" Games

"When playing house my child usually assumes the role of:"

	"Feminine" boys (N = 51)*	"Tomboy" girls (N = 34)	"Masculine" boys (N = 31)
Total male	24%	47%	91%
Father	14	21	55
Brother	2	15	10
Other Male	4	12	16
Self (boys)	4	0	10
Total female	63	21	0
Mother	41	18	0
Sister	8	0	0
Other female	14	0	0
Self (girls)	0	3	0
Other	14	32	10

Total: Chi Square 48.361, p $<$ .001
"Feminine" boys vs. "Tomboy" girls: Chi Square 14.672, p $<$ .001
"Tomboy" girls vs. "Masculine" boys: Chi Square 14.624, p $<$ .001

* These numbers vary from previous tables because only those children who play house-type games are included.

female role. This pattern falls between that of the "feminine" boys and the "masculine" boys ("tomboy" girls are reported to take masculine roles in house games more often than the "feminine" boys, but less often than the "masculine" boys). This is shown in Table 7.

CONCLUSION

Sexual identity is a complex and fundamental personality component. Its formation begins very early in life and has a strong impact on interaction throughout the life cycle. Some males and females do not develop a culturally typical identity. Retrospective accounts of adults with atypical sexual patterns recall the atypicality as beginning early in life. However, retrospective accounts of childhood behaviors are subject to various types of distortion. A more valid strategy for tracing patterns of early behavior to later behaviors is a longitudinal one, evaluating individuals as children and then periodically mapping their development.

It is not unexpected that the "tomboy" behaviors shown in the tables were manifest, in that these girls were recruited for such specific behaviors. The research described here represents the initial evaluation of female and male children whose gender-role behaviors are, to varying degrees, atypical and resemble those described by adults with an atypical sexual identity and of male children whose behaviors are culturally typical. Of interest in this preliminary report is the comparison of the behaviors of the "tomboy" girls with the behaviors of the typical and atypical male groups.

Future reports will focus on other aspects of this research. The next phase of analysis will be a comparison between the "tomboy" girl and the "feminine" girl families to see in what ways, if any, the two differ. Of longer interest is the monitoring of the continuing psychosexual development of all the groups of children. As they are followed through adolescence and into adulthood, we will have a greater understanding of the development of both typical and atypical patterns of sexual identity.

SUMMARY

This study describes three groups of children aged 4 to 12: sixty "feminine" boys, fifty demographically matched "masculine" boys, and forty-five "masculine" girls (a "feminine" girl group is being generated). The atypical children engage in gender-role behaviors considered typical of the other sex. The "feminine" boys avoid sports and rough, aggressive activities. They prefer the company of girls, playing with girls' toys and dressing in girls' clothes. They role-play as females when playing house or imitating characters from books or television. The "tomboy" girls behave in a culturally masculine manner. Sports, especially when played with boys, is a favorite activity. They are less interested in playing with dolls than with trucks and guns. If they play house-type games, they often take a male role. Their gender-role behavior closely resembles that of the "masculine" boy group. The descriptions provided are based on the initial evaluations of these children and will be supplemented by periodic reevaluations.

FOOTNOTE

*This research is supported by National Institute of Mental Health Grant number 5 RO1 MH26598-04. We acknowledge the considerable assistance of Michael Diringer and Jay Harper in the data collection for this project.

REFERENCES

Bell, R., and N. Darling (1965), "The prone head reaction in the human newborn," *Child Development* 36:943–949.

Benjamin, H. (1966), *The Transsexual Phenomenon*. New York: Julian Press.

Colley, T. (1959), "The nature and origins of psychological sexual identity," *Psychological Review* 66:165–177.

Ehrhardt, A., and S. Baker (1974), "Fetal androgens, human central nervous system differentiation, and behavior sex differences," pp. 33–51 in R. C. Friedman, R. M. Richart, and R. L. Vande Wiele (Eds.), *Sex Differences in Behavior*. New York: Wiley.

Freud, S. (1935), *A General Introduction to Psychoanalysis*. New York: Boni and Liveright.

Gagnon, J. (1977), *Human Sexualities*. Glenview, Ill.: Scott, Foresman & Co.

Garai, J., And A. Scheinfield (1968), "Sex differences in mental and behavioral traits." *Genet. Psychol. Monogr.* 77:169–299.

Goldberg, S., and M. Lewis (1969), "Play behavior in the year old infant: Early sex differences," *Child Development* 40:21–31.

Green, R. (1974), *Sexual Identity Conflict in Children and Adults*. New York: Basic Books.

——— (1976), "One-hundred ten feminine and masculine boys: Behavioral contrasts and demographic similarities," *Archives of Sexual Behavior* 5:425–446.

———, and J. Money (1960), "Incongruous gender role: Nongenital manifestations in prepubertal boys," *J. Nerv. and Ment. Dis.* 131:160–168.

——— (1961), "Effeminacy in prepubertal boys: Summary of eleven cases and recommendations for case management," *Pediatrics* 27:286–291.

Kagan, J. (1958), "The concept of identification," *Psychological Review* 65:296–305.

Kinsey, A. C., W. Pomeroy, and C. Martin (1948), *Sexual Behavior in the Human Male*. Philadelphia: Saunders.

———, and P. Gebhard (1953), *Sexual Behavior in the Human Female*. Philadelphia: Saunders.

Kleenman, J. (1971a), "The establishment of core gender identity in normal girls, I," *Archives of Sexual Behavior* 1:103–161.

——— (1971b), "The establishment of core identity in normal girls, II," *Archives of Sexual Behavior* 1:117–129.

Maccoby, E., and C. Jacklin (1974), *The Psychology of Sex Differences*. Stanford: Stanford University Press.

Mischel, W. (1966), "A social learning view of sex differences in behavior," in E. Maccoby (Ed.), *The Development of Sex Differences*. Stanford: Stanford University Press.

Money, J., J. Hampson, and J. Hampson (1955), "An examination of some basic sexual concepts: The evidence of human hermaphrodism," *Bull. Johns Hopkins Hospital* 97:301–319.

———, and A. Ehrhardt (1972), *Man & Woman/Boy & Girl*. Baltimore: Johns Hopkins University Press.

Moss, H. (1967), "Sex, age, and state as determinants of mother-infant interaction," *Merrill-Palmer Quarterly* 13:19–36.

Prince, V., and P. M. Bentler (1972), "Survey of 504 cases of transvestism," *Psychological Reports* 31:903–917.

Saghir, M., and E. Robins (1973), *Male and Female Homosexuality: A Comprehensive Investigation*. Baltimore: Williams and Wilkins.

Stoller, R. (1968), *Sex and Gender: On the Development of Masculinity and Femininity*. New York: Science House.

——— (1972), "Etiological factors in female transsexualism: A first approximation," *Archives of Sexual Behavior* 2:47–64.

PART II

CHILDREN BEING FOLLOWED INTO ADULTHOOD

FACTORS IN CHILDREN'S BEHAVIOR AND MENTAL HEALTH OVER TIME: THE FAMILY RESEARCH PROJECT*

Thomas S. Langner, Elizabeth D. McCarthy, Joanne C. Gersten, Ora Simcha-Fagan, Jeanne G. Eisenberg, †

COLUMBIA UNIVERSITY

The Family Research Project was born out of a concern that the associations found between adult mental disorder and familial variables in the Midtown Manhattan Study might be a function of adult disorder causing distorted reporting or perception of childhood experiences rather than a result of early familial environment causing adult disorder. The project which arose from this concern has been studying children during the time they are growing up, relying on mother's reports of the child's behavior and environment, in addition to the child's report, psychiatric and questionnaire interviews of the child, school data, police and probation reports, and data from other social agencies. The use of multiple sources and various techniques to get at the etiology of behavioral disorders in

Research in Community and Mental Health, Vol. 1, pp 127–181.

children and to trace the course of these behaviors to determine whether they are part of usual developmental changes or constitute prodromal stages of adult mental disorder has been in progress for ten years. To get at causality, changes in stress have been related to changes in strain (or disordered behavior) over time. There have been many issues of substance and method which arose during the study, and many of these issues have yet to be resolved or even approached. This overview of the project contains several sections, some of which deal primarily with substantive findings—such as the predictors of behavior in children, both concurrent and prognostic; the prevalence of behaviors in welfare children vs. children from a cross-section of the population, and how they changed over time; the relationship of family structure to child behavior and longitudinal data on the shift to single-parent families across social classes. Greater emphasis on method and its effect on the data is shown in sections on the measurement of antisocial behavior using questionnaire and record data, and in a section dealing with true historical change in child behavior over time, using age cohorts. While these sections are necessarily brief, they give some idea of the scope of the project and of the data and techniques involved. Some of the implications for theory, intervention, and social policy are suggested, though in a very limited way.

In order not to be repetitive, a methods section describes the techniques and measures common to all the sections. Additional methodological details are given within each section.

METHOD

Samples

Cross-sectional Sample: Time I   The sample area was defined as the area between Houston Street and 125th Street on the East and West sides of Manhattan, New York City. This area included all the major ethnic and income groups of Manhattan. The sample was broken down into health areas, blocks within each health area, and dwelling units in each block. The total number of dwelling units in each block was translated into terms of clusters, where, on the average, each cluster consisted of eight dwelling units. Thus, the sample was one of systematic cluster sampling, stratified by health area. A team of enumerators contacted each household that fell into the sample to determine if it contained a child between the ages of 6 and 18 and thus was eligible for the study. When an eligible household fell into the sample, an appointment was made by the enumerator for a trained interviewer to come and interview the mother of the household. The sample was completed with the relatively low refusal rate of 15.6 percent. The breakdown by the major ethnic groups of the final cross-sectional sample of 1,034 families was 56 percent white, 29 percent Spanish-speaking, 14 percent black, and 1 percent other.

Welfare AFDC Sample: Time I   The Welfare AFDC households were selected randomly from welfare rolls which covered the same area of Manhattan as that of the cross-sectional sample. Eligibility was once again determined by the presence of a child between 6 and 18 years old in the family. The sample was stratified by ethnic background, to approximate equal thirds of the major ethnic groups (27 percent white, 36 percent Spanish-speaking, 37 percent black) in the final sample of 1,000 AFDC families. The refusal rate for this sample was a low 8 percent.

In both the cross-section and welfare samples each age group except the oldest comprised nearly one-thirteenth of the sample, and males and females were fairly evenly distributed across the thirteen age groups.

Follow-up Study: Time II   Approximately five years later, the two samples were followed up. The first wave of interviewing was conducted in 1966 and 1967, the second wave in 1971 and 1972. The follow-up was conducted in such a manner as to ensure constancy of the ethnic proportions at both time points. This rule set a lower bound to the follow-up, since many of the Spanish-speaking families had moved out of the city and could not be located. In the cross-sectional sample, a total of 732 families or 71 percent of the original sample was reinterviewed. In the welfare sample, a total of 661 families or 66 percent of the original sample constituted the follow-up sample. The follow-up (or Time II) samples did not differ significantly from the Time I samples on any of the central measures, namely, age and sex of the study child, demographic characteristics, marital and parenting dimensions, and child behavior dimensions. The follow-up samples thus represented unbiased subsamples of the original samples.

Procedure

The Mother's Interview   In both Time I and Time II, mothers were interviewed for an average of two and one-fourth hours. The questionnaire was, for the most part, a structured instrument, with some verbatim response material included. The questionnaire was designed to elicit information on the development and current behavior of the study child, aspects of parental character and the marital relationship, child-rearing practices, and a broad range of demographic variables. The questionnaires for the welfare and cross-sectional samples were identical except for an additional section in the welfare questionnaire on welfare-related attitudes and behavior. The entire questionnaire was translated into Spanish for the large number of Puerto Rican respondents, and interviewers and respondents were matched by ethnic background in the interest of establishing maximum rapport.

Psychiatrist's Rating of Questionnaire At Time I, a computer summary of the questionnaire information dealing only with the child's behavior (654 items) was used by two of the three project psychiatrists to rate each child on a five-point total impairment rating scale where 1 equaled well, or minimal impairment, and 5 equaled severe impairment. The distribution of ratings from each rater was transformed into a distribution of standard scores. The reliability for the average of two psychiatrists for the total impairment rating (TIR) was .84. Validity information for this rating was summarized earlier (Langner, Gersten, Greene, Eisenberg, Herson, and McCarthy, 1974).

Factor Analysis of Questionnaire Data The total pool of 654 child items in the mother's questionnaire was reduced by first eliminating those items with low frequencies and age or sex contingency. A second group of about 200 items was collapsed into a set of composite scores (number of fears, illnesses, etc.). Independently of their psychiatric evaluation, the 287 items which remained were then factor analyzed (orthogonal varimax rotation), forming eighteen dimensions using a total of 222 items. This analysis was conducted on the cross-sectional sample pool. The welfare sample data were recoded and scored on each item. This was done to allow direct comparisons on the factors between samples. (For a detailed description of the child factors see Eisenberg, Langner, and Gersten, 1975.) The internal consistency reliabilities for Time I ranged from .72 to .94 (cross-section) and .57 to .92 (welfare). At Time II they were .56 to .93 (cross-section), .57 to .93 (welfare).

Familial Factors Questionnaire items describing the marital relationship, the character and personality of the mother and father, and the mother's physical and emotional health were factor analyzed at Time I. A total of ninety-one items comprised eight parental factors. Questionnaire items describing the parent-child relationship, child-rearing practices, etc., were also factored. Five parent-child factors included eighty-one questionnaire items. This analysis was conducted on the cross-section item pool. The welfare sample data were coded and scored on each item. Standard Z scores were computed for the Time I and Time II sample data on each of the thirteen familial factors. The internal consistency reliability coefficients for the familial factors at Time I ranged from .66 to .88 (cross-section) and .42 to .85 (welfare); at Time II: .58 to .85 (cross-section), .36 to .87 (welfare).

PREDICTORS OF CHILD BEHAVIOR AND THEIR IMPLICATIONS FOR SOCIAL POLICY

Thomas S. Langner

Though there are literally thousands of studies of children's behavior and emotional health, there are very few which begin to qualify as etiological studies. Major problems of method and design make most of the literature on children inadequate to isolate the sources of behavioral disorder. The most common problems are that these studies (1) have focused on child patients who are preselected and unrepresentative of children in general; (2) are not longitudinal; (3) concentrate on isolated or individual symptoms, making for unreliability; and (4) while they may control for one or two variables, they do not test the simultaneous predictive power of the many factors in the child's environment to discover which of them really contributes to the prediction of behavior and to what extent. In addition, (5) reliable classification systems are lacking for children, so that the development of behavior types based on clustering of behavior dimensions as well as on clinical judgment has become a necessity. There has always been (6) a tendency to focus on a narrow band of behavior, so that the specificity of predictors for contrasting types of behavior, such as anxious vs. antisocial, withdrawn vs. aggressive is obscured.

Those studies which are most helpful, despite having some of these inherent faults from which they, and our project, suffer, are: Douglas, 1964, 1966; Lapouse and Monk, 1958, 1964; Long, 1941; MacFarlane et al., 1954; Rutter et al., 1970; Shepherd et al., 1971; Robins, 1966; Thomas et al., 1970; Tuddenham et al., 1974; Kellmer-Pringle et al., 1966. These studies are among the best of the surveys, as they do not focus on patient populations. A few are prospective, though Robins' study is a "follow-back" design. Some deal with a narrow age range or a small sample. Most stop either at the level of symptom counts or at demographic correlates. Each study has its strong points and its deficits, dictated by design, and the limitations of time, funding, and range of professional staff skills. Family life variables, such as marital and parental behavior, tend to be slighted by all but a few surveys, leaving this to more intensive investigations. Good measures of physical health based on direct examination (notably lacking in our project) are present in a few cases. In all these studies, including ours, social-psychological concepts and their measures are notably absent: self-image, aspiration level, model internalization, reference groups, and support networks, etc. Perhaps it is too early to expect these variables, which are difficult to measure, to appear in studies other than those which focus primarily on a single one of these concepts.

In our own study, the factor-analyzed predictor variables which survived the rigorous multiple-regression analysis, and did in fact make some contribution (greater than 1 percent) to variation in child behavior, came from three groups of predictors: the demographic (forty-five variables), the parental (eight characteristics of parents and their marriage), and the parent-child (five child-rearing and home atmosphere variables). Table 1 gives the relative power of 11 major variables both concurrently (predictor at Time I, child behavior at Time I) and prospectively (predictor at Time I, child behavior at Time II). The ranks were assigned on the basis of the number of dependent child behaviors to which a specific independent variable contributed at a level of at least 1 percent unique variance. Lower ranks indicate that more dependent child behaviors were associated with the independent variable according to the criterion noted.

Table 1

Final Rank Order of Predictors by the Sum of Concurrent
and Forecasting Ranks

		Ranks[a]		
		Concurrent	Forecasting	Sum of
Rank	Predictor	Time I	Time II	Ranks
1	Spanish-speaking	3	1	4
2	Parents Punitive	4	2	6
3	Parents Cold	2	4	6
4	Black	6	3	9
5	Mother Excitable - Rejecting	1	9	10
6	Mother's Physical and Emotional Illness	5	6	11
7	Large Number of Children in Household	9	7	16
8	High Rent	8	8	16
9	Mother Traditional - Restrictive	11	5	16
10	High Number of Addresses	7	10	17
11	Number of Natural Parents	10	11	21

[a] 1 = highest number of associations; 11 = lowest number of associations.

Given a design which purposely included a wide range of independent (environmental) and dependent (behavioral) variables, it is important not to ignore the specificity of these associations. In brief, being Spanish-speaking was currently associated with more isolation, less membership in groups, more (toilet) training difficulties, mentation problems (concentration, memory, speech), and compulsivity. In forecasting behavior, it predicted Dependency and group nonmembership five years later. Being black was linked to present Mentation Problems and Demandingness (asking parents to do or give things), and it forecast being Dependent and Repetitive Motor Behavior (spinning, head-banging, etc.). Being white forecast greater Conflict with Parents. The common forecast of Dependency for the minorities is of particular interest. While ethnic background contributes to those behaviors independently of social class and all twenty-five other factors or variables included in the predictor sets, such correlates of minority status as low birth weight, poor physical health, and discrimination not included in the predictors might have "explained away" a lot of the ethnic variance. Parental Coldness was linked with behavior which expressed conflict with others; in the family, such as parents and siblings, and in the school and larger community, such as conflict with peers (Fighting) and Delinquency.

Parental Punitiveness, in keeping with many studies which focused on delinquency, was concurrently tied to Fighting, Conflict with Parents, and Regressive Anxiety. It forecast both Fighting and Conflict with Parents, as well as Delinquency. Of interest is that the forecasting rank of Parental Punitiveness is so high, and that it was not strongly associated with Delinquency at Time I, but was at Time II. Punishment of children, especially severe physical punishment, may have a "sleeper effect" as current fighting develops into more socialized forms of aggressive behavior or simply moves from the family into the street as the child ages.

Excitable Mothers had most of its strength concurrently. It would show up as a major factor in prevalence studies, but as less powerful in longitudinal studies which emphasized forecasting of adult behavior. A preponderance of behaviors relating to the self was associated at Time I (Self-Destructiveness, Mentation Problems, Anxiety, and Isolation). In addition, behaviors involving conflict with others (parents, siblings) and Fighting were associated with "excitable" mothers at Time I. Only Conflict with Parents was associated at Time II with having had an "excitable" mother at Time I. The association of parental aggressiveness, inconsistency, and lability (screaming, "flying off the handle") with antisocial behavior in the child is found in the literature (McCord, McCord, and Howard, 1961; Andry, 1960; Bandura and Walters, 1959). As mentioned before, a multidimensional dependent variable allows us to see an association between Mother's Excitability and more neurotic-like dimensions for the child (self-destructive, anxious, isolated).

Mother's Physical and Emotional Illness (primarily psychophysiological complaints associated with loss of role functioning in adults) was tied to Fighting concurrently and to Anxiety at both times. If measures of the mother's antisocial behavior had been included, they might have given us better prediction of children's antisocial behavior. This relationship is being tested using police record data. Having Traditional-Restrictive Mothers forecast Dependency, but had no significant strength concurrently.

A large Number of Children in the household was related to reduced competition (and to a rating of the children's School Impairment). Since this is the unique contribution of a large family, it is not simply a function of social class differences. The Number of Natural Parents was associated only with Delinquency, and only concurrently. (This finding is examined in more detail in a separate section of this paper.) This reflects myriad other studies, but does not come up with the additional finding of many studies of anxiety and depression being linked to father loss. This may be a function of treated samples, as opposed to this random community sample. Moving (High Number of Addresses) was also tied to increased Delinquency and to Fighting as well, possibly as a result of uprooting. Of great interest would be the ratio of gang vs. solo delinquency, to test whether moving uproots peer relations as well as positive influences of teachers and other neighborhood nonpeer authorities.

High Rent was the only variable associated with high socioeconomic status which showed any association with greater pathology. Children who came from families paying higher rent showed greater Conflict with Parents and greater Isolation from other children concurrently. At Time II, however, they showed *less* Dependence. Perhaps less exposure to peer norms, and more assertiveness with parents, who may encourage such behavior (at least verbal assertiveness) are part of the prodromal middle-class success pattern. One might expect these children to be more independent as adults, and perhaps even to develop into entrepreneurial rather than bureaucratic types (see Miller and Swanson, 1958).

The specificity of the association of environmental factors with child and adolescent behavior is clearly demonstrated by these findings. This should not deter us from ignoring the variations in association between environmental factors and specific child behaviors. When a ranking in terms of the overall power of a factor is wanted (predicting a large number of behaviors well), the specific associations may be obscured. From a public health standpoint, intervention related to these 11 variables is worth considering; however, in many cases such action would be difficult, if not impossible. Ethnic background may rank first in predictive power, but changing minority status is, of course, not a present government possibility. Programs designed to change parental behavior would seem to be in line with stated goals of the administration to support the American family. However, support for families is often interpreted as noninterference with the family. This is particularly true at a time when government control or intervention in general is suspect. Teaching parental behavior—less punitiveness, less coldness, less excitability, less restrictiveness, as well as emphasis on persuasion and reward for control, warmth, and physical contact, control of parental anger or limits to its expression, and allowing more freedom for the child's expression—appear to be quite the opposite of the current political and child-rearing trends.

Is there enough evidence in this or other studies to develop a base for interventive policy? Three questions bear on this point.

First: Is the evidence consistent enough across studies, including ours, to warrant an association between particular predictors and particular behavioral outcomes? The answer would be "definitely" for the relationship of both loss of father and excessive punishment in connection with antisocial behavior (Biller, 1970; Bacon, Child, and Barry, 1963). In addition, parental coldness, in many studies, has been tied to antisocial behavior dimensions (Andry, 1960; Bandura and Walters, 1959). We found, to the contrary, that it was not predictive of depression and withdrawal. This may be because coldness formed a factor quite independent of rejection and punishment, while in other studies the separate aspects of "bad parenting" are often obscured in the form of a general rating, because the item pool of parental behaviors is not large enough to derive separate factors. Parental aggressiveness, inconsistency, and excitability-rejection (as our factor was labeled) is frequently associated with antisocial behavior in the literature, and in our data (McCord, McCord, and Howard, 1961; Andry, 1960; Bandura and Walters, 1959).

In general, the evidence that a mother's (or father's) emotional illness affects child behavior and disorder is overwhelming (Jenkins, 1966; Shields and Slater, 1961; Bennett, 1960). The nature of the psychophysiological measures of mothers illness we used (i.e., neurotic and psychosomatic measures) probably explains the fact that mother's emotional illness predicted (or accounted for variance in) only two child behavior dimensions, fighting and depression. Children of depressives, schizophrenics, and various types of neurotics have been found to have a higher risk of disorder. In the more serious diseases genetic factors may be operative instead of or in addition to whatever role learning plays. Perhaps the child learns to imitate some of the more serious behavior patterns. What portion is learned and what portion is genetic is still unknown, but the children who are at such high risk must not be ignored.

Evidence for the unique negative effects of moving and having a large family over and above social class membership is not found in the literature. Our data show that these factors make contributions independent of social class. All in all, there is good agreement that these eleven variables are associated with behavioral disorder in children.

Second: Is the overall relationship between these predictors and child behavior strong enough to make them part of a preventive program? The answer is a definite "Yes." While individual factors account for a maximum of 10 percent of the unique variance (or a correlation of .32), and many are around 1 percent (or $r = .10$), it must be remembered that these are unique contributions based on partial correlations. This means that only the portion of that particular child behavior which is accounted for by the particular predictors, *excluding* some twenty-five other factors in the equation, shows in the percentage. When the unique variance and the variance which these predictors have in common are considered, they amount to a maximum of 45 percent for one child behavior, or one dependent variable at Time I (a multiple correlation of .67). When Time II predictors are added to the Time I predictor set, as high as 60 percent of the variance in a particular Time II child behavior may be accounted for (multiple R of .78). If we can account for 60 percent of a child behavior measure using just environmental factors, we have done well, since many aspects of the environment, and probably most of the genetic prediction factors, have been left out of our study. If we could change even a small portion of antisocial behavior or depression by changing the factors we have isolated, it would be greatly beneficial. This is true from an economic standpoint as well as a moral one, for it is estimated that from half to three-quarters of visits to doctors are for complaints which are essentially psychogenic.

Third, if these predictors are merely associated with mental disorder but are not causal factors, wouldn't such a preventive program be a colossal failure? This argument is an important one, but there is strong evidence for causality in these data, although replication in other longitudinal samples would increase our confidence. What we have presented so far are associations; now we turn to an analysis of change over time which allows us to get closer to causal explanations. The standardized regressed change score can be used to indicate if a change has occurred which is independent of initial standing and thus regression toward the mean has been controlled. Indeed, findings show that if parents became warmer or less rejecting over the five-year period, their children demonstrated reductions in Conflict with Parents, Regressive Anxiety, Fighting, Mentation Problems, Isolation, and Delinquency. Furthermore, changes in Parental Coldness and Excitability were tied to changes in children's aggressive behavior in all settings. Changes in Parental Punitiveness were related only to changes in children's intrafamilial aggression, but not in aggression toward peers or society in general. Whether these reductions in pathological behavior are based upon imitation of changing role models, or on reduction of frustration in the child, or both, is crucial for building more detailed theory, but the fact that changes in parents are *followed* by changes in child behavior is enough for us to support a program which involves educating for better parenthood.

How can these changes be implemented? To actually affect the desired changes would involve complex issues. While it is not the purpose of this paper to discuss policy options thoroughly, some general suggestions can be outlined briefly. Physical punishment, a major component of our "parental punitiveness" score, should be mitigated. Only three states and New York City prohibit physical punishment by teachers, despite this strong evidence that punitiveness is related to aggressive behavior within the unit administering the punishment (family), and by this token probably within the school or classroom as a similar unit. The Supreme Court, ignoring the strong evidence of many studies, including the many television-and-violence findings (for example, see McCarthy et al., 1975), and the experimental evidence (see Bandura and Walters, 1963), has condoned and encouraged models of violence by ruling that teachers may use physical punishment. If nonfamily members can do this to children, while police may not legally beat adult criminals, then surely a parent can beat a child with impunity. Judges and teachers, both authority figures in the larger community, are often models for the parent.

Other approaches can be suggested briefly. It is possible that parental coldness can be modified through physical contact and discussion of the origins of anger. Excitable parents may benefit from behavior therapy, with group reinforcement. Currently, family size is declining generally, a trend which may well help to reduce the proportions of children suffering from anxiety and school impairment. (The latter is perhaps also a function of organicity in later births, as well as the lack of individual attention in large families, and parental anger at later unwanted children.) Many factors contribute to the frequent moves of some families, a problem which is linked to children's delinquency, fighting, and school impairment. Rehabilitation of neighborhoods rather than bulldozing could lessen some of this uprooting. Finally, support of the family, through massive employment and job training programs, and welfare reform, might help to reduce loss of father by divorce, separation, and abandonment; and job safety programs could reduce paternal deaths (5 percent of our sample), perhaps thereby reducing delinquency.

To many observers, policy as it concerns children and adolescents appears severely neglected. National fears are acted upon irrationally in this area. The overwhelming focus is on law and order, as crime escalates in degree and frequency. Yet the Supreme Court of our land encourages behavior which appears to contribute to violence in children. Minorities and welfare recipients are blamed for our national problems, but the job and welfare reforms which might aid positive change are delayed or underfunded. Fear of inflation and war may be realistic, but preserving the quality of life is also crucial and in our view cannot be accomplished without massive social programs. National medical care for all age groups has also been postponed. The early screening programs and school-based medical care programs are now in shambles, especially in large cities. Concern for people should be primary. The minorities—various ethnic groups, women, the aged, and children—all need special programs.

In a social system, as in a multiple regression equation, a change in one independent variable will produce changes in others. Whether information gleaned from the myriad studies of people is put to use is no longer just a question of whether this information is adequately accurate or scientific; *some* of it doubtless is. The basic question is whether the public really wants to ameliorate the lives of the majority of Americans, including their own children.

FAMILY STRUCTURE: ITS RELATION TO SOCIAL CLASS AND CHILD BEHAVIOR

Elizabeth D. McCarthy

U.S. Census reports indicate that single-parent families have increased seven times as fast as the traditional two-parent or nuclear family in the decade between 1960 and 1970. Trends toward single-parent families have taken place among lower and middle-class families. These trends raise questions with respect to changes in child-rearing patterns and the effects of such changes on child behavior and development. Longitudinal data will be examined with reference to these national trends: To what extent are trends toward single-parent families class-related? What are the effects of class and family structure on child behavior?

In an earlier study, using the first-wave data from the welfare sample and a subsample of the cross-section sample, family structure was found to be related to the behavioral functioning of children and their mothers (McCarthy et al., forthcoming). The effect of father absence and the effect of the presence of a father surrogate in the home were found to differ within the two social class groups studied. The evidence suggested that while children benefit from the presence of both natural parents in the home, the greater the general hardships impinging on a child, the less additional harm is felt by the absence of a father. There was a clear-cut relationship between children's dysfunctional development and the presence in their homes and lives of father surrogates in both the welfare sample and the cross-section lower to middle class sample. The children of surrogate fathers revealed significantly more behavioral difficulties than those reported for children living with no father in the home. The effects of father absence were found to differ between mother and child. In general, the mother who was an only parent reported less interaction with her child and fewer expressions of warmth. However, according to the mothers' own reports on their children, these parental characteristics did not appear to have a direct or negative effect on the children.

Family Structure and Social Class
Income data for Time I were arranged in five groups which approximate the following social class categories: lower, lower-middle, middle, upper-middle, and upper class. The Time II data were also grouped in this manner. The middle class groups include both the Mean ($\overline{X}$) and median income values for the Time I and Time II data, respectively.

Data on the study children were based on mothers' reports; therefore, each of the three groups which comprise the family structure variable includes the presence of the child's mother in the home: natural father; surrogate father; no father (or single-parent household). The frequency distributions for Time I and Time II for income group and family structure appear on Table 2.

The data for Time I and Time II show clearly that families with no father (single-parent families) are significantly overrepresented in the lowest income group and that father absence is strongly and inversely related to higher social class membership. While 21 percent of the Time I sample reported no father in the home, 47 percent of this group was in the lowest income group (23 percent in the middle-income group; only 7 percent in the highest income group). The percent of single-parent families increased by 5 percent during the five-year interval. However, the distribution of single-parent families among the five income groups remained relatively unchanged, with a 4 percent decrease in the lowest income group and an increase of 6 percent in the lower-middle income group.

Ten percent of the total samples at each time reported father surrogates in the home. This includes stepfathers, male relatives, and unrelated males living in the household. Father surrogates were fairly evenly distributed across income groups at both time periods. The only income group evincing change over time was the lowest income group, where the presence of a surrogate father in the home decreased 6 percent.

An examination of the proportions of the highest-income families with both natural parents in the household indicates that membership in the upper-income families strongly overlaps with being a two-parent family. Eighty-one percent and 84 percent of the highest-income groups reported two natural parents in the home at the two time periods. In addition, the

Table 2

Sample Proportions with Income and Family Groups for Time I and Time II

INCOME		FAMILY STRUCTURE						TOTAL			
		Natural Father		Surrogate Father		No Father		Time I		Time II	
		Time I	Time II	Time I	Time II	Time I	Time II	N	%	N	%
Lower											
T I	$780 – $ 3,899	35[a]	26	12	9	53	65	190	18[b]	118	17
T II	$780 – $ 5,199	9[b]	7	23	17	47	43				
Lower-Middle											
T I	$3,900 – $ 5,199	69	60	10	9	21	31	153	15	119	18
T II	$5,200 – $ 7,799	15	16	16	17	15	21				
Middle											
T I	$5,200 – $ 9,199	74	70	10	10	16	20	299	29	208	31
T II	$7,800 – $15,499	30	33	30	34	23	23				

	Income							N	%
Upper-Middle									
T I	$9,200 – $15,499	83	82	6	4	11	14	155	15
T II	$15,500 – $30,499	18	25	10	8	8	11	131	19
Upper									
T I	$15,500 +	84	81	9	15	7	4	236	23
T II	$30,500 – $100,000	28	19	21	24	7	2	101	15
N_T		719	436	100	64	214	177	1,033	677
		70[a]	64	10	10	21	26	100	100

NOTE: A five-way income break was employed for T I and T II.
The middle income group for T I and T II include the $\bar{X}$ and the median income values.
AST incomes $\geq$ $15,500 were grouped in the initial data, a breakdown of those in this category was not possible.

[a] Row percents
[b] Column percents

only income groups where there was a decrease in the proportion of two-parent households over time were the two lowest income groups (9 percent for each of these groups).

Over half of the lowest income families in Time I reported no father in the home. The proportion of single-parent families within the other income groups decreased steadily from 21 percent in the lower-middle income group to only 7 percent in the highest income group. Either the chance for a child of living in a single-parent household steadily increases as the income level diminishes or the income level decreases as the chance of not having a mate increases. In addition, households headed by women comprised 21 percent of all households in the Time I sample; they constitute 53 percent of the families of the so-called poverty group. And while the proportion of female-headed households represented in the total sample indicates a 5 percent increase at Time II, these families comprised 65 percent of the families of the poverty group.

Effects on Child Behavior
The literature on social class differences in children's personality characteristics and behavioral patterns, while extensive, has been described as lacking methodological and conceptual clarity (Hess, 1970). With regard to one area of study, it has been suggested that the relative effects of social class and "family disorganization" should be evaluated in order to ascertain which is the most important explanatory factor. This interpretation suggests that social class operates through the intermediary of the family (Bastide, 1972), but that a research design should include both class and familial influences in order to ascertain the effects of each on child behavior. Studies evaluating the effect of single-parent families on child behavior have often neglected to control for the effects of social class. Two studies in particular have reviewed this and other methodological limitations of single-parent family research (Spray, 1967; Herzog and Sudia, 1968). An additional problem arises from the diverse findings on the effects of family "disruption" (Hollingshead and Redich, 1958; Sanua, s.d.).

In the preceding section, single-parent families have been found to be characteristically lower class. In the analysis which follows, we will examine the separate and combined effects of social class and family structure on six measures of child behavior. These six scores have been found to be predictive of behavioral impairment (TIR) at both Time I and Time II for our cross-section sample (Gersten et al., 1976). The six scores described the following types of child behavior: Mentation Problems, Conflict with Parents, Regressive Anxiety, Fighting, Delinquency, and Isolation.

Of the six child factors, three showed a significant main effect for the family structure variable at Time I: Mentation Problems, Fighting, and Delinquency. (These are shown on Table 3.) Children of surrogate fathers had mean scores indicative of greater pathology on each of the three factors. This supports the finding of the earlier study discussed above, where children of surrogate fathers revealed significantly more behavioral difficulties than those reported for children living in female-headed households (McCarthy et al., forthcoming). In the preceding section, it was reported that the variable Number of Natural Parents was one of the ten variables in the demographic set with the highest predictive power in relation to the overall impairment rating (TIR). Our present findings suggest that the variable effect was a function of the presence of a surrogate father in the home more than a function of the single-parent family.

Two of the three behavioral scores showed significant main effects for the income variable at Time I: Mentation Problems and Conflict with Parents. A review of the means showed an *inverse* relationship between social class and Mentation Problems; i.e., the lower the income level, the greater the number of mentation problems reported. The dimension of Mentation Problems deals with thought processes, speech, and school achievement problems. This finding is consistent with studies which have found SES differences in children's cognitive abilities. However, since our own factor describes several different types of cognitive and language skills, the conclusions drawn from this can only remain tentative. This is particularly true since SES differences in cognitive and learning skills have been found to be associated with a number of other factors such as patterns of interaction with parents and peers as well as with broader factors such as subcultural and media influences (Hess, 1970).

The mentation factor was the only behavioral score examined found to be related to both income and father type. Other studies which have examined the relationship of both social class and father absence-presence to cognitive and learning skills have found that children without fathers performed more poorly in these areas than children with fathers. While these differences were found within the same socioeconomic groups, the differences were more marked within the lower socioeconomic stratum (Deutsch and Brown, 1964). In Kriesberg's study (1970), he examines explanations for such interaction effects. Our own findings show that children of surrogate fathers from low-income families had a greater risk of mentation difficulties than lower-class children from single-parent families or families with both natural parents.

In addition to the separate effects of father type and income, an interaction effect was observed for the mentation factor. This interaction effect is explained in terms of a reversal in mean trends for the two independent variables. In general, as the main effects show, children of surrogate fathers and children from low-income families had a greater risk of menta-

Table 3

Mean Score for Child Factors with Significant Effects for
Father Type and Income

MAIN EFFECTS

Child Factor			Father Type			
			Natural father	Surro-gate father	No father	F-Value
3.	Mentation Problems					
	T	I[b]	137.98	133.85	136.29	5.98+
2.	Fighting T	I	125.39	122.70	124.23	4.21*
15.	Delinquency					
	T	I	132.15	127.40	128.84	12.21†
	T	II	130.87	129.23	126.50	3.41*

Child Factor			Income					
			Low 1	2	3	4	High 5	F-Value
3.	Mentation Problems							
	T	I	133.84	135.08	136.45	140.14	140.44	15.07†
	T	II	136.70	138.77	140.31	140.45	141.33	2.62
4.	Conflict with Parents T	I	177.59	176.57	175.49	171.19	169.31	4.07+

INTERACTION[a]

Child Factor			Surrogate Fathers					
			Low income 1	2	3	High income 4	5	Interaction F-Value
3.	Mentation Problems							
	T	I	126.74	132.81	133.80	141.20	139.00	1.96*
18.	Isolation							
	T	I	40.57	38.94	40.10	43.90	42.71	2.51+

Note: Lower scores are indicative of more behavior of the type labelled by the factor.

[a] Means are given for the surrogate father group only: for Factor 3 a reversal in mean trends for the two independent measures is shown; for Factor 6 the surrogate father group includes the highest and lowest $\overline{X}$ scores for the total sample.

[b] Time I sample (T I); Time II sample (T II)

* $p \leq .05$
+ $p \leq .01$
† $p < .001$

tion difficulties than children in the other groups represented. There was a reversal in this trend in the upper-middle class groups, where children from single-parent families had means indicative of the greatest number of mentation difficulties and children of surrogate fathers were the *healthiest* in this group. In fact, children of surrogate fathers had means indicative of the greatest number of mentation difficulties in each income level *except* that of the upper-middle class.

Conflict with parents was found to increase directly with social class. This finding is consistent with an earlier study which examined the differences in these behaviors between the cross-section and welfare samples at Time I (Eisenberg, 1975). Aggressive and conflicted relations with parents occurred with greater frequency among cross-section children than children from the welfare sample.

One of the six scores, Isolation, showed no main effects but an interaction with the two independent measures. A review of the fifteen means showed that children of surrogate fathers had the highest *and* lowest mean scores within the fifteen cells examined. Children of surrogate fathers of the lower-middle class were described as the most isolated from peers and lacking in friendships, while children of surrogate fathers in the two highest income groups were the *least* isolated in the sample. These effects are not present in Time II. This suggests that age may be a factor contributing to this effect, although it does not clarify the particular effect that surrogate fathers have for a child's peer relationships. Age has been found to be a mediating factor in other studies where social class position was found to be clearly related to rejection of peers only among younger children (Neugarten, 1946; MacDonald et al., 1949). This is consistent with findings discussed in the welfare section of this paper, where behavioral difficulties associated with group activities were observed to improve over time for both cross-section and welfare children.

The regressive anxiety score was found to have no relation to the family structure or income variables. The items on this factor are equivalent to "neurotic symptoms of childhood" as described by Slater and Roth (1969). The relation of neurotic symptomatology and SES has been cited in two studies of adults (Hollingshead and Redlich, 1958; Rennie et al., 1957). However, the findings for childhood neurosis are far from conclusive. The literature suggests that different types of anxious-neurotic symptoms are characteristic of children from all social classes. Neuroses expressed behaviorally in deviance or expressed somatically have been associated with lower-class groups, and neuroses with anxiety and depression are more frequent among upper-income groups (Freedman, 1962). For this reason the lack of specificity in our own anxiety factor could explain the lack of effects with income.

The Time II data show significant main effects for two of the six behavioral measures. Delinquency is found to be characteristic of children from single-parent families at Time II, but shows no effect with the income variable. Mentation Problems, the only behavioral measure to vary significantly with each of the independent measures at Time I, is clearly related to membership in low-income groups at Time II. Perhaps the most important finding with respect to the Time II data is the reduction in the number of behavioral measures with significant effects with income and father type when the data for the two time periods are compared. This suggests that time may in fact reduce the effects of the influence of such factors as father type and social class. That is, as children get older and other influences such as peer relations, teachers, and school environment intervene in their lives, the role of one's father and even the income level of one's parents, may very well affect one less directly than in one's early years. The nature of the data only allows speculation here, since the groups examined do not include all of the same people at the two time points. However, as almost half of the sample at Time II are between the ages of 18 and 23, this suggestion is credible.

The findings with respect to father type certainly support Kadushin's statement (based on his 1968 review of studies on the one-parent family) that "the association between single-parent familyhood and psychosocial pathology is neither strong nor invariable." In our own study only one of the six behaviors reviewed was found to be related to living in a single-parent family: Delinquency (at Time II). On the other hand, children living with surrogate fathers were found to manifest more mentation difficulties, fighting, and delinquent behaviors (at Time I) than children from single-parent families or families with both natural parents. These findings suggest that the role of the surrogate father in the family be further explored. The lack of data in this field is surprising in light of the fact that in the mid-1960's one out of nine children in the U.S. was a "stepchild"; and two out of every 100 children in our society are reared by adoptive parents (U.S. 1970 B. Census). As one-third of all marriages in the U.S. end in divorce, this alone would produce a very large proportion of single-parent families or families with one step-parent.

THE WELFARE CHILDREN:
AN OVERVIEW OF LONGITUDINAL FINDINGS
Jeanne G. Eisenberg

This section focuses on the welfare child and faces two basic issues: first, the relative prevalence of disturbed behaviors in a sample of welfare children as compared to a sample of children from a cross-section of the population; second, differences in children in short-term and long-term welfare families. The longitudinal data demonstrate that the children in families that got off welfare were functioning significantly better even while their families were still on welfare than children in the long-term welfare families. The findings suggest that familial qualities may be more critical for the welfare child than the effects of welfare labeling per se.

Research in the area of social class and child behavior has been extensive, but there are many issues still to be clarified (Beiser, 1972). The research generally, but not always, shows a relationship between high child impairment or symptomatology and low socioeconomic status. While some studies have reported population rates of children's psychiatric impairment (Rutter and Graham, 1966; Langner et al., 1974), others have focused on reports of specific symptoms or symptom areas (Frierson, 1965; Lapouse and Monk, 1964; Sewell and Haller, 1959). The studies dealing with the lower class have not adequately distinguished *types* of lower-class families (Miller, 1964). Little is known about welfare children as a particularly disadvantaged group within the lower class, or about the special effects of welfare status on children.

In this section, some highlights of the data from the longitudinal survey of welfare Aid to Families with Dependent Children (AFDC) will be presented. Many advantages were seen in obtaining a sample of welfare families that was comparable in method and procedure to the longitudinal cross-sectional sample. The latter provided a data base from a cross-section of the urban population to which the behavior and development of welfare children could be compared and contrasted in terms of the relative prevalence of a range of behaviors.

Several issues were of central importance. How did children in the two vastly different socioeconomic samples compare in terms of the prevalence of both healthy and disturbed behaviors? How did results of such comparisons change as the children grew older? Was the developmental course of the various behaviors similar or different for the children in two different samples? How did the behavioral dimensions combine in specific children to form *types* of children? Were the social and familial predictors of the behaviors similar for the children in the two samples, or did some factors assume more importance for children in different sociocultural settings?

In addition, in view of the growth and extent of the welfare phenomenon in the United States (Rein, 1974), it seemed increasingly important to examine patterns of welfare assistance through time, particularly in terms of differences in children in long-term welfare families and in families that were able to become free of public assistance. In the current paper, data will be presented which suggest rather strongly that there are some distinct differences between long-term and short-term welfare families and children, and that this may be one useful distinction between types of lower-class families. Another issue is that of the effects of welfare assistance upon families and children. The data will suggest that the effect of welfare status *per se* is not the main issue, but rather the personal and social factors which enable some families to become free of public assistance while others remain on welfare.

METHOD

The Time I welfare sample (1966–1967) contained 1,000 cases randomly selected from AFDC rolls in Manhattan. That geographic area matched that of the cross-sectional sample. In Time II (1971–1972), 661 of the original AFDC cases were located and the mothers were reinterviewed about the randomly chosen child in the family. The data to be presented here focus on 522 AFDC cases interviewed at both time points.[1] For comparisons with the cross-sectional sample, the 732 cases interviewed at both time points in the cross-section have been used. It should be pointed out that in the Time II welfare sample, 27 percent of the families were no longer on any type of public assistance, and these cases later formed the "short-term" group versus the 73 percent "long-term" welfare cases. However, in the general comparisons of the cross-sectional and welfare samples, these cases are included in the welfare sample, since the interest was in comparing a group of disadvantaged children with a cross-section of the population through time.

The welfare sample was viewed as representing one broad type of unstable lower-class urban family. The children were considered to be disadvantaged (relative to the cross-section children) on a number of variables or family characteristics. A total of 73 percent had no father figure (as compared with 21 percent in the cross-sectional sample), and all were at the extreme base of the economic and occupational ladder. For the most part, mothers were heads of households of generally three or four dependent children. The welfare sample, too, by design contained a large proportion of ethnic minorities. Thus, while all of the welfare families were at the base of the economic scale, two-thirds of the sample were also the targets of racial prejudice. The welfare sample of 522 cases contained 28 percent white, 34 percent black, and 38 percent Spanish-speaking, while the cross-section contained 56 percent white, 14 percent black and 29 percent Spanish-speaking.

This discussion centers on fifteen of the eighteen child behavior factors described in the Method section.

Time I Data: Comparisons of Cross-Sectional and Welfare Children
The question of the relative prevalence of disturbed behaviors in the two samples of children at Time I has been addressed in detail in an earlier

Table 4

Child Behavior Factors: Time I and Time II Means for Welfare Sample (with T-Values for Differences between Means and F-Values for Time II Welfare Status Main Effect by Child Factor at Time I and Time II

	Factor Means†		Differences between means: t value $	Analysis of variance for Time I factor scores: F values for welfare status Time II main effect⋆	Analysis of variance for Time II factor scores: F values for welfare status Time II main effect⋆
	Time I	Time II			
Self-destructive	67.75	66.65	6.85+	4.99*	2.96
Mentation problems	135.92	138.08	4.68+	114.75+	.00
Parental conflict	176.66	170.56	8.54+	39.06+	6.38*
Dependence	13.29	13.70	1.68	.00	.03
Regressive anxiety	114.17	115.59	2.93+	97.34+	10.02+
Weak group membership	6.80	8.28	8.38+	.00	3.93*
Compulsivity	10.34	9.25	3.88+	.00	.14
Undemandingness	13.78	14.12	1.61	.34	8.11+
Repetitive motor behavior	38.60	39.46	4.18+	2.09	.23
Fighting	124.48	122.84	3.64+	114.27+	11.07+
Delusions-hallucinations	106.01	112.55	33.89+	1.29	1.05
Competition	5.44	5.35	.59	4.80*	.91
Delinquency	130.10	127.77	5.00+	22.73+	4.30*
Sibling conflict	41.48	42.79	5.05+	4.84*	8.88+
Isolation	41.55	42.55	4.37+	.00	5.23*

*   Significant at the .05 level or better.

+   Significant at the .01 level or better.

†   **A lower means score indicates *more* of that dimension.**

$ The test for correlated samples was used.

⋆   A two-way analysis of variance for unweighted means was conducted for Time II welfare status and ethnic background by each child behavior dimension.

publication (Eisenberg et al., 1975). In brief, when the welfare children were compared with the cross-sectional children on Time I child behavior factors, the rather surprising result obtained was that the children in the two very different samples showed no difference in prevalence on many of the child factors tapping rather serious symptomatology. For example, Mentation Problems, Isolation, Repetitive Motor Behavior, Delusions-Hallucinations, and Fighting showed no significant differences between samples. Some of the factors did, however, show differences, and a pattern emerged of behaviors that tended to be more characteristic of welfare children than of children from the general urban population. For example, welfare children showed significantly *more* Dependence, Weak Group Membership, and Delinquency, but significantly *less* Conflict with Parents, Conflict with Siblings, Regressive Anxiety, and Compulsivity than the cross-sectional children. However, the intercorrelations of the child factors tended to be quite similar in the two samples. For example, in both samples Regressive Anxiety, Conflict with Parents, and Delinquency were highly and positively correlated, but all of these behaviors were negatively correlated with Dependence. On the basis of these prevalence data it appeared that two types of children were fairly common in the welfare population: the dependent child and the delinquent or aggressive child. This was supported when a welfare child typology was later constructed with a totally different statistical procedure[2] (Eisenberg et al., 1976).

The findings from the Time I data (Eisenberg et al., 1975) further indicated that the familial predictors of the various child behaviors were amazingly consonant in the two extremely different socioeconomic samples. A multiple regression analysis indicated that two of the strongest familial predictors of aggressive disorders in children in both samples were two familial dimensions (from a factor analysis of child rearing practices): Parental Coldness and Mother Excitable-Rejecting. In both samples these parental qualities were highly and uniquely predictive of aggressive disorders both inside and outside the home: Conflict with Parents, Conflict with Siblings, and Delinquency. In addition, the Mother Excitable-Rejecting quality was also important for Regressive Anxiety in both samples, as was Parental Punitiveness. The Dependence child factor and the Weak Group Membership factor, however, were predicted by mothers who tended to be Traditional and Restrictive in their child-rearing practices. The striking similarity of results in the two samples argued for the generalizability of parent-child dynamics across two very different socioeconomic contexts. In other words, the aspects of parental behavior that were stressful for the nonwelfare child appeared to be rather equally stressful for the welfare child.

The Time II Data: Changes in the Prevalence of Child Behavior Through Time
The longitudinal nature of the study made it possible to examine differences in prevalence of the behavioral disturbances through time. Table 4 contains the mean factor scores for the child behavior factors for the welfare sample in both Time I and Time II. Twelve of the fifteen factors showed either mean increases ·or decreases over time which were significant at the .01 level or better. Mentation Problems, Repetitive Motor Behavior, Delusions-Hallucinations, Noncompulsivity, and Regressive Anxiety decreased over time, as did Isolation, Weak Group Membership, and Conflict with Siblings. Dependence, Undemandingness, and Competition showed no change in prevalence over time. Finally, four important aggression-related behaviors *increased* over time: Fighting, Delinquency, Conflict with Parents, and Self-Destructive Tendencies. In sum, these data indicated that there was a general decrease in many problematic child behaviors in the welfare children as they grew older, *but this was not true of the major problems of aggression.*

How did the results for the welfare children compare with the findings for the children within the cross-sectional sample? In short, the patterns were extremely similar. *The same results, using the .01 significance level, were obtained for twelve of the fifteen child behavior factors when Time I and Time II means were compared within the cross-sectional sample.* The three behavior dimensions that showed a different pattern in the cross-sectional sample were as follows: Cross-section children showed no significant change in Compulsivity and Fighting behavior, and a significant decrease in Demanding behavior. However, the strong over-all consonance of these findings in the two different samples suggested that the developmental trends of children in different socioeconomic environments were highly convergent. It must be remembered, however, that we were dealing here only with behavior *prevalence* in a group of children not tracking the course of the behaviors in specific children. Work integrating stability and change information has been conducted for the cross-sectional children (Gersten et al., 1976), but still remains for the welfare children.

The above discussion dealt with changes in the prevalence of child behaviors through time *within* each sample. Earlier, the relative prevalence of the various child behaviors *between* the welfare and cross-sectional samples in Time I was discussed. Now the latter must be considered in terms of the Time II data, where the children were roughly five years older than they were in Time I. The discussion will be limited to five of the most central and important child behavior factors, where results were extremely clear-cut.[3]

As mentioned above, the Time I data resulted in a general picture of the welfare children as being either more Delinquent or Dependent than the nonwelfare children, and characterized by *less* Anxiety and Conflict with Parents. *In the follow-up samples, Delinquency and Dependence remained significantly more prevalent in the welfare than in the cross-sectional children.* However, Conflict with Parents did *not* show a significant mean difference between samples in the Time II data as it did in Time I (the cross-section children showing more of this behavior). Further, an interesting reversal occurred on the Anxiety factor. The welfare children showed significantly more of these behaviors than did the cross-sectional children in Time II, a complete turnabout from the Time I data. Finally, the Fighting dimension changed from no difference between samples at Time I, to significantly more of this behavior for welfare children at Time II.[4] (And, as noted above, the welfare children increased significantly on the Fighting dimension through time, while the cross-sectional children did not.)

The above findings suggest that the welfare children were not faring as well as the children from the general population as they grew older. In the Time I data we did not see more disorder in the welfare children than in the cross-sectional children, only somewhat different patterns of behavior (Eisenberg et al., 1975). Following Beiser (1972), it was suggested that the family may be a fairly successful buffer for lower-class children at early developmental stages and at these stages the inequities of the larger social system do not severely damage many of the children. It was further suggested that the welfare child's problems may become more pronounced at later developmental points as he comes more in contact with the larger society, particularly in the schools. The longitudinal data have supported this hypothesis.

The above findings leave us with some important questions in regard to welfare children. What are some of the specific factors associated with their poorer showing through time on some problematic child behaviors? We must learn more about specific kinds of children in specific kinds of welfare families. Such an approach will shed light on the findings regarding prevalence of behaviors.

As has been stressed, the Time I data suggested that two fairly prevalent types of welfare children were the delinquent and the dependent. The children showing high Delinquency tended to show high Conflict with Parents and Anxiety, while the Dependent children tended to be low on these dimensions. These correlations held in the Time II data. If we now bring the Fighting dimension into consideration, where there was a considerable increase for welfare children over time, we see that it was also highly correlated with this constellation of behaviors. (The Time II first-order correlations were as follows: Fighting and Delinquency .37; Fighting and Regressive Anxiety .45; Fighting and Conflict with Parents .60;

and Fighting and Dependence $-.17$.) A great many of the items on the Fighting factor had to do with school behavior in relation to classmates: "does not get along with other children at school," "starts fights with other children," "thinks teachers and other children are against him," and so on. This was in contrast to the Delinquency factor which had more extreme items: "has been arrested," "plays hooky," "has been expelled," and so forth. If it is true that the welfare child's problems increase as he encounters the larger society, then we would expect the increase to occur on factors heavily laden with items which reflect this larger environment, namely Fighting and Delinquency. Further, the welfare children perhaps did not decline in Regressive Anxiety at the rate the cross-sectional children did because of their increasing problems in school and the social environment outside the home. Anxiety was also correlated with the increasing Conflict with Parents ($.34$), perhaps indicating that life in the home was being affected adversely as well. The Dependent children, on the other hand, seemed to be rather untroubled by these problems, their scores being negatively correlated with all of the above factors. Typical items on the dependence scale were "never stands up for rights with siblings," and "never acts independently of mother." Here the problem may be one of passivity or withdrawal, in that the Dependence factor correlated negatively with Group Membership ($-.13$) and Competitiveness ($-.32$).

Short-term and Long-term Welfare Families
It is an empirical question whether or not welfare can be viewed as a separate entity on the social class ladder. Coser has put forth a rather strong position about how those on welfare may be qualitatively different from those who are not. He states, "The poor are men who have been so defined by society and have evoked particular reactions from it. In modern societies the deprived are assigned to the core category of the poor only when they receive assistance" (1965:141). Further, "in the very process of being helped and assisted, the poor are assigned to a special career that impairs their previous identity and becomes a stigma which marks their intercourse with others" (1965:145).

The advantage of a longitudinal welfare study is that it is possible to examine families that change in welfare status through time in terms of factors associated with such change *both before and after the change in status*. All of the families in the sample were on welfare AFDC assistance in Time I. However, during the five-year interval between interviews, 27 percent of the 522 families interviewed at both time points had been able to get off welfare. A central question for the analysis was whether children in the two kinds of welfare families (those that remained on welfare and those that got off welfare) were different in terms of their behavior and functioning at both time points. If the Time I behavior scores for the children were significantly different for the children in the two kinds of welfare families, *before* the one type later got off welfare, this would support the idea that it was not welfare status *per se*, but perhaps more importantly, something about the families which was associated with different behavioral outcomes in the children.

This hypothesis was pursued in a two-way analysis of variance design where ethnic background was included along with change vs. nonchange in welfare status when examined for differences in the fifteen child behavior factors. (Recently, analyses with the ethnic variable had indicated that it was a factor of paramount importance in understanding differences in welfare families and children.)[5] Table 4 contains the results of the analysis of variance tests for the welfare status variable, conducted for both Time I and Time II data. It should first be noted that for the Time II data, the welfare status variable accounted for significant differences in eight of the fifteen child behavior dimensions. In other words, *families that were later to get off welfare had children that were functioning differently than those that stayed on welfare, even before the former got off welfare*. There is no question about the direction of the scores. For all eight factors, children whose families would later get off welfare were functioning better than those in the long-term welfare families. For the Time II analysis, *after* the families had gotten off welfare, eight of the fifteen child behavior dimensions again showed differences between groups (though not in all cases the same dimensions). But note some of the factors that remained typical for children in the long-term welfare families: Fighting, Delinquency, Conflict with Parents, and Anxiety, the same characteristics the welfare children tended to increase on through time! In sum, there seems to be quite a difference in children of short-term and long-term welfare families.

These data suggest that the welfare labeling process does not seem to be as important a determinant of functioning in the children as perhaps some aspects of the family. Preliminary analyses have already shown that characteristics of the parents (emotional illness, child-rearing practices, and so on) are quite divergent in the short-term and long-term welfare families, with the latter showing more problems. A further way to investigate this issue is to examine the behavior factor means for the children in the two kinds of welfare families in regard to the cross-sectional children. In general, the means for the children in the short-term welfare families were closer to the means for the cross-sectional children than they were to the means of the long-term welfare children. The data strongly suggest that a central variable in future analyses must be the distinction between long-term and short-term assistance, perhaps delineated in terms of family types.

Summary and Conclusions
These results must be viewed from two perspectives. For the broader comparisons of the welfare and cross-sectional samples, it was useful to view the welfare children as simply a disadvantaged group within the lower-class population. How the children in the two samples varied in terms of prevalence of behaviors through time related more to the issue of social class differences in child behavior. The second perspective was in the welfare sample itself, in terms of long-term and short-term welfare families.

From the comparisons of prevalence of child behaviors at the two time points in the two different socioeconomic samples, we were left with a cautioning fact: Comparisons of the behavior of lower-class or welfare children with children from the general population are heavily dependent upon the age-range of the children being compared. In the Time I data, the balance of more or less symptomatology did not fall on either sample. Welfare children presented one pattern of being either more dependent or more delinquent than the average nonwelfare child, but the latter was found to have heightened problems of anxiety, compulsivity, and conflict with parents and siblings. When the children were approximately five years older, however, the balance began to shift, and the children from the welfare families began to show generally heightened symptomatology. This supported the hypothesis that the family serves as a fairly effective buffer for the lower-class child, and that his problems increase as he meets the larger society, particularly in school.

However, differences seen in the children in the two samples should not obscure the overriding conclusion of similar behavior dynamics in the two very different samples. First, the familial predictors of child behavior were extremely similar in the two samples. Second, the intercorrelations of the various child dimensions were similar. Third, the patterns of change in prevalence through time on the different dimensions were extremely similar for the two samples. Aggressive disorders increased while many other serious disorders decreased in both samples.

The more specific analysis of short-term versus long-term welfare families yielded provocative findings. Children in families that later got off welfare showed less behavior difficulties than children in long-term welfare families, *even while their families were still on welfare.* This finding suggested to us that welfare labeling may not be as important an issue for child behavior as parental characteristics and family functioning, which appear to have been important factors with respect to staying on public assistance. This hypothesis was supported when scores on parental and familial dimensions were examined for the short-term and long-term welfare families. Mothers who would later stay on welfare showed significantly more physical and emotional illness, unhappy marriages, and punitiveness with their children than mothers who would later be able to get off welfare (though these data were not formally presented in the current report). It would seem that future analyses with the welfare sample data will offer some clues regarding the prediction of long-term and short-term welfare status. Such information could identify probable long-term families and suggest points of intervention and supportive services.

THE ROLE OF HISTORICAL CHANGE IN THE DEVELOPMENT OF TYPES OF BEHAVIORAL DISTURBANCE
Joanne C. Gersten

Developmental changes in types of behavioral disturbance arise either from historical-generational or ontogenetic sources. Determination of which source accounts for changes seen over time is essential in the delineation of the domain, and those factors of change within that domain, responsible for the change. It was examined whether cultural changes during the period of 1967–1972 could account for the longitudinal trends evidenced by six types of behavioral disturbance and if its role, if any, was consistent for both sexes.

The elaboration of the life-span developmental perspective in recent years (cf. Baltes and Schaie, 1973; Datan and Ginsberg, 1975; Goulet and Baltes, 1970; Huston-Stein and Baltes, 1976; Nesselroade and Reese, 1973) has resulted in renewed emphasis on a number of issues of critical import for research on the development of behavioral disturbances. These issues are not confined to research which studies children and/or adolescents, but instead have relevance across the entire life-span from infancy to old age. This section addresses only one of these issues, but excellent presentations of others are available (cf. Baltes, 1973; Huston-Stein and Baltes, 1976).

The issue addressed, which has been clearly sharpened by the life-span perspective on both theoretical and methodological levels, concerns the relationship between historical-generational and ontogentic sources of change in behavioral disturbance. It is widely recognized (cf. Wohlwill, 1970; Nunnally, 1973)[6] that cross-sectional designs in which different age cohorts are compared cannot be used to estimate ontogenetic age changes because of confounding cohort-generational differences. Schaie (1970) dramatically demonstrated this when he showed that the decline in intellectual functioning in later life inferred from cross-sectional studies could in large part be attributed to cohort differences and not the aging process. However, a simple longitudinal study of one cohort is not a solution to the concern of separating ontogenetic from historical sources of change. The cohort is itself in a historical context and changes over time may as readily reflect the sociocultural changes in that context as ontogenetic change or, even possibly, an interaction between historical events and ontogenetic development. An additional problem with this design is that it severely limits the researcher's ability to generalize about the change found, whether arising from ontogenetic or historical sources, to other age groups and other historical periods.

A longitudinal study which incorporates a number of cohorts can determine the generalizability of change found across age cohorts. The problem still exists, however, given identical times of measurement of the types of disturbance, that any observed change may reflect not ontogenetic change but historical-generational changes during the historical period intervening between measurements to which all cohorts were exposed. Whether the changes in disturbed functioning can be ascribed to this historical period can be determined by examining different cohorts or generations of identical age, one measured before and the other after the historical period.

Historical differences or cohort effects have been found to play an important role in accounting for change, for example, in adolescent personality and intelligence measures (Baltes and Nesselroade, 1972; Nesselroade and Baltes, 1974), social play measures of preschoolers (Barnes, 1971), and adult personality and intelligence (Schaie, 1970; Schaie and Gribbin, 1975). These findings clearly foretell the potential importance of historical change in accounting for any changes noted in disturbed functioning. In order to ascertain the precise domain of factors responsible for behavioral change, a research design must then either rule in or out the potential effects of historical change. Historical change would direct attention for actual factors to the domain of broad social forces and institutions and their changes, while responsibility for ontogenetic change would lie in factors such as maturational processes, changes in individual familial constellations and dynamics, modeling, and learning experiences.

Gersten et al. (1976) determined the changes with aging and stability of six dimensions of behavioral disturbance for 732 children and adolescents who constituted the sample reassessed after five years of an original cross-sectional sample of Manhattan youth 6 to 18 years old. Change was examined both on the total sample level and differentially by six age cohorts which ranged from 6.7 years to 16.4 years with about two-year intervals between adjacent cohorts. Membership in the cohorts was limited to those children or adolescents whose time of measurement interval was within 4.5 to 5.5 years. The six dimensions subjected to this analysis were selected from a total of eighteen factor analytically derived dimensions, because they had the highest correlations with a rating of total impairment made by psychiatrists, had uniformly high reliabilities at both times of measurement (.80 or better), and accounted for 90 percent of the total variance predicted by all dimensions in the total impairment

rating. The change found over time on the total sample level was replicated across all six age cohorts for four of the six dimensions, and across
two-thirds of the age cohorts for the other two dimensions. Thus, in
general, the changes with aging or longitudinal change did not evidence
cohort specificity. In other words, the longitudinal finding of change was
generalizable across different age groups who differed in their historical
experience up to the initiation of the study in 1967. For the most part then
the differential cumulative historical exposure associated with the cohorts
was not reflected in differential change patterns and its importance was
considered minimal. The role of exposure across cohorts to the same
historical period of 1967–1972, and the cultural changes which occurred in
that period, in accounting for the longitudinal changes was still at issue
and the objective of this section is to determine that role.

METHOD

The reader is referred to the earlier research reported above (Gersten et
al., 1976) for a detailed exposition of the sample and procedures.

Information about the child's behavior at both time points was obtained
from a structured questionnaire about the child and the family which was
administered to mothers in the selected households. At Time I, two project psychiatrists used a computer summary of only the items of child
behavior to rate each child on a 5-point total impairment rating scale. The
items were also independently factor-analyzed and resulted in eighteen
dimensions. Only six dimensions of behavioral disturbance are of concern
here; the reasons for their selection were given above. The six dimensions
were Mentation Problems, Conflict with Parents, Regressive Anxiety,
Fighting, Delinquency, and Isolation.

The six age cohorts examined in the earlier study, in which the first
value is the mean age at Time I and the second value is the mean age at
Time II, were: (1) 6.7–11.5; (2) 8.4–13.4; (3) 10.6–15.4; (4) 12.6–17.5; (5)
14.4–19.6; and (6) 16.4–21.5. To address the question if the longitudinal
changes found on the six dimensions reflected historical change during
1967–1972, the following procedure was used. Independent groups of
children were selected from these cohorts whose mean age at either time
was within one year. In other words, the mean age of the children was
similar, they differed in the time of measurement, one measurement reflecting the historical exposure and the other not, and no group of children
was involved in more than one comparison. Two sets of comparison
groups were developed. In the first, called 11-year-olds, the younger generation (the generation who developed during the specific historical period
under consideration) was represented by the Time II measurement of the

first cohort ($N=92$), and the older generation was the Time I measurement of the third cohort ($N=75$). In the second set of comparison groups, labeled 13-year-olds, the younger generation was the Time II measurement of the second cohort ($N=98$), and the older was the Time I measurement of the fourth cohort ($N=78$). Each of the generation groups was then divided into males and females in order to determine if the effects of historical change varied as a function of sex as has been found in other work (Nesselroade and Baltes, 1974). More importantly, sex was included to determine if sex differences were generalizable across generations or historical periods, a question of considerable importance, since the period under examination (1967–1972) was characterized by considerable changes in sex values and mores.

RESULTS

Due to the unequal number of subjects in the two generation groups for both 11- and 13-year-olds, unweighted-means analyses of variance were used. Specifically, a 2×2 (Sex$\times$Generation) unweighted analysis of variance was done for each of the six dimensions in each of the two age sets. The 11- and 13-year-olds were not combined into one analysis, since that would have introduced cross-sectional differences of little interest and doubtful meaning. The results of the analyses are presented in Table 5.

Before the results in Table 5 are discussed, the longitudinal age changes

Table 5

F-Values from the Analyses of Variance on
Dimensions of Disturbance for Two Age Cohorts[a]

Dimension of disturbance	11-Year-Olds		13-Year-Olds	
	Generation	Sex	Generation	Sex
Mentation problems	4.39*	2.30	6.16*	0.84
Conflict with parents	6.99+	10.49+	4.97*	0.50
Regressive anxiety	0.73	0.97	0.02	9.32+
Fighting	0.64	7.78+	2.06	0.09
Delinquency	9.72+	4.34*	2.12	0.05
Isolation	0.80	– 0 –	0.73	0.19

[a] All interactions between sex and generation were not significant and hence are not entered in table.

* $p < .05$; + $p < .01$

found on both a total sample level and across six cohorts for each of the six dimensions are now given. This provides the background against which the importance of the historical-generational differences demonstrated can be better evaluated. Significantly greater pathology at the later time ($p<.001$) was found on the dimensions of Conflict with Parents and Delinquency. Significant decreases in disturbance over time ($p<.001$) were noted on the dimensions of Mentation Problems, Regressive Anxiety, and Isolation. The dimension Fighting showed no significant mean change over time.

Turning now to the results in Table 5, no significant historical-generation effect was found in either 11- or 13-year-olds on three of the dimensions of disturbance: Regressive Anxiety, Isolation, and Fighting. The finding with respect to fighting was expected, since no longitudinal age change had been found. The lack of a historical effect in combination with the lack of a cohort-specific effect provides strong evidence for the conclusion that the decline in pathology over time noted on the dimensions of Regressive Anxiety and Isolation represents true ontogenetic change.

Significant generation effects were found in both 11- and 13-year-olds for the types of disturbance labeled Mentation Problems and Conflict with Parents. At both ages (11 and 13), the older generation showed significantly more pathology on the dimension of Mentation Problems than did the younger generation. In other words, the children developing through the five-year period of 1967 to 1972 had significantly less of this type of disturbance. The historical effect was in the same direction as the longitudinal change noted for this disturbance, i.e., toward decreasing levels. On the dimension of Conflict with Parents at both ages the younger generation had significantly more disturbance than did the older generation. In this case the historical effect was opposite to that noted on the dimension of Mentation Problems. The two dimensions were identical, however, in that the direction of the historical change matched the direction of the longitudinal change.

The type of disturbance measured by the factor of delinquency presented a more complicated picture. A significant generation effect was found only at the younger age, and the younger generation showed significantly less of this disturbance than did the older generation. In other words, the historical effect appeared dependent upon the part of the age-span through which the child was developing during the period. Surprisingly, however, the direction of this effect, i.e., toward lower levels of Delinquency, was opposite to the longitudinal trend, which was toward higher levels.

Looking now at sex differences, it was found that sex never modified the historical effect, or the interaction between the two factors was non-significant across all dimensions and both ages. Alternatively, any significant sex differences found were upheld across the generations studied or generalizable generationally. The pattern of significant sex differences was clearly dependent upon the age of the children, or the significant sex differences were not generalizable from preadolescence to early adolescence or vice versa. Only the dimensions of Mentation Problems and Isolation evidenced findings with regard to sex which were generalizable across the generations and ages studied; namely, there was no significant difference between the sexes for either dimension.

For the 11-year-olds, all dimensions which tapped aggression or conduct type of disorders, namely Conflict with Parents, Fighting, and Delinquency, showed a significant sex effect, in each case boys showing more of the disturbance than girls. No significant differences were found between sexes for these types of conduct disorders at the older age of 13. In contrast, among the older children girls showed significantly more of the neurotic type of disturbance covered by the dimension of Regressive Anxiety (fears, sleep disturbance behaviors, and psychophysiological complaints as stomach aches, headaches, sweating, and flushes) than did boys. This sex difference was not found for the younger children.

DISCUSSION

The importance of historical change over a five-year period from 1967 to 1972 in accounting for longitudinal age change in types of behavioral disturbance was not as pervasive as might have been expected from earlier research which investigated a portion (1970–1972) of the period (Nesselroade and Baltes, 1974). However, historical change did appear to play the primary role in accounting for the changes with aging on the dimensions of Mentation Problems and Conflict with Parents. In other words, the results strongly suggested that change in these types of behavioral disturbance occurred from 1967 to 1972 because the cultural socialization context for children changed during this period.

Of course, it becomes an exercise in speculation, without further data, to delineate those specific aspects of change within the socialization context responsible for the primarily historical trend in these disturbances. Nevertheless, certain domains of factors come to mind to direct future investigations. Mentation Problems, a factor containing many items dealing with school achievement, speech difficulties, and reasoning ability, evidenced a declining historical trend or the prevalence of the problematic behaviors it comprises decreased over the 1967–1972 historical period. This period was characterized on the educational level by increased spending for diverse programs in educational remediation, and expanded screening and training programs in learning disabilities. These programs, instituted as part of the Johnsonian Great Society and continuing through the Nixon years, may have resulted in a decline in intellectual deficits and problems, although the evidence on this effect is conflicting. In contrast, Conflict with Parents, the intrafamilial aggression factor, evidenced a historical trend of increase during this period. Since the other two dimensions tapping aggressive or antisocial behavior did not evidence this historical trend, possible explanatory factors would appear to lie more in changes in either parental patterns of interaction with their children, which operated across social levels ("the generation gap phenomenon of the late sixties and early seventies"), or in changes in parental sensitivity to and hence perception of such problems rather than in such sociocultural factors as changes in television viewing or the heavy exposure to the war violence of this period. Finally, however, only systematic investigation can ascertain whether these *post hoc* suggestions of explanation have validity, but the historical trends delineated make it clear that a substantial portion of the influences on the development process of certain disturbances may lie outside the person and on the broad societal level.

The changes in childhood neurotic behaviors (Regressive Anxiety) and isolative withdrawn behaviors (Isolation) over time clearly stemmed from ontogenetic sources. Both types of disturbance declined with aging, a finding congruent with other research at other historical periods (e.g., Lapouse and Monk, 1958; McFarlane et al., 1954). Thus, these declines appear to be a function of the developmental experiences common to children across generations or historical periods such as a growing mastery of the environment with its attendant decline in uncertainty and expanding exposure to and experiences with peers (cf. Kohlberg et al., 1972). In the same vein, the increase in delinquent, antisocial behavior with aging was seen to arise primarily from ontogenetic sources, since the historical trend was counter to the longitudinal trend and confined to one age cohort.

None of the historical trends found varied as a function of sex; therefore, the changes in the socialization context underlying the trend operated for both genders. The sex differences found in level of disturbance strongly agreed with past research. It has been fairly well established by observations in a variety of cultures and using a variety of measures that males are more aggressive than females (Maccoby and Jacklin, 1974). Males at preadolescence (11 years old) in this study evidenced greater intrafamilial, peer-directed, and antisocial aggression than did females, but no significant differences existed at early adolescence. However, a review of studies (Maccoby and Jacklin, 1974: 230–233) indicated almost none that studied this specific age. It would appear that early adolescence is a developmental point at which an earlier sex difference disappears to reappear later and as such the significance of this period of age for females should be more fully explored. Findings with respect to fear and anxiety have been ambiguous, with either no difference between the sexes or, if a difference, one favoring greater levels for females (Maccoby and Jacklin, 1974: 182–190). Only the adolescent females, not the preadolescent females, had higher anxiety scores than the males in this study. As with the aggressive findings, this requires further exploration as to whether it represents a true gender difference in the developmental process.

In summary, this section has demonstrated that historical change over as short a period as five years can be of paramount importance in accounting for the changes in certain types of disturbed functioning as the person develops and ages. Its importance behooves social scientists to consider its role in more clearly defined ways than is presently the case. This entails not only movement toward designs which permit its assessment but also careful and systematic description of the changes in the sociocultural milieu which occur during the course of the study.

THE PREDICTION OF DELINQUENT BEHAVIOR OVER TIME: SEX SPECIFIC PATTERNS RELATED TO OFFICIAL AND SURVEY-REPORTED DELINQUENT BEHAVIOR

Ora Simcha-Fagan

Various social, school-related, familial and psychological characteristics have been separately related to delinquent behavior. Yet the social-behavioral pattern (or patterns) leading to delinquent behavior remain largely unclear; neither are we able to empirically account for a substantial amount of the variance in delinquent behavior. Some of the major barriers have been the tendency to rely on retrospective information, to focus exclusively on a given domain of behavior, and, most importantly, the inability to curb the error introduced into the measurement of delinquent behavior. The present study attempts to deal with these problems and proceeds to investigate the extent to which delinquent behavior is predictable over time, and the major antecedent patterns involved.

Considering the plethora of empirical studies on the "causes of delinquent-antisocial behavior," the information on etiological processes is scant. Furthermore, even those findings which have been replicated are open to doubt in terms of their etiological significance, as they are subject to common methodological constraints.

Two such analytical problems predominate. Until recently, studies concerned with etiology tended to use matched designs comparing "known cases" (as determined by police records, institutionalization, or clinical diagnosis) with nondelinquent controls from comparable social, ethnic, and age categories (e.g., Glueck, 1950; Andry, 1960; Empey, 1971). Such designs truncate socioeconomic dimensions as well as their behavioral correlates. Important predictors are thus excluded and the relative weight of various predictors cannot be assessed. The absence of a population sampling-frame further imposes limitations on the analysis and on the ability to draw generalizations. The tendency in such studies to use information concurrent with public labeling (or that which is collected retrospectively) raises questions of contamination and essentially leaves the direction of the relationship observed unknown (Hirschi and Selvin, 1967, and Nye, 1958, provide a relevant discussion and pertinent examples). A certain improvement in studies which rely on a controlled comparison was gained by selecting controls on the basis of information which predates publicly recorded antisocial behavior (e.g., Robins, 1966). Such "follow back" designs, however, have only limited information which predates diagnostic/legal labeling, in that they are dependent on routinely collected information—mostly in school records and on parental official records.

A second and related problem which affects the validity of the above noted etiological studies as well as of prevalence studies, is the lack of agreement on an acceptable criterion measure of delinquent-antisocial behavior. Robisons's pioneering work (1936) revealed some of the difficulties in using "official" record information as a basis for measuring *delinquent behavior*. Nevertheless, much of the work that ensued over the next two decades used official delinquency/crime records to determine the prevalence and correlates of delinquent behavior. Moreover, such correlates provided the basis for the dominant theoretical perspectives in delinquency (Merton, 1957:131; Cloward and Ohlin, 1960; Cohen, 1955; Miller, 1958). As empirical research expanded, however, dissatisfaction with official records as the basic datum measuring delinquent criminal behavior grew stronger and several researchers initiated studies using self-reported information (Nye and Short, 1957; Gold, 1970; Hirschi, 1969).

Data from self-report studies indicate that official statistics vastly underestimate the extent of delinquent behavior (Erickson and Empey, 1963; Elliott and Voss, 1974). They also demonstrate that some of the most important correlates of officially known delinquent behavior (most notably, socioeconomic status) are considerably attenuated when self-reported information is used (Nye, 1958; Hirschi, 1969). Such observations suggest that the relationship with publicly known delinquency is artifactual and reflects differential treatment by the agencies. Proponents of the use of official data contend that while only a sample of delinquents is identified, the criterion for selection is primarily guided by frequency and severity of offense (Wolfgang et al., 1972; Terry, 1967). They point out the difficulties in establishing the validity of self-reported information and particularly criticize the inability of self-report instruments to measure serious crime.

At least some of the criticism advanced by each of these divergent approaches remain salient in the face of further empirical data and efforts at conceptualization. Inasmuch as delinquent behavior is defined in most relevant studies as well as in this analysis by reference to [all] acts in violation of the law, there is considerable evidence that official record information contains only a meager portion of the relevant data. On the other hand, in examining self-reported versus officially recorded delinquent behavior, several studies report a substantial (15–17 percent error) level of underreporting (Clark and Tifft, 1966; Gold, 1966). Such underreporting was found in one of the more detailed analyses to be positively related to seriousness, introducing a substantial error in the measurement of severe crimes (Elliott and Voss, 1974:73). When it is considered that the items included in self-report instruments and hence available for such comparisons do not include the whole range of severe crimes, such underreporting may hint of an even greater problem. Moreover, officially recorded delinquent behavior bears a quality of face validity; it is not surprising, therefore, that it has been used as an external criterion in validating self-report. As put by one of the proponents of self-report,

. . . the records of the police are, on a priori grounds, a weaker measure of the *commission* of delinquent acts than presumably honest self-reports. But the relation between self-reported delinquent acts and police records has significance for validity beyond confirming that persons reporting certain acts are more likely to have committed them: the agreement between "commission" and "detection" affirms that the acts are *delinquent* as the term is defined (Hirschi, 1969:64).

Considering these divergent but interrelated approaches, the difficulties in establishing an acceptable criterion measure are expectedly considerable. Since the criterion provides the standard against which the relevant predictors are identified, the lack of agreement on an acceptable criterion of delinquent behavior presents a stumbling block to etiological research. Furthermore, at this point, given the tendency in research to rely on only one or the other criterion measure—that is, police-recorded or survey-reported—the extent to which they represent overlapping or continuous dimensions of behavior cannot be assessed.

The following analysis attempts to deal with the major problems noted above. It employs a prospective design and includes social, familial, and individual-behavioral information which predates public recognition of delinquency. The time ordering facilitates causal interpretation, and the relative importance of various antecedents can be assessed within a larger framework. In terms of the criterion measure(s), survey-reported information by the mother[7] and police-recorded information are used. These two independent measures of the criterion are first examined for antecedents separately; a similar investigation is then made when the criterion is a conjoint function of the two measures.

Following this strategy several focal questions can be more directly explored:

1. To what extent can later delinquent behavior be accounted for when social, familial, early school, and home behaviors are jointly considered?

2. What are the common and differential predictors of police vs. survey-reported delinquency?

3. Can the relationship between police and survey-reported delinquency be used to circumvent some of their shortcomings, hence providing a more valid criterion?

4. To what extent do we improve our ability to account for and explain the development of delinquent behavior by reducing the error in measuring the criterion?

5. Do sex differences further clarify the predictive pattern(s) involved?

Method and procedure

The reader is referred to the introductory statement for a description of the procedure used in drawing the cross-sectional sample. The sample drawn at Time I is an area probability sample of 1,034 Manhattan children age 6 to 18. At Time I, the mothers of children in the sample were interviewed using a structured questionnaire about the child and family. At Time II, on the average five years later, the sample was followed up and the mothers were reinterviewed. The follow-up sample was designed to maintain the original ethnic proportions, and constitutes 71 percent of the original sample. The follow-up sample of 732 children and the original sample of 1,034 children do not significantly differ on a host of Time I variables as well as in terms of official record information. The follow-up sample of 732 children is used in the longitudinal analysis reported here.

School records were obtained for 88 percent of the children in the follow-up sample. The *continuous* school record was obtained and the coding system applied to each year of the child's school career, noting its temporal relationship to the Time I and Time II interviews.

Information on officially recorded delinquent/criminal behavior was collected via a search of the records of Family Court and the Police Department (both youth and adult records). Information from agency records was transformed into a coding form. The coding-measurement indicated the date of occurrence for each event, relevant aspects of its content, and the offense charge(s) applied. For the purposes of the following analysis a police event (on a given date) was counted as a single charged offense, although various types of charges might have been involved.

Independent variables used in the prediction of delinquent behavior were derived from the Time I interview with the mother and from Time I school data. Specifically, *five sets of Time I variables* were included: *social characteristics* (four variables); *parental behavior* (three dimensions); *parent-child relationship* (four dimensions); *child behavior* (nine dimensions); and *school behavior* (six variables). The list of variables is presented in Table 7. The selection of variables to be included in each of the sets was primarily guided by relevant empirical research and by our earlier findings (Simcha-Fagan et al., 1975; Schwartz and Gersten, 1976). The overall set of variables, however, is explicitly meant to provide for more than one type of antecedent pattern leading to delinquent behavior.

The reliability of the behavioral dimensions used is high, with their alpha coefficients ranging between .74 and .94. It should be noted that among the eighteen child-behavior factors extracted from Time I data, one was labeled delinquency. This dimension includes survey report of arrest as well as other "trouble with the police." To avoid overlap between the predictors and the measure of police-recorded delinquency, this dimension was excluded from the analysis.

Three types of criterion variables measuring delinquent behavior were constructed. The first utilizes only official record information and provides the *Frequency of Officially Reported Offenses*. All officially known offenses which preceded the time of the first survey interview were deleted. Individuals with two or more official offenses prior to the Time I interview were excluded from the analysis.

The second measure, *Mother-Reported Delinquency Score,* is a composite score of fifteen equally weighted survey items pertaining to delinquent behavior. The items were chosen on the basis of their equivalence with "chargeable" behaviors. They cover the behaviors addressed in the Nye self-report instrument (Nye, 1958), excluding those pertaining to aggression against peers.[8] The items included are: refuses when directed by father, mother; takes sums of money that do not belong to him/her; takes things other than money that do not belong to him/her; teacher complains about X——'s absences; plays hookey; expelled from school or left for an extended period; X—— lies so often that cannot believe anything he/she says; runs away from home; drinks alcoholic beverages; smokes marijuana; uses drugs other than marijuana; smokes cigarettes; bad home behavior; and doesn't come home at the promised time. Responses were coded either as a dichotomy or on a three-point scale— never, sometimes, and often.

The items contained in this index were asked both at the Time I and Time II interviews. Using each of these data sets (Time I; Time II), two equivalent measures were separately constructed and standardized.[9] Change on this measure is being used for a developmental analysis of delinquent behavior. In the present context, however, a survey-reported measure comparable in nature to the cumulative official record was sought. For this purpose Time I and Time II survey scores, which were individually standardized, were used in determining the total mother-reported delinquency score.

The third measure of delinquent behavior considers both officially recorded and survey-reported information. Using the two independent measures of delinquent behavior, a *congruence sample was constructed for which both sources indicate non/moderate/highly delinquent behavior.*

Table 6

Mother Reported Delinquency Score by
Frequency of Officially Charged Offenses

Frequency of officially charged offenses	Mother Reported Delinquency Score*					
	Low (1)	Mild (2)	Moderate (3)	Moderately High (4)	High (5)	
0	267[a] (93.4)[b]	159 (86.9)	105 (90.5)	50 (86.2)	54 (62.8)	635 (87.1)
1	12 (4.2)	11 (6.0)	5 (4.3)	5 (8.6)	8 (9.3)	41 (5.6)
2	4 (1.4)	5 (2.7)	1 (0.9)	3 (5.2)	7 (8.1)	20 (2.7)
3 − 4	2 (0.7)	4 (2.2)	3 (2.6)	0 (0)	8 (9.3)	17 (2.3)
5+	1 (0.3)	4 (2.2)	2 (1.7)	0 (0)	9 (10.5)	16 (2.3)
	286	183	116	58	86	729

Chi Square test significant at .001 level.
Contingency coeff. (c) = .32

*   (1) Greater than ½ s.d. below $\overline{X}$ (2) ½ s.d. below to $\overline{X}$.
    (3) $\overline{X}$ to ½ s.d. above $\overline{X}$ (4) ½ s.d. to 1 s.d. above $\overline{X}$
    (5) More than 1 s.d. above $\overline{X}$

[a] Number
[b] Column percents

The relationship between these two measures is presented in Table 6. Those who are both low on the survey measure and have no official record provide the group of nondelinquents and can be thought of as "true negatives." Those who are both above the mean (a score ≥ 3) on the survey measure and have official offenses can be considered "true positives" and were divided into moderate and highly delinquent, using a cutting point of three or more official offenses. The congruence sample encompasses slightly less than half of the total sample ($N=318$ of 729 available for prospective analysis).

RESULTS

To what extent can delinquent behavior be predicted over time?
The most general concern was to establish the extent to which delinquent behavior could be predicted by jointly considering social, familial, early behavioral characteristics, and school behavior. The question was particularly important, since previous studies tended to consider only one or two of these predictor sets at a time, and the question remained open as to whether the large unexplained variance in delinquent behavior was due to the absence of "other" relevant predictors or, alternatively, that the predictive power of the variables considered was greatly attenuated by errors introduced into the criterion measure.

The analysis performed here indicates that the five sets of predictors, which include a total of twenty-seven independent variables, account for a significant amount of the variance in each of the criterion variables measuring delinquent behavior (see Table 7). There are, however, important quantitative and qualitative differences among the predictions. The amount of variance explained in officially recorded delinquency is relatively low ($R^2 = .28$) and is not significantly larger than that accounted for in studies using mainly sociodemographic and school variables as predictors (e.g., Wolfgang, Figlio, and Sellin, 1972). On the other hand, a substantial amount of the variance in survey-reported delinquency (in this case, mother-reported) is accounted for ($R^2 = .44$ and .48 for males and females, respectively). Finally, when delinquency is measured in the congruence sample, for which the validity of the criterion has been established by reference to two independent measures, the prediction is extremely powerful ($R^2 = .59$ and .63 for males and females, respectively). The analysis clearly indicates that the independent variables selected within this framework are predictive of later police-known and survey-reported delinquency. The ability to identify the relevant predictors and their proper weighting is increased when error in the criterion measure is reduced.

What are the common and differential predictors of officially recorded vs. survey-reported delinquent behavior?

For each of the dependent variables, a simultaneous multiple regression was performed using the twenty-seven independent variables.[10] Given this set of independent variables, what are the most important predictors of each dependent variable? That is, which predictors account for the largest proportion of *unique* variance—variance not accounted for by any other predictor? The unique contributions of Time I independent variables are presented in Table 7. Focusing initially on the prediction of *Officially Reported Offenses* and of *Mother-Reported Delinquency,* important differences are observed.

For males, the unique predictors of each criterion measure exhibit little overlap. Race and income level are uniquely related to official delinquency but not to survey-reported delinquency. This differential relationship confirms previous findings (Hirschi, 1969; Gold, 1970). Residential mobility, in contrast, is an important predictor of survey-reported delinquency. Parental and parent-child variables make no unique contributions to the variance explained in police-known delinquency. On the other hand, parents' punitive practices are uniquely related, though the relationship is not statistically significant, to survey-reported delinquency.

Major differences are observed in the child behavior predictors for the two measures. Two dimensions of child behavior, mentation problems, and unanxious noncompulsive behavior, are uniquely related to publicly known delinquency/criminality in males. The former dimension consists of difficulties with speech, memory, and concentration as well as some specific signs such as blank spells and stuttering. The latter dimension is defined by lack of concern with order, being on time, or checking over one's performance; it also includes some explicit antisocial behaviors, namely, stealing and misbehavior at school. This latter dimension also contributes uniquely to the prediction of survey-reported delinquency and as such is a common predictor. The other unique and differential predictors of male survey-reported delinquency are conflict with parents, fighting (with peers and siblings), and self-destructive behavior (talks of killing self now/past). School variables make no contribution to officially known delinquency but some to survey-reported—most notably, dropping out of school and the existence of a confidential file.

Overall, male officially recorded delinquency is uniquely related to ethnic and socioeconomic differentials, to early difficulties in developmental-mental functioning which affect primary skills, and to early noncompulsive antisocial behavior. Survey-reported delinquency is, on the other hand, uniquely related to aspects of the parent-child relationship and to child behaviors indicating early schism from parents, tension in the relationship with peers and siblings, and considerable emotional pathology. Noncompulsive behavior is, as indicated, a common predictor across the measures. The behavioral pattern predictive of male survey-reported delinquency is, with the exception of early noncompulsive behavior, highly reminiscent of the pattern identified in an earlier study (Simcha-Fagan et al., forthcoming) investigating the antecedents of *self-reported* illicit drug use; this pattern was primarily associated with multiple drug use which excluded the use of heroin.

For females, the predictors of officially recorded and survey-reported delinquency exhibit a large degree of overlap. The differential relationship of the criterion measures with race and ethnic group, which clearly distinguish male police-recorded and survey-reported delinquency, is not observed for females. Some differences are evidenced in terms of parent-child relationship; maternal rejection is uniquely related to survey-reported delinquency, while the mother's traditional and restrictive attitude appears important for police-recorded delinquency. In terms of the child behavior predictors, there is considerable commonality across the criterion measures. To some extent, the common predictors are masked in the final simultaneous prediction, which includes an additional variable (Time I mother-reported delinquency) used only in the prediction of publicly known delinquency/criminality.

The most prominent predictors of survey-reported female delinquency are conflict with parents, fighting, and self-destructive behavior; unanxious noncompulsive behavior has a significant but substantially lower contribution than that identified for males; and, finally, early delusions and hallucinations have some unique predictive power. In the prediction of officially known delinquency, Time I mother-reported delinquency is of major importance. The relationship indicates an earlier crystallization and a stronger relationship between Time I survey-reported and subsequent police-reported delinquency for females. When this predictor is excluded, however, and the same predictors are used across the criterion measures, early fighting and delusional behavior are significantly and uniquely related to officially reported delinquency and identify common predictors for female delinquency. As for males, school behavior makes some, but not a large, unique contribution to female survey-reported delinquency. For females then, differences are observed in the social and parental predictors of the two measures, but a large degree of overlap is evident among the child behavior predictors. The unique predictors of female delinquency (particularly as measured by survey-report) largely conform with the etiology described for "Unsocialized (or psychopathic) Aggression" (Hewitt and Jenkins, 1946).

Table 7

Percent of Total Explained Variance (R^2) in Delinquent Behavior and Unique Contributions of Time I Independent Variables

Time I Predictors	Number of Officially Reported Offenses		Mother - Reported Delinquency Score		Delinquency Score In Congruence Sample	
	Male (N = 374) r^2_p	Female (N = 355) r^2_p	Male (N = 374) r^2_p	Female (N = 355) r^2_p	Male (N = 150) r^2_p	Female (N = 168) r^2_p
Time I Demographic Variables						
Age	0.4	0.9	8.7†	5.7†	9.7†	0.3
Race Spanish-speaking	0.3	0.1	0.1	0.5	0.0	3.0*
Race Black	2.9+	0.8	0.0	0.5	0.4	0.0
Number natural parents	0.3	0.4	0.7	0.5	0.3	0.0
Number of addresses	0.3	1.1	2.6+	0.3	3.0	0.4
Family income	1.7*	0.0	0.1	1.0	1.3	0.1
Time I Parental Factors						
Isolated parents	0.3	0.0	0.4	0.7	0.6	0.1
Unhappy marriage	0.6	0.0	0.0	0.3	4.9*	0.3
Mother's physical emotional illness	0.1	0.1	0.2	0.0	0.0	0.5
Time I Parent-Child Factors						
Parents cold	0.0	0.3	0.4	0.0	0.1	1.1
Mother traditional - restrictive	0.3	0.9	0.1	0.0	1.0	2.7
Parents punitive	0.4	0.2	0.9	0.5	1.7	0.0
Mother excitable - rejecting	0.0	0.1	0.5	1.3*	0.0	0.4

172

Time I Child Factors						
Mentation problems	1.9+	0.0	0.0	0.1	3.5*	0.1
Conflict with parents	0.2	0.5	3.9†	5.9†	0.4	5.8+
Regressive anxiety (low)	0.5	0.4	0.1	0.0	1.0	1.0
Unanxious noncompulsive	1.9+	0.6	5.1†	1.8*	10.2†	0.9
Fighting	0.0	0.0	3.0+	6.1†	1.6	6.6+
Delusions - hallucinations	0.2	1.2	0.5	1.1	0.0	12.6†
Conflict with siblings	0.2	0.8	0.1	0.0	0.0	0.1
Sex curiosity	0.0	0.1	0.0	0.1	0.7	0.5
Self-destructive tendencies	0.0	0.2	2.9+	3.7†	1.5	3.4*
Time I Mother-Reported Delinquency Score φ	0.1	7.5†	—	—	—	—
Time I School Variables						
Dropout up to Time I	0.6	0.5	1.6*	1.2*	2.0	0.1
Absenteeism	0.2	0.5	0.8	1.2*	2.5	2.1
Confidential file	0.1	0.0	1.4*	0.5	0.2	1.5
Self-control	0.0	0.1	0.0	0.6	0.6	0.0
Obeys rules	0.4	1.5*	0.3	0.1	3.7*	3.0*
Held over at or before Time I	0.4	0.2	0.0	0.5	2.6	0.0
Total R	.5272	.5369	.6606	.6946	.7649	.7929
Total R² (percent)	27.8†	28.8†	43.6†	48.2†	58.5†	62.9†
Adjusted R² (shrunken)	21.9†	22.7†	39.2†	43.9†	49.3†	55.7†

* p < .05 + p < .01 † p < .001
φ Included only in prediction of number of officially reported offenses.

To what extent can the relevant predictors be better identified by using a congruence sample? And what are the major predictive patterns?

One of the major difficulties in relying on the prediction of officially reported offenses for the identification of etiological variables is, specifically, the inability to determine the extent to which the predictors identified are artifacts of the error introduced by agency bias. Moreover, the amount of unexplained variance which remains casts further doubt on the validity of any interpretation.

To circumvent some of these difficulties a congruence sample was identified for which police and survey-reported information are in agreement. True negatives and true positives as determined by both sources are included. The continuum of delinquency, as measured in the congruence sample, represents survey delinquency, which is also likely to become publicly known.

The total explained variance in delinquency for the congruence sample is extremely high, indicating the relevance of the framework used. Before turning to the prediction for each of the sex groups, the major differences in the contribution of age to male and female delinquency are worth noting. Across the criterion measures there is a strong indication that delinquency in males is more age-related than among females. This further enchances the above-noted results which suggest earlier crystallization of female delinquency. It also, of course, identifies the great need for developmental research in delinquency.

Considering first the group at higher risk, males, the prediction in the congruence sample helps identify the potential etiological patterns involved. It should be noted that when social variables alone are taken into account, race and income are significantly related to delinquency. However, as indicated from the results presented, when other variables are simultaneously considered, the variance explained by race and income is exhausted by other relevant characteristics. Most important among the parental behaviors which surface as a unique predictor is the dimension labeled unhappy marriage. This dimension includes items indicative of the mother's extreme frustration with marriage and life, the father's inadequacy in work roles and at home as well as disagreements concerning drinking. The unique contribution of parental punitive practices is noteworthy but does not reach statistical significance. Child behaviors which contribute significantly replicate those identified in the prediction of male officially reported offenses, namely, mentation problems and unanxious noncompulsive behavior. Low regressive anxiety, (high) fighting, and self-destructive behaviors also contribute uniquely but not significantly. Of the Time I school variables, difficulties in accepting authority (rules and regulations) make the largest and most significant contribution. Overall, the prediction points to an antecedent pattern emphasizing the importance of: parental behavior—notably unhappy marriage and modeling of antisocial behavior; parental punitive practices; early mentation problems; and antisocial behavior. The set of factors indentified supports previous propositions on the development of "socialized delinquency" (Quay and Werry, 1972; Robins, 1975). It should be noted, however, that the familial environment rather than a social or ethnic "subculture" appears to generate the crucial (proximal) socializing effect.

The predictors of male delinquency identified here only partially overlap with those which contributed to the prediction of survey-reported delinquency. Most prominent among the common predictors is early unanxious noncompulsive behavior. As a group, however, the predictors of survey-reported delinquency did not identify a strong effect of parental pathology. Instead, variables related to parent-child relationship and child behaviors indicating early emotional difficulties and social maladjustment were of greater importance. There is a strong indication in these data that even after the ethnic and class differentials are removed two overlapping but relatively distinct etiologies may be involved—one emphasizing social modeling and early mental development and the other primarily determined by early emotional-social adjustment problems.

For females, the unique predictors in the congruence sample further verify those identified in predicting survey-reported delinquency. Certain ethnically related differences are observed: namely, being Spanish and mother-traditional-restrictive are more important for the prediction which takes publicly reported information into account while lower class and maternal rejection contribute to survey-reported delinquency. The child behaviors which contribute uniquely are, however, identical, with the only difference being the considerably larger contribution of delusion-hallucination to delinquency in the congruence sample. For adolescent females, then, it appears that a fairly uniform etiology operates across (or independent of) the criterion measure used. Early severe emotional pathology seems of crucial importance.

CONCLUSION

The analysis clearly demonstrates that social, familial, and early child behaviors reported before the onset of publicly recorded delinquency, and excluding the effect of concurrent peer influence, are highly predictive of later delinquent behavior. It also indicates that by refining the criterion measure, particularly that derived from official records, greater accuracy in the measurement and prediction of delinquency can be achieved.

Inasmuch as any classificatory system ultimately relies on its relationship with an identifiable etiology, delinquent behavior among males does not appear to constitute one overlapping or continuous dimension of behavior. Instead, two relatively distinct antecedent patterns appear to be involved. In contrast, for females a relatively uniform pattern accounts for antisocial delinquent behavior.

Considering the results of previous studies and their implications in terms of prevention, the dominant lesson suggests that analyses focusing on isolated variables or variable sets may be etiologically misleading. As indicated in this analysis, school behavior to which much attention has been devoted in delinquency research is, when other early behaviors are considered, not of great unique importance. In light of earlier studies, then, it might be necessary to more clearly distinguish the most accessible and practical setting for intervention—whether school, home, or an alternative setting—from the etiological factors which should be considered in setting treatment and prevention plans.

FOOTNOTES

*This research comes from the Division of Epidemiology, Columbia University School of Public Health. This investigation was supported by U.S. Public Health Service Project Grant MH 11545 and MH 18260 of the National Institute of Mental Health, Center for Epidemiologic Studies; by the U.S. Department of Heath, Education, and Welfare, Social and Rehabilitation Service, Cooperative Research and Demonstration Grants Branch, grant SRS-CRD-348 (SRS-56006); by the Office of Child Development, grants OCD-CB-348 and OCD-CB-480; and by the National Institute of Mental Health, Center for Studies of Crime and Delinquency, grant MH 28182. The principal investigator was supported by Career Scientist Awards I-338 and I-640, Health Research Council of the City of New York, and is currently receiving Research Scientist Award MH 20868, NIMH.

†Thomas S. Langner, Ph.D., Professor of Clinical Psychiatric Epidemiology (in Public Health) and Director, Family Research Project (FRP), Elizabeth D. McCarthy, M.A., Staff Associate in Epidemiology, Joanne C. Gersten, Ph.D., Associate Professor of Public Health (Epidemiology) and Associate Director, FRP, Ora Simcha-Fagan, D.S.W., Assistant Professor of Public Health (Epidemiology), Jeanne G. Eisenberg, M.A., Senior Staff Associate in Epidemiology.

1. A total of 139 cases were dropped from the welfare sample because of extreme follow-up sample time-interval problems between the two interviews and because some of the families moved from AFDC to some other type of public assistance.

2. Using a hierarchical profile analysis, the Time I data yielded six behavioral *types* of welfare children: Mildly Dependent, 51 percent of the sample; Aggressive Backward Isolate, 24 percent; Competitive-Independent, 14 percent; Delinquent-Aggressive, 6 percent; Self and Other Destructive, 2 percent; and Delusional, 2 percent. The strength of this procedure is that it allowed us to move from a discussion of the prevalence of various traits in welfare children to a classification of *kinds* of welfare children. This technique thus has obvious implications for planning and intervention in the population being studied.

3. In comparing the Time II samples, rigid controls must be made for length of time between interviews; otherwise the ages of the children and some other variables are no longer comparable. Due to time and funding problems, the welfare sample was necessarily completed with a somewhat shorter length of time between interviews than the cross-

sectional sample. To assure strict comparability between the Time II samples, a special analysis was conducted with 222 welfare cases that were rigidly matched to the 732 cross-sectional cases. The results obtained when the sample of 222 was compared to the cross-sectional sample were identical to the results obtained when the welfare sample of 522 was compared to the cross-sectional sample on the five central factors being discussed.

4. The means for the five central child behavior factors under discussion in the Time II data were as follows, for the cross-sectional and welfare samples, respectively. (A lower score indicates *more* of that behavior.) Delinquency, 129.64 and 127.77; Dependence, 15.80 and 13.70; Conflict with Parents, 169.95 and 170.56; Regressive Anxiety, 117.01 and 115.59; and Fighting, 125.01 and 122.84.

5. The Time II data has indicated that the developmental paths of children in the welfare sample differ by ethnic group. These processes, for the different behavioral areas, are extremely intricate and are currently being analyzed in depth and prepared for publication. Generally, the Spanish-speaking welfare children showed the greatest improvement through time, relative to the black and white welfare children. Concerning the problem of the broader comparisons of child behavior over time between the welfare and cross-sectional samples, the proportion of Spanish-speaking children in the welfare sample, 38 percent was somewhat larger than the proportion of Spanish-speaking children in the cross-section, 29 percent. However, since the Spanish-speaking children showed the greatest relative improvement through time, the more general finding of poorer functioning of the welfare child through time was a conservative estimate, because of the greater proportion of Spanish-speaking children in the welfare sample than in the cross-section.

6. *Ontogenetic* indicates the origin and course of development of an individual organism; it denotes the abstract general problem of origin and development within the organism's life history.

7. Self-reported information on delinquent behavior was collected for a subsample in late adolescence. Overall, the relationship between mother's and child's report of delinquent behavior is high ($r = .70$). There are, however, discernible differences with regard to certain types of behaviors, particularly when the data are examined within ethnic subgroups. An analysis focusing on the triangular relationship of mother, child, and police-reported delinquent behavior is being reported separately.

8. A separate index of violent behavior against peers as well as within the family was constructed and is included in a broader analysis of antisocial behavior.

9. The reliability, internal consistency, of the measure as determined by coefficient alpha, is .58 at Time I and .71 at Time II. The Time I measure excludes some of the detailed items concerning type of illicit drug used.

10. An additional variable—Time I mother-reported delinquency score—was used in predicting later police offenses.

REFERENCES

Andry, Robert G. (1960), *Delinquency and Parental Pathology*. Springfield, Illinois: Charles C. Thomas.

Bacon, H. K., I. L. Child and H. A. Barry (1963), "A cross-cultural study of correlates of crime," *Journal of Abnormal and Social Psychology* 66:291–300.

Baltes, P. B. (Ed.) (1973), "Life-span models of psychological aging: A white elephant?" *Gerontologist* 13:457–512.

Baltes, P. B., and J. R. Nesselroade (1972), "Cultural change and adolescent personality development: An application of longitudinal sequences," *Developmental Psychology* 7:244–256.

Baltes, P. B. and K. W. Schaie (Eds.) (1973), *Life-Span Developmental Psychology: Personality and Socialization.* New York: Academic Press.

Bandura, A., and R. Walters (1959), *Adolescent Aggression.* New York: Ronald Press.

—— (1963), *Social Learning and Personality Development.* New York: Holt, Rinehart & Winston.

Barnes, K. E. (1971), "Preschool play norms: A replication," *Developmental Psychology* 5:99–103.

Bastide, Roger (1972), *The Sociology of Mental Disorder* (Tr. Jean McNeil). New York: David McKay Co.

Beiser, Morton (1972), "Etiology of mental disorders: Sociocultural aspects," in B. B. Wolman (Ed.), *Manual of Child Psychopathology.* New York: McGraw-Hill.

Bennett, I. (1962), *Delinquent and Neurotic Children: A Comparative Study.* New York: McGraw-Hill.

Biller, H. B. (1970), "Father absence and the personality development of the male child," *Developmental Psychology* 2:181–201.

Clark, John P., and Larry L. Tifft (1966), "Polygraph and interview validation of self-reported deviant behavior," *American Sociological Review* 31:516–523.

Cloward, Richard, and Lloyd E. Ohlin (1960), *Delinquency and Opportunity: A Theory of Delinquent Gangs.* Glencoe, Illinois: The Free Press.

Cohen, Albert K. (1955), *Delinquent Boys: The Culture of the Gang.* Glencoe, Illinois: The Free Press.

Coser, L. (1965), "The sociology of poverty," *Social Problems* 13:140–148.

Datan, N., and L. H. Ginsberg (Eds.) (1975), *Life-Span Developmental Psychology: Normative Life Crises.* New York: Academic Press.

Deutsch, Martin, and Bert Brown (1964), "Social influences in Negro-white intelligence differences," *Social Issues* 20:24–35.

Douglas, J. W. B. (1964), *The Home and the School.* London: Macgibbon & Kee.

—— (1966), "The school progress of nervous and troublesome children," *The British Journal of Psychiatry* 112:1115–1116.

Eisenberg, J. G., J. C. Gersten, T.S. Langner, E.D. McCarthy, and O. Simcha-Fagan (1976), "A behavioral classification of welfare children from survey data," *American Journal of Orthopsychiatry* 46:447–463.

——, T. S. Langner, and J. C. Gersten (1975), "Differences in the behavior of welfare and non-welfare children in relation to parental characteristics," *Journal of Community Psychology,* Monograph 48 (October).

Elliott, S. Delbert, and Harwin L. Voss (1974), *Delinquency and Dropout.* Lexington, Mass.: Heath Lexington Books.

Empey, LaMar T., and Steven G. Lubeck (1971), *Explaining Delinquency: Construction, Test and Reformulation of a Sociological Theory.* Lexington, Mass.: Heath Lexington Books.

Erickson, Maynard C., and LaMar T. Empey (1963), "Court records, undetected delinquency and decision-making," *Journal of Criminal Law, Criminology and Police Sciences* 54:456–464.

Freedman, L. Z. (1962), "Psychopathology and poverty," Thirteenth Annual Human Development Symposium at the University of Chicago (April).

Frierson, E. (1965), "Upper and lower status gifted children: A study of differences," *Exceptional Children* 32:83–89.

Gersten, J. C., T. S. Langner, J. G. Eisenberg, O. Simcha-Fagan, and E. D. McCarthy

(1976), "Stability and change in types of behavioral disturbance of children and adolescents," *Journal of Abnormal Child Psychology* 4:111–127.

Glueck, Sheldon, and Eleanor Glueck (1950), *Unraveling Juvenile Delinquency*. New York: Commonwealth Fund.

Gold, Martin (1966), "Undetected delinquent behavior," *Journal of Research in Crime and Delinquency* 3:27–46.

—— (1970), *Delinquent Behavior in an American City*. Belmont, California: Brooks Cole.

Goulet, L. R., and P. B. Baltes (Eds.) (1970), *Life-Span Developmental Psychology: Research and Theory*. New York: Academic Press.

Herzog, Elizabeth, and Cecelia Sudia (1968), "Fatherless homes: A review of research," *Children* 15 (September):177–182.

Hess, Robert D. (1970), "Social class and ethnic influences on socialization," in Paul H. Mussen (Ed.), *Carmichael's Manual of Child Psychology,* Third Edition. New York: Wiley

Hewitt, L. E. and R. L. Jenkins (1946), *Fundamental Patterns of Maladjustment: The Dynamics of Their Origin*. Springfield, Illinois: Green.

Hirschi, Travis (1969), *Causes of Delinquency*. Berkeley, Calif.: University of California Press.

——, and Hanan C. Selvin (1967), *Delinquency Research: An Appraisal of Analytic Methods*. New York: The Free Press.

Hollingshead, A. B., and F. C. Redlich (1958), *Social Class and Mental Illness, a Community Study*. New York: Wiley.

Huston-Stein, A., and P. B. Baltes (1976), "Theory and method in life-span developmental psychology: Implications for child development," in Hayne W. Reese (Ed.), *Advances in Child Development and Behavior,* Vol 11. New York: Academic Press.

Jenkins, R. L. (1966), "Psychiatric syndromes in children and their relation to family background," *American Journal of Orthopsychiatry* 36:450–457.

Kadushin, Alfred (1968), "Single-parent adoptions: An overview and some relevant research." New York: Child Welfare League of America.

Kellmer-Pringle, M. L., N. R. Butler, and R. Davie (1966), *11,000 Seven Year Olds. The National Child Development Study.*London: Longmans, Green & Co.

Kohlberg, L., J. LaCrosse, and D. Ricks (1972), "The predictability of adult mental health from childhood behavior," in B. B. Wolman (Ed.), *Manual of Child Psychopathology*. New York: McGraw-Hill.

Kriesberg, Louis (1970), *Mothers in Poverty: A Study of Fatherless Families*. Chicago: Aldine Publishing.

Langner, T. S., J. C. Gersten, E. L. Greene, J. G. Eisenberg, J. H. Herson, and E. D. McCarthy (1974), "Treatment of psychological disorders among urban children," *Journal of Consulting and Clinical Psychology* 42:170–179.

Lapouse, R., and M. A. Monk (1958), "An epidemiological study of behavior characteristics in children," *American Journal of Public Health* 48:1134–1144.

—— (1964), "Behavior deviations in a representative sample of children: Variation by sex, age, race, social class and family size," *American Journal of Orthopsychiatry* 34:436–446.

Long, A. (1941), "Parents' reports of undesirable behavior in children," *Child Development* 12:43–62.

Maccoby, E. D., and C. G. Jacklin (1974), *The Psychology of Sex Differences*. Stanford: Stanford University Press.

MacDonald, M., C. McGuire, and R. J. Havighurst (1949), "Leisure activities and the socioeconomic status of children," *American Journal of Sociology* 54: 505–519.

MacFarlane, J. W., L. Allen, and M. P. Honzik (1954), *A Developmental Study of the Behavior Problems of Normal Children between Twenty-one Months and Fourteen Years*. Berkeley: University of California Press.

McCarthy, E. D., J. C. Gersten, T. S. Langner, J. G. Eisenberg, and L. Orzeck. (Forthcoming), "The effects of father absence on children and their mothers: A test of the culture of poverty thesis."

——, T. S. Langner, J. C. Gersten, J. G. Eisenberg, and L. Orzeck (1975), "The effects of television on children and adolescents: Violence and behavior disorders," *Journal of Communication* 25(4):71–85.

McCord, W., J. McCord, and A. Howard (1961), "Familial correlates of aggression in non-delinquent male children," *Journal of Abnormal and Social Psychology* 62:79–83.

Merton, Robert K. (1957), *Social Theory and Social Structure*, New York: The Free Press.

Miller, S. M. (1964), "The American lower class: A typological approach," *Sociology and Social Research* 48:1–22.

Miller, Daniel, and Guy Swanson (1958), *The Changing American Parent*. New York: Wiley.

Miller, Walter B. (1958), "Lower class culture as a generating milieu of gang delinquency," *The Journal of Social Issues* 14:5–19.

Nesselroade, J. R., and P. B. Baltes (1974), "Adolescent personality development and historical change: 1970–1972." Monographs of the Society for Research in Child Development 39 (I. Serial No. 154).

——, and H. W. Reese (Eds.) (1973), *Life-Span Developmental Psychology: Methodological Issues*. New York: Academic Press.

Neugarten, B.L. (1946), "Social class and friendship among school children," *American Journal of Sociology* 51:305–313.

Nunnally, J. C. (1973), "Research strategies and measurement methods for investigating human development," in J. R. Nesselroade and A. W. Reese (Eds.), *Life-Span Developmental Psychology: Methodological Issues*. New York: Academic Press.

Nye, F. Ivan (1958), *Family Relationships and Delinquent Behavior*. New York: Wiley.

——, and James F. Short, Jr. (1957), "Scaling delinquent behavior," *American Sociological Review* 22:326–331.

Quay, Herbert C., and John S. Werry (1972), *Psychopathological Disorders of Childhood*. New York: Wiley.

Rein, M. (1974), "The welfare crisis," in L. Rainwater (Ed.), *Social Problems and Public Policy: Inequality and Justice*. Chicago: Aldine.

Rennie, T. A. C., L. Srole, M. K. Opler, and T. S. Langner (1957), "Socioeconomic status and mental disorder in the metropolis," *American Journal of Psychiatry* 113:831–837.

Robins, Lee N. (1966), *Deviant Children Grown Up*. Baltimore, Md.: The Williams and Wilkins Co.

——, Patricia A. West, and Barbara L. Herjanic (1975), "Arrests and delinquency in two generations: A study of black urban families and their children," *Journal of Child Psychology and Psychiatry* 16:125–140.

Robison, Sophia M. (1936), *Can Delinquency Be Measured?* New York: Columbia University Press.

Rutter, M. and P. Graham (1966), "Psychiatric disorder in 10 and 11-year old children," *Proceedings of the Royal Society of Medicine* 59:382–387.

——, J. Tizard, and K. Whitmore (1970), *Education, Health and Behavior*. London: Longman.

Sanua, Victor (s.d.), "The epidemiology and etiology of mental illness and problems of methodology: A review of the literature." New York: Yeshiva University (Unpublished).

Schaie, K. W. (1970), "A reinterpretation of age-related changes in cognitive structure and functioning," in L. R. Goulet and P. B. Baltes (Eds.), *Life-Span Developmental Psychology: Research and Theory*. New York: Academic Press.

―――, K. Gribbin (1975), "Adult development and aging," *Annual Review of Psychology* 26:65–96.

Schields, J., and E. Slater (1961), "Heredity and psychological abnormality," in H. J. Eysenck (Ed.) *Handbook of Abnormal Psychology*. New York: Basic Books.

Schwartz, Madelyn, and Joanne C. Gersten (1976), "Antecedent Familial Conditions of School Drop-outs." New York: Columbia University (unpublished).

Sewell, W., and A. Haller (1959), "Factors in the relationship between social status and the personality adjustment of the child," *American Sociological Review* 24:511–520.

Shepherd, M., B. Oppenheim, and S. Mitchell (1971), *Childhood Behavior and Mental Health*. New York: Grune & Stratton.

Simcha-Fagan, Ora, Joanne C. Gersten, Thomas S. Langner, and Jeanne G. Eisenberg (Forthcoming), "Antecedents and correlates of illicit drug use in a sample of urban youth."

―――, Thomas S. Langner, Joanne C. Gersten and Jeanne G. Eisenberg (1975), "Violent and antisocial behavior: A longitudinal study of urban youth," Report of the Office of Child Development. OCD-CB-480.

Slater, E., and M. Roth (1969), *Clinical Psychiatry,* Third Edition. London: Cassell.

Spray, Jetse (1967), "The study of single parenthood: Some methodological considerations," *The Family Life Co-ordinator* 16 (January–April):29–34.

Terry, Robert (1967), "The screening of juvenile offenders," *Journal of Criminal Law, Criminology and Police Science* 58:173–181.

Thomas, A., S. Chess, and H. Birch (1970), "The origins of personality," *Scientific American* 223:102–109.

Tuddenham, R. D., J. Brooks, and L. Milkovich (1974), "Mother's reports of behavior of ten-year olds: Relationship with sex, ethnicity and mother's education," *Developmental Psychology* 10(6):959–995.

U.S. Bureau of the Census (1970), "Selected characteristics of persons and families, March 1970." Current Population Reports, Population Characteristics, Series P-20, No. 204 (July 13).

Wardle, C. J. (1961), "Two generations of broken homes in the genesis of conduct and behavior diorders in children," *British Medical Journal* (July–August): 349–354.

Wardrop, K. R. H. (1967), "Delinquent teenage types," *British Journal of Criminology* 714:371–380.

Wohlwill, J. F. (1970), "Methodology and research strategy in the study of developmental change," in L. R. Goulet and P. B. Baltes (Eds.), *Life-Span Developmental Psychology: Research and Theory*. New York: Academic Press.

Wolfgang, Marvin E., Robert M. Figlio, and Thorsten Sellin (1972), *Delinquency in a Birth Cohort*. Chicago: University of Chicago Press.

THE IMPACT OF PARENTAL
MENTAL ILLNESS ON
CHILDREN[1]

John A. Clausen and Carol L. Huffine, UNIVERSITY OF
CALIFORNIA AT BERKELEY

The mental illness of a loved one is a life-disrupting experience at any age.
For a child, the impact of the mental illness of a parent may range from
short-term traumatization to domination of the child's early life experience. Most research on the impact of mental illness on children has
tended to focus either on the behavior of mentally ill mothers (usually
soon after a period of hospitalization) toward young children or has
sought evidence of psychological disturbance through cross-sectional
study of mentally ill parents. The current report is derived from a study
with a broader focus on the impact of mental illness on the family, as
assessed soon after a husband or wife's initial hospitalization, with subsequent follow-up of one cohort of patients fifteen to twenty years later.

Research in Community and Mental Health, Vol. 1, pp 183–214.
Copyright © 1979 by JAI Press Inc.
All rights of reproduction in any form reserved.
ISBN 0-89232-063-X

We shall be dealing with two groups of patients, one hospitalized in the 1950's and the other in the early 1970's both comprised largely of functional psychotics who had not been previously treated for mental disorder.

The questions to be addressed here fall into two categories, one dealing with the family situation in the period antecedent to and during the patient's initial hospitalization and the other dealing with the children's later development and current situation. For the earlier period we sought to delineate the ways in which the initial symptomatology of the patient impinged upon the children, as reported by the spouse, the orientation of the well spouse to the children's needs, and the ways in which family functioning appears to have been influenced by the initial episode of illness. The second set of questions relates to the long-term implications for the children's development, as assessed through follow-up interviews with the spouse (or occasionally the patient or even one of the children) in which we sought to secure detailed data on the current status and developmental history of each of the children in the family.

Prior studies leave no doubt that parental mental illness, and especially that of the mother, leads to severe deficits in the ability to respond to offspring and may be accompanied by child abuse as well as neglect. Research on behaviors of mothers toward their offspring following an initial period of treatment for an acute schizophrenic episode suggests that many of these mothers are unable for some months to respond appropriately to the needs of the child (Garmezy, 1974; Grunebaum et al., 1974; Rodnick and Goldstein, 1974). Heavy dosage with ataractic drugs is often implicated in the lack of responsiveness of the mother. Weissman and Paykel (1974) also report considerable impairment of mother-child relations among depressed women, who show a high frequency of hostility and guilt.

Elizabeth Rice and her associates (1971) focused specifically on the impact of parental mental disorder on the children, with data obtained from the well parent or other child caretaker. Many instances of child neglect and child abuse on the part of the patient came to the attention of the workers, but less than half of the caretakers were aware of behavior problems or other symptoms of psychological disturbance in the children. Rogler and Hollingshead (1965) also reported widespread neglect and child abuse in their study of lower-status Puerto Rican families with a schizophrenic parent. These authors noted also that mothers married to schizophrenic men seemed to be coping successfully with the family problems their husbands' illness had forced upon them and that there were fewer serious behavioral problems where the father was the patient than where the mother was. In families where the mother was hospitalized, fathers tended largely to ignore their children; in these families there was almost universal evidence of school retardation and of severely disturbed behavior in the children.

E. James Anthony (1971) reported several distinct types of reaction in preadolescent children of parents hospitalized for mental illness. It was his impression that chronically psychotic patients had less severely disturbed children than did parents with acute disturbances, that children were more disturbed by parental acting out than by parental avoidance and neglect, and that children's adaptations and adjustment were markedly enhanced when the nonpsychotic parent was oriented toward being helpful to them. Rutter (1966) found that psychiatrically ill children were three times as likely to have psychiatrically ill parents as were children seen in dental and pediatric services. Children who were disturbed came more often from families where: (1) the mother was the patient; (2) the children were directly involved in the patient's symptoms; (3) the other parent was also psychologically disturbed; and (4) the parent's illness was long-lasting. In another study, Rutter (1971) found a higher than expected incidence of antisocial behavior among sons of mental patients, especially in families characterized by marital discord.

Several of the papers reviewed by Garmezy (1974) suggest that children who are under three at the time of the mother's initial hospitalization are especially vulnerable, both because of the likelihood that the mother is unable to provide loving care and because of the critical consequences of separation of child and mother in the early period after a close bond has been established.

As earlier noted, most of these studies have assessed parents or children or both at a single point in time. An exception is the long-term research of Bleuler (1974), as yet only partially reported in English, on the course of schizophrenia and its consequences for parents and children. Knowing in considerable detail the life histories of his patients and their children, Bleuler was more struck with the resilience and emotional strength of the offspring than by their pathology. Acknowledging that many of the children had suffered damage to their self-esteem and had difficulties in relating to the opposite sex, Bleuler nevertheless regarded three-fourths of them as "mentally sound and non-eccentric."

One of the very few studies to assess the long-term impact of parental mental illness on the development of children was a fifteen year follow-up of children of schizophrenic mothers by Miller, Challas, and Gee (1972). These investigators relied primarily on a search of records of schools, courts, and mental health facilities in the community to which a group of schizophrenic mothers returned in 1956. The follow-up, conducted in 1971, sought evidence of problems among children of schizophrenic mothers as compared with children of samples of welfare mothers, control families at the same socioeconomic level as the schizophrenic mothers, and a random sample of urban families. The sample of patients was predominantly nonwhite and overwhelmingly working class. The investigators concluded that the children of schizophrenic mothers differed little in developmental deviance from children of other lower-class families. If anything, children of schizophrenic mothers showed fewer school problems and a smaller proportion of serious deviancy than children of either welfare mothers or controls matched on socioeconomic status. In the words of these investigators: "Residential transience, welfare, foster and adoptive homes, black skin—*these* are the truly important variables, beside which the schizophrenia of a mother pales in comparison." While this study did not deal directly with the experience of the children, it presents a crucial argument overlooked in most of the literature, namely that the social context within which the schizophrenia occurs and the resources available to the family may be of overwhelming importance in determining outcomes for the children.

Summarizing the somewhat varied findings of prior research, there is reason to anticipate more difficulties among children of psychotic mothers than among those of psychotic fathers, among children who are directly involved in the patient's symptomatic behavior (especially hostile behavior), among those whose well parents are unable to be supportive and understanding, and in families characterized by marital conflict. Severe problems can be expected far more often in working-class than in middle-class families. Insofar as possible, we have examined these issues in our own data analysis, but our objective has also been to delineate the nature of the social situation facing parents and children when one parent becomes mentally ill and the ways in which the well parent tends to balance the several sets of needs—home, patient's and children's—in attempting to cope with the immediate problems posed by mental disorder.

THE RESEARCH

The current report draws upon data from a two-phase study of the impact of mental illness on the family. Phase I was carried out in the 1950's at the Laboratory of Socio-Environmental Studies at NIMH and entailed interviews with husbands or wives of white, native-born patients, aged 20 to 49, who had recently been admitted to a mental hospital for the first time with a diagnosis of functional psychosis or severe psychoneurosis. These were serially selected (i.e., successive admissions meeting the criteria) during periods of interviewer availability; less than 10 percent of the wives of male patients refused to be interviewed while about 20 percent of the husbands of female patients denied interviews.

In the course of the original study, we shifted from a sequence of up to fifteen semi-structured interviews over the period of the patient's hospitalization (first thirty-three families)[2] to a set of four structured interviews. In all, eighty-eight families were seen, but some did not meet the sample specifications by virtue of diagnosis, age of patient or evidence of an earlier episode of mental disorder. The present report deals with the sixty-three families in the original group who met sampling specifications plus seventeen families of schizophrenic women hospitalized from the San Franciso Bay area in the late 1950's who were studied intensively by Sampson, Messinger, and Towne (1964) in a separate but roughly parallel project. Both groups of families (i.e., eighty in all) were followed up in 1972–1974 as Phase 2 of the research.

In the follow-up, we interviewed the spouse, the patient, or another relative in sixty-six of the eighty families who constituted the Phase I basic sample, and secured at least some data on the situation of eight other families. In most instances where there were interviews, data were obtained on the current status and developmental histories of the children (in large families focusing on the oldest four children). Some interviews had to be conducted by telephone, and for these it was not always feasible to secure complete developmental histories of the children. Overall, however, we were able to secure at least some information as of follow-up on 149 children.

The interviews at time of initial breakdown inquired into child-care arrangements during the patient's hospitalization, communication with the children concerning the patient's illness, signs of upset in the children, and, for a part of the sample, the relationship between the patient and the children after the patient's return from the hospital. The follow-up interview inquired into the current whereabouts of the children, the nature of each child's current relationship with patient and spouse, the level of education completed, age at leaving home and evidence of developmental problems.

A number of the children were interviewed, either separately or with siblings, in instances where parents had indicated a willingness or even desire for such interviews. In several instances where the patient and spouse were both dead or were inaccessible, our primary respondent was an adult son or daughter of the patient. Such respondents usually volunteered some information on the ways in which the parent's illness had affected their own development.

Phase II of the research also entailed study of a new cohort of forty families of patients entering treatment in the 1970's. We shall draw upon the data from this group of families for limited comparisons with the earlier cohort.

The original sample of eighty families included thirty-six in which the husband was the patient (twenty diagnosed schizophrenic and sixteen affective disorders or other diagnoses) and forty-four in which the wife was the patient (thirty-eight diagnosed schizophrenic and six affective disorders). Seventy-one of the families had children at the time of the patient's initial hospitalization and at least seventeen of these families added one or more children after the patient's return home. The current

Table 1

Characteristics of Patients by Sex and Diagnosis

	Male		Female	
	Schiz.	Other	Schiz.	Other
Total Number of Children	20	16	37	6
Age at admission:				
Less than 30	7	4	13	3
30 – 39	11	5	16	2
40 – 49	2	7	8	1
Not ascertained	–	–	1	–
Education:				
Less than high school graduate	5	5	16	2
High school graduate	6	3	11	3
College, any amount	9	8	7	–
Not ascertained	–	–	4	1
Duration of marriage at hospitalization:				
Less than 5 years	8	6	8	1
5 – 9 years	6	3	14	2
10 – 14 years	5	2	8	1
15 years and over	1	5	4	2
Not ascertained	–	–	4	–
Duration of hospitalization:				
Less than 3 months	5	6	16	2
3 up to 6 months	9	6	11	1
6 months to 1 year	3	3	6	1
1 year or more	2	1	3	1
Not ascertained	1	–	2	1

number of children is unknown for eight of the families who were not interviewed in recent years.

Table 1 indicates certain of the demographic characteristics of our patients, by sex and diagnosis. Except for the nonschizophrenic males, the large majority of each group of patients were under 40 years of age. Educational status of the hospitalized women was somewhat lower than that of the male patients (and the social status of the husbands of the female patients was lower than that of the male patients).

More than one-third of the patients had been married at least five years and nearly two-thirds had been married ten or more years. Thus, on the whole we are dealing with marriages that had endured long enough for the spouses to have developed relatively stable expectations.

Duration of hospitalization tended to be least for schizophrenic women, of whom nearly half were hospitalized less than three months. This was not, however, an indication of lesser severity of illness. Rather it reflects a sharp change in policy and practice with reference to duration of hospitalization after the introduction of tranquilizers in the mid-1950's. Our research began with the families of male patients in 1952, before the use of tranquilizers; no female patients were seen before 1955. While half of our male patients had been admitted by late 1954, half of our female patients were not admitted until 1958. In the intervening period, the mean duration of hospitalization for first admission patients dropped by nearly one-half in the hospitals included in the research. Data on the initial episode of illness and on subsequent symptomatology suggest that the female patients were in fact more seriously disturbed and more persistently symptomatic than were the male patients.

For families with children in the group followed up, the mean number of children at follow-up was 2.2 for schizophrenic males, 2.0 for males with other diagnoses, 2.8 for schizophrenic females, and 1.8 for the small group of females with affective disorders. The age distribution of the children at the time of the parent's initial hospitalization is given in Table 2.

Before turning to a discussion of findings, a cautionary note relating to interpretation of the data is called for. The impact of a parent's mental illness upon the children may reflect both genetic and experiential features. In the present study, the children of female schizophrenics would seem to be doubly vulnerable to impairment in that the mothers are more likely than the fathers to have poor prognoses. They have experienced much longer durations of symptomatic behavior and impaired functioning in the years since initial hospitalization.[3] Moreover, men who marry and father children are a very select subsample among schizophrenic males, since establishment of a relationship with the opposite sex is perhaps the best single indicator of favorable prognosis. Such men are, then, more

Table 2

Age Distribution of Children at Time of Patients' Initial
Admission, by Sex and Diagnosis of Patient

| | Male | | Female | |
	Schiz.	Other	Schiz.	Other
Under 2	7	1	15	3
2 through 5	8	5	21	2
6 through 12	13	4	25	2
13 through 17	2	5	6	1
18 and over	–	4	1	1
Number of Children	30	19	68	9

likely to have a disorder of limited duration and there is reason to believe
that genetic vulnerability plays a less important role in their breakdown
(Rosenthal, 1971). The children of the schizophrenic fathers would thus
be less likely to inherit a tendency toward schizophrenia than would those
of schizophrenic mothers. At the same time, since children tend to be
closer to their mothers than to their fathers, we might expect more upset
when the mother is the patient. There is no way in which we can distinguish effects of heredity from those resulting from life experience.

THE FAMILY SITUATION ANTECEDENT TO HOSPITALIZATION

As previously noted, the median duration of marriages in this group of
first admission patients was between five and ten years for both male and
female patients. We attempted to ascertain the degree of marital satisfaction prevailing in these families prior to the spouse's first perception that
"something was wrong" with the patient. Dissatisfaction and conflict
were more often evident in the families of female patients; less than one-
fifth of the marriages were rated happy (on the basis of spouses' reports
and information available for hospital records), and many had been
characterized by long-standing, pervasive conflict. Most of the marriages
of male patients, on the other hand, were rated happy and only one-tenth
had been characterized by long-standing conflict.

Symptoms of emotional disturbance were more long-standing in
families where the wife was the patient. Husbands of a majority of these
women, in both happy and unhappy marriages, dated the onset of

symptomatic behaviors more than a year before entry into the hospital (though at the time they often had not interpreted the symptoms as manifestations of an emotional disorder). Where the husband was the patient, only one-fourth had been seen as showing symptomatic behavior for more than a year prior to admission, and none of these couples was rated "happily married."

The patient's early symptomatology gave rise to confusion, annoyance, and anger in most families, for it was more often interpreted as intentional deviance or weakness than as mental disorder. A core of sympathetic response was found in roughly half of the families where the marital relationship had been good but in very few families where it had been poor.

In families of female patients in which the marital relationship had been very poor, three-fourths of the husbands responded to their wives' symptomatic behavior with overtly expressed anger. Conflict often built up to explosive levels and resulted in the wife's making a suicide attempt or venting rage destructively in a number of families.

We emphasize that even when the marital relationship had been good, there was much anger and confusion during the period antecedent to hospitalization. Most often the children were not directly involved in the patient's first manifestations of symptomatic behavior, so that the turmoil of conflict and the preoccupation of the well spouse may well have been the most salient features of the early stages of the parent's mental disorder. Serious neglect of the children or abusive behavior was not uncommon in *later* stages and was often a precursor to arranging for hospitalization, especially in the case of mothers.

The relationship between patient and children was reported to have been affected prior to hospitalization in roughly two-thirds of the families. When the mother was the patient, and the marital relationship was good, the mother's relationship with the children was seldom reported to have been seriously affected until shortly before hospitalization. Where the marital relationship had been poor, however, the mother-child relationship was significantly ($p < .05$) more often said to have been affected for more than three months prior to hospitalization. A similar trend held for fathers, but this would be expected by virtue of the longer duration of symptoms when the marital relationship was poor. Thus, it appears that in the presence of a good marital relationship a mother's symptomatic behavior impinged less directly upon the children.

When we asked directly about the children's reactions to the patient, however, the spouses' reports did not vary appreciably according to ratings of the marriage. Roughly a third of the children in each group were reported to have been upset or frightened by the patient's behavior. Nearly a fifth were reportedly unaware of the problem despite being old enough to understand and the remainder were reported to be either too young to understand or to have accepted the patient's behavior with little reaction. As in the research by Elizabeth Rice, we found that many of the well parents seemed almost totally oblivious of signs of upset in their children, despite (or perhaps because of) their own marked emotional upset in the face of the patient's behavior.

We did not record in sufficient detail the ways in which the patient's behavior impinged on the children in our original study, but did so for the forty families studied more recently. Male patients tended either to withdraw from the children and not to respond to them or to become more critical. Mothers were also sometimes less responsive but more often were reported to be critical, severe, or (occasionally) hostile or bizarre in dealing with the children. Where the mother was the patient, more than half of the children were reported to have been either frightened by or angry in response to their mothers' symptomatic behaviors.

Very few of the well parents were able to discuss the nature of the patient's problem with the children. Prior to hospitalization, many were unable to define the nature of the problem for themselves; subsequently, most avoided telling the children that the patient's problem was a mental or emotional disorder. Wives of male patients were somewhat more likely than husbands of female patients to explain the true reason for hospitalization, but the majority either glossed over the nature of the patient's problem or ascribed it to physical illness.

In the recent cohort, thirty families had children beyond infancy living at home. Again we found that only about a third of the wives of male patients and less than a fourth of the husbands of female patients explained to the children that the other parent was suffering from a mental or emotional problem. When asked why they had not offered some explanation of the patient's disturbing behavior at home and subsequent hospitalization, our recent informants gave the same reasons that we had received twenty years ago. Some felt that the children "knew what was going on" and therefore it wasn't necessary to talk about it. Others, with children of comparable age, reported that the children were "too young to understand." A few acknowledged that they were either too upset themselves or simply weren't able to talk about the problem.

Thus, despite increased public information about mental illness and the availability of informational materials on what to tell a child whose parent is mentally ill (Arnstein, 1960), there appears to have been little change in the guidance provided children facing the bewildering sequence of events that led to hospitalization of one of their parents. Only a very few parents, mostly mothers, seemed aware of the possibility that a child might feel that he or she was to blame for the angry or upset behavior of the patient before hospitalization. Interviews with some of the children, to be reported later, revealed that some had felt guilty and others angry, though the well spouse had reported lack of reaction in the child or said that the child "knew what was going on" and needed no explanation.

Care of Children During Initial Hospitalization
In the early years of the research, the duration of a man's initial hospitalization often exceeded six months. Women whose husbands were hospitalized and who did not already have jobs or have adequate financial resources were often advised to take employment. Roughly one-third had already been working, and at least another third did take jobs within a month or two of their husband's hospitalization.

Whether or not they worked, a majority of the wives maintained their regular quarters and kept their children with them. A few moved in with their parents, and a few left the children during the day with their mothers, or more rarely, with the patient's mother, but by and large the wives managed to keep their children near by.

Where the wife was the patient, however, the family was less frequently kept together. A somewhat higher proportion of children were cared for by grandparents or other relatives, some of whom lived at a considerable distance. Thus, children whose mothers were hospitalized and who were sent to stay with relatives were more often deprived of the immediate availability of both parents. Very young children were far more likely to be placed outside the family home when the mother was the patient than when the father was the patient. Even when wives of male patients worked, they gave higher priority to the child's needs than did husbands of female patients.

By the 1970's, the duration of hospitalization does not usually exceed three weeks, and among the families we have recently studied it is quite unusual for any children to be placed with relatives except for daytime care. Arrangements tend to be temporary, except in the few instances where the patient remains seriously symptomatic. In no instance did a wife seek a job in the period immediately following her husband's hospitalization. On the contrary, a substantial proportion of mothers who had been working took time off from the job or put in shorter hours. This was equally true of husbands of female patients in the group of families studied in the early 1970's.

Returning to the families studied in the 1950's, where the children remained at home, older children tended to become confidants of the well spouse, especially when that spouse was the mother. Our data on hospital visiting by the children were not systematic in the original study. Many were taken to visit the patient when the hospital was near-by. But several of the hospitals from which we drew patients in the 1950's were relatively inaccessible unless the family had a car. Even when families did have a car, not all wives drove. Those children who did visit tended to do so infrequently.

In the 1970's, most of the hospitals are more readily accessible, and the great majority of patients in our present study group were visited by children, usually several times a week, as might be true if the patient were hospitalized for physical illness. Men who took children to visit their mothers tended to report that there had been "no problems" connected with the visit for the children—that they were not in any way nervous or upset. Women who took children to visit their hospitalized fathers more often reported that the children were apprehensive or nervous. Because of the small samples these differences are not statistically significant. No child was reported to have been *markedly* upset by a hospital visit.

Finally, in the group of families recently studied, we asked about the children's responses to the patient's absence. Most of the wives of male patients said that the children were visibly concerned or upset and two reported seriously upset behavior that persisted for some time. Husbands of female patients, on the other hand, reported lack of concern almost as frequently as concern or upset. In a couple of families with long-standing conflict or stress, they reported the children were relieved. Only one father reported an acutely disturbed child, though our interviewers either observed or inferred (from other statements made by fathers) three other instances of serious disturbance which the father did not recognize as such. In only one instance (in which the father was the patient), was psychiatric help sought for a child.

There is reason to believe that the amount of turmoil experienced by the children was much greater than the spouse-respondents indicated, and this was especially true when the mother was the patient. Our evidence on the meaning to a child of a parent's hospitalization for mental disorder is less adequate than we would wish. However, the observations of the children, which will be presented later, make clear that relatively few parents are able to perceive, no less respond to, the needs of their children when the other parent enters a mental hospital.

THE FAMILIES AND CHILDREN AT FOLLOW-UP

At the time of follow-up, the children in these families ranged in age from 8 to 35, with the majority in their late teens and early to mid-20's. Most of the children under 15 had been born after the patient's return from the hospital. We shall be concerned here only with the children who had been born at the time of the patient's initial hospitalization and who had resided with the study families at that time. The median and modal ages of the children varied little by sex and diagnosis of the patient, being in every instance between 20 and 22 years. Thus, most of the children were through adolescence but were still early in the period of maximum likelihood of breakdown from schizophrenia or other mental disorder.

Before examining in detail the data secured on the current status and developmental histories of these children, it may be helpful to summarize our findings with reference to the recurrence of symptomatology and the status of the marriage during the fifteen to twenty years intervening between initial hospitalization and our follow-up. More than 80 percent of the women and roughly half the men were rehospitalized one or more times in the intervening period. For the most part, these hospitalizations were of relatively short duration—a few weeks or at most a few months—but a number of the patients were persistently symptomatic and were being carried in outpatient treatment during their stays in the community.

Separation and Divorce
Twenty-six of the eighty couples separated prior to our follow-up. Separation most often came after a rehospitalization of the patient, an event frequently preceded by bizarre or hostile behavior. Four of the nine women with minor children who separated from their mentally ill husbands said that they did so partly because of fear for the children. Such fear was reported by only two of the husbands (after severe child abuse had already occurred), but in several other instances the husbands reported almost total neglect of the children by the sick mother.

Persistent or recurrent symptomatology in the patient was much more likely to lead to separation and divorce in the case of male patients whose work performance was thereby markedly impaired. A substantial proportion of their wives sought separation and/or divorce within three years of the husband's return from initial hospitalization. Husbands who did not manifest severe symptomatology after their initial hospitalization tended to have orderly careers and stable marriages; these couples not only stayed together but seemed predominantly happy.

Persistent symptomatology was less clearly related to termination of the marriage of female patients or even to the happiness of the marriage among those couples who remained together. Separation was not a clear-cut event in many of these families. Subsequent hospitalizations of the mother resulted in the children being placed with relatives or in foster care and in some instances the home simply was never reconstituted.

Husbands who separated from persistently symptomatic wives seldom secured formal divorces unless and until they planned to remarry. Minor children sometimes stayed with the mother as long as she was able to provide for them (often with some help from the father), but they were equally likely to remain under the father's nominal care, often lodged with a grandparent, a sibling of patient or spouse, or other relative. Sometimes, an older daughter took over the role of mother and maintained the home for her father and siblings. Some families were so amorphous that it would be hard to say whether or not they remained intact. Patient or spouse would periodically desert and there might be talk of divorce, but the couple would live alternately together or with one or another of the children once the latter were on their own.

To our surprise, our ratings of the happiness of the marriage in the prehospital period (prior to the spouse's awareness of the initial symptoms of mental disorder) were not significantly related to the intactness of the family at follow-up for patients of either sex. Some of the most conflict-ridden marriages persisted at follow-up or until the death of either patient or spouse. In other instances, marriages that had seemed highly rewarding to both patient and spouse at the time of our initial contacts subsequently ended in separation. Also contrary to our expectation, separation or termination of the marriage was more frequent among middle-class families of both male and female patients, though more markedly so in the case of female patients.

Very few of the divorced wives of male patients remarried, while a majority of the divorced husbands of female patients eventually did so. The new marriages seldom constituted a home base for the children, though in some instances older children lived recurrently with their fathers and stepmothers. Very few of the stepmothers appear to have been warmly receptive of the children.

Intact Families
As noted above, intact families of male patients tended to be characterized by infrequent recurrence of symptomatology, by occupational stability, and by relatively smooth relationships between husband and wife. Much less stability was found in the intact families of female patients. There was, as already noted, a much higher level of persistent or episodic symptomatology on the part of the patients who were mothers. Thus, there were periodic disruptions of living arrangements; also, the children were more often subject to neglect at times when their mothers were at home.

On the whole, wives of male patients seemed to cope much more competently with the dual roles that were thrust upon them when their husbands were incapacitated than did the husbands of female patients. The husbands were more likely to turn to alcohol or to absent themselves from the home, leaving the children to cope with their mother's difficulties. In a few families, the men were as seriously disturbed as their wives and they berated and physically abused both wives and children. In fully a third of the families where the wife was the patient, the marriage was characterized by a mutual pathological dependence that held the pair together despite frequent displays of hatred and abuse.

This is not to say that there were no happy intact marriages among the women patients. A number of the husbands were not only sympathetic and attentive but were devoted both to their recurrently symptomatic wives and to their children. A few of the husbands modified their own careers in order to be more available to their wives and children. But unlike the intact families of male patients, where marital happiness tended to be highly associated with effective functioning of the former patient, the happy marriages of female patients were most often characterized by persistent or at least episodic symptomatology on the part of the wife and mother.

Over the period of childhood, then, children of male patients in intact families were more likely to have two parents who performed competently, a once-hospitalized father who held a steady job and a mother who was relatively sympathetic and supportive. The family regime was stable and often highly routinized. On the other hand, when the wife had been the patient, the children were more often faced with episodes of upset, demonstrations of lack of competent performance on the part of the mother and angry, unsupportive behavior on the part of the father.

Where the father had been the patient, the mother was almost always the primary source of discipline and support for the children; where the mother had been the patient, there was often conflict over discipline and limit setting. Thus, the socialization process was markedly more problematic in the families where the mother had been the patient, though experience might differ considerably from family to family, depending not only on the availability of the father as a source of support and stability but on the strength and competence of older siblings and the availability of other relatives.

Educational Attainment of the Children
The career potentialities of both men and women depend very substantially on educational attainment. Several of the studies cited earlier suggest that the mental illness of a parent frequently leads to school problems on the part of children. Since the advent of "high risk" studies, a number of investigators have examined the school records of children of schizophrenics on the assumption that poor school performance may be an early sign of individual vulnerability (e.g., Roff and Garmezy, 1974). Results have been somewhat mixed, though decrements in performance have frequently been found.

Lacking a matched control group of children whose parents are not mentally ill, we cannot readily assess the degree of deficit in school performance among the children in our own study group. We can, however, make comparisons among subgroups within our sample, and we can examine the educational attainment of the mature children in these families relative to that of their parents.

In general, parental social status is the most potent influence on a child's orientation to and performance in school. This is as true of families with mental patients as it is of the population as a whole. Thus, among children over 18 in our sample, 78 percent of those from middle-class families but only 55 percent of those from working-class families graduated from high school. College graduates and students currently in college are found very largely among the middle-class families.

There has been a steady increase in the educational level attained by each generation in the United States in the twentieth century, so we would expect the proportion of our patients' grown children who graduated from high school to exceed the proportion of their parents who did so. Among families of schizophrenics, however, the mean educational level of the parents is remarkably similar to that of their grown children. The proportion of high school graduates is almost identical: 74 percent for parents vs. 73 percent for children in families of male patients, and 51 percent for parents vs. 56 percent for children in families of female patients. On the other hand, children of patients who received diagnoses of affective psychosis or severe psychoneurosis clearly exceeded their par-

Table 3

Mean Number of Years of School Completed by Children over 18,
by Sex of Patient, Social Class and (a) Diagnosis and
(b) Intactness of Family

	Male		Female	
	Middle class	Working class	Middle class	Working class
(a) Diagnosis				
Schizophrenia	12.9*	11.9	12.7*	11.0
Other diagnoses	15.5	11.3	16.0	12.4
(b) Intactness of Family				
Intact families	14.1	12.0	13.5	12.0+
Broken families	13.5	11.3	12.9	10.4

*   Differences within class and sex group significant at p $<$ .05.
+   Differences within class and sex group significant at p $<$ .01.

ents in level of educational attainment. Ninety percent of the grown children vs. 75 percent of the parents had graduated from high school and substantially more children attended college as well.

When social class and sex of patient are both controlled, the mean number of years of schooling completed by children 18 years of age and over tends to be lower in families of patients with a diagnosis of schizophrenia than in families of patients with other diagnoses, and lower in families that have been dissolved than in intact families (Table 3). Although the number of cases involved when we control for both sex of patient and social class is small, several of the differences are statistically significant. The educational levels achieved by children in families of male patients tend to be slightly higher than those in families of female patients, but these differences are not significant, nor do they become significant when social class alone is controlled. If we combine the sexes, diagnosis shows a highly significant relationship ($p<.01$) with level of education completed by children in middle-class families, and intactness of the home shows a similarly powerful relationship with level of schooling completed by children in working-class families. Sons and daughters do not differ appreciably in level of education attained within groups classified by sex and diagnosis of patient, social class, or status of the marriage.

Overall, our examination of the school performance of the older children of our patients reveals that social class differences among subgroups are far more substantial than differences by sex and diagnosis of patient, sex of child, or intactness of the home. It appears that children whose parents have a diagnosis of schizophrenia drop out of school earlier than do children whose parents have other diagnoses, and this is especially so in the middle class, where higher levels of educational achievement would be expected. In the working class, however, intactness of the family seems to make a greater difference, especially for children of female patients. Although we cannot assess the possible effect of genetic vulnerability in the children themselves, the pattern of differences that we have found suggests that social circumstances confronting the child in the home clearly mediate the effects of parental mental illness upon the children's educational performance.

Age at Leaving Home
Children almost always leave home permanently at the time of marriage or when they take a job in a different community. Youngsters who are not doing well in school or who are in sharp conflict with their parents may leave the parental home before completing school. In addition, early marriage on the part of girls is frequently a mode of escape from an unhappy parental home, and this course was taken by a number of the daughters of our patients. At least four of the daughters married after they became

pregnant (two by age 15) and another threatened to get pregnant in order to obtain permission to marry at the same age.

As Table 4 indicates, both sons and daughters were much more likely to leave home before age 18 ($p<.05$) in instances where the parental marriage was eventually broken than where it remained intact.

Early departures from home were most frequent in working-class families of female patients. More than half of these children were gone from the home before age 18. Many of the fathers in these families were extremely unsympathetic to their wives. Some were brutal in their treatment of wives and children. We have no way of knowing whether a child's early departure from home was precipitated by the mother's emotional problem or the father's behavior, but as we shall shortly document, the children are more likely to retain a positive relationship to their mothers than to their fathers.

In several instances where children left home early, the parents remained together only until the children left. Conflict was rife in these families. In one, the schizophrenic mother indulged her three daughters and encouraged them to be sexually provocative. The parents' separation was precipitated when the mother invited her 16-year-old daughter's

Table 4

Age at which Children Left Home, Among Children 18 and Over,
by Sex of Patient, Intactness of Family, and
Sex of Child

	Male Patients				Female Patients			
	Intact* home		Broken home		Intact home		Broken home	
	Sons	Dtrs.	Sons	Dtrs.	Sons	Dtrs.	Sons	Dtrs.
15 or earlier	—	—	—	—	—	—	2	2
16 – 17	—	—	2	3	—	3	1	3
18 – 19	2	4	1	—	1	3	1	3
20 and over	3	3	1	1	2	2	1	2
Still in home	4	6	3	—	4	3	1	3
Number of children	9	13	7	4	7	11	6	13

* Differences between children in intact vs. broken homes (overall) significant at p $<$ .01.

lover—a drifter—to come and live with her at home. The husband, after battling unsuccessfully to prevent this, moved out.

Another instance in which parental separation followed a child's departure entailed long-standing conflict not only between the parents but between the schizophrenic mother and her daughter. The daughter had been quite young when her mother was hospitalized initially and was preadolescent when the mother was rehospitalized. When the patient again returned home, conflict became acute, and the daughter sought attachments outside. She became pregnant at age 15, which was the occasion for her marriage and departure from home. The father then left his wife and they were subsequently divorced.

Perhaps as impressive as the number of children who left home before age 18 is the number who are still in the parental home beyond age 20. This is especially true of the intact families. To remain at home is not, of course, to be problem-free. Several of the most deviant and disturbed of the children were living in the parental home beyond age 18, either because of convenience (e.g., a schizophrenic mother looks after her daughter's illegitimate child while the daughter works) or because of intense dependencies, often coupled with strong hostility.

Parent-Child Relationships
We asked our respondents both about their current relationships with children no longer at home and about problems in parent-child relationships or difficulties that the children had in the course of growing up. Problems of parent-child communication were reported more often in families of schizophrenics than in those of patients with other diagnoses. They were also strongly sex-linked, being most acute in families where the mother was the patient and the child was a son. Almost without exception there was poor communication and tension reported between son and parents in these families, whereas communication with daughters was reported to have been good throughout childhood and early adolescence in half the families where the mother was the patient.

Current relationships are more often reported to be positive with at least one of the parents for children whose fathers were hospitalized (Table 5). Relationships between children and both parents are predominantly warm only in intact families of male patients. The lack of data adequate for coding in the case of so many children of female patients is itself telling, since our failure to elicit data from our respondents often suggested estrangement and lack of significant contact with the child. It is evident that regardless of which parent was the patient, children are more often reported as having a warm relationship with the mother. This is especially true of daughters. Sons are more often reported to have only

Table 5

Percentage Distribution of Grown Children's Reported
Relationship with Parents, by Sex of Patient
and Intactness of the Home

	Male Patients		Female Patients	
	Intact family	Broken family	Intact family	Broken family
Warm relations with:				
both parents	61	7	50	36
mother only	21	71	12	23
father only	5	–	–	5
Fair or poor relations with				
both parents	13	22	38	36
	100%	100%	100%	100%
Number of children for whom adequate data exist	(38)	(14)	(26)	(22)
Number for whom data were inadequate to code	(5)	(4)	(16)	(9)

fair relationships with their mothers and poor relationships with their
fathers or to be unaccounted for in our data.

Problems of the Children
We did not attempt to interview children in most of these families. Especially in those families where the patient had not been symptomatic in
recent years and where the topic of the earlier breakdown was never
discussed, an inquiry into the child's perceptions would have been
threatening to the parents. For evidence of developmental problems,
then, we must rely then on the parents' responses to our direct questioning and on our ability to pick up evidence indirectly or from records.

This group of children as a whole is not exceptionally problematic, but
roughly a fourth have (often recently) had serious emotional problems or
been involved in significant deviance (delinquency, illegitimacy, etc.).
Table 6 shows the distribution of various types and degrees of emotional

Table 6

Distribution of Emotional Problems or Deviance as of Follow-up Among Children Born Prior to Hospitalization of Patients by Sex and Diagnosis of Patient

	Male Patients		Female Patients	
	Schiz.	Other	Schiz.	Other
Total Number of Children	<u>30</u>	<u>19</u>	<u>69</u>	<u>8</u>
*Psychotic episode, hospitalization	2	—	5	—
*Psychiatric treatment or other direct evidence of non-psychotic disturbance	2	1	5	—
*Illegitimate pregnancy	—	—	3	—
*Other serious deviance	1	—	3	—
*Indirect evidence of severe emotional disturbance	—	—	5	—
Minor or transitory emotional problem	7	5	17	—
Psychosomatic disorder	1	—	3	—
No apparent problem	15	9	16	6
Inadequate data	2	4	12	2
Total with adequate data	(28)	(15)	(57)	(6)
Percentage with serious problem**	17	7	37	0

*Defined as serious problem.
**Different between children of male and female patients significant at p < .05.

disturbance or deviance by sex and diagnosis of the patient. Serious problems are more frequently reported for offspring of schizophrenic female patients than for any other category. There are reports of psychotic episodes with hospitalization, of prolonged or intermittent psychiatric treatment for emotional disturbance, of serious delinquency or of illegitimate pregnancy for 28 percent of the children of schizophrenic mothers for whom data are available and there is indirect evidence of serious emotional disturbance for another 9 percent. The indirect evidence comes sometimes from reports of parental concerns, as in the instance of an apparent hallucinatory experience on the part of the daughter, and sometimes from incidental comments, such as a sibling's report of his brother's "weird behaviors."

Some children appear to have had an early period of considerable upset or vulnerability but to have fared well in recent years. These have been classified under minor or transitory problems. Other children so classified are reported to be extremely high strung or vulnerable, but have thus far shown no serious psychological disturbance.

Where the father was the patient, neither social class nor intactness of the marriage was related to serious psychological problems or deviance in the offspring, nor was there any clear patterning by age of the child at the time of the parent's initial hospitalization. Where the mother was the patient, however, serious problems are substantially more frequent in working-class families than in middle-class families (44 percent vs. 9 percent). Intactness of the marriage is not related to serious emotional problems and deviance among the children of schizophrenic women, despite its relationship to educational attainment and age of leaving home.

Surprisingly, we find the highest prevalence of serious problems not among those children who were under 2 at the time of the mother's initial hospitalization but among those who were 2 to 6. Seven of ten such children in working-class families with female patients appear to have had serious problems, as against none among eight children who were under 2 at the time of the mother's initial hospitalization. Children who had been 6 to 12 also showed a high frequency of problems in the families of working-class female patients (almost all schizophrenics). Because of the small number of cases involved, we might be inclined to dismiss these findings were it not for the recent publication by Inbar (1976) which suggests that the age range from 5 or 6 to 11 or 12 may be a period of high vulnerability to crises and displacements.

INTERVIEWS WITH THE CHILDREN

We were able to interview thirteen children from nine families, and these interviews reveal additional facets of the impact of parental mental illness on the child as well as nuances of the children's perceptions that parents could hardly report. The themes that emerged from these interviews on recollections of family life during childhood relate specifically to: the dawning of awareness of the parent's problem; feelings of resentment, guilt, and occasionally terror; problems deriving from the behavior of the parent who had *not* been hospitalized; and, above all, uncertainty. We shall touch briefly on these, illustrating them through direct quotations.

The Dawning of Awareness of Parental Mental Illness

In families where the children were young at the time of a parent's initial hospitalization and where there had been no recurrence of serious symptomatology, the children may remain ignorant of the parent's ever having had a problem. Where there have been recurrences, a number of the children have become aware only gradually, as new episodes occur and as the well parent chooses to disclose the past history. Older children frequently become the confidants of the well parent, especially children of the same sex. They may be involved in surveillance of the returned patient, looking for danger signals, or in helping to cope with a symptomatic episode:

> As I got older, when Daddy would start getting sick, my mom would ask my opinion. You know, we would collaborate and try to figure out if this was a false alarm or something was really going to be happening—should we have people come over and help us.

Smaller children might know initially only that the parent had been away or was "in the hospital." Although a number had visited their mothers or fathers in the mental hospital, they seldom reported any feelings about the hospital as such. Moreover, in only one instance did a child report having been made to feel acutely uncomfortable by other children because of the parent's hospitalization. Often, of course, that hospitalization was not known to their playmates, but several reported that they found it necessary to explain to their peers the nature of the problem. This was particularly true if the peers were to be brought into the home, where they might witness bizarre acts.

Two of the offspring whom we interviewed expressed strong resentment at not having been told early in childhood about a parent's mental illness. One knew only that some things that she did evoked very strong negative responses in her mother.

> There were many things that were never sayable in this household, and many clothes, many colors, I could never wear in front of (father). No red, no pink, no purple, no brown. And there were many kinds of jokes that could never be said, and unfortunately I often didn't find out about them until after I had made them. And then my mother would jump down my throat . . . so finally when I was about eight she explained the whole set of circumstances to me.

Some children explicitly recognized how hard it is for the other parent to talk about hospitalization:

As for Mom's condition or anything, he's never said anything to us about it. But then, we've never really been able to talk to Dad, you know? And he's never really been able to talk to us. I mean, we've all stuck together—we love each other the way we did, and we love Dad (but) . . .

Resentment, Guilt, and Terror

Even when a grown son or daughter appreciates that a parent is mentally ill, it may be difficult to cope with parental symptoms and defenses. Thus, two of the children expressed great annoyance with their symptomatic schizophrenic parents, in one case the father, in the other the mother, for their "dishonesty." They realized that the parent's use of denial or refusal to discuss matters that were painful were symptoms of the mental illness, yet these children could not accept such behavior in everyday life. Thus the comment: "Like my father hides his liquor, she hides her thoughts." In the other instance, the father would invoke his paranoid delusions whenever his daughter wanted to do something that her father disapproved of or that threatened him.

Several children mentioned their discomfort when their mothers talked incessantly to themselves. A young woman remembers that when she was in junior high school:

Mom didn't seem any worse—but she was never any better. You know, she still talked to herself a lot . . . And a lot of times I would just try to think of something to say to her, to keep her from talking to herself. Because it just bothered me, you know, if she talked to herself.

Equally disconcerting, though it elicited the opposite response, was another mother's obliviousness to the child's efforts at communication:

She'd hear it but then it'd go right through her, you know. It really got to bug my younger brother, after a while. He used to tell me, "God, you know," he said, "it'd get me where I don't even want to talk to her about anything any more."

Several children who were older at the time of the parent's initial breakdown reported that they had felt responsible for it. A son who was teen-aged when his mother was first hospitalized reports:

I was a wild youth, you know. And for a while I thought it was my fault, you know. I mean, some of the things were my fault. It was sorta, you make your mom worry kind of thing, you know.

And younger children might be made to feel that even if they hadn't been in any way responsible for the first episode, their behavior could cause a subsequent trip to the hospital. Thus, a college student who had been 2 when his father was hospitalized reports that in later years his mother incessantly invoked the father's vulnerability as a means of social control:

> My mother said, "If you keep this up, he'll end back in a mental institution . . ." I never got a chance to just be a kid, you know.

Memories of childhood among our offspring respondents range from its being viewed as a relatively pleasant or uneventful period to a preoccupation with its horrors. Pleasant memories are in general associated with relatively little symptomatology beyond the initial hospitalization and having a nonpatient parent who was sympathetic and supportive. Horrible memories are most often reported when protracted disabling symptomatology in the patient is coupled with abusiveness or unavailability in the other parent. Thus, the child of a schizophrenic mother and a hard-drinking, abusive father reports that on those occasions when she gets together with her several siblings, they can talk about little except the "hell" they went through together. Such meetings are always followed by nightmares. All of the children in this family appear to suffer from emotional problems, though the only ones we have recorded as problematic were designated as seriously problematic in clinical records. None has, to our knowledge, received treatment. Indeed, a daughter reports that no member of the family "will ever go near a psychiatrist."

Happier memories are reported from another family, where the father was the patient and experienced a single hospitalization. His daughters see him as grumpy and unsocial but one recalls:

> Remember, when we were teen-agers, how friendly Daddy used to be all the time to our friends? . . . But after we got older, well, he doesn't like to meet people. He likes to sit at home and read, and think. But I've known families that had worse fathers.

There were times of terror in some homes. The following quote, with its denial nicely belied by grammatical "slips," is from an interview with three young adults who were all less than 8 years old when their mother was first hospitalized for schizophrenia. The oldest recalls an episode:

> I knew she had bought a gun. Because she was—well, she said she was afraid somebody would try to break in the house—that she didn't have any protection . . . Well, you know, I remember thinking at the time that people say that a person who's sick

like that always tried to hurt the people they love the most. But I wasn't afraid she would try to hurt us—I thought she might try to hurt herself. 'Cause I don't believe she would ever do anything—to hurt herself (sic) because she always put us before anybody else. But I was always—I was never afraid, I never believed that she would ever do anything to hurt us . . . So (sibling) and I found it (and hid it).

What evidence we have of physical abuse of the children at the hands of the patient comes primarily from clinical records. One child was brain-damaged when the mother threw it against a wall; this child remains in a state institution. In another instance a mother was alternately overprotective of her children and hostile toward them. On one occasion she believed that the house was being filled with poison gas to kill her children. She broke windows to let in fresh air and then attacked the children with a broom handle.

On the whole, however, except during episodes when delusions guided their behavior, the patients abused the children less than did some of the spouses, especially husbands who were heavy drinkers.

Problems Deriving from the "Well" Parent

Husbands and wives of the former patients were not infrequently emotionally vulnerable themselves. Roughly a sixth have, in the intervening period since the index patient's first hospitalization, received psychiatric help. Others have turned to alcohol as a means of handling their feelings of inability to cope. In such families the children have a double burden to bear, and it is our impression that some of these have had the most difficult time emotionally. In one instance a young adult daughter requested an interview after learning that her father had been seen in the follow-up because she wanted to counter the lies she was sure her father would tell the interviewer. The father, a sadistic man who beat his wife and children, had reported that the children were all against him, explaining, "It's natural that no matter how rotten their mother is, they side with her." He had never explained anything about the mother's illness to the children despite recurrent hospitalizations over a fifteen-year period. He was exceedingly strict with his daughters, who regarded him as being at least as sick as their mother.

In other instances, the parent who was not a patient was relatively unavailable to the children by virtue of taking on activities that would minimize contact with the patient. Thus, the children might be called upon to cope with the patient's minor upsets and idiosyncrasies while the other spouse—husband or wife—invested energies heavily outside the family. In such families children expressed bitterness toward both parents.

Uncertainty and Personal Involvements

At very least, the mental illness of a parent tends to introduce profound uncertainty into the lives of children. Younger children whose mothers were hospitalized were often separated not only from the mother but from the father and sometimes siblings as well. For most preadolescent children it was not clear what was going on at the time of the parent's first admission. Conflict and recrimination frequently pervaded the family life space. With no explanation from a trusted caretaker, those children fortunate enough to have siblings seem often to have clung to each other for support and hope.

Yet many children learned to cope with uncertainty and, indeed, to achieve a sense of competency and maturity far beyond what would normally be expected at their ages. Again our data suggest that a supportive parent or other close relative was a prime ingredient in such achievements. Where the other parent leaned heavily on a child for support, however, or where the child was made to bear the burden of the patient's condition, rebellion or despair were more likely outcomes than competent coping.

In several instances, almost all among working-class families, adolescent daughters were pressed into service as a surrogate mother to younger siblings and as housekeeper and cook. One reports:

> I don't remember what we ate until I managed to learn how to cook, but he didn't like for me to cook because I was only—what—twelve . . . But, uh, the lady across the street helped me. She taught me to cook a roast and the lady on the other side taught me to cut up a chicken and fry it. And, well, from then on I kinda learned on my own . . . And (father) got so he'd let me pick out the groceries when we'd go to the grocery store, and cook, and I'd always wash the clothes.

Some of the daughters who took responsibility for caring for younger siblings or running the household are matter-of-fact in describing what they did. A few express resentment at a lost childhood, though if the siblings had close relationships and the well parent was supportive, warm feelings about family life may persist despite great hardships and uncertainties. Occasionally there is even a note of resentment at giving up the autonomy derived from taking over for a sick mother. Some of the patients themselves felt that they had lost authority by virtue of hospitalization for mental disorder, but our impression was that competent performance was the primary basis for the maintenance of parental authority.

DISCUSSION AND CONCLUSIONS

Children of mental patients inhabit families that are subject to periodic disruption and to levels of conflict and uncertainty that must seriously impair the socialization process. The nature of the evidence that we have been able to gather probably understates the degree of turmoil and the emotional traumatization of the children, for we have secured our data from parents who naturally wish to give the best possible account of themselves. Yet it is evident that many of the parents—both patients and spouses—could not provide role models for competent performance and emotional control.

Most of the children have not yet entered the period of maximum risk of mental disorder. The timing of our follow-up obviously does not permit any conclusion as to the proportion of children who will ultimately show serious psychological problems. At least three have already been hospitalized briefly, and several other, including a couple who have been high achievers in school, appear to us to be extremely vulnerable. On the other hand, several of the children who had turbulent times in early adolescence have as young adults shown considerable growth. Thus, one daughter who became pregnant and dropped out of school at age 14 decided within the next few years that she wanted a college education and, although she in now the married mother of several children, she is studying part-time to get a degree.

We have seen that children whose mothers are hospitalized are particularly subject to changed living conditions and to having to cope with recurrent immobilization and upset of their mothers. When the fathers are supportive and sympathetic, most of these children do seem to find ways of coping. We do not know enough about the relatives, teachers, or friends who were available to help children handle the problems that confronted them. Our data suggest that middle-class children have a considerable advantage in this respect over working-class children, for they manage to stay in school longer and show considerably less deviance and somewhat less emotional distress.

Children of schizophrenic parents manifest more problems than those of parents with affective psychoses and psychoneuroses in a number of respects. Whether this is because of genetic vulnerability, because of the nature of the parental personalities and the marital relationship itself or because of lesser parental care and affection, we cannot say. Again, however, social class makes a difference. Though we did not systematically code our data in such a way as to test such a generalization, it is our impression that children of schizophrenic parents tended to respond somewhat differently to the problems of their families than did children of parents with other diagnoses. Many of the children of schizophrenic mothers, for example, turned outside the home for personal response and intimacy, often in precocious love affairs. Others rebelled and quit school to enter the service or to drift outside the family. On the other hand, it appears that children of patients with affective diagnoses more often threw themselves into their schoolwork. A manic depressive father might be a terror to live with at some times, but at other times he might be seen as "a knight in shining armor"—to use the words of one of the grown sons we interviewed. Periods of acute symptomatology might be interspersed with periods of extremely effective functioning, something much less apparent in the case of schizophrenics.

Children from intact homes tended to remain in the home and to stay in school longer than did those from broken homes, especially in working-class families. This finding is not as obvious as it might seem, since the level of conflict in a number of the intact homes would have suggested that many children would leave at the earliest possible time. Where conflict was most bitter and pervasive a number *did* leave, and, as noted, separation of the parents came after the child's departure in several instances. Therefore, our finding of differences between intact and separated families should not be interpreted as if they reflected broken homes at an early age. Our sample is simply too small to produce adequate statistical analysis of the complex sequence and web of relationships.

Similar considerations apply to our findings in regard to the marital relationship antecedent to the onset of mental illness. It will be recalled that this relationship affected the timing and intensity of the impact of the patient's initial symptoms upon the children and mediated the well parent's responses and communication but did not predict either the long-term stability of the marriage or outcomes for the children. Perhaps this is yet another indication of the fluidity of interaction process and the adaptability of human behavior to changing situations. Both husbands and wives frequently changed their styles of interacting and coping. The growth and later needs of the children themselves posed problems of decision-making in which the patient's symptoms and the options available to the spouse had to be weighed.

The finding that psychological problems were *not* most frequent or acute among the youngest children at the time of the parents' hospitalization again suggests the salience of long-term developments and not just the crisis of initial breakdown and separation. Implicit in this finding may also be support for the conclusion arrived at by Anthony (1973) that hostile behavior on the part of acutely disturbed mothers was more devastating to the children than the withdrawal and neglect manifested by a "process" schizophrenic. Children who were old enough so that their demands and behaviors were intrusive and could not be ignored may well have drawn more harsh and hostile responses than infants.

Our interview data do not bear on the specific deficits of mothering of young infants during episodes of acute symptomatology. We certainly observed such deficits, especially in visiting a chronically schizophrenic patient who was caring for her nine-month-old grandson. She picked him up and shook him when he was playing contentedly and she ignored him when he whimpered because of getting tangled up in his playpen. Kagan (1977, p. 37) has recently observed that "a caretaker does not ordinarily impose constraints when the child seems occupied and happy." One would expect that the infant or child who gets unpredictable feedback from the primary caretaker would have many subsequent difficulties in learning and in relating to others, but we know too little about possibilities of compensating for such experiences through other relationships.

That parental mental illness often impairs the child's normal development can hardly be doubted. But most of the problems that it poses may not be by any means unique to parental mental disorder. Conflict and disruption characterize many homes. Child neglect and child abuse occur in many families. It is perhaps the persistence of chaotic situations in the families of recurrently ill mental patients that most sets off these families, though as Miller and her associates (Miller, Challas, and Gee, 1971) point out, such persistence (and child problems) may be as frequent in families of welfare parents or convicted criminals.

Socialization for competence calls for a substantial measure of firm parental regulation coupled with involvement of the child in decisions that directly affect it and with warm acceptance of the child. When one parent is mentally ill, it takes a strong and competent spouse to provide such regulation and support for the children while still coping with the problems posed by and the needs of the patient. The wives of male patients far more often showed such strength and competence than did the husbands of female patients. Both social-class placement and marital-selection processes seem to play a part in accounting for this relationship. Our data leave many questions unanswered, but they attest as much to the resilience of the developing child as to the deficits that parental mental illness may entail for the child.

One finding is particularly dismaying to a long-time student of the impact of mental illness on the family. Neither in the 1950's, when this research was first undertaken, nor in the 1970's, when we returned for follow-up and also studied a new group of families confronting mental illness, have we found significant evidence of an awareness on the part of treatment personnel that the family and especially the children need help. It appears that no one now takes the time to meet with the well spouse and the children, to assess their needs for information and guidance. With all the lip service to community mental health, we find this a distressing state of affairs. Surely the high risk of psychological disorder among the children of mental patients should make this group a prime target for preventive services.

FOOTNOTES

1. The research here reported has been supported from 1971 to date by Grant MH-19649 from the National Institute of Mental Health through the Institute of Human Development, University of California, and by supplementary assistance from the William T. Grant Foundation from 1975 to date. We are grateful to Nancy Pfeffer and Bruce Turetsky for handling our computer analyses and for helpful comments on the manuscript.

2. Early publications of the study were based exclusively on this initial group of thirty-three families. See Clausen and Yarrow (1955).

3. For example, 81 percent of the schizophrenic women but only 47 percent of the schizophrenic men traced had been rehospitalized one or more times, though most were in the community at follow-up.

REFERENCES

Anthony, E. J. (1971), "A clinical evaluation of children with psychotic parents," pp. 224–256, in R. Cancro (Ed.), *The Schizophrenic Syndrome*. New York: Brunner/Mazel.

Arnstein, H. S. (1960), *When a Parent is Mentally Ill: What to Say to Your Child*. New York: Child Study Association.

Beisser, A. R., N. Glasser, and M. Grant (1967), "Psychosocial adjustment in children of schizophrenic mothers," *Journal of Nervous and Mental Disease* 145:429–440.

Bleuler, M. (1974), "The offspring of schizophrenics," *Schizophrenia Bulletin*, No. 8:93–107.

Clausen, J. A. (1975), "The impact of mental illness: A twenty-year follow-up," pp. 270–289, in R. T. Wirt, G. Winokur, and M. Roff (Eds.), *Life History Research in Psychopathology*, Vol. IV. Minneapolis: University of Minnesota Press.

———, and M.R. Yarrow (Eds.) (1955), "The impact of mental illness on the family," *Journal of Social Issues* 11: No. 4. Entire issue.

Garmezy, N. (1974), "Children at risk: The search for the antecedents of schizophrenia. Part 1. Conceptual models and research methods," *Schizophrenia Bulletin*, No. 8:14–90.

Grunebaum, H., et al. (Eds.) (1974), *Mentally Ill Mothers and Their Children*. Chicago: University of Chicago Press.

Inbar, M. (1976), "The Vulnerable Age Phenomenon," *Social Science Frontiers*, No. 8. New York: Russell Sage Foundation.

Kagan, J. (1977), "The child in the family," *Daedalus* 106:33–56.

Miller, D., G. Challas, and S. Gee (1972), "Children of deviants: A fifteen year follow-up study of children of schizophrenic mothers, welfare mothers, matched controls and random urban families." San Francisco: Scientific Analysis Corp. (mimeo).

Rice, E.P., M.C. Ekdahl, and L. Miller (1971), *Children of Mentally Ill Patients: Problems in Child Care*. New York: Behavioral Publications.

Rodnick, E., and M. Goldstein (1974), "Premorbid adjustment and the recovery of mothering function in acute schizophrenic women," *Journal of Abnormal Psychology* 83: 623–628.

Roff, J. E., and N. Garmezy (1974), "The school performance of children vulnerable to behavior pathology," pp. 87–107, in D. F. Ricks (Ed.), *Life History Research in Psychopathology*, Vol. IV. Minneapolis: University of Minnesota Press.

Rogler, L. H., and A. B. Hollingshead (1965), *Trapped: Families and Schizophrenia*. New York: Wiley.

Rosenthal, D. (1971), "A program of research in the heredity of schizophrenia," *Behavioral Science* 16:191–201.

Rutter, M. (1966), *Children of Sick Parents: An Environmental and Psychiatric Study*. London: Maudsley Monograph No. 16.

Sampson, H., S. L. Messinger, and R. Towne (1964), *Schizophrenic Women*. New York: Prentice-Hall

Treudley, M. B. (1946), "Mental illness and family routines," *Mental Hygiene* 30:235–249.

Weissman, M. M., and E. S. Paykel (1974), *The Depressed Woman*. Chicago: University of Chicago Press.

PART III

ADULTS AND MENTAL HEALTH

SOCIAL SOURCES OF EMOTIONAL DISTRESS

Leonard I. Pearlin, NATIONAL INSTITUTE OF MENTAL

HEALTH

Morton A. Lieberman, UNIVERSITY OF CHICAGO

The proper work of social science, according to Mills (1959), is to illuminate the connections between personal problems and social problems. However, the manner in which the study of human behavior has been traditionally divided among academic turfs masks these connections. There are those who study personal problems, relying on speculation in drawing connections of these problems to the social milieu of people and, correspondingly, those who study the structure of society and its institutions and guess about their consequences for the emotional lives of people. This report strives to bring together these issues by empirically tracing the links joining the psychological distress of people to the experiences they have within the context of major social roles.

Research in Community and Mental Health, Vol. 1, pp 217–248.
Copyright © 1979 JAI Press, Inc.
All rights of reproduction in any form reserved.
ISBN 0-89232-063-X

There is a substantial body of research, of course, whose purpose is similar to our own. Nevertheless, in some pivotal respects the present inquiry is quite different from other studies, even from those with which it shares common goals. These differences can best be highlighted by providing a summary overview of earlier work. Any general summary of such a large and established area of research, however, must of necessity ignore many studies altogether, give scant attention to others, and ignore the nuances and distinguishing features of all. With this caveat in mind, we shall discuss what we believe are three distinct types of research.

One type of investigation, in its search for the contribution of social factors to psychological distress, has emphasized correlations between the status characteristics of people and various indicators of psychological disturbance (Hollingshead and Redlich, 1958; Gurin et al., 1960; Srole et al., 1962; Dohrenwend and Dohrenwend, 1969). Characteristics such as sex, race, marital status, and socioeconomic class indicate where people are positioned in the society. Such information is of paramount importance, for the ways that people's experience becomes organized and structured depend significantly on who they are and where they are located in the broader social order. The important conditions of life and the wide variety of experiences that unfold in life are typically associated with the social statuses of people. Paradoxically, it is the very richness of circumstances associated with status characteristics that makes knowledge of the characteristics alone a limited basis for identifying the social factors that affect psychological well-being. That is, status characteristics carry so much circumstantial and experiential freight that it is quite difficult to know with any precision what is contributing to their relationships with other attributes of people. To explicate these relationships, the circumstances and experiences associated with the status need to be recognized, delineated, and measured at the outset. With information of this sort, it becomes possible to interpret empirically a relationship between the status and a dependent variable.

It is accurate to assert that mental health research has depended too much on simply establishing associations between the status characteristics of people and their psychological states, then relying on conjecture to identify reasons for such associations. When we describe our own work, it will be seen that we attempt to go beyond this kind of reliance.

A second type of research into social factors underlying mental health has come into prominence in the past decade. It is pioneered in the work of Holmes and Rahe (1967) and other workers (Myers et al., 1971) who have attempted to identify events in the lives of people that contribute to emotional stress and physical illness. They have delineated over forty events, each having a weight based on lay people's judgments of their required adjustment demands. Correlations have been found between the total scores of events people have experienced and their reports of various physical ailments and psychological upset.

There are many methodological and conceptual problems associated with this instrument, most of which have been cogently discussed elsewhere (Brown, 1974; Rabkin and Struening, 1976). Yet, viewed against the background of the first type of study we discussed, the search for significant life-events can be seen as representing some forward movement. Specifically, it bespeaks the need to know more than the characteristics of people who are distressed; we also need to know the experiences that contribute to their distress. However, though the life-events instrument has succeeded in alerting us to gaps in our knowledge, it has thus far failed in closing these gaps. Aside from its serious methodological shortcomings, the major reason for this failure lies in its rather crude conceptual specification of events and experiences. Essentially events are treated as conglomerates of experience, unrelated to each other except by chance occurrence. To the extent that it is important to reconstruct the structure of experience from a patterning of events impinging on people over time and through space, the instrument is of limited usefulness. It provides only a score, a score that is producible by many different combinations of life-events. Research that seeks to understand the organization of events predictive of distress, not merely to assemble whatever information enhances prediction, cannot rely on life-event scales in their present form.

A third and final type of research that can be identified is distinguished from the foregoing by its exclusive concern with the psychological impact of but a single event. In terms of the sheer quantity of research into the social antecedents of distress, this is probably the most common. It includes, for example, studies of the psychological effects of such experiences as separation or divorce (Bachrach, 1975), losses resulting from death (Kastenbaum, 1974), struggling to earn a Ph.D. (Mechanic, 1962), having a first child (Smith, 1974), facing the "empty nest" (Deutscher, 1964), making the transition from high school to college (Silber et al., 1961), relocation of the elderly (Lieberman, 1975), and so on.

The intensive examination of single, traumatic, and threatening situations has helped to enrich theories of psychological distress while contributing to an understanding of particular situations and their consequences. What we cannot know from these studies is the extent to which processes surrounding one event may be generalizeable to other events, or how the impact of an event may be regulated by other events taking place at the same time. As a result, the psychological effects that we might be attributing to a single event, may, in fact, be produced by several events occurring across a person's social roles. Ideally, of course, it would be desirable to observe all of the significant events and experiences impinging upon the lives of people through time, for such observation would help us to understand more completely both the confluence of social factors to which people are exposed and their resultant psychological states. Our data fall far short of this ideal, but they do take us a step in its direction.

This broad overview identifies some of the major currents in a rather vast literature that has developed over many years. Its purpose is to create a backdrop against which certain features of the present work can be highlighted. From the issues that we have selectively emphasized it is probably apparent, first of all, that in seeking to identify sources of emotional distress we shall look beyond the status characteristics of people and consider as well the events and circumstances they experience. In specifying these events and circumstances, secondly, we shall avoid the buckshot approach by attempting to conceptualize life-problems as they are structured through time and space. The third difference, obvious from the second, is that we shall examine a broad range of events and circumstances, not a single life-change. Central to this work, therefore, is the specification and measurement of different sources of distress. Here we shall give only a general description of these sources, reserving until later a more detailed treatment.

We begin by distinguishing two major types of events. One is represented in the gains and losses of major alterations of roles that predictably occur in the course of the unfolding life-cycle. We refer to these as *normative events* in order to underscore the expectedness and regularity of their occurrence. The second type of event we refer to as *nonnormative;* these are often crises that, although they commonly occur, are not easily predictable by people because they are not built into their movement across the span of life. Some of these relatively eruptive events may lead to loss, such as being fired from one's job or being divorced. Other nonnormative events, such as illness, are disruptive without necessarily entailing role loss. In addition to the normative and nonnormative events of life, we shall examine *persistent role problems*. These are not events having a discrete onset in time but, on the contrary, acquire their presence insidiously and become relatively fixed and ongoing in daily role experiences. Problems of this order are often chronic, low-keyed frustrations and hardships that people have to contend with in their occupations, their economic life, and their family relations. The normative and nonnormative events and the more persistent role problems collectively constitute what we occasionally call life-strains.

It is around these three types of circumstances, we believe, that much of the social experience affecting the psychological well-being of people is organized. The analysis that we shall present is concerned in part with learning the extent to which each of them—normative role transitions, nonnormative events, and durable role problems—affects psychological distress. In addition, we shall seek to learn how their effects are exercised. Specifically, we shall be attempting to identify the mechanisms through which events come to result in emotional distress. Is it because important change always produces an inner disequilibrium or psychic imbalance, or are there different processes that determine the impact of life-events? Finally, we need to know how life-strains are distributed in a population. To the extent that these strains grow out of fundamental conditions in the larger social order, they are not spread randomly among people, but are likely to impinge on some groups more than others. An important aspect of the analysis is to observe how the problems and events of life are distributed among those who are differentially located in the society. Before turning to these tasks, it is necessary to describe the background and methods of the study and to specify in greater detail the conceptualization and measurement of the life-strains of the psychological distress.

BACKGROUND AND METHODS

The study to be reported here has been under way since 1972. In that year scheduled interviews were conducted with 2,300 people representative of the adult population of the Census-defined urbanized area of Chicago. These interviews had three main foci: the assessment of a wide range of problems and hardships people experience as workers and breadwinners, as husbands and wives, and as parents; the identification of resources and responses they bring to bear in coping with these life-strains; and the enumeration of symptoms indicative of emotional stress and psychological disturbance. Many of the strains and coping repertoires about which respondents were questioned were first identified in open-ended, unstructured discussions with over 100 subjects. As people would describe some of the vexing and problematic experiences in different areas of their lives, they would be asked how they attempted to deal with these problems. From a thematic analysis of the content of these discussions the outlines of a number of strains and coping responses repeatedly surfaced. Questions were then developed around these issues and were put through a succession of pretests leading to the development of the final scheduled interview.

A cluster technique was used to draw the 1972 sample, each cluster consisting of four households per block. Since the total sample of 2,300 was to be made up of clusters of four households, the interviewing was done in 575 blocks, one-fourth the size of the sample. The 1970 Census (U. S. Bureau of the Census, 1972) reports that there are 2,137,185 households in the Chicago Urbanized Area, and when this total is divided by the total number of blocks in which households are to be chosen (575), the result, 3,716, is the skip-factor for the selection of households. After each 3,716th household was selected, three additional households from the same block were chosen by dividing the total number of households on the block by four and using the result as the factor for counting from the initially selected address. In anticipation of refusals—30 percent of those contacted—and to make allowance for households where contact could not be established within three call-backs, substitute addresses in each block were also prelisted. The sex of the person to be interviewed in each household was predesignated in order to have as equal a number of males and females as possible. Finally, only those between 18 and 65 were included, producing a sample still actively engaged in occupational life.

At the time of the 1972 interview, subjects were asked if they would be willing to be reinterviewed in the future. Eighty-eight percent, approximately 2,000 of the original sample, agreed to this. In 1976–1977 a subsample of over 1,100 people was drawn whose social characteristics, it can be seen in Table 1, differ only slightly from the original. Specifically, the subsample contains 5 percent fewer nonwhites than the 1972 sample, 4 percent fewer nonmarried, 6 percent fewer whose education is less than high school, and 3 percent fewer unskilled workers. There is also some difference in the economic make-up of the subsample. In 1972, 29 percent of our sample had annual family incomes of $8,000 or less; but only 21 percent of the subsample are drawn from that category, with a corresponding increase at the higher levels. Finally, there was a slight loss of the youngest group of respondents; whereas 15 percent of the original sample should presently be in their twenties, 11 percent of the subsample are actually in that age rank. The current subsample, therefore, is slightly older than it would be if it were perfectly representative of the original sample, somewhat more highly placed in socioeconomic status, whiter, and a bit more likely to be married. To a small extent it mirrors less accurately the population characteristics of the Chicago Urbanized Area, but its discrepancies will not distort the kinds of relationships we shall be examining.

The follow-up survey, like the first, is also broadly concerned with the problems and challenges that converge on the lives of people and their psychological effects. The 1972 interview, however, emphasized the persistent problems of everyday life, while the scope of the 1976–1977 survey was enlarged to include as well the events which we shall also be analyzing here: life-cycle transitions through which people had passed and the crises they had confronted in the four-year period following the first interview. The specification and measurement of the three types of life-strains need to be described in some detail.

Table 1

Comparison of Social Characteristics of 1972 Sample
and 1976 Subsample

Social characteristics	Original 1972 sample (N = 2,299)	1976 Follow-up (N = 1,106)
Race		
White	75%	80%
Non-white	25	20
Marital status		
Single	13%	9%
Married	69	75
Separated	4	3
Divorced	6	5
Widowed	7	8
Education in 1972		
Less than high school	32%	26%
High school	32	33
More than high school	35	41
Occupational status in 1972		
Unskilled	9%	6%
Semi-skilled	17	15
Skilled	15	15
Clerical, Sales	31	29
Administrative, Minor Professional	13	14
Managers, Proprietors	11	15
Executive, Major Professionals	4	6
Sex		
Male	41%	39%
Female	59	61
Income in 1972		
Less than $8,000	29%	21%
$ 8,000 to $13,999	38	37
$14,000 to $19,999	20	24
$20,000 to $25,999	7	10
More than $26,000	6	8

Table 1 (cont.)

Social characteristics	Original 1972 sample (N = 2,299)	1976 Follow-up (N = 1,106)
Age in 1976		
Twenties	15%	11%
Thirties	25	27
Forties	22	22
Fifties	18	20
Sixties	20	20

TYPES OF LIFE-STRAIN

In Figure 1 we have outlined the circumstances that we shall be consider-ing in relation to psychological distress. Within each of the three role areas we shall examine: (1) nonnormative events, the relatively unex-pected and occasionally eruptive exigencies; (2) normative events bound to life-cycle changes and attendant role transitions; and (3) the more per-sistent problems embedded within roles.

Some of the nonnormative events may involve the loss of a role, and others may involve only a disruption of normal activities within a role. Thus, in the occupational realm, being fired or laid-off entails the loss of job, however temporary the loss may be; divorce and separation also involve loss, both of marriage partner and of martial status. In the paren-tal area, the only nonnormative event resulting in role loss is the death of a child. Among the nonnormative events not entailing role loss are move-ment within occupation or between jobs and the serious illness of a spouse or child. Regardless of whether or not they involve loss, the central fea-ture of events of this type is their somewhat unpredictable occurrence. This is not to say that such events are uncommon; on the contrary, they may be widely experienced. But their intrusion into the lives of individu-als is neither expected nor is the timing of such events, when they do erupt, likely to have been forcast.

Normative transitional events are those junctures of life-cycle that typi-cally (though not always) involve either the loss or gain of roles or—and this is an important feature of some transitions to which we shall make reference later—both loss and gain. Normative loss in the occupational realm is represented in retirement because of age, or exiting from an occupation to have or raise children and engage in homemaking or to seek training. Normative loss in marriage can result only from the "timely" death of a spouse. In the parental area we treat the departure of children

Figure 1

Types of Life-Strains in Different Roles

Occupation

A. Nonnormative events
1. Job movement — changes from one job to another resulting from promotion, movement to another job.
2. Loss of job — role loss resulting from elimination of job, being fired, laid off, or illness.

B. Normative role transitions
1. Gain of role — first job or reentry to labor market after giving birth, following full-time homemaking, or training.
2. Loss of role — exit from occupational life and into retirement or homemaking.

C. Persistent occupational problems
1. Noxiousness of physical working environment.
2. Job pressures, role overloading.
3. Deprivation of rewards.
4. Depersonalizing work relations.

Marriage

A. Nonnormative events.
1. Serious illness of spouse.
2. Loss of marriage and currently single as a result of divorce or separation.

B. Normative role transitions.
1. Gain of marital role
2. Loss of marriage and currently single as a result of death of spouse.

C. Persistent role problems.
1. Lack of marital reciprocity.
2. Nonfulfillment of role expectations.
3. Nonacceptance of one's self by spouse.

Parenthood

A. Nonnormative events.
1. Serious illness of child.

B. Normative role transitions.
1. Gain of role by becoming parent for first time.
2. Progressive movement toward independence within role; entering school, becoming adolescent.
3. Loss of role resulting from last child leaving home or marrying.

C. **Persistent role problems.**
1. Unacceptable general comportment.
2. Children's failure to act toward goals or values.
3. Children's failure to be attentive, considerate of parents.

from home as a normative loss, although one certainly does not yield one's parental role when one's children leave. However, departure obviates so many of the familiar role definitions that for our purposes it is reasonable to categorize it in this manner. With regard to normative role gains, they are represented in the entry or reentry into the labor force, by marriage or remarriage, and by giving birth. It will be noted that we have further identified in the parental area events that we consider to be transitional, although they do not involve role gain or loss. These are the benchmarks of development that stand as important turning points in children's movements toward the eventual establishment of their own independent lives outside the parental home. Whatever their particular substance may be, the principal feature of all transitional events is that they are part of people's normative expectations.

The third type of life-strains being observed in each role entails those circumstances that are not events in the sense of having a clear temporal onset or termination. They are the more persistent, though certainly not immutable, problems with which people collide in their daily lives as workers, marriage partners, or parents. There is a wide variety of such problems, both within and across roles and a number of these have been identified. Figure 1 indicates the problem areas for which measures have been constructed, but the measures themselves are presented in Appendix 1. Their examination will reveal that the ingredient common to each of the persistent problems, regardless of whether they are job or family problems, is that they are experienced by ordinary people engaged in ordinary activities. They represent the rather dogged hardships that people commonly confront in the course of doing what they are expected—even required—to do.

PSYCHOLOGICAL DISTRESS

Our ultimate goal is to move toward some broader picture of the kinds of outer conditions that affect our inner psychological well-being. There are many feelings that come together to establish a level of well-being in individuals, and there are many ways to evaluate and measure these feelings. The measure employed here is made up of twenty-three symptoms, reproduced in Appendix 2. These symptoms were originally identified from the presenting complaints of patients receiving psychiatric treatment (Lipman et al., 1969; Derogatis et al., 1971). When the symptoms are factor-analyzed, those numbered 1 through 12 form an anxiety factor; the remainder of the symptoms constitute a depression factor. Here, however, they are combined in order to create a more global measure of psychological distress. The scoring is done in Likert fashion, where the larger the number of symptoms frequently experienced, the larger the score.

The amalgam of anxiety and depression in this measure enables us to evaluate the impact of life-strains on fundamental aspects of mental health. In this regard it is necessary to raise a warning signal. Given that the scale was developed from the presenting symptoms of people undergoing psychiatric care for diagnosed anxiety and depression, it is understandable that people in treatment typically receive high scores on the measure. However, one cannot extrapolate from this to a normal population. That is, in a community sample, such as ours, people with high scores are not necessarily in need of psychiatric care. The only thing of which we can be certain is that the larger the number of intense symptoms people possess, the greater is their psychological distress.

SOCIAL DISTRIBUTION OF LIFE-STRAINS

The types of life-strains under examination here do not by any means embrace all of the invasive problems and misfortunes that can seriously affect well-being. People are struck by lightning, they are killed and maimed in wars, they may be victims of accidents and of other types of "bad luck." But although we are looking at only a partial range of the many events and conditions potentially inimical to mental health, those that we have selected are not simply randomly scattered misfortunes or happenstance tragedies. Instead, they can be thought of as being structured along several dimensions. First, some are structured by their occurrence in a relatively orderly sequential pattern through the life-span. Others are structured to the extent that they are attached to social roles, the domains around which much of experience is organized through space and time. Finally, and of present concern to us, they are structured in that they are differentially experienced by groups and collectivities having common social characteristics.

Table 2 indicates what kinds of people are likely to be exposed to the various life-strains that were arrayed in Figure 1. Gamma coefficients are used to indicate the magnitude of the associations, since most of the variables are either nominal classifications or ordinal measures. In each role area people were divided into those who experienced a particular kind of event or transition and those whose lives were free of any of the events over the past four years. Thus, the gamma coefficients represent the association between the various social characteristics of people and whether or not they have been exposed to the nonnormative events or the normative transitions. The persistent problems, however, are not discrete events but are continua on which all people within a particular role are

Table 2

The Association of Life-Strains in Different Roles
with the Social Characteristics of People (Gammas)*

Role areas	Number experiencing circumstance	1972 Socio-Economic Statuses				
		Age	Sex	Education	Occupation	Income
Occupational strains (N = 634)						
A. Nonnormative events						
1. Job loss resulting from:						
a. Being fired, laidoff	(81)	-.27ϕ	.24ϕ	-.32+	-.31+	-.45+
b. Health problems	(11)	.16	.30	-.64+	-.44ϕ	-.38
2. Job movement involving:						
a. Promotion	(168)	-.45+	.14	.14ϕ	.10	-.07
b. Changed place of employment	(157)	-.48+	.25ϕ	.06	.06	-.11
c. Demotion	(20)	-.15	-.37	-.12	-.04	.13
B. Normative transitions						
1. Job loss to take up:						
a. Retirement	(43)	.97+	.10	-.29ϕ	-.10	-.11
b. Homemaking	(79)	-.47+	1.00+	-.41+	-.07	-.16
2. Job gain resulting from:						
a. Entry, re-entry into job market	(87)	-.67+	.79+	.02	-.05	-.25
C. Persistent job problems						
1. Job pressures, overloads	(634)	-.13†	-.26+	.10ϕ	.11ϕ	.10ϕ
2. Inadequate rewards	(634)	.06	.21+	-.10ϕ	-.03	-.15+
3. Depersonalizing work relations	(634)	−.11†	-.23+	.09ϕ	.11ϕ	.01−†
4. Noxious work environment	(634)	-.04	-.10	-.40+	.41+	-.22+
Marital strains (N = 782)						
A. Nonnormative events						
1. Loss of spouse from divorce, separation	(41)	-.40+	.30	-.18	-.19	-.15
2. Illness of spouse	(206)	.12ϕ	-.05	.04	.01	.03
B. Normative transitions						
1. Loss of spouse from death	(20)	.64+	.75+	-.09	-.16	.05
2. **Marriage, remarriage**	(41)	-.53+	.14	.07	.02	-.54+
C. Persistent marital problems						
1. Nonfulfillment of expectations	(782)	-.08ϕ	.14ϕ	.03	.03	-.02

Table 2 (cont.)

Role areas	Number experiencing circum- stance	Age	1972 Socio-Economic Statuses			
			Sex	Educa- tion	Occu- pation	Income
2. Lack of reciprocity	(782)	-.04	.16†	.03	.05	-.02
3. Nonacceptance by spouse	(782)	-.14†	.15†	.01	.01	-.04
Parental strains (N = 924)						
A. Nonnormative events						
1. Illness of child	(236)	-.21+	.09	.15$^\phi$	.03	.13$^\phi$
2. Death of child	(7)	.03	.11	-.36	-.20	-.28
B. Normative transitions						
1. First child born	(51)	-.93+	-.25	.47+	.14	.01
2. Movement						
a. Last child enters school	(132)	-.52+	-.08	.20†	.01	.18$^\phi$
b. Last child becomes teenager	(126)	-.11	.04	.09	.08	.22†
3. Role loss from:						
a. Last child leaving home	(60)	.34+	.00	.24$^\phi$	.04	.40$^\phi$
b. Last child marrying	(27)	.40+	.11	.17	-.06	.12
C. Persistent parental problems						
1. Unacceptable general comportment$_a$	(924)	-.41+	.07	.12$^\phi$	.08	.17+
2. Failure to act toward goals$_b$	(848)	-.11$^\phi$	.08	.02	.02	.07
3. Disrespectful, inconsiderate of parents$_c$	(836)	-.31+	.01	.18+	.15+	.13†

*   Minus sign (-) indicates that men, younger people, people with less education, lower income and lower occupational status experience the events and circumstances more often.

a   Measured for parents of children of all ages
b   Measured for parents with a child over 5 years of age
c   Measured for parents with a child 5 — 16 at home, or a child living away from home

+ p $<$ .001; -† p $<$ .01; ϕ p $<$ .05

measured. The gammas of these persistent problems, consequently, indicate the association between certain social characteristics and the level of intensity with which such problems are experienced. The N's in Table 2 also require some explanation. Next to each social role heading is the N showing the total number of people in our subsample who are occupied, married, or parents. This "N" is the one upon which the gammas and tests of statistical significance are based. The parenthetical N's next to each of the events and transitions are comparatively small, for they indicate only the number who have experienced the particular circumstance. Since we have measures of the intensity of the more persistent problems for all people in each role, the parenthetical N for this type of life-strain is the same as for the total number of people in the role.

What is the distribution of these life-strains? We shall not answer this question in detail but shall identify only the more prominent patterns in Table 2, indicating which characteristics are most likely to bring people into contact with the various strains in the different roles. Because the number of people involved in some of the events and transitions is quite small, even substantial relationships may be unstable. For this reason we are indicating the level of statistical significance of each association.

Age   It is quite evident that in the occupational realm younger workers are more likely than older workers to experience disruptions in employment, change of jobs, and, to a slight extent, the more intense persistent job problems. The one appreciable exception, of course, is in retirement, which almost exclusively involves older workers. Occupational strains, then, are most likely to affect those in the process of establishing their work lives and careers. For most people the world of work becomes more stable and less eventful with age, not more so. Turning to the marital and parental areas, the pattern of associations with age are seen to parallel the life-cycle even more closely. Thus, younger people are more often involved both in the formation and dissolution of marriages, while it is the older who are obviously the more likely to be confronted with an ill spouse and with death. Similarly, as parents, the younger have to deal with all of the exigencies and transitions that occur early in life, while the older are more often engaged in seeing their children depart from the nest. Furthermore, it is the younger people who bear the brunt of the persistent problems of parenthood, clearly, many important events and transitions are firmly anchored in the life-cycle.

Sex   Women are more likely to fired or laid off, to leave one job for another, to give up outside employment for homemaking, and to be entering or reentering the labor force. They are, therefore, more actively caught up in both the loss and acquisition of jobs. They also are more apt to experience occupational reward deprivations, while men are more often exposed to overloads and depersonalizing experiences on the job. In marriage each of the significant relationships involves women. Specifically, women are more vulnerable to the durable problems of marriage and, as we know, the chances are good that they will survive their husbands and be widows for some time. Differences among men and women in the events and circumstances they experience as parents are quite minimal, as could be expected, with none reaching statistical significance.

Socioeconomic status There is some variation among the three indicators of status—education, occupation, and income—but they can for present purposes be discussed together. These indicators, it should be noted, are based on 1972 information so that we could be sure that the statuses do not result from later events and conditions but, instead, are a basis on which the events and conditions are likely to arise and be distributed. It should be further noted that race, a characteristic of considerable importance in society, is not included in the table. The pattern of associations between race and the various events and circumstances is very similar to that found for income and for this reason does not appear.

In occupation we see that job instability is more common among people with lower statuses. They are notably more open to being fired or laid off and having to withdraw from occupational life for health reasons. It is also evident that leaving employment for retirement or for homemaking is especially apt to occur among those with limited educations. In marriage, it is consistently suggested across the three indicators of socioeconomic status that the disprivileged have a greater chance of being divorced or separated. None of these associations, however, reaches statistical significance. Among parents, it is the better placed who are more likely to experience the various transitions of childhood. This may be an artifact of family size, for the fewer the children in families of child-rearing age, the greater the chances that a last child will be traversing a critical dividing line in the life-span. Parents in the higher-status ranks are also more apt to experience behavior problems and a lack of consideration and respect from their children. Perhaps this reflects a more general involvement in and monitoring of children's development among middle-class parents.

By and large, then, the events, transitions, and persistent role problems are not scattered helter-skelter throughout the population, but tend to be more or less prevalent among groups having distinguishing social characteristics. Some life strains, such as those in occupation, may be associated with a full range of characteristics, and others may be associated with fewer. Overall, however, the results support the assumption that if there is a social epidemiology of psychological distress, there should also be an epidemiology of major life-strains. But, of course, this assumption is predicated on there being an actual influence of life-strains on the well-being of people. It is to the evaluation of these influences that we now turn.

THE RELATIVE IMPACT OF DIFFERENT LIFE-STRAINS

Table 3 shows the relationship between the various life-strains people have encountered and the level of their psychological distress. The measure of distress, it will be recalled, is based on symptoms of anxiety and depression. People were scored according to the number and intensity of their symptoms, and these scores were then grouped into five categories of approximately equal size. The most general and apparent finding of Table 3 is that life-strains—that is, events, transitions, and persistent problems—do indeed affect the emotional well-being of people. However, there is substantial variation in the magnitude of their effects, both within and between roles.

Looking first at occupation, it is evident that each of the three types of life-strains represent important sources of stress, for the nonnormative events, normative transitions, and persistent role problems are each closely associated with emotional distress. The only exceptions are represented in promotion and retirement, which produce very modest associations. Many of the most potent of the occupational strains tend to entail nonnormative loss: being fired or laid off, exiting from work because of health, and being demoted. However, it is not the nonnormative character of these events alone that accounts for their effect, for promotion, which also has no normative basis in the life-cycle, is only slightly related to distress, nor is it loss alone that accounts for their effect, for job loss resulting from retirement is inconsequentially related to distress. It is perhaps the combination of unexpectedness and loss that is most productive of emotional affects. Yet, there are occupational circumstances other than nonnormative loss whose impact needs to be recognized, too. Giving up outside employment for homemaking, in particular, is outstandingly distressful, as is movement to a new job and entry into occupational life. Work overload and depersonalization, finally, are the persistent problems of work likely to exact the most costly emotional toll. The central place of occupation in the lives of people is confirmed by these data; they rather convincingly indicate that in this arena there are many changes and conditions which can stimulate anxiety and depression.

The relationships existing within the marital role encompass several contrasts. One is that the loss of a spouse, either through divorce, separation, or death is, as could be expected, quite distressful. It is perhaps less

Table 3

Life-Strains and Psychological Distress in Different Roles
(Gammas)

Role areas	Number experiencing circumstance	Gamma
Occupation (total employed: 634)		
A. Nonnormative events		
1. Job loss resulting from:		
a. Being fired, laidoff	(81)	.31*
b. Unemployed with health problems	(11)	.74*
2. Job movement involving:		
a. Promotion	(168)	.14†
b. Change in place of employment	(157)	.22+
c. Demotion	(20)	.41+
B. Normative transitions		
1. Job loss to take up:		
a. Retirement	(43)	.10
b. Homemaking	(79)	.30*
2. Job gain resulting from:		
a. Entry, re-entry into job market	(87)	.21†
C. Persistent job problems		
1. Job pressures, overloads	(634)	.23*
2. Inadequate rewards	(634)	.14*
3. Depersonalizing work relations	(634)	.32*
4. Noxious work environment	(634)	.06
Marriage (total married in 1972: 782)		
A. Nonnormative events		
1. Loss of spouse from divorce, separation	(41)	.23*
2. Illness of spouse	(206)	.05
B. Normative transitions		
1. Loss of spouse from death	(20)	.31
2. Marriage, remarriage	(41)	.07
C. Persistent marital problems		
1. Nonfulfillment of expectations	(782)	.40*
2. Lack of reciprocity	(782)	.34*
3. Nonacceptance by spouse	(782)	.40*
Parenthood (total parents: 924)		
A. Nonnormative events		
1. Illness of child	(236)	.16*

Table 3 (cont.)

Role areas	Number experiencing circumstance	Gamma
2. Death of child	(7)	.56+
B. Normative transitions		
1. First child born	(51)	.05
2. Movement involving:		
a. Last child entering school	(132)	-.05
b. Last child becoming teen-ager	(126)	-.01
3. Role loss from:		
a. Last child leaving home	(60)	-.05
b. Last child marrying	(27)	-.21
C. Persistent parental problems		
1. Unacceptable general comportment$_a$	(924)	.18*
2. Failure to act toward goals$_b$	(848)	.26*
3. Disrespectful, inconsiderate of parents$_c$	(836)	.18*

a Measured for parents of child of all ages
b Measured for parents with a child over 5 years of age
c Measured for parents with a child 5 − 16 at home, or a child living away from home

* $p < .001$; + $p < .01$; † $p < .05$

expected that key problems persisting within intact marriages are even more likely than the disruption of marriage to produce distress. Another interesting finding concerns the newly married, who, regardless of whether they are marrying for the first time or remarrying, do not show any upsurge in anxiety or depression. Despite marriage representing what is undoubtedly one of life's most critical transitions, the emotional rewards are apparently sufficiently abundant to balance the distress that may otherwise result from the role change.

Some of the events commonly viewed as representing trials and vicissitudes of parenthood turn out not to be. The illness and death of children are indeed distressful events, but the normative transitional events generally have but a trivial effect on symptoms of distress. Indeed, although the number of cases is too small to show statistical significance, it is nevertheless interesting to note that seeing one's first child marry is negatively related to distress. Parents not only are unperturbed by the thinning out of the nest, but they also seem to gain some positive emotional boost when it is finally empty. It's a somewhat different story with the more durable problems of child-rearing. As in each of the other role areas, the greater the intensity of the day-to-day problems encountered in this domain, the higher are the levels of anxiety and depression.

Generally, the findings of Table 3 indicate that confrontations with unexpected events, experiences with life-cycle transitions, and struggles with chronic problems are, in one or more areas of life, capable of arousing psychological distress. But, of course, this general summary ignores variations between and within roles. The same type of event, for example, may have an appreciable effect in one role and very little or none in another. When it comes to explaining psychological well-being, it is clear that different life-strains do not have equivalent effects. Much of the analysis that follows deals with some of these variations. In particular, it focuses on differences in the psychological impact of events, attempting to learn what makes one event more potent than another.

HOW DO EVENTS COME TO MATTER?

A rather accepted view of social life and adult development is one of people being psychologically bombarded by a parade of changes. According to this view, change of all kinds imposes an inner need for readjustment; whenever and however it occurs, it is likely to produce in people the signs and symptoms of distress. The explanation for distress is thus placed with the event itself and its interference with established habits and equilibria. It is our contention, however, that events and transitions affect people by altering the more enduring circumstance of their lives. Emotional disturbance is most likely to surface when events adversely reshape important life-circumstances with which people must contend over time. Thus, the event does not act solely or directly upon inner life, but through the reordering of more enveloping circumstances. The impact of events, we submit, is largely channeled through the persistent problems of roles.

These statements can be buttressed by a variety of data. We begin by taking as an illustration people who, in the past four years, have experienced the unexpected and untoward events of being fired, laid off, demoted, or being forced to give up work because of ill health—occupational events shown in Table 3 to have substantial associations with symptoms of distress. However, in addition to the changes they directly entail, these very events are also capable of creating persistent dislocations in the work role, in household financial matters, and in family relations. Such dislocations, we suggest, in part underlie the associations between the events and psychological distress. If this contention is accurate, we should first find that the experiencing of the events is related to exposure to intense, persistent role problems and, second, that when the effects of these problems on psychological distress are taken into account, the association between the events and distress is diminished.

To demonstrate this process we have computed total scores of *persis-*

tent problems for occupation, household finances, and marriages.[1] For occupation and marriage this was done by simply summing individuals' scores on the persistent problems that in preceding tables had been presented separately under category "C" in each case. Problems in household finances are measured by a special scale reproduced in Appendix 3. The intensity of these role problems, we next learn, is considerably greater for those who have been fired, laid off or demoted, or who lost work because of illness than for people whose work lives in the past four years have been uneventful. Thus the nonnormative, relatively eruptive occupational losses are often accompanied by more enduring role problems.

To what extent do these persistent role strains explain the relationship between the events and psychological distress? One way to answer this question is by observing whether this relationship is reduced when the effects of the role problems are statistically removed. Combining into a single group people who have been through any of the four occupationally eruptive events, there is a gamma of .31 between experiencing such an event (compared to those who experienced no events) and psychological distress. When the effects of concomitant financial hardship are controlled, the resulting partial gamma is .16, a reduction of almost 50 percent. The partial gammas emerging when similarly controlling for persistent occupational problems (among those currently employed) and for persistent marital problems (among those currently married) are, respectively, .19 and .15.

Another way of assessing the mediating effects of role problems is to utilize analysis of covariance, comparing the same group of individuals who have been fired, laid off, demoted, or experienced job loss during the past four years to those who have not encountered any such events. Analysis of variance between these two groups for level of psychological distress yielded an F of 16.4, significant at a .001 level. When the levels of persistent strains in the occupational, economic, and marital areas were entered as covariates, the F value for a comparison between the two groups on symptoms was reduced to 2.2, short of statistical significance. A series of covariance analyses examining specific role problems clearly indicates that of the problems taken into consideration, economic hardship is the major mediator. Thus, it is largely through the effects of economic strain that the events come to affect levels of symptomatology. When the same occupational events occur without these problems also being present, the events then appear to have little impact on level of psychological distress. Furthermore, when parallel analyses are made of the effects of divorce, separation, and widowhood, it is similarly the persistent problems, economic hardship in particular, through which these marital disruptions exert much of their distressful impact.

The foregoing data illustrate one mechanism through which external events and inner emotional states become joined. When people are beset by rather persistent difficulties in important areas of their lives, they come to manifest symptoms of anxiety and depression. Although these difficulties may have many roots, they can be precipitated by major life-events, such as events threatening occupational continuity. The problems that the events bring into being are quite diffuse and overlap role boundaries. Events in occupation, for example, create durable problems in family relations and financial affairs as well as on the job (for those remaining employed). Because of this diffusion, single events can result in an enveloping range of problems that erode psychological well-being. Economic hardships emerge as particularly potent in this regard.

There are three events involving role loss that suggest a second and somewhat different mechanism through which events also come to exert their effects on psychological well-being. Two of the events are normative transitions from occupation—one involving retirement and the other becoming a full-time homemaker; the third is the loss of a marital partner through divorce, separation, or death. By their very nature, these events involve more than yielding an old role or status; they also entail the acquisition of a new role or status and an accompanying exposure to a new set of conditions. The new roles and statuses may harbor circumstances every bit as difficult as those experienced prior to the transitions. We have devised separate measures of the problems people encounter in retirement, in homemaking, and as unmarried men and women (see Appendix 3). With these measures it is possible to ascertain whether it is the movement out of the old roles that provokes emotional distress or the quality of people's experience within their new roles.

The issue with which we are dealing here is logically the same as that which we addressed earlier. We are still interested in learning if we can account for the relationship between events and distress by the more durable circumstances brought about by events. Despite the similarity of their logic, it is not possible to use the same kinds of statistical controls that we employed in observing the effects of persistent role problems. Whereas those problems are independent of whether or not people experienced the eruptive events, the problems that people find in retirement, in homemaking, and in singleness are not shared by people who have remained employed or married. Therefore, a somewhat different strategy has to be adopted to assess the effects of the newly encountered problems of people who have made role transitions.

This strategy is incorporated into Table 4, which deals with people who in the past four years have left occupational life to take up either retirement or homemaking. The left-hand part of the table compares the symptom levels of people who have had uneventful employment with the levels of those who have departed their jobs. If we were to look only at

Table 4

Role Loss in Occupations, Intensity of Problems as Retirees
and Homemakers, and Symptoms of Distress (percent)

| | | | Intensity of problems encountered by new retirees and new homemakers | |
| | Stably employed | All new retirees and homemakers | | |
Symptoms			Low	High
Low 1	33	20	25	15
2	18	20	25	15
3	22	20	24	15
4	17	26	15	38
High 5	09	14	10	18
	100%	100%	100%	100%
N =	(273)	(120)	(59)	(61)
	$X^2 = 11.6$; 4 d.f. gamma = .23	p < .05;	*$X^2 = 2.4$; n.s gamma = .05	*$X^2 = 21.6$; p < .002 gamma = .40

* Compared to 273 stably employed.

this part of the table, we could reasonably conclude that the transitions lead to an exacerbation of symptoms, for those who have left occupational life are more disposed to distress than people still in active employment, there being a gamma of .23. However, when the new retirees and homemakers are further divided by whether they are below or above the median on the measures of their respective role problems (see Appendix 3), it is seen that the former (below the median) are essentially no different from the stably employed (gamma = .05). However, those whose problems in their new roles have an intensity higher than the median are considerably more symptomatic (gamma = .40). From these differences it is quite evident that it is not the transitional event as such that accounts for the distress, for people who were engaged in the same transitions are very different with regard to the level of their symptoms. What matters more than the passage itself is the quality of experience at the transitional destinations, for where people who have made the passage find relatively benign conditions in their new roles, they are every bit as likely to enjoy mental health as people whose occupational lives are stable. But if the new conditions are highly problematic, then these symptoms will be at a much more elevated level than those of the stable group. It is not the tearing away from old roles that matters to well-being, but what is discovered in the context of the new roles.

Essentially the same conclusions can be drawn from the results of Table 5. This table is constructed in the same way as the preceding table, first comparing all people who in the past four years have become unmarried with those whose marriages have been continuous, and then subdividing the newly single into those below and those above the median on the measure of problems confronted as unmarried men and women (Appendix 3). In the first comparison it is evident that as a group people who have lost their marriage partners in the past four years are more susceptible to distress (gamma = .27). Once again, however, it can be noted that those whose problems in singleness are higher than the median are the sole contributors to this relationship (gamma = .61). The trauma of loss alone does not propel the formerly married into a state of distress; it is, instead, the trauma of moving into a new status in which there are intense problems and hardships. These findings, furthermore, are entirely consistent with recent studies seeking to account for the frequently observed relationship between marital status and psychological disturbance (Radloff, 1975; Warheit et al., 1975; Pearlin and Johnson, 1977).

Table 5

Role Loss in Marriage, Intensity of Problems as Non-Married
People, and Symptoms of Distress (percent)

Symptoms		Stably married	All new divorcees widowed, & separated	Intensity of problems encountered as unmarried people	
				Low	High
Low	1	27	24	32	12
	2	21	08	15	—
	3	24	19	18	20
	4	19	27	29	24
High	5	09	22	06	44
		100%	100%	100%	100%
N =		(549)	(59)	(34)	(25)
		X^2 = 15.9; p <.01; 4 d.f. gamma = .27		$*X^2$ = 3.7 n.s. gamma = .00	$*X^2$ = 35.9 p <.001 gamma = .61

* Compared to 549 stably married.

The illustrative data we have examined have placed us in a somewhat better position to answer the question of how life-events come to matter to the psychological well-being of people. It is clear that complex causative processes are involved that require analysis more formal and systematic than the present treatment. Our findings, however, plausibly indicate that to an appreciable extent the impact of events is channeled through relatively durable problems impinging on the lives of people. There are at least two mechanisms that seem to link events to these enduring, problematic experiences. First, events themselves may trigger or contribute to the formation of such problems. Being fired, for example, has wide ramifications: It may reduce economic resources—a circumstance of central importance, result in marital conflict, create strain in relations with one's children, and so on. Some events thus give rise to circumstances that are nonevents, and the nonevents may be mainly responsible for emotional distress. The second mechanism pertains especially to events involving the departure from one role and the acquisition of another. The passage alone appears to be far less predictive of distress than does the quality of experience one finds in one's new role. In this kind of instance, the event merely signals that a transitional change has occurred; but it is the durable conditions that one finds at the final leg of the passage that are primarily responsible for eventual distress.

DISCUSSION

One of the major considerations underlying this analysis is the certainty that to understand better how societies contribute to or take away from the emotional well-being of their members, we first have to identify the important dimensions of structured experience. The identifications we made were largely guided by perspectives of life-cycle and social role, enabling us to differentiate experience that arises both through time and across space. We believe that conceptualized distinctions among events and circumstances represent a sorely needed departure from the uncritical collection and scaling of large numbers of random events. And, by looking at these life-strains as they contribute to distress in different major roles, we were able to encompass a much broader view of sources of distress than is reflected in the studies dealing with but one event in one area of life.

Yet, it is clear that knowledge of life-strains alone, no matter how they are conceptualized, is not sufficient to predict fully their psychological outcomes. In addition, it is necessary to take into account the ways in which people recognize and respond to the events and circumstances that arise in their lives. The manner in which people cope with their life-strains determines in large measure the effects that the strains will eventually have on them. We have some knowledge of the coping repertoires and the coping efficacy of individuals struggling with persistent role problems that lace their daily lives (Pearlin and Schooler, 1978). These primarily involve cognitive and perceptual devices that function to shape the meaning of experience in ways that neutralize what are otherwise stressful effects. But virtually nothing is known of the anticipatory learning and prior preparation that would enable people to cope with normative role transitions when they occur in the future. Similarly, little is known of the use of social networks and formal helping agents, aspects of coping that are probably especially pertinent in dealing with eruptive crises. The adult portion of the life-span is peppered with problems and strains. To understand fully their effects on well-being, we need to understand how they are experienced and coped with.

In contemplating many of the findings we have presented, the question of directionality is very likely to arise. We have been assuming that it is the life-strains that eventuate in psychological distress. But is it not also reasonable to argue that a state of psychological distress may result in unfavorable events, especially those that are outside of normative change? Instead of job loss causing distress, for example, distress may cause people to lose their jobs. It is not necessary to rely completely on conjecture in coming to grips with this serious problem. Identical information concerning psychological distress was gathered both in 1972 and 1976–1977, and these longitudinal data permit us to gain some purchase on the issue of directionality. Thus, in looking at the nonnormative, unexpected events, it could be determined that these events bear no appreciable relationship to the level of symptomatology preceding the event, but are closely related to symptoms measured following the event. In occupation, to take one example, the gamma is .10 between being fired or laid off and the earlier symptom level, but .31 between the events and the later symptomatology. The vagaries of life, it appears, are not very likely to follow from earlier emotional disturbance, but emotional disturbance is quite likely to follow from these vagaries. The patterns of these relationships hardly constitute proof, but they indicate that distress is much more likely to flow from conditions of life than to give shape to these conditions.

It is important that what we learned about the social distribution of life-strains be brought together with what we learned of their distressful impact. Ten life-strains can be identified in Table 3 that are associated with distress at gamma levels of .25 or stronger and that are statistically significant at .05 or better. Five are in occupation, three in marriage, and two in the parental area. They are disproportionately concentrated among women, for fully eight out of the ten are more commonly experienced by females, five of them at a statistically significant level. The ten outstanding strains are located with equal uniformity among younger people. There is, however, a wider distribution of these highly distressful strains across the socioeconomic echelons. In the occupational realm there is little doubt that those of lower standing are more exposed to the severe strains, the only exception being depersonalizing experiences. However, the remainder of the severe strains, those existing in the marital and parental areas, are divided among groups of different status, none being statistically significant. In general, then, women, the young, and—most clearly in occupation—those of low socioeconomic position are most vulnerable to the severest life-strains. These kinds of patterns underscore the utility of examining the social distribution of life-strains. Such a distribution, first, indicates that the sources of these strains may reside in conditions that vary for different groups and collectivities; and, second, it indicates that once strains are generated, whatever their source, some groups and collectivities are more likely than others to suffer their consequences. The study of events and circumstances affecting well-being is inseparable from the study of larger social organization.

It should be emphasized that the life-strains delineated here do not by any means exhaust all of the important social sources of distress among adults. People express a good deal of concern with conditions in their community milieux: neighborhood deterioration, crime, pollution, noise, transportation, and so on. They feel ceaselessly victimized as consumers in the marketplace. And relatives outside the nuclear family unit can occasionally present overwhelming problems and concerns. It also should be recognized that not all the strains that are affecting our lives at any particular moment in time have clearly discernible anchorages in the external social world. Many of the important life-strains may be stimulated by what has already been accumulated in our psychic interiors. Our roles may remain the same, there may be no untoward events that disrupt the continuity of our lives, and yet from within come new perceptions, new meanings, new disaffections, and new searchings. We ourselves, by virtue of prior development, can be considered to be among the important sources of our own change and, perhaps, our own emotional distress.

FOOTNOTES

1. Parenthood is omitted not for any substantive reasons, but because the separate problems measured were developed for somewhat different age groups. This presents some problem in creating a unified score of strain resulting from persistent problems in this area.

REFERENCES

Bachrach, Leona L. (1975), *Marital Status and Mental Disorder: An Analytical Review.* Washington, D.C.: DHEW Publication No. (ADM) 75-217. Government Printing Office.

Brown, George W. (1974), "Meaning, measurement, and stress of life events," pp. 217-243, in Barbara S. Dohrenwend and Bruce P. Dohrenwend (Eds.), *Stressful Life Events.* New York: Wiley.

Derogatis, L. R., R. S. Lipman, L. Covi, and K. Rickles (1971), "Neurotic symptom dimensions," *Archives of General Psychiatry* 24: 454-464.

Deutscher, Irwin (1964), "The quality of post-parental life," *Marriage and the Family* 26:52-60.

Dohrenwend, Bruce P., and Barbara S. Dohrenwend (1969), *Social Status and Psychological Disorder.* New York: Wiley Interscience.

Gurin, Gerald, Joseph Veroff, and Shiela Feld (1960), *Americans View Their Mental Health.* New York: Basic Books, Inc.

Holmes, Thomas H., and Richard H. Rahe (1967), "The social readjustment rating scale," *Journal of Psychosomatic Research* 11:213-218.

Kastenbaum, Robert (1974), "Is death a life-crisis? On the confrontation with death in theory and practice," pp. 19-50, in Nancy Datan and Leon Ginsberg (Eds.), *Proceedings of Fourth Life-Span Developmental Psychology Conference: Normative Life Crises.* New York: Academic Press.

Lieberman, Morton A. (1974), "Adaptive processes in late life," pp. 135-159, in Nancy Datan and Leon Ginsberg (Eds.), *Proceedings of Fourth Life-Span Developmental Psychology Conference: Normative Life Crises.* New York: Academic Press.

Lipman, R. S., K. Rickles, L. Covi, L. R. Derogatis, and E. H. Uhlenhuth (1969), "Factors of symptom distress," *Archives of General Psychiatry* 21: 328-338.

Mechanic, David (1962), *Student Under Stress.* New York: The Free Press.

Mills, C. Wright (1959), *The Sociological Imagination.* New York: Oxford University Press.

Myers, Jerome K., J. J. Lidenthal, and M. P. Pepper (1971), "Life events and psychological impairment," *The Journal of Nervous and Mental Disease* 152:149-157.

Pearlin, Leonard I., and Joyce S. Johnson (1977), "Marital status, life-strains and depression," *American Sociological Review* 42:704-715.

————, and Carmi Schooler (1978), "The structure of coping," *Journal of Health and Social Behavior.* 19:2-21.

Rabkin, Judith G., and Elmer L. Struening (1976), "Life events, stress, and illness," *Science* 194:1013-1020.

Radloff, Lenore (1975), "Sex differences in depression: The effects of occupation and marital status," *Sex Roles* 1: 249-265.

Silber, Earle, George Coehlo, Elizabeth B. Murphey, David Hambur, Leonard I. Pearlin, and Morris Rosenberg (1961), "Competent adolescents coping with college decisions," *Archives of General Psychiatry* 5:517-527.

Smith, Candyce Russell (1974), "Transition to parenthood: Problems and gratifications," *Journal of Marriage and the Family* 36:294-301.

Srole, Leo, Thomas S. Langner, Stanley T. Michael, Marvin K. Opler, and Thomas A. C. Rennie (1962), *Mental Health in the Metropolis: The Midtown Manhattan Study.* New York: McGraw Hill.

U.S. Bureau of the Census (1972), *Census of Housing: 1970 Block Statistics; Financial Report HC(3)-68, Chicago, Illinois-Northwestern Indiana Urbanized Area.* Washington, D.C.: U.S. Government Printing Office.

Warheit, George J., Charles E. Holzer, III, Roger A. Bell, and Sandra A. Arey (1976), "Sex, marital status and mental health: A reappraisal," *Social Forces* 55:459-470.

APPENDIX 1

Occupational Persistent Role Problems

A. Noxiousness of physical work environment.

How much of the time:

1. Do you have a lot of noise on the job?
2. Do you work in a lot of dirt or dust?
3. Are you in danger of illness or injury on the job?
4. Do you do the same thing over and over again?

B. Job pressures, role overloading.

How much of the time:

1. Do you have more work than you can handle?
2. Are you under pressure to keep up with new ways of doing things?
3. Do you work too many hours?

How often:

4. Do people come to you for your opinions about how the work should be done?
5. Do you have to do tasks that no one else wants to do?

C. Deprivation of rewards.

How much do you agree or disagree that:

1. The income I earn is just about right for the job I have?
2. I can count on a steady income?
3. My chances for increased earnings in the next year or so are good?
4. The work I'm doing now is preparing me for a better work situation later?
5. My work has good fringe benefits such as sick pay and retirement?
6. There is always a chance I may be out of a job?

D. Depersonalizing work relations.

On your job, how often:

1. Do people act toward you as if you are a person without real feelings?
2. Do people treat you in an unfriendly way?
3. Are you told that you're doing a good job?
4. Are you treated unfairly by another person?

Marital Persistent Role Problems

A. Lack of marital reciprocity.

How much do you agree or disagree that:

1. My husband/wife) insists on having (his/her) own way?

2. My (husband/wife) usually expects more from me than (he/she) is willing to give?
3. My (husband/wife) usually acts as if (he/she) were the only important person in the family?
4. Generally, I give in more to my (husband's/wife's) wishes than (he/she) gives in to mine.

B. Nonfulfillment of role expectations.

How much do you agree or disagree that my (husband/wife is someone:

1. I can really talk with about things that are important to me?
2. Who is affectionate toward me?
3. Who spends money wisely?
4. Who is a good (wage earner/housekeeper)?
5. Who is a good sexual partner?
6. Who appreciates the job I do as a (wage earner/housekeeper)?

C. Nonacceptance of one's self by spouse.

How strongly do you agree or disagree with these statements:

1. My (husband/wife) seems to bring out the best in me?
3. My (husband/wife) appreciates me just as I am?
3. My marriage doesn't give me enough opportunity to become the sort of person I'd like to be?
4. I cannot completely be myself around my (husband/wife)?

Parental, Persistent Role Problems

A. Unacceptable general comportment.

Children age 5 or less. How often does it happen that your child:

1. Cries without your knowing why?
2. Has a poor appetite?
3. Has difficulty sleeping?
4. Demands too much from you?
5. Does things slow for his age?
6. Doesn't want as much attention as you want to give?
7. Is hard to control?
8. Doesn't play well with other children?

Children ages 5 to 16. How often do you have to give some attention to the correction of:

1. Misbehavior in the house?
2. Your child(ren) having the wrong kinds of friends?
3. Your child(ren) failing to get along with others the same age?
4. Your child(ren) being careless about personal appearance?

Children older than 16. As a parent how often do you wonder if your child(ren):

    1. Might be tempted by others to try illegal drugs?

    2. Might be using too much alcohol?

B. Failure to act toward goals or values.

Children ages 5 to 16. How often do you have to give some attention to the correction of:

    1. Poor school work?

    2. Poor use of spare time?

Children older than 16. As a parent how often do you wonder if your child(ren):

    1. (Is/Are) living too much for the present and thinking too little of what lies ahead?

    2. (Is/Are) showing too little interest in religion?

    3. (Is/Are) not practicing the moral beliefs that are important?

    4. (Is/Are) not trying hard enough to prepare for the life ahead of (him/them)?

    5. (Is/Are) not headed for the success you want for (him/them)?

    6. May not be headed for a good family life?

C. Failure to be attentive, considerate of parents.

Children ages 5 to 16. As a parent, how often do you have these experiences:

    1. You are treated without proper respect?

    2. Your advice and guidance are ignored?

    3. You are helped with household chores without asking?

    4. You are disobeyed?

Children living away from home. How often:

    1. Do you receive a phone call or letter from your child(ren)?

    2. Do(es) your child(ren) visit you?

    3. Are you invited to visit your child(ren)?

APPENDIX 2

Psychological Distress Scale Items

In the past week, how often did you:

1. Have headaches or head pains?

2. Have an upset or sour stomach?

3. Have tightness or tension in your neck, back, or other muscles?

4. Feel faint or dizzy?

5. Sweat when not working hard or overheated?

6. Notice your hands trembling?

7. Have to avoid certain things, places, or activities because they frighten you?

8. Have your heart pound or race when not physically active?

9. Feel nervous or shaky inside?
10. Have trouble getting your breath?
11. Feel tense or keyed up?
12. Feel fearful or afraid?
13. Lack enthusiasm for doing anything?
14. Have a poor appetite?
15. Feel lonely?
16. Feel bored or have little interest in doing things?
17. Lose sexual interest or pleasure?
18. Have trouble getting to sleep or staying asleep?
19. Cry easily or feel like crying?
20. Feel downhearted or blue?
21. Feel low in energy or slowed down?
22. Feel hopeless about the future?
23. Have any thoughts of possibly ending your life?

APPENDIX 3

Economic, Persistent Problems

At the present time are you able to afford:
1. A home that is large enough and comfortable enough for (you/your family)?
2. Furniture or household equipment that needs to be replaced?
3. The kind of car you need?

How often does it happen that you don't have enough money to afford:
4. The kind of food (you/your family) should have?
5. The kind of medical care (you/your family) should have?
6. The kind of clothing (you/your family) should have?
7. The leisure activities that (you/your family) want(s)?
8. How much difficulty do you have in meeting the monthly payments on (your/your family's) bills?
9. In general, how do (your/your family's) finances usually work out at the end of the month? Some money left over? Just enough to make ends meet? Not enough to make ends meet?

Retirement, Persistent Problems

How often does your retirement result in:
1. Having too much time with not enough to do?
2. Not having the money to be able to do some of the things you used to do?
3. Your being by yourself?
4. Your missing a daily routine?

5. People treating you as if you don't know what's going on?
6. Being more free to do what you like?
7. People paying less attention to your opinions?
8. Your not having a chance to be with and talk to younger people?

Homemaking, Persistent Problems

In your experiences as a homemaker, how often are you:
1. Not appreciated for your work in the house?
2. Uninterested or bored with doing housework chores?
3. Tired out from doing your housework?
4. Lonely for the company of adults during the day?
5. Really enjoying the work you do at home?
6. Using your talents and abilities in doing your housework?
7. Able to have free time for yourself?

Singleness, Persistent Problems

As a single person, how often:
1. Do you feel out of place in a social situation because you are not married?
2. Are you without anyone to talk to about yourself?
3. Are you without anyone you can share experiences and feelings with?
4. Do you have a chance to have fun?
5. Do you stay at home because you are afraid to go out at night?
6. Do you wonder if you may not be an interesting person?
7. Do you feel that you are not having the kind of sex life you would like?

ECONOMIC DEPRESSION AND POSTWAR OPPORTUNITY IN MEN'S LIVES: A STUDY OF LIFE PATTERNS AND HEALTH*

Glen H. Elder, Jr., Richard C. Rockwell, BOYS TOWN RESEARCH CENTER, OMAHA

As a field of inquiry, the study of life chances has dealt mainly with the constraints and options associated with differential position in the class structure, a perspective that varies from research on social mobility to sophisticated analyses of class, values, and psychological functioning.[1] In recent years this approach has been elaborated by historical and demographic considerations through developments in the sociology of age and the life course.[2] Age locates individuals in the social structure by means of age-related criteria and in historically specific cohorts according to birth year. With members of a birth cohort, one encounters a distinct array of historical experiences, options, and disadvantages. Cohorts that are differentiated by social change, size, and composition establish differing

Research in Community and Mental Health, Vol. 1, pp 249–303.

contexts of life opportunity, a point well illustrated by the small Depression cohort which came of age during a period of increasing prosperity and the large postwar cohorts that entered adulthood at a time of economic decline.

This contrast brings to mind Harris' argument (1969:183–185) for a model of change that represents fluctuations in opportunity within the developmental course of American society. "Sometimes men have thought, and said, that they lived in a land of opportunity which surpassed and improved upon the conditions of former years. At other times other men have maintained that opportunity was not what it had once been." Such diverse outlooks are part of the historical record on young adults who apparently shared everything (class position, life stage) except cohort membership and the times. One thinks of the bleak experience of 20-year-olds in 1932 and the workers' market of their counterparts during the mid-1920s; in the words of a Depression veteran "the essence of being in your twenties in the Thirties was that no matter how well tuned up you were, you stayed on the ground," (MacLennan, quoted in Elder, 1974:273). From historical evidence on demographic and mobility patterns, Harris finds abundant support for the proposition that within the long-term course of societal development "opportunity *did* alternately open up or close up significantly for young Americans in successive groups of years."

The sociological perspective on age identifies other temporal considerations that bear upon life chances, in particular the career stage of the cohort and its members at points of social change. Historical change has differential consequences for persons of unlike age and social roles, a difference which entails variations in adaptive resources and options, and thus in developmental outcomes. An example of such variation is provided by a comparison of children, adolescents, and middle-aged parents during the Great Depression of the 1930s. For young children, the potential disadvantage of economic misfortune stemmed from their critical developmental stage and total dependence on family support made unpredictable and insufficient by the stress of survival requirements. Within this age category, the risk of family hardship is likely to have taken the form of impaired development, cognitive, social, and motivational. Such impairment is less probable among adolescents, who were beyond the vulnerable years of early dependence, as suggested by evidence on one cohort of youth (Elder, 1974) who grew up in Oakland, California (birthdates, 1920–1921). For the fathers of these adolescents, income loss and unemployment represented a direct threat to hard-earned financial independence, assets, and security in the latter years of life (cf. Thernstrom, 1973). Frequently, men who lost their job were forced out of their customary line of work in order to acquire employment.

This comparison identifies two related outcomes of Depression hardship by life stage at the point of drastic change; alterations in the life course and in psychological health. Change in the life course had psychological consequences which impinged on subsequent life events. Thus in the Oakland study, cited above, unemployed fathers were least likely to regain stable employment when their adaptations included prolonged emotional depression, social withdrawal, and heavy drinking. The life course and health states of these men also established an explanatory chain of conditions and influences between family deprivation, on the one hand, and the life experience of their sons, on the other. The Depression experience and life prospects of the Oakland boys were thereby linked to the economic hardship and adaptations of their parents. The impact of family deprivation and its adverse psychological effects persisted into the adult years of men from the working class, damaging life prospects in education and health.

Our objective in this study is to carry out a more restricted longitudinal analysis of the Depression experience in the life patterns and health of eighty-three males who were born in Berkeley, California (1928–1929), an investigation which will nevertheless permit selected *intercohort* comparisons of this historical change in social experience and psychological functioning. By comparing outcomes from the Berkeley cohort with those obtained from similar analyses of the Oakland men (birthdates, 1920–1921), we shall be able to test a *life stage* hypothesis: *that Depression hardship entailed more adverse and enduring developmental outcomes in the lives of men who encountered this event as young children than as adolescents* (see Figure 1). The Oakland youth left home for school, work, and marriage at the end of the 1930s; the Berkeley adolescents at

Figure 1 Interaction of Depression Hardship and Life Stage: A Comparison of the Berkeley and Oakland Cohort

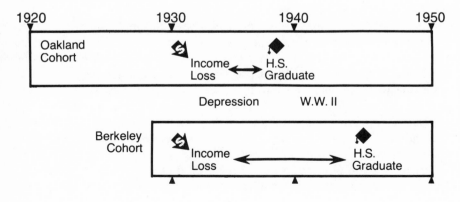

the end of World War II. The latter were more vulnerable than their Oakland counterparts to family strains and disruptions in the Depression and they were exposed to a longer phase of economic hardship and its persistence up to departure from home. The psychological significance of this difference in timing becomes clear when one realizes that the subjects from the Berkeley cohort were probably dependent as young childen on significant others who were often unpredictable, sullen, and perhaps even hostile.

This hypothesis may appear to conflict with Michael Inbar's (1976) conclusion that it is children in the 6- to 11-year age category who occupy the most vulnerable stage relative to drastic change and its adverse effects on learning and formal education. However, Inbar's interpretation is based largely on studies of geographic mobility, especially immigration, and on the cultural discontinuity of such change in the child's ability to communicate and perform effectively in school settings. Movement across cultural boundaries is most damaging to the education and development of children who are just beginning their schooling. By contrast, our concern is with family rather than school change, a decremental change that entailed severe hardship for many Berkeley families throughout the 1930s and even into the war years. Such change may, of course, lead to greater strength if mastered, but it is precisely this outcome which is least likely among children who grew up in a "hurtful" world that seemed out of control.

The life stage of a child in the Great Depression generally indicates his adaptive potential in coping with drastic change. A broader measure of this potential is provided by the class position of the child's family as the economy collapsed. Economic loss posed a greater status threat to middle-class families and they could not match the experience of lower-status families with setbacks of this type. Nevertheless, evidence on the Depression years indicates that middle-class families had greater access to resources, social and material, that could moderate the impact of heavy income loss. Thus, while middle-class children were less prepared for economic adversity, they were better equipped in family support, skills, and inner resources to work out adaptive responses to family change.[3] Consistent with this account, the Oakland study found adult health to be most negatively influenced by Depression hardship among men who grew up in the working class. Accordingly, we shall test the *class hypothesis: that adverse developmental effects of family deprivation in the Berkeley cohort are concentrated in the lives of men from the lower strata; in their developmental course through adolescence, in education and worklife accomplishments, and in adult psychological functioning.*

The focal point of our analysis is centered on the process by which the Depression experience of young boys in the Berkeley cohort influenced their response, as young adults, to the unparalleled opportunities of the postwar era, and, consequently, their life course and health to middle age. These men came of age at a time of expanding opportunity in the mid to late 1940s, but they did not enter this new world with the resources and outlook of a common background in the depressed 30s. Some boys in middle- and working-class families experienced the full impact of severe economic hardship, which may have produced a legacy of disadvantage for educational and occupational prospects, especially when family deprivation continued into the War years; a legacy of failure encountered through family members which undermined their adaptive capacity relative to the decisions and pressures of late adolescence and the young adult years. Once established, this developmental course could handicap even the most able youth's response to opportunities in the postwar era. By contrast, the offspring of families that suffered minimal hardship in the 30s were exposed to a life path which typically offered "smooth sailing" up through wartime adolescence and perhaps through the end of formal education; a life course in which setbacks and developmental tests were more likely to occur in the adult years.

At issue in a comparison of men who grew up in relatively nondeprived and deprived families is the assumed primacy of early experience in shaping the course of life-span development, a perspective long entrenched in psychoanalytic thought and developmental psychology. More recently, this position has been effectively challenged by empirical research and theory on personal change through the life course (Baltes and Schaie, 1973). Despite impressive evidence on personality continuity (Block, 1971), longitudinal research has begun to document the varied developmental paths in which childhood promise is not matched by well-being or accomplishments in the adult years, and dismal life prospects among youth are at least partially repaired by growth-inducing experiences later on in life (Furstenberg, 1976; Vaillant, 1972, 1974). Lee Robins (1966) has identified marital support and autonomy in work life as key factors in stabilizing the lives of men who were diagnosed in adolescence as sociopathic. Likewise, George Vaillant's (1974; 1975) longitudinal study of Harvard alumni indicates that both marriage and work life provided developmental experiences which enabled some men to surmount the handicap of inadequate childhoods. Consistent with a life-course model of human development, we shall investigate the effects of Depression hardship in two phases of the Berkeley cohort's life span, the early years, which extend from childhood through the completion of formal education; and a subsequent adult phase, which extends from school leaving to midlife, a phase structured most significantly by work life. The relation between education and work life achievement in this neglected life stage has been described by Kerckhoff (1976: 377) as "the greatest challenge" in understanding the process of status attainment. Very little is known about the life course between school leaving and occupational attainment during the middle years.

As we move from childhood to school completion and middle age, life events and adaptations are progressively removed from the orbit of constraints associated with family hardship in the Great Depression. This change and the historical context of the Berkeley cohort provide sufficient grounds for a general hypothesis on the *timing of effects: that the principal handicap of family deprivation and its persistence into the war years were expressed during the early life course of the men, as manifested through impaired psychological functioning and school performance, low aspirations, and an educational disadvantage.*

These outcomes would imply a continuing pattern of relative disadvantage in work life for men from deprived households, if only because a man's education structures options on career beginnings. However, prior results indicate that most of what a man does in his work to mid-life is not explained by his educational history, and this is even more true of his sense of well-being, relationships, and living standard. In fact, we find that the work life of the Oakland men (see Elder, 1974: Chapter 7) generally countered whatever educational handicap they had experienced as a result of family deprivation in the Great Depression. Given what we know about postwar opportunity, the work life phase of the Berkeley cohort may well yield a very different picture of the Depression legacy than its childhood or adolescent stage. In this regard, it is important to take note of the unique historical context of the cohort as we briefly describe the study itself and the setting.

THE BERKELEY COHORT AND ITS HISTORICAL CONTEXT

Members of the Berkeley Guidance Study were selected for a study of normal development from a cross-section of births in the city during an eighteen-month period in 1928–1929 (Macfarlane, 1938). The original sample of 248 infants was divided into two subgroups of equal size, an intensively studied group which provided detailed annual information on socioeconomic conditions and family patterns, and a less intensively studied group which was matched on social and economic characteristics. The basic cohort includes 214 children and their families who participated in the study through the 1930s and up to the end of World War II—102 of these are boys. Most of the children were Caucasian and Protestant, and two-thirds came from middle-class families. Three-fourths of the families were headed by native-born parents. The average IQ based on a median of scores from annual Stanford-Binets (ages 6–15) is 118. The archive of childhood and adolescent data includes socioeconomic information over the seventeen-year period, annual records of scholastic performance, teachers ratings, periodic interviews with mother and son, and psychological ratings. Eighty-three of the 102 *S*s provided life history information at the age of 40. Most of these men participated in two adult follow-ups. Both follow-ups (1959–1960 and 1969) entailed lengthy interviews and a battery of psychological, medical, and mental tests. Educational, occupational, and family histories were constructed from the interview materials. A comparison of the childhood and adult samples produced no reliable differences in IQ, 1929 social class, and ethnicity.

In 1929 family income averaged $2300 and all but a few of the fathers were fully employed. Some three years later, in the trough of the Great Depression, family income had declined by 30 percent, a figure which is comparable to that of California families in general (Medical-Economic Survey, 1937). Between 1929 and the low point of the Depression, the number of Berkeley families at the bottom of the economic ladder (below $1500) more than tripled. Using income records by year for the intensive Berkeley sample, we find that families were most likely to reach the bottom of their economic descent in 1933, followed at a distance by 1932 and 1934. Though economic changes between the three lowest years (1932–1934) were relatively minor, we relied upon the low-year figure since it provides the best estimate of maximum change. Family deprivation thus refers to a decremental change in economic status, in contrast to the usual association of deprivation with chronic poverty (Elder, 1974:9; Jordan, 1974). Economic decline among the Berkeley families was generally followed by at least some recovery as the economy responded to the stimulus of wartime mobilization. Unlike chronic poverty, this type of change offered children and families a broad range of adaptive options and resources during the 1930s, particularly among those who were positioned in the middle class as of 1929.

Two factors were influential in identifying families that were truly economically deprived; change in cost of living and loss of family assets. Data assembled by the U.S. Bureau of Labor Statistics indicate that the cost of living among Bay Area communities declined by at least 23 percent as of 1932. On the basis of this trend, economic losses up to one-fourth of pre-Depression income would not qualify as hardship. In fact, two of the Berkeley mothers cited the much lower cost of living as the main reason for the well-being of their families in the face of salary cuts amounting to nearly a fourth of their 1929 income. Substantial deprivation of one kind or another occurred as the income loss exceeded one-third of the 1929 figure. These deprivations include both general and severe budgetary restrictions (moving to a cheaper rental, etc.), rapidly mounting indebtedness, exhaustion of savings and credit, and the loss of assets, from insurance policies to furniture, the family car, and home. Among families in this general category, we find repeated references to the piling up of debts; as one of the mothers exclaimed, "I could lose my mind if I let myself think about it."

These effects were also observed in a Depression study of middle- and working- class families in Oakland (Elder, 1974:45); in both social classes, families with an income loss greater than 34 percent were classified as economically deprived. From the evidence at hand, the division between the relatively nondeprived and deprived seems equally appropriate for the Berkeley families, and enables us to classify all families in the Berkeley "matched" sample—only slightly more than half of these families had complete income records during the Depression. By using unemployment and public assistance data, we were able to assign the residual families to a deprivational category. Despite the limitations of this alternative, the percentage of deprived families in the middle and working class, as of 1929, turns out to be identical for the intensive and less intensive samples (36 and 57). No meaningful differences have been observed to date in comparisons of the effects of economic change within the two samples. Income declined between 1929 and the low year by approximately 15 percent among nondeprived middle- and working-class families, and by 55 percent among deprived families.

The general course of economic recovery between the 1930s and World War II provides a rationale for differing interpretations of Depression hardship in the subsequent life course of the Berkeley men. One focuses on family deprivation throughout the 1930s and its adverse developmental consequences; the other on economic recovery and orientations toward a future of more abundant opportunities. The former perspective stresses the imperatives of family survival in the Depression era which called forth adaptations and ways of life that may have run directly contrary to long-range interests and goals, such as a father's desire to ensure a more beneficent life for his son. Though hard-pressed parents may have favored higher education for their sons, the coercive realities of economic deprivation and their stubborn persistence suggest a different outlook based on correlated strains, emotional and socioeconomic, that undermined school performance and aspirations, a sense of competence and security, and financial support (Mechling, 1971; Elder, 1974; Sacks, 1975). Observations on family responses to economic loss in the 30s have documented a substantial increase in financial and psychological strain, disorganization of household routines, and a shift in family patterns in which father became a less attractive parental figure to both sons and daughters. Through gainful employment and earnings, adolescent boys played a significant role in the economy of deprived households, in some cases to the detriment of their own education. From this vantage point, an understanding of the wartime adolescence of the Berkeley men and their life options at the time requires knowledge of their childhood experience during the Great Depression. Family strains and the developmental outcomes of economic deprivation are likely to be expressed in an educational and health disadvantage among men who grew up in deprived families within the middle and working class.

Three conceptual aspects of these strains have particular relevance to an understanding of the survival predicament of young children in the Depression: (1) loss of control of desired outcomes, experienced through seemingly inexplicable parental distress and behavior; (2) social ambiguity or ambivalence, as manifested through relational uncertainties and conflicts, extreme mood swings, inconsistent discipline and demands; and (3) relative loss of the father as a nurturant, strong, affirmative male figure. Under such conditions, both the family environment and the child's resources would favor a survival course of withdrawal from conflict, hypersensitivity to others, and passivity. The safest course for a young child in a world made unpredictable and hurtful is to avoid action that impinges on significant others. Miller and Swanson (1960:79) describe such a world in their analysis of a boy whose mother demands obedience to regulations that are not explained. "His world soon consists of high fences bounding any little spaces from which he can escape only by risking her disapproval. In new situations he cannot afford the risk of arriving at his own judgments. Because he often does not understand the purposes of his mother's regulations, he cannot tell whether she will condemn the actions he takes on his own initiative."

Such developmental outcomes are consistent with theory that links family patterns to the adaptive requirements of concrete situations, with the critical developmental stage of the Berkeley men at the time of family hardship, and with studies that have reported a negative association between the downward mobility of fathers and the achievement behavior of sons (Smelser, 1963; Douglas, 1964). This research also directs attention to the potential counterinfluence of family recovery from the Depression on the developmental course and life options of sons; it suggests that the most adverse effect of economic deprivation was concentrated among men who grew up in families that failed to regain their pre-Depression standing, especially by the end of Wordl War II. But whatever the recovery status of families, a modest upswing in the economy during the last half of the 1930s (excluding the depressed years of 1937–1938) provides sufficient reason to consider adaptations to the anticipated future in the 1940s, with its greater promise for the younger generation.

A long-standing assumption in socialization theory holds that parents rear their children in terms of the world they expect them to enter. Responses to everyday pressures and constraints are structured in terms of the future. Accordingly, Inkeles (1955:14–15) argues that parents in times of drastic change will intentionally adapt their "childrearing practices to train children better suited to meet life in the changed world as the parents see it." This account assumes a substantial degree of future awareness, rationality, and choice in parental behavior, conditions which were not favored by the emergency requirements of family survival in the Depression. Nevertheless, one might expect more evidence of this future orientation among the Bekeley parents and sons during the late 1930s and prosperous war years, as expressed by aspirations and the boys' school performance.

Within this historical context, a background of economic hardship may well have reinforced belief in the importance of advanced education as a path to financial security and control over one's destiny. Studies have found a strong attachment to class of origin among working-class fathers who were brought up in the middle class, an identification reflected in goals for children if not in actual child-rearing behavior (Elder, 1968:92; cf. Allingham, 1967). Such evidence and its broader implications suggest that parent aspirations for adolescent sons were not constrained by Depression hardship, and, in fact, may have become more conscious and emphatic in the education-aware middle class. By insisting that offspring be successful and plan for college in the face of continuing hardship, middle-class parents would project a favored world in keeping with economic growth and also profit from the image—"we are not down and out." Whether such aspirations were present during World War II or implied family recovery, *they could have unintended consequences by intensifying the psychic damage of a deprived childhood which lacked male "models of resilience"* (see Murphy, 1974:94). Children socialized amidst family strain and examples of failure are not likely to be well equipped for accentuated pressures and decisions on life matters in the adolescent years.

Berkeley is itself an education-conscious city, and families are known to have chosen to settle in the city in order to offer their children a better chance for entering the local state university. The state of California also offered all youth with a high-school diploma an extraordinary opportunity for higher education; a tuition-free place in an institution of higher learning (Smelser and Almond, 1974:14–27). Though only the most able had access to the state universities, junior and state colleges were available to the average or borderline student. One consequence of this system is that California has led all states for many years in the proportion of its college-age population in educational institutions. Another important implication is that we would expect the educational constraints of family deprivation in the 1930s to be manifested in the lives of equally able students primarily *during the course of their college career,* and perhaps in the type of school attended, from the lowly junior college to the prestigious state university. Even qualified boys from hard-pressed families may have been able to manage the initial costs of higher education if they boarded at home. This option was available to the Berkeley men since the Bay region offered a broad selection of institutions at all levels, from the University of California to junior colleges. However, even with this option and free tuition, each year of higher education meant greater financial pressure on students from a Depression background of economic hardship, both through rising economic demands (books, clothes, activities) and earnings foregone. Among some families that barely managed to survive the 30s, the price of advanced education would surely have included the sacrifice of financial aid which they would otherwise have received from an older son.

Opportunity in California's system of higher education may also apply to work in its booming, full-employment economy of the postwar era. Wages and salaries more than doubled between 1940 and the mid-40s, a trend which continued upward in the postwar years, though at a more moderate pace. Rapid corporate expansion was coupled with pronounced growth in professional, managerial, technical, and service jobs.[4] Labor demands and mobility opportunities were such that men could advance to prestigious occupations without the credentials of a four-year college program. In view of these considerations, there is some reason to doubt whether any developmental or educational handicap from the Depression era would carry over to work life progress. It is noteworthy that this transfer of disability did not occur in the lives of men who experienced the Great Depression as adolescents in Oakland (Elder, 1974:Chapter 7). Economic deprivation restricted educational opportunity primarily among the sons of working-class parents, but even in this group the effect did not handicap work life achievement up to middle age. California's economic growth of the postwar years undoubtedly qualifies as one of the equalizing factors in this outcome.

Such opportunities cannot of course explain why some young men were more likely than others to take advantage of them or to use their formal education, as credentials and acquired skills, to greater effect in their work life. What social experiences and developmental change would enable men from deprived backgrounds to surmount educational and psychological disabilities in their careers and health at mid-life? Clues may be found in adult responsibilities and rewards, and we have suggested the growth experience of work life as a primary factor, though military service, marriage, and parenthood are also plausible sources of personal consolidation and development. Among the Oakland men, the disability of economic hardship was countered by experiences that proved valuable in the world of jobs and employers. Reality testing in vocational development came early to the boys from deprived households; though no more ambitious than the nondeprived, they were more likely to have paid jobs in adolescence, to crystallize their vocational commitments during early adulthood, and, subsequently, to enter a stable career line at an earlier age. This life course may appear to have little relevance to the Berkeley men, who were young children during the worst phase of the Depression. But at the very least, one might expect a childhood of scarcity to magnify the importance of work as *the* route to economic independence, security, and recognition. This would be even more likely among those youth who lost out in education.

Overview of Analysis

In turning to our analysis of the Great Depression in life prospects, we begin with the early life course of the Berkeley men, their educational history, and personality development, and then branch out to their work life accomplishments and psychological functioning up to mid-life. Three general hypotheses informed by theory and research, are at issue: (1) that Depression hardship more adversely influenced the life course and health of the Berkeley men, when compared to the lives of the Oakland men, as described in *Children of the Great Depression;* (2) that this outcome in the Berkeley cohort will be most pronounced among men who grew up in the working class (class position hypothesis); and (3) that such outcomes will be manifested primarily in the early life course of the Berkeley men, in an educational disadvantage and impaired psychological functioning.

The latter hypothesis on the timing of impact suggests contrasting developmental paths and timetables to mid-life status and health (cf. Offer and Offer, 1975). It implies that some men from hard-pressed families will repair the damage of their Depression childhood through adult experience (especially work) and in such cases the middle years (age 30+) will be regarded as more rewarding than either childhood or adolescence. For the children of relative privilege, the nondeprived, adulthood is apt to bring far more setbacks and disappointments than they had encountered to that point, and, consequently, may not be viewed as positively as their earlier years.

EDUCATIONAL CAREERS AND DEVELOPMENTAL PATTERNS

The early life course of the Berkeley cohort vividly shows the imprint of postwar opportunity. Some program of higher education became a reality for most of the boys (80 percent), a level of attainment well above that of their fathers and the Oakland men (45 and 66 percent, respectively). Three-fourths of the college entrants enrolled in a four-year institution (one-third at U.C., Berkeley) and all but five began their careers in the state of California. Approximately 30 percent of the total cohort completed one to three years of higher education and less than a third did so within a junior college; thus some college does not merely reflect the achievement constraints of a two-year institution. Twenty-nine percent of the cohort ended up their educational career with a bachelor's degree, and slightly more than a fifth pursued some type of postgraduate work, for the most part only up to the Master's level. As implied by such achievement, our explanatory task is less one of accounting for college entrance than of explaining variations in progress beyond that point and their consequences for occupational careers and psychological health. Other events are prominent in structuring this phase of the life course and provide a useful context in which to assess the enduring impact of family origins.

Socioeconomic Origins in Early Life Events

Three early life events illumine the cohort's timetable relative to educational experience and also differentiate levels of attainment by their temporal arrangement. They are full-time entry into the labor force, age at first marriage, and entry into the armed services. Among the men who ever married, approximately half entered the labor force before the end of the 1940s, and were both married and out of school by 1951 (Table 1). Three-fourths of the men served in the military, mainly during the Korean War. According to sequence, military experience is the only event that was more likely to occur before the completion of education—57 percent. From available evidence, we know that the G.I. Bill provided educational benefits for some men and we suspect that they were far more prevalent than our sketchy records on this issue imply. In any case, this sequence and that of work entry before school leaving appear with greatest frequency among men in two career categories; some college and postgraduate. For nearly 60 percent of these men, higher education was interrupted by periods of full-time employment or military service. A central theme of economic need and self-support is suggested by the early life pattern of the college entrants who did not complete four years; unlike the college graduates and postgraduates, these men were unlikely to marry before departing from school or before entering the labor market. Marital delay seemingly represents an adaptation to persistent hard times, and we find support for this interpretation in the family history of these men.

Although the times were unusually generous to the Berkeley men in terms of advanced education, those who came from the working class or from households that suffered heavy income losses in the 1930s were far less likely to experience such good fortune. As noted earlier, income

Table 1

Early Status Transitions and Sequences in the Life Course of the Berkeley
Men by Their Educational Attainment, in Percentages and Medians

Timing and Sequence of Life Events	Early Status Transitions and Sequences by Educational Attainment, in Medians and Percentages				
	Total[a] (N = 75)	High school or less (N = 16)	Some college (N = 22)	College (N = 21)	Post-graduate N = 16
Median age at:					
Full-time employment	**21.8**	**18.2**	**20.3**	**23.0**	**25.7**
First marriage	**23.8**	**22.0**	**24.0**	**24.1**	**24.3**
Entry into military	**22.3**	**20.7**	**21.0**	**22.4**	**23.0**
Completion of education	**23.1**	**18.6**	**21.7**	**23.3**	**29.0**
Status sequences:					
Education exit - work entry					
Education then work	13	6	4	33	6
Same year	44	62	42	38	39
Work then education	43	31	54	29	56
	100	99	100	100	101
Education exit – marriage					
Education then marriage	44	69	59	38	6
Same year	16	19	14	19	12
Marriage then education	40	12	27	43	81
	100	100	100	100	99
Work entry – marriage					
Work then marriage	57	75	77	48	25
Same year	15	12	18	14	12
Marriage then work	28	12	4	38	62
	100	99	99	100	99
Education exit – military entry					
Education then military	24	57	28	21	7
Same year	19	14	11	42	–
Military then education	57	28	61	37	93
	100	99	100	100	100

[a] We have restricted this analysis to ever-married men since first marriage is included in our assessment of status sequences. The number of cases is smaller than indicated for the comparison of education exit and military entry – only three-fourths of the men entered the service.

losses were especially widespread in the childhood experience of men from the working class, but their educational disadvantage appears well before hard times in the Depression. In 1930–1931, working-class parents ranked well below parents in the middle class on achievement standards and encouragement (Macfarlane, 1938). We see the main effect of lower family origin in termination of formal education at the high school level and in the type of institution of higher learning attended; with but one exception, the men who enrolled in junior colleges did so from the working class and none of them later transferred to a four-year college or university. This social background, with its cultural and resource limitations, turns out to be far more influential than family losses during the Depression in putting an end to educational careers before college or in junior college; 56 percent of the working-class sons followed this course, compared to only 8 percent from the middle class.

As a barrier to higher education, Depression hardship appears among boys who enrolled in college, and is expressed primarily in failure to complete a four-year program. This outcome, it should be noted, is not due to the type of entry institution, whether two- or four-year; men from deprived households were not more likely than the nondeprived to enroll in a junior college. If we restrict our analysis to college entrants, the likelihood of completing a four-year program is substantially higher among the sons of nondeprived parents when compared to the deprived, a difference which persists even with adjustments for class background and mental ability. Among the college entrants, the educational disadvantage of family deprivation (beta $= -.27$) is roughly equivalent to that of lower-class origin (beta $= -.24$), and is far greater than that observed among the Oakland men (beta $= -.09$). Both of these influences correspond with an economic interpretation of event sequences among men who ended up with some college, a majority of whom entered the labor force or the military before school leaving and married thereafter.

It is not obvious how family deprivation in the early 1930s could shape the course of educational outcomes some fifteen years later; the Depression's impact on families peaked well before the Berkeley men encountered the immediate financial problems of advanced education. However, such problems do represent a plausible element in our account if Depression hardship persisted in the war years through work life instability and the depletion of resources. These effects would include a dominant mother and problematic father, the necessity for self-support and possible aid to parents, as well as dismal prospects for a college education. Though qualified youth could enter a state college or university at minimal expense, owing to free tuition, inadequate economic support from a hard-pressed family would make full-time progress toward a four-year degree highly problematic. Whatever the type of institution attended, "some

Table 2

Educational Attainment in Relation to Class Origin and Family Deprivation,
in Percentages and Beta Coefficients

Education by Class and Deprivation in Percentages and
Beta Coefficients

Educational Attainment	Class origin		Middle-class origin		Total sample	
	Middle I,II,III	Working IV,V	Non-deprived	Deprived	Non-deprived	Deprived
Postgraduate	30	11	32	25	24	18
College, 4 yrs.	43	11	45	38	40	16
Some college	21	39	13	38	16	45
H.S. or less	6	39	10	—	20	21
	100(47)	100(36)	100(31)	101(16)	100(45)	100(38)

$$r = .50 \qquad r = -.27 \qquad r = -.39$$
$$\text{beta} = .35^a \qquad \text{beta} = -.23^b \qquad \text{beta} = -.27^b$$

[a] The full range of educational attainment (postgraduate, college, some college, high school, less than high school) is included in our calculation of zero — order correlation and beta coefficients. The beta coefficient represents the main effect of class origin (as measured by Hollingshead's five-level index based on father's education and occupation in 1929 — full range included) on educational attainment with economic deprivation (0 = nondeprived, 1 = deprived) and the boys' median IQ (age 6 - 14) included in the equation.

[b] The effect of family deprivation is restricted to the men who entered a program of higher education, and mainly differentiates those who did not complete four years of college from all other college entrants. In order to represent this effect, we coded educational attainment among the college entrants as college completion (score of 1) and some college (score = 0). The beta coefficient thus indicates the main effect of family deprivation on college completion, with class origin and IQ controlled. Though heteroscedasticity becomes a problem when a dependent variable is dichotomized, our results do not differ from those obtained from other modes of analysis which avoid this difficulty, such as probit analysis.

college" may reflect a compromise between aptitude and economic reality in the lives of men from deprived homes. The evidence at hand indicates that they were just as capable on measured intelligence as the sons of nondeprived parents, with class origins taken into account.

In lieu of evidence on the decision process at the time, we gain some understanding of economics in the scheduling of early events among men from deprived homes. Within the some college group, work entry before school leaving turns out to be relatively common among both the deprived and nondeprived. However, men with deprived backgrounds are distinguished by their pronounced tendency to assume a full-time job well before marriage (at least one year) and to enter military service prior to the completion of education; average differences of 20 and 55 percent, respectively, when compared to the nondeprived. Both of these differences represent a contrast that is independent of class background. The prominence of military service among the sons of deprived parents (25 percent higher than the nondeprived) and its scheduling before school leaving in their lives seem to point to educational benefits (G.I. Bill) as a motive, though one suspects other functions that can only be understood within the developmental course of their lives. For youth confused about past and future by a troubled family history, the military may have had special appeal as a "psychosocial moratorium" from commitment pressures (Erikson, 1968), a legitimate term away from school, job, and family in which to sort matters out, to consolidate and acquire mature self-certainty as their own person. A good many of the deprived boys undoubtedly resolved matters of self and occupation during this life phase, for work life began in earnest shortly after they left the Armed Forces.[5]

Graduation from college (four years +) and some college represent the primary contrast by Depression hardship, apart from class variations, and the graduates show very little evidence of the economic pressure that we have inferred from the pattern of events among men with lower achievement. Only one-fourth followed the general sequence of labor force or military entry, education exit, and first marriage, a life course that applies to nearly three-fourths of men with some college. If economic constraints from the Depression years largely account for this difference and for the educational disadvantage, one would expect the effect of economic loss and unemployment in the 1930s to be expressed through evidence of family hardship which *persisted* into the 1940s. The Depression's legacy thus takes the form of a continuing handicap at a time of war-generated prosperity, perhaps through paternal impairment, lack of economic recovery or advancement, and depleted assets in savings and investments.

To explore this legacy, we constructed an index of the family's socioeconomic career between 1929 and 1945, using selected aspects of the father's work life. Fathers who suffered a heavy income loss (classified as deprived) experienced a more unstable work life into the war years than the nondeprived, as indicated by multiple jobs and employers, one or more shifts in line of work, less time in a consistent line of work, a fluctuation in occupational status (e.g., movement down, up, down), and status loss between 1929 and World War II. These aspects of the family career are highly interrelated (average $r = .46$) and formed a satisfactory index of persistent hardship through a principal axis factor analysis with iterations (eigenvalue = 3.28); each work life item was equally weighted to produce a composite score with a reliability (omega) of .90 and a validity coefficient of .95.

According to this measure, persistent hardship represents a substantial link between family deprivation during the early 1930s ($r = .56$) and lack of completion of college in the postwar years ($r = -.32$). The disadvantage of persistent hardship is most pronounced among sons from the middle class, where institutionalized career paths are particularly disrupted by a disorderly work life. Among college entrants from this social class, the effect of initial economic deprivation upon completion of college is due entirely to the persistence of hard times in family life; the main effect of deprivation is $-.06$ (beta) with persistent hardship and IQ included in the regression equation. However, even in the total sample of college entrants, it is persistent hardship resulting from family deprivation during the early 1930s that largely accounts for the educational disadvantage of men from deprived families. Two-thirds of the deprivational effect on attainment in higher education occurred through a pattern of socioeconomic troubles that extended into the war years.

These results carry us some distance toward specifying constraints that link two events which are widely separated in historical time and context, family deprivation during the early 1930s and failure to complete four years of college during the postwar years of generalized prosperity. Thirty-one percent of all families in the sample experienced some form of instability or hardship between 1930 and the end of World War II, as indicated by our measure of persistent hardship; and, with few exceptions, these families suffered economic misfortune during the Great Depression.

Depression Hardship and Developmental Outcomes

The persistence of family deprivation into the war years does not offer a precise account of the process by which this condition restricted achievement in higher education. Was this effect expressed mainly through a lack of parental support, economic and social; through developmental handicaps in early school achievement, aspirations, and personality—self-image, competence, etc.; or did it occur through a combination of these outcomes? In lieu of explicit evidence on economic support of son's education, whether by expense account or board and room, we must estimate this factor indirectly through tests of alternative hypotheses. Data are available on two such interpretations; that Depression hardship and its persistence (1) discouraged parental aspirations for son's higher education and (2) produced developmental costs in the boy's own school achievement and psychosocial maturation.

At first thought, low parental aspirations seem to offer a most implausible interpretation, since college entry was equally common among boys from both deprived and nondeprived families. Annual interviews with the Berkeley mothers from 1940 to 1945 included an open-ended question concerning parent ideals for offspring. The question did not mention educational or occupational goals, though such aspirations were verbalized by approximately half of the mothers over this time period. From a review of all maternal responses to this question, we noted that references to aspirations generally occurred in family contexts that made such achievement both problematic and important, such as the deprived middle class. Using the list of statements, we coded each boy in terms of whether his mother reported high aspirations (professional, managerial), lower aspirations, or no goals.

High aspirations were more prevalent in the responses of middle-class mothers, when compared to mothers from the working class (44 percent vs. 23 percent), and within the middle class they were most often expressed by mothers who experienced hard times in the Depression (53 percent vs. 36 percent, nondeprived). Among working-class families, high aspirations were associated with the more privileged position of nondeprived households, but the difference is too small to be reliable. This class difference suggests that maternal aspirations varied according to recovery from hard times in the Depression; that mothers were most likely to espouse high goals for their sons under conditions of economic recovery, a change for the better which is concentrated among deprived families in the middle class.

Whatever the pressures associated with persistent hardship, we find *no* evidence that they lowered maternal aspirations; on the contrary, ambition for son tended to flourish under such conditions (beta = .16), and the effect is strongest among mothers in the middle class. It is misery, not personal fulfillment, which fed such ambition; a desire to achieve compensation for life frustrations and husband's failure by living through the accomplishments of sons. The more ambitious mothers with deprived histories were likely to occupy a dominant position in family affairs during the 1930s, to have impaired and nonsupportive husbands, and to value lofty economic standards before hard times (average beta = .34). These women also found the traditional family role too confining and unrewarding. By contrast, their counterparts from nondeprived homes were distinguished by a sense of life gratification; their husbands were emotionally supportive during problem situations in the 1930s, participated in family activities, and assumed a leading role on family decisions (average beta = .32). Yet despite such varied developmental roots, it is apparent that maternal ambitions for sons do not in themselves enable us to account for the educational disadvantage of a deprived background.

If maternal aspirations are ruled out as a factor in the divergent educational careers of men from deprived and nondeprived families, do we gain some insight from their early school record, aspirations, and psychological development? Do we find any evidence of a cumulative disadvantage from childhood through adolescence? To answer these questions, we used the following measures on the boy's developmental history: (1) Stanford Achievement Test scores in reading and arithmetic, annual scores averaged for grades 1–2 and 5–6; (2) 7-point ratings by the boy's elementary school teacher on attitude toward school, leadership, and mood, annual ratings averaged for grades 5–6; (3) an interviewer's rating of the boy's emotional stability and social adjustment, annual ratings averaged for grades 5–6; (4) grade-point average in high school, averaged across all years and standardized; (5) a 9-point rating of aspiration level in adolescence, an average of two interrelated ($r = .67$) ratings—"has high aspirations" and "genuinely values intellectual and cognitive matters"; and (6) indices of psychological functioning in adolescence, as constructed from a set of Q ratings (scores range from 1 to 9). These personality measures are described more fully in the context of our analysis.

The boys entered first grade at a time when Depression hardship was still very much a source of family instability, yet we find no evidence of this strain in their school performance, emotional state, and social relationships during grade school. Throughout this time period, boys from the working class fared less well on reading tests than students from the middle class ($p < .05$), but neither test scores nor psychosocial development varied by economic deprivation within each stratum. These outcomes had far more to do with the class position and cultural resources of families, and perhaps the supportive environment of grade school, than with hard times in the Depression. But even with negative effects at this point, their long-range implications would depend on whether they carried over to the high school years and influenced critical decisions. In this life stage, which coincided with World War II, we observe a less positive future among deprived youth, when compared to the nondeprived. Among the boys who eventually entered college, family deprivation is linked to lower aspirations and grades ($r_s = -.18$ and $-.30$), an association which occurs primarily through a pattern of continuing hardship.

This causal chain is represented in Figure 2 by a path-analytic model for all boys who embarked on higher education. Class origin and economic deprivation are defined as antecedent to the boys' intellectual functioning (as indexed by IQ) and persistent hardship in the family; senior high GPA and aspirations constitute potential linkages between these four variables and level of educational attainment beyond college entrance—some college, four years of college, and postgraduate studies. Each path with a beta coefficient greater than .09 is retained in the model (e.g., by this criterion, family deprivation does *not* have a direct effect on the boys' performance on IQ tests), and is described by a beta coefficient and a

Figure 2 Linking Economic Deprivation to Educational Attainment

Regression Coefficients in Standard Form
(r correlations within parentheses)
—Trimmed Model N = 66, College Entrants Only

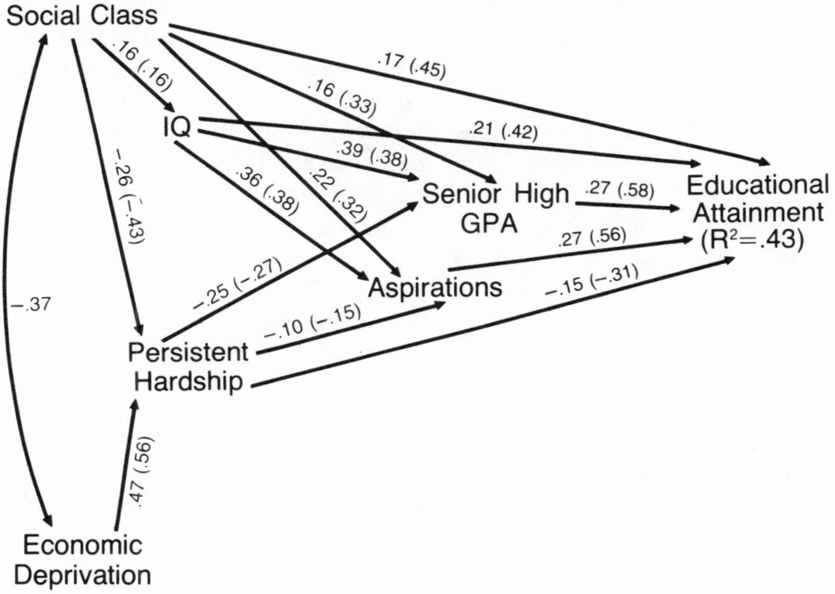

zero-order correlation coefficient (within parentheses). The diagram charts the two major influences, class origin and family deprivation, and their pathways to outcomes in higher education. Middle-class origin is linked to success in higher education through achievement capacity, as indexed by IQ, scholastic performance, and adolescent aspirations. Depression hardship restricted higher education when hard times persisted into the war years and lowered both aspirations and grades. Though family deprivation is negatively related to advancement in higher education ($r = -.32$), it has no direct effect in this regard (beta = .04) or on IQ, high school grades, and aspirations. To an equal extent, both economic and developmental constraints interpret the relationship between Depression hardship and failure to complete college in the Berkeley cohort. Economic constraints are expressed in the direct cost of persistent hardship; a developmental handicap in the negative effect of such hardship on grades and aspirations in high school.

From our analysis to date, childhood and adolescence tell a very different story concerning the life prospects of deprived youth who managed to continue their education beyond high school. The developmental costs of family hardship emerge *only* during the boys' adolescent years in World War II, a period of rising prosperity. Does this apparent change in behavioral outcome reflect the cumulative impact of life in a hard-pressed family, a change in developmental course marked by stress and uncertainties that proved costly in undermining the boys' self-confidence, adaptive capacity, and vision of the future? Lower aspirations among the deprived boys may be symptomatic of defenses and coping responses that were shaped by a family history of scarcity and personal trauma, of insecurity fashioned by adult figures who failed and were not to be counted on or emulated. Lacking male examples of dependability and emotional support at a young age, deprived boys may have learned to manage the "hurt" in their lives by lowering what they expected out of life, by avoiding commitments that entail risks, and by closing off the world of adversity through denial or withdrawal. Such responses are commonly part of a clinical syndrome of impaired self-esteem (Rosenberg, 1965), hypersensitivity to criticism, and self-pity in feeling cheated or victimized by events.

Some of these orientations toward self and others were observed in the lives of Oakland boys whose families suffered heavy losses in the Great Depression (Elder, 1974: Chapter 6). Drastic change tends to heighten sensitivity to others by making relationships uncertain, and we find this behavior among deprived boys in the Oakland cohort. Compared to the nondeprived in both middle- and working-class families, the deprived were more often described by their mothers as self-conscious, vulnerable to hurt feelings, worrisome, and subject to angry outbursts when frustrated. Despite such differences, family hardship was not expressed in self-disparagement, low aspirations, or impaired relations with age-mates. Both the younger age of the Berkeley boys and their longer exposure to family misfortune before leaving home—from the early 1930s to the war years—support the expectation that family deprivation had more adverse and enduring consequences for their adolescent development.

This expectation is generally borne out by a clinician's assessment of the boys' psychological functioning in adolescence, an appraisal based on selected nine-point ratings from the California Q Sort.[6] The clinician's judgments were informed by a thorough review of all case materials on each boy from childhood to the adolescent years; these include staff observations and interviews with the boys and their mothers. Among boys who continued their education beyond high school, we find considerable evidence in adolescence of a developmental pattern shaped by the Depression experience (Table 3). Whatever their class origin before hard times, youth who grew up in deprived households are characterized more by a lack of self-esteem and personal meaning in life; by a tendency to withdraw from adversity, avoid commitments, and employ self-defeating tactics; and by a sense of victimization and vulnerability to the judgments of others. These attributes appear in the behavior of nondeprived as well as deprived adolescents, but they are clearly more prevalent among the latter, especially in the middle class. By comparison and contrary to our hypothesis, family losses made substantially less difference in how working-class youth felt about themselves or responded to life's problems. The lower the class position of families before the Depression, the less boys were judged responsible and considerate of others (average $r =$ $-.21$), and family misfortune reinforced this behavior pattern in the working class. But beyond such outcomes, the psychic costs of Depression hardship are concentrated within the middle class.

Judging from this outcome and results to this point, it is apparent that

Table 3

Adolescent Personality Ratings in Relation to Family Deprivation by Class Origin: Regression Coefficients (College Entrants Only)

Adolescent personality ratings.[a] (California Q Set)	Effects of Family Deprivation on Adolescent Personality[b] by Class Origin: Regression Coefficients			
	Unstandardized Coefficients		Standardized Coefficients	
	Total	Middle class	Total	Middle class
	(N = 61)	(N = 41)	(N = 61)	(N = 41)
Responsible: dependable, gets things done	-.41	-.24	-.10	-.06
Considerate of others: giving toward others, has warmth, etc.	-.06	.44	-.02	.12
Withdraws from adversity: not assertive, withdraws in face of frustration, submissive	.53	.93	.13	.23
Low self-esteem: concerned with adequacy, not satisfied with self, basically anxious	.39	.78	.14	.25
Feels victimized: feels cheated and victimized by life	.88	1.11	.22	.25
Lacks personal meaning: feels a lack of personal meaning in life	1.04*	1.59+	.24*	.35+

Table 3. (cont.)

Adolescent personality ratings.[a] (California Q Set)	Effects of Family Deprivation on Adolescent Personality[b] by Class Origin: Regression Coefficients			
	Unstandardized Coefficients		Standardized Coefficients	
	Total	Middle class	Total	Middle class
	(N = 61)	(N = 41)	(N = 61)	(N = 41)
Reluctant to commit self: tends to delay or avoid action	1.02	1.34	.19	.25
Thin-skinned: vulnerable to anything that can be construed as criticism or slight	.87*	1.24+	.24*	.34+
Self-defeating in relation to goals	.71	.88	.19	.24

* $p < .10$, + $p < .05$

a   Each of the first four characteristics is indexed by an average of scores on nine-point Q ratings: Responsible — "is genuinely dependable and responsible person" and "is productive; gets things done" (two items, average $r = .78$); Considerate — "behaves in a giving way toward others (regardless of motivation involved)," "behaves in a sympathetic or considerate manner," and "has warmth; is compassionate" (three items, average $r = .78$). Withdraws from adversity — "gives up and withdraws where possible in face of frustration and adversity," "behaves in an assertive fashion in interpersonal situations" (reflected), "basically submissive" (three items, average $r = .48$); and Low self-esteem — "is overconcerned with own adequacy as a person, either at conscious or unconscious levels," "feels satisfied with self" (reflected), and "is basically anxious" (three items, average $r = .52$). The other five characteristics are indexed by a single rating, as described in the table.

b   To remove the effects of class origin in both the total and middle-class analysis we included the Hollingshead index of social position in each set of regression equations. Three strata within the middle class (I, II, III) both required and enabled statistical control of intraclass variations.

our initial thinking failed to give sufficient weight to class variations in the psychological transition between economic depression and war-generated prosperity. If the insecurity and stresses of Depression hardship left boys ill-equipped to cope with parental achievement pressures in adolescence, such pressures were mainly the fate of middle-class youth. According to the limited evidence at hand, mothers in the deprived sector of this stratum were most emphatic in ambitions for sons, particularly when family realities called for some restraint. The psychological functioning of these boys reflects an accommodation to the disparity between lofty maternal claims and their perceived reality, between what their mother wanted and what they felt capable of accomplishing or in fact desired. The boys display symptoms of what Durkheim once called "the malady of unlimited aspirations." "What could be more disillusioning," he observed, "than to proceed toward a terminal point that is nonexistent, since it recedes in the same measure that one advances?. . . Pessimism always accompanies unlimited aspirations" (quoted by Nisbet, 1965:101). It is pessimism, not hopefulness, that stands out in the life style of adolescent boys from the deprived middle class. Instead of decisive action and mastery, we observe indecision, avoidance, and withdrawal—a syndrome resembling Erikson's concept of identity diffusion. It is a syndrome that also brings to mind a circle of causation (Smith, 1968:277) in which failures, experienced and anticipated, make one "hesitant to try. What to others are challenges appear to him as threats; he becomes preoccupied with defense of his small claims on life at the expense of energies to invest in constructive coping."

Some aspects of this behavior pattern are more strongly associated with family deprivation among the sons of ambitious mothers[7] and are correlated with hardship that persisted into the war years. Low self-esteem, self-defeating actions, and a sense of victimization are linked to deprivation in the 1930s through persistent hardship.[8] Continuing hardship also had consequences for a boy's sensitivity to criticism, his reluctance to commit himself to a course of action and his acquiescence or withdrawal in the face of adversity, but it is primarily the initial experience of family deprivation that accounts for these psychological states. Each of these characteristics are part of the small claims that deprived boys held on their future. Among both middle- and working-class youth, those who expected very little out of life (low aspirations) were judged least responsible, decisive, and assertive. A sense of victimization and meaninglessness were also part of their world view (average $r = .41$). This psychological pattern also appears in the behavior of boys who encountered academic problems in their high school career. Adolescent aspirations and achievement are thus embedded in developmental configurations that have roots in the Depression experience, either the psychological inadequacy of an adolescent who grew up amidst deprivation and emotional strain or the self-confident, coping posture of one blessed with a relatively secure and stable family situation.

By extending these developmental paths to the years of higher education, we gain suggestive insights concerning the process of early school-leaving among deprived youth. Judging from our materials, these boys entered college with a lower sense of adequacy, purpose, and ambition than the offspring of more affluent families; their scholastic record was not as strong and they undoubtedly harbored the belief that college for them meant unusual sacrifices on the part of their parents, if only in terms of earnings foregone. Within this framework, academic difficulties would tend to affirm misgivings and doubts, weaken commitments to the ideal of earning a four-year degree, and perhaps support the wisdom of time out for military service or civilian employment. Early school-leaving would thus relieve the presumed family burden of prolonged education. Among the college entrants, those who dropped out were characterized in adolescence by lower self-esteem, a tendency to withdraw from adversity, indecisive and self-defeating behavior, and a sense of victimization (average r = .18, with educational level). Though meaningful in fleshing out an account of early school-leaving, these factors do not enhance our statistical explanation; they are much too aligned with the syndrome of low aspirations and poor grades to provide additional information.

Review and Interpretation

Up to this point, we have examined evidence which bears upon two of the three general hypotheses that inform our study; variations in the effect of Depression hardship by *life stage* and *class position*. The third hypothesis on the timing of impact (the main effect will occur during the early life course) awaits analysis of the adult years to middle age. The Berkeley youth occupied a more vulnerable developmental stage at the time of family deprivation, when compared to their older counterparts in the Oakland cohort, and Depression hardship did entail more substantial educational and psychological disadvantages for members of the Berkeley cohort. However, the processes leading to this outcome yielded some unexpected results. Income losses drastically altered the childhood environment of a large percentage of the Berkeley boys, and yet the adverse effect of this change only appears during their wartime adolescence. Neither academic performance in grade school nor evidence of childhood impairments are linked to family deprivation. In retrospect, this finding corresponds with the proposition that developmental limitations are likely to surface when children encounter demanding situations that call upon their adaptive resources, as in the transition from the protective environment of an elementary school to the achievement pressures of adolescence. This transition coincided with a number of other changes in the social experience of the Berkeley youth (increasing prosperity, rising aspirations, etc.), and it is at this point that we begin to see adverse effects from the Depression experience. Though contrary to our initial expectations, this psychological pattern is concentrated among the sons of parents in the deprived middle class, a subgroup which was most subject to the discontinuity between scarcity conditions and the aspirations of wartime America.

The diverse psychological paths of the nondeprived and deprived bear upon the degree of synchrony between adaptive potential and situational demands or requirements. The risk of adolescents from the protected environment of a nondeprived family is based on a childhood where demands seldom challenged adaptive capacities. Their relative well-being in adolescence may tell us very little about how they managed the stresses of work, family, and civic obligations in adulthood (Sanford, 1966:30). By comparison, boys with a history of family deprivation were exposed to the developmental risk of demands and stresses which surpassed their adaptive resources, and it is this disparity which seems more pronounced and costly in the Berkeley cohort than among older youth in the Oakland cohort. Nevertheless, we ought not discount the possibility that the Depression experience offered some developmental benefits, perhaps in the form of preparation for the stresses of adult responsibilities.

From a life course perspective, the incompetent self that appears in adolescence may indicate a painful phase which did not close off options for subsequent growth in self-integration, resilience, and meaningful direction, despite a handicap in formal education. In this regard military service acquires significance as a potential developmental context for young men who lacked hopeful feelings about themselves and the future. This experience and that of work may counter the simple equation that early disadvantage equals more of the same in adult life; that the educational and psychological limitations of men with deprived histories will carry over to their adult experience up to middle age. As Vaillant (1974:22) reminds us, "damaged children when adult can find ingenious ways to compensate for early deprivation. . . . The adaptive capacity of the ego may reflect the difficulties it has mastered as often as it reflects the assets with which it was blessed." Such mastery is not apparent in the early lives of the Berkeley boys who grew up in deprived families, but childhood and adolescence do not make a life.

An adequate test of the Depression experience in the Berkeley cohort thus entails broadening our scope to questions concerning experiences beyond education. It is not a matter of how little deprived youth were able to achieve in formal education, when compared to the nondeprived, but rather what both groups have done with their education and lives up to middle age. Most important in this regard is the arena of work life. Depression hardship and the precarious task of earning a living had important formative implications for a young boy's ideas about work, job security, and getting ahead. The Berkeley youth were too young in the 1930s to be gainfully employed, and we know very little about how father's unemployment and income losses influenced their thoughts and preferences on matters of work and self-support. Nevertheless, there is good reason to expect a high priority on stable work among the sons of deprived parents, and their early entry into the labor force is consistent with this interpretation. With appropriate opportunity, both early career beginnings and persistence favor a course of advancement that could minimize or reduce educational handicaps, just as it did among men who grew up in hard-pressed families within the city of Oakland.

FROM EDUCATION TO WORK AND HEALTH AT MID-LIFE

As the Berkeley men completed their education and military service in the postwar years, employment prospects looked very bright indeed, even for those who lacked a college degree. The Pacific Coast states and especially California were in the midst of rapid economic growth fueled by a boom-ing defense industry. Between 1950 and 1960, employment in professional-technical occupations expanded by 83 percent (Manor, 1963), and a significant number of the Depression children were part of this growth. By mid-life (1968), nearly three out of five middle-class sons occupied jobs in the professional-managerial stratum, as did a fourth of the men who grew up in the working class. At this stage, the working class included only three men from middle-class homes and a third of the sons of blue-collar fathers. Class differences in occupational achievement most clearly reflect differences in edication, but we find surprisingly little evidence of this handicap in the work life achievement of men who experienced Depression hardship.

College entrants from hard-pressed families did not advance as far in their education as their more privileged counterparts (beta = − .27), but we observe no reliable evidence of this in occupational status at mid-life (age 40, beta = − .05) after adjustments for class origin. Even among all men in the sample, family deprivation left no discernible mark on status attainment (beta = − .02). As in the Oakland cohort, the evidence points to work life experiences as an important pathway around the educational limitations of a deprived family history. Thus, among the college entrants, the occupational disadvantage of family hardship diminished between the first job after education to mid-life status (from beta − .12 to − .05) with class background taken into account. This change is more striking when educational inequality and class origin are eliminated from the picture; under this condition, deprived men actually gained more in their work lives than the sons of nondeprived parents, a differential which is more pronounced at mid-life than after the completion of education (beta = .06 and .24). The paradox here is that men whose adolescent behavior seemed least promising for a productive life—the children of Depression hardship—have apparently refuted this prognosis in their occupational accomplishments, even to the point of surmounting an educational handicap by achieving parity with the offspring of more fortunate childhoods, the nondeprived.

The well-established connection between level of education and occupational placement is commonly interpreted from an allocation perspective; ". . . that apart from anything they have learned, people are allocated to adult roles involving authority and efficiency on the basis of education, in modern societies" (Meyer, 1976:4). Whatever the dynamics of this process, the Berkeley cohort and other evidence points to considerable slippage between education and occupational status. A man's education is strongly related to his occupational position in our cohort ($r =$ .66), but men with varied Depression experiences are not uniformly distributed around the "best fitting line" between these variables. Men with deprived family histories were more likely to do better than one would predict from their education, whereas the reverse tendency is more applicable to the lives of the nondeprived. What a man did with his education, then, in terms of work status at mid-life, represents a key distinction between the adult experience of men who grew up in deprived and nondeprived families.

To investigate this difference in life experience, we defined two types of adult achievement (high and low) relative to given levels of education; the category of high achievement includes men whose occupational status at least equaled or surpassed the expected level. Two classification procedures were employed in assigning men to one of these categories: (1) a prediction equation in which mid-life status was regressed on educational attainment; and (2) a clinical evaluation of work life histories involving independent judgments by project analysts—differences were resolved by a third judge. The first approach was applied to the large group of men who entered college but did not continue beyond four years or a bachelor's degree. To assess the mid-life status of these men by education, we obtained predicted levels of achievement from a regression analysis that included educational level as well as IQ, senior high GPA, and adolescent aspirations. The high achievement group included men whose actual status did not fall below their predicted score by 1.0 or more; twenty-eight out of forty-four men were so classified.

A clinical approach was used to classify achievements at opposite ends of the educational ladder, the postgraduates and men with less than college. In different ways, the work lives of these men were constrained by initial educational position (e.g., a high school graduate had less distance in which to move down than in which to move up the occupational strata), and the seven levels of the Hollingshead occupational index tended to magnify such constraints. By relying upon detailed work histories, we were able to utilize information concerning movement relative to education within general occupational strata that would otherwise have been lost to the classification. This includes career advancement in occupational prestige and authority, productivity, and reputation. Differences along these lines are reflected in the careers of two men with very similar training in medicine; one ended up as a staff member among many in an outpatient clinic of a hospital, the other as professor of medicine and a

Table 4

Selected Characteristics of College Entrants and Less Educated Men by Achievement Level Relative to Education, in Means and Percentages

Characteristics	Men's Characteristics by Education Category and Achievement Level, in Means and Percentages			
	College Entrants		Less than college	
	Low Ach. (N=26)	High Ach. (N=40)	Low Ach. (N=8)	High Ach. (N=8)
Early Factors				
Class origin, 1929: $\overline{X}$	3.7	3.0 L>H*	2.0	2.4
Economic deprivation: % deprived[a]	31%	55% L<H*	63%	38%
IQ: $\overline{X}$	123	125	107	103
Senior high GPA: $\overline{X}$	49	49	36	35
Adolescent aspirations: $\overline{X}$	4.6	4.6	2.3	2.4
Educational attainment				
Mean score: (1 = low, 7 = high)	6.0	5.8	2.9	2.4
Occupational status				
First full-time job after education: $\overline{X}$	4.2	5.4 L<H+	2.3	1.8
Mid-life status, 1968: $\overline{X}$	4.8	5.9 L<H+	3.3	4.3

* $p < .05$ + $p < .01$

[a] The main effect of family deprivation on achievement level for the college entrants is .20 (beta), with class origin and IQ included in the regression equation.

member of the school's board of directors. Two research associates achieved 80 percent agreement in their placement of the cases; 60 percent of all men in the cohort were classified as high achievers.

Men with deprived origins among the postgraduates and college group (graduates and some college) were most likely to be classified as high achievers (73 percent vs. 50 percent for nondeprived); but this life pattern does not apply to men who failed to enter college (38 percent vs. 62 percent for nondeprived), typically sons of working-class parents. Hard times resulting from the Depression did not account for the restricted schooling of the latter group, but these conditions were detrimental to their work life experience relative to education. It is Depression hardship in a context of low-class origin and limited educational skills that damaged the work life prospects of men in the cohort; despite a similar handicap on education, the nondeprived advanced to a higher position in their work life by age 40 (beta = .37). From this high school group to the college entrants and beyond, evidence of early achievement potential does not distinguish between those who were more or less successful in adult work life (Table 4). For analytical purposes, the low and high achievers are identical on measured intelligence, high school grades, and aspirations, and even level of formal education.

Adult Achievement and Work Life
Does work life yield clues to the divergent accomplishments of deprived men who entered college and those who failed to do so? Were the latter, for example, more attached as earners to the deprived economy of their family of origin, when compared to the nondeprived with comparable educational skills? Such ties and concerns might be expressed by early entry into the labor market, hasty acceptance of any job with adequate pay which is later discovered to offer no chance for advancement, and perhaps restricted job options through lack of geographic mobility. The data are consistent with this interpretation, though it is difficult to arrive at a satisfactory account, given archival limitations and subgroup size. We find that men with a deprived background did enter the labor force at an earlier age, spent a larger proportion of their work life in manual jobs and were more likely to switch both employer and line of work up to mid-life.[9] They established a stable pattern of work later in life than the nondeprived, and thus followed a single line of work for a shorter period of time. This unstable work life and prolonged earner status relative to the parental family jointly favor marital delay, and a late transition to adult status is strikingly characteristic of deprived men who never entered college. Extended support of aging parents and related emotional dependencies thus qualify as a plausible account of their lifetime disadvantage in work achievement.

Table 5

Life Course Attributes of Men by Achievement Level and Family Deprivation,
in Means, Percentages, and Regression Coefficients: College Entrants Only

Life Course Attributes by Achievement Level,
in Means and Percentages

Aspects of Life Course	Achievement level		Probability level	Deprivation effect[b]
	Low	High		
	(N = 26)	(N = 40)	(L vs. H)	beta
Timing of transitions				
($\overline{X}$ age in yrs.)				
Labor force entry	23.0	21.7	.09	-.09
Completion of education	26.2	24.6	.28	.15
First marriage	23.9	24.3	.71	.13
Work life[a]				
No. of jobs: $\overline{X}$	2.7	2.8	.80	.06
No. of employers: $\overline{X}$	2.3	2.0	.38	.18
Career delay, in yrs.: $\overline{X}$	10.6	7.8	.01	-.15
Duration of work line, in yrs.: $\overline{X}$	12.0	15.2	.00	.15
% work time in manual jobs: $\overline{X}$	26.0	12.0	.09	.13
Break in work line: %	33%	20%	.24	.13
Status fluctuations: %	33%	14%	.12	.02

a Number of jobs and employers refers to the period from 1956 through 1968. Career delay is indexed by the number of years between 1946 and year of entry into a relatively
stable line of work (followed for six years or more) — cases of no stable career were
given the maximum value by age at completion of education. Duration of work line refers to the total number of years a person has followed a single line of work (function-
ally related jobs), from 1946 through 1968. Percentage of time in manual jobs was calculated according to age at first full-time job after education. Break in work line refers
to discontinuity (one break or more) between completion of education and mid-life.
Lastly, status fluctuation depicts a course in which the worker moved first in one status
direction (up or down) and then in the opposite direction — the percentage of men with
at least one such pattern.

b Class origin is included in each regression equation.

Having entered college, men with deprived histories were more likely than the nondeprived to embark on a course that produced substantial work life achievement, and they did so without the advantage of more years of education or any detectable asset through adolescence. As a group, the high achievers entered full-time work and completed their education at an early age (Table 5), when compared to the less successful, and this accelerated beginning also extends to career entry, persistence, and stability. Successful men generally made a swift start in all areas except marriage, and we find some evidence of this pattern among the work careers of deprived men who entered college. They were slower than the nondeprived in marrying and completing their education, but they established a stable career line at an earlier age and tended to ply a consistent line of work over a longer time span. These two aspects of work account for approximately half of the association between Depression hardship and adult achievement (from beta = .20 to .11); early career entry and persistence proved to be even more important to the work life success of deprived men than to that of the nondeprived. We also detect some evidence of work life disorder among the deprived (more employers, breaks in line of work), but these events generally occurred early in work life and did not as a rule impair their occupational ascent.

The timing of career entry, persistence, and stability have obvious implications for a man's occupational advancement, but they are not sufficient in themselves as an explanation for the differential achievement of men who grew up in deprived and more affluent families. Men observed in adolescence as unambitious, submissive, and indecisive do not come to mind as workers who quickly established themselves career-wise and stayed with their line of work over an extended period of time. On the contrary, one would expect to see evidence of floundering and vacillation, a disorderly work pattern of frequent job shifts, periods of idleness, and status fluctuations. How, then, do we connect two phases within a life course that appear to have so little in common? How did a good many of the sons of deprived parents manage to achieve occupational success from a background of educational limitations and maladaptive behavior in adolescence?

Adult Achievement and Development

For the college boys with a background of Depression hardship, we suggest that developmental gains occurred in adaptive functioning between adolescence and the end of their third decade, the twenties; and that such change in the model of late development enables us to understand the disparity between their adolescent psychology and productive work life. This change may have been prompted by adult independence and work, or by marriage, parenthood, and the "psychosocial moratorium" of military service. The tendency to drop out of college for work or military service could be interpreted as symptomatic of floundering; and also as valuable maturing experience that enabled some men to achieve a sense of direction and purpose in life. The precise source of change will be difficult to establish, given the materials at hand, but the important question is whether developmental gains are primarily associated with the life course of college boys who grew up in hard-pressed families during the 1930s.

This question is placed in context by relevant differences and similarities between the life course of the Berkeley and Oakland cohorts. Nearly a decade older at the time of the Great Depression, the Oakland men, as adolescents, displayed no adverse effect of family deprivation on their outlook, aspirations, and vocational perspective; class origin influenced such views, but not family losses. As 20-year-olds, the economically deprived showed greater vocational certainty or crystallization than the nondeprived in both social strata, and were more likely to establish a stable career line at an early age. This developmental course led to an achievement advantage among men from the deprived middle class, and effectively countered an educational disadvantage in the adult lives of men with origins in the hard-pressed working class. Depression hardship thus influenced the two cohorts in ways which differed most during the early phase through schooling and least during the post-education years. These men started out life along contrasting paths, with pathological outcomes of family deprivation concentrated among the younger Berkeley group; but once they left school we observe substantial work life convergence up to mid-life. Perhaps reflecting their maturity in the Depression, the Oakland men show far greater life-span continuity on development pertaining to a successful occupational career than do the Berkeley men.

In view of the unpromising adolescence of Berkeley men from deprived homes, their adult accomplishments seem likely to be most critical in determining health at middle age. The greatest psychological change should appear among those who were relatively successful in work despite the handicap of background and early development, the high achievers. By contrast, continuity is suggested by a life history of Depression hardship, maladaptive behavior in adolescence, and an undistinguished or unrewarding work life. We begin our analysis with aspirations, a sensitive gauge of life situation and prospects, and then enlarge the scope to include both clinical and personal reports on psychological health. As noted in relation to the adolescent years, our measure of aspiration level is based on two interrelated nine-point Q-sort ratings; "has high aspiration level for self," and "genuinely values intellectual and cognitive matters." To compare aspirations in adolescence and the adult years, we developed corresponding measures from items in the two adult *Q*-sorts, 1959–1960 and 1969–1970 (see Haan and Day, 1974). Values on each item were averaged to yield a single score.

Between adolescence and middle-age, high aspirations became more salient among the characteristics of men who entered college (Table 6). Most of this upward trend occurred before the age of 30 and is concentrated among men who achieved success in their work life, a change that may reflect the increasing substantive complexity and rewards of their work (Kohn, 1976). Compared to the low achievers, these men show both a more pronounced temporal gain in the salience of high aspirations and greater instability up to middle age; their adolescent aspirations are less predictive of this orientation at age 30 and 40 than in the group which failed to achieve much headway in work after formal education. Consistent with our expectations, this contrast is most striking in the lives of men who experienced Depression hardship; those who followed a course of low achievement changed little in aspiration level over the life span, from adolescence to middle age, a pattern that differs markedly from the upward trend among successful men. The ambitions of these men bear little resemblance to their more pessimistic outlook in adolescence; the correlation coefficient between aspiration level in adolescence and mid-life is only .16 among achievers with a deprived background compared to .40 for the total sample. Within the limitations of subgroup size, variations in adult achievement sharply differentiate the aspiration trajectory of men who grew up in hard-pressed families, and they do so to a far greater extent than among the offspring of more affluent families.

This evidence of change in the perspective of successful men from deprived families supports an expectation of correlated developmental gains in self-evaluation, competence, and health between adolescence and mid-life. To what extent do these men also display greater resilience and well-being than we observed in adolescence? Were the social and psychic benefits of adult achievement sufficient to repair the developmental damage of hard times in the 30s? To explore these questions, we assembled nine identical measures of psychological functioning across three time periods (Adolescence, 30 years, and 40 years), as described in Table 3. Four measures (Responsible, Considerate, Withdrawal from Adversity, and Low Self-esteem) represent a composite of nine-point ratings from *Q* sets in each time period. Single ratings index the other characteristics—Feels Victimized, Lacks Personal Meaning, Reluctant to Commit Self, Thin-skinned, and Self Defeating. *Q*-sort descriptions for the two adult periods are based upon extensive interviews, ranging from approximately twelve hours in length for age 30 to about four hours in the 1968–1970 interview. Both the interviewers and the reliability raters (psychologists or psychiatric social workers) were restricted in their work

Table 6

Men's Aspirations Across Time by Achievement Level and
Family Deprivation, in Mean Scores and Correlations: College Entrants Only

Mean Aspiration Level by Achievement and Family Deprivation

Time period	Achievement level			Low achievement			High achievement		
	Low (N = 16)	High (N = 29)	Probability level	Nondep. (N = 10)	Deprived (N = 6)	Prob. level	Nondep. (N = 11)	Deprived (N = 15)	Prob. level
Time periods: $\overline{X}$									
Adolescence	5.0	4.6	.52	5.1	4.7	.72	5.2	4.2	.11
30 yrs. (approx. 1959 - 1960)	5.4	5.8	.30	5.6	5.0	.45	6.1	5.6	.40
40 yrs (approx. 1969 - 1970)	5.6	6.3	.12	6.0	4.8	.15	6.6	6.2	.47

Period comparisons

1 Adol. vs. 30 yr.						
Mean difference	.52	1.11	.64	.30	.84	1.30
Prob. no diff.[a]	.14	.00	.14	.75	.11	.00
r correlation	.82	.50	—	—	—	—
2 Adol. vs. 40 yr.						
Mean difference	.67	1.62	.89	.08	1.16	2.00
Prob. no diff.[a]	.07	.00	.06	.53	.03	.01
r correlation	.55	.26	—	—	—	—
3 30 yr. vs. 40 yr.						
Mean difference	.23	.39	.50	-.22	.56	.25
Prob. no diff.[a]	.44	.22	.19	.75	.22	.70
r correlation	.62	.52	—	—	—	—

[a] Wilcoxon Signed Ranks Test

285

to one time period. Two judges or raters per case were generally sufficient to produce a reliability coefficient of .65 or higher for the Q-sort composite.

Two approaches were employed in the analysis. We first compared the achievement groups across time periods, and then assessed the main effect of family deprivation on psychological functioning by time period for all men and the high achievers. For purposes of consistency, we restricted the sample to college entrants in the cohort; only three other men had psychological measures in adolescence *and* adulthood. The first strategy is addressed to the question of whether adult achievement is associated with increasing competence from adolescence to mid-life. Temporal change in the effects of family deprivation represents the focal point of the second approach, with emphasis on life contexts such as occupational achievement. Is Depression hardship less strongly associated with evidence of ill-health in adulthood than in adolescence, and does work life success make a difference in this temporal pattern?

From adolescence to adulthood, the overall trend is toward greater competence and health (Table 7). Compared to their adolescence, the Berkeley men are described as more responsible and productive, responsive to others, and compassionate; and their outcomes in work made very little difference in such judgments. The primary temporal correlate of work life success occurs in aspects of pathogenic functioning (except for being thin-skinned); such aspects became less prominent in the personality of successful men from adolescence to middle-age. Low self-esteem, feelings of victimization, reluctance to commit self, and self-defeating behavior show the most striking differential change by adult achievement. Across these measures, the mid-life portrait of achievers bears no relation to their assessment in adolescence (average $p = .07$, Wilcoxon test); a change which stands out when compared to the degree of personal stability (average $p = .71$) observed among the less successful.

In turning to the effects of Depression hardship, we discover evidence which provides clues as to why adult achievement made so little difference in responsible behavior, consideration of others, and vulnerability to criticism. The least responsible adolescents were characterized as opportunistic, inclined to stretch limits, and less able to control impulses; a behavior pattern which persists into the adult years among the economically deprived and especially among those who managed to achieve in work. Likewise, consideration for others and resilience in the face of criticism are not among the personal assets of the deprived in adolescence or in middle age. These temporal patterns offer little assistance toward understanding how some men from hard-pressed families were able to succeed in their careers and did so from a position of educational inequality. Men who are not dependable, productive, or able to take criticism seem unlikely prospects for an orderly progression in occupational status.

One answer to the ascent of deprived men is suggested by developmental gains in other areas. By the age of 30, they are much less likely to resemble their adolescent portrait of low self-esteem, indecision, and withdrawal from adversity than are the nondeprived who also moved upward in work life. At this stage, the children of deprived families remain more vulnerable to the judgments of others, when compared to the nondeprived, but they are no longer distinguished by feelings of inadequacy and meaninglessness, by self-defeating behavior, and a reluctance to commit self to a course of action. In these respects at least, we see evidence of relatively greater inner strength, effectiveness, and purpose than was observed in adolescence; note the change in sign of deprivational effects across time periods. The developmental course of successful men from deprived families is characterized by a mixture of strengths and weaknesses, of developmental gains since adolescence and persistent deficits; and some pathogenic traits are more prominent at middle age than in the early adult years, e.g., lacks personal meaning, self-defeating. Nevertheless, they have accomplished far more than one would have expected from their early background and lives.[10]

Jean Macfarlane (1963:338), the long-time director of the Berkeley Guidance Study, may have been referring to some of these men when she observed that nearly half of the men turned out to be "more stable and effective adults than any of us with our differing theoretical biases had predicted . . ." Most noteworthy, she concluded, are the number of men whose poor scholastic records in adolescence "completely belie the creative intelligence demands of their present position (italics removed)." A large proportion of the "most outstandingly mature adults in our entire group . . . are recruited from those who were confronted with very difficult situations and whose characteristic responses during childhood and adolescence seemed to us to compound their problems" (1964:121). In retrospect, Macfarlane (1963) cites two practices which contributed to the inaccuracy of early staff predictions: (1) overweighting the presumed negative influence of early pathogenic aspects of development, at the expense of recognizing hardship experiences as maturity inducing—"we have learned that no one becomes mature without living through the pains and confusions of maturing experiences"; and (2) insufficient awareness of such experiences in the adult years, coupled with the potential of late development for changing the course of lives. Consistent with our observations, Macfarlane notes that a good many of the Berkeley children did not achieve a sense of ego identity until adult situations "forced them or presented an opportunity to them to fulfill a role that gave them a sense of

Table 7

Men's Psychological Functioning Across Time Periods by Achievement Level and Family Deprivation: Means and Regression Coefficients (College Entrants Only)

Indicators by[a] time period	Psychological Functioning by Achievement Level in Means			Effect of Family Deprivation in Regression Coefficients[b]			
	Low	High	Probability level	High achievers	Total	High achievers	Total
	(N = 16) X̄	(N = 29) X̄	Low vs. high	(N = 29) beta	(N = 45) beta	(N = 29) b	(N = 45) b
Responsible							
Adolescence	5.9	6.4	.43	-.25	-.11	-.92	-.45
30 years	6.2	7.3	.04	-.26	-.12	-.66	-.40
40 years	6.4	6.9	.32	-.31	-.23	-1.00	-.74
Considerate							
Adolescence	4.5	4.7	.62	.03	-.12	.11	-.44
30 years	5.4	5.1	.52	-.16	-.22	-.42	-.63
40 years	5.2	5.2	.87	-.30	-.32+	-.88	-.90+
Withdraws from adversity							
Adolescence	5.0	5.4	.41	.07	.16	.31	.65
30 years	4.9	3.9	.02	-.10	-.04	-.27	-.11
40 years	4.2	3.2	.06	-.07	.06	-.17	.19
Low self-esteem							
Adolescence	6.3	6.0	.51	.24	.07	.63	.19
30 years	6.6	6.2	.35	-.04	.01	-.12	.02
40 years	5.5	4.6	.16	-.06	-.07	-.24	-.27

288

Feels victimized						
Adolescence	3.7	3.7	.92	.02	.19	.08	.75
30 years	4.3	3.8	.39	.18	.27	.68	.96
40 years	4.0	2.9	.02	.01	-.07	.03	-.22
Lacks personal meaning						
Adolescence	4.1	3.8	.59	.30	.28	1.24	1.19*
30 years	4.7	4.3	.52	-.22	-.04	-.74	-.14
40 years	4.5	3.7	.14	.10	.15	.35	.56
Reluctant to commit self						
Adolescence	4.6	4.8	.79	.27	.28*	1.33	1.49
30 years	5.2	3.9	.02	-.23	-.13	-.82	-.44
40 years	4.5	3.8	.24	-.39*	-.12	-1.29*	-.50
Thin-skinned						
Adolescence	5.7	6.1	.52	.17	.21	.63	.77
30 years	6.0	5.7	.51	.16	.11	.42	.28
40 years	5.0	4.7	.25	.19	.09	.47	.22
Self-defeating						
Adolescence	4.7	4.3	.38	.35*	.27*	1.13*	.93*
30 years	4.9	3.9	.07	.01	-.01	.04	-.03
40 years	5.0	3.2	.00	.29	.08	1.04	.31

* p < .10, + p < .05, † p < .01

a The first four adult indicators are similar in construction to those reported in Table 3; for the two adult periods, the average inter-item correlation per index ranges from .54 to .80.

b To maximize the stability of the regression coefficients, we have restricted the analysis to the total group of college entrants and to those in the high-achiever category.

worth . . ." She refers to this group as the "late bloomers" and singles out the developmental importance of their departure from home and community in permitting them to "work through early confusions and inhibitions." In this regard, our analysis underscores the value of military service, a rewarding work life, and possibly the emotional support and gratifications of marriage and family life. In the successful group, men from deprived families were no less the beneficiaries of a stable, satisfying marriage than the offspring of more privileged family backgrounds.

Our assessment of psychological functioning is structured by interest in the effects of Depression hardship, and consequently provides a restricted view of adult health. It is not clear at this point how the findings relate to a more general clinical appraisal of psychological health in adulthood. Such a measure was constructed by Livson and Peskin (1967) for research on the Berkeley cohort. In the two adult periods, psychological health is measured by the correlation between the men's individual Q sorts and a criterion composite of the psychologically healthy adult; a composite of Q sorts by clinical psychologists employing the 100-item California Q set. Livson and Peskin describe the measure as representing "an underlying dimension of psychological health, one which may be regarded as genotypic in its referent, permitting a variety of healthy (and unhealthy) expressions" (p. 513). The pool of items that are most and least characteristic of psychological health includes a number that are part of the set of nine indicators, but it also enlarges the scope considerably. Among the positive attributes are: "seems to be aware of the impression he makes on others," "genuinely dependable and responsible," "socially perceptive," "behaves in an ethically consistent manner," and "appears straightforward, forthright." The least characteristic traits include "brittle ego-defense system," "feels cheated and victimized by life," "gives up and withdraws where possible in face of frustration and adversity," "negativistic," "self-defeating," and "aloof, keeps people at a distance."

Table 8 shows the main and joint effects of Depression hardship and achievement level on psychological health in the two adult periods, with mean scores adjusted in a multiple-classification analysis for the influence of class origin. Family deprivation did increase the health risk of men in the adult years, as our prior analysis suggests, and this effect appears in both achievement contexts, high and low, at the ages of 30 and 40, with the primary cost showing up in the early adult lives of relatively unsuccessful men. The years beyond 30 were good ones from a health standpoint among the offspring of deprived parents; whether successful in work or not, they achieved sizeable gains in well-being up to middle age, and the same relative change appears among the nondeprived achievers—their health status improved. Thus we observe a convergence in psychological well-being up to middle age among low achievers from

Table 8

Adult Psychological Health by Time Period, Family Deprivation, and Achievement Level, in Means Adjusted for Social Class in Multiple Classification Analysis

Adult Psychological Health by Time Period, Deprivation, and Achievement Level, in Mean Values

Achievement level	30-year Assessment			40-year Assessment		
	Non-deprived	Deprived	beta[a] (deprivation)	Non-deprived	Deprived	beta[a] (deprivation)
Total	.21(28)	.02(24)	.26	.31(31)	.22(22)	.13
Low	.19(11)	-.10(8)	.39	.20(16)	.12(8)	.12
High	.21(17)	.08(16)	.19	.40(15)	.29(14)	.17
beta[a]						
(achievement	.02	.17		.31	.13	
ment						

[a] These values are partial standardized regression coefficients from a multiple-classification analysis. Since the coefficients are based on groups that vary markedly in size, their meaning is best appraised through comparisons rather than by a test of significance which is influenced by group size.

nondeprived and deprived families; over time, Depression hardship became less consequential relative to their work life disadvantage. Benefits from work life advancement are generally reflected in the health status of successful men at the age of 40, but so also is the advantage of a nondeprived background. Whether successful or not, men with deprived family histories do not equal the nondeprived in health at mid-life. In this and the preceding analyses, it is clear that work life accomplishments are correlated with developmental gains among the sons of deprived parents, but that such increments do not eliminate the health disadvantage of Depression hardship.

Extremes in psychological health are defined by the relations between Depression experience and subsequent work life. Throughout the adult years, the greatest risk is found among men whose occupational career bears some resemblance to the hardship of family deprivation—the unsuccessful from deprived families. Their childhood, adolescence, and adult years stand in sharp contrast to the privileged life history of nondeprived men who fulfilled their early promise in a productive and gratifying career. Men with this family background were not as likely as the deprived to make the best of their assets at the end of formal education, but those who did are among the healthiest at middle age. *Both childhood and adult experience, then, make a difference in the health of the Berkeley men and neither is sufficient to offset completely the psychological damage of the other.* This observation applies to men from the middle and working class even though they followed different life paths. By middle age, it is not class origin but experience in the Depression and adult years that matters for assessments of health.

These outcomes at middle age correspond with the men's own responses to selected interview questions (1969–1970) on health problems and life evaluations. This stage of life, as a transition between career beginnings and building to consolidation in the later years, is commonly marked by what Daniel Levinson and his colleagues (1976:24) have termed "the experience of disparity" between one's "life structure and the self": "The sense of disparity between 'what I've reached at this point' and 'what it is I really want' instigates a soul-searching for 'what it is I really want.' " Aspects of the self that were suppressed by the requirements of work and family begin to surface at this point (cf. Brim, 1976). A large percentage of the Berkeley men were aware of bodily decline, and also reported efforts to obtain professional help in working through problems. Slightly more than half reported some health problem or impairment, more than 40 percent acknowledged therapeutic help over the recent past, and approximately 30 percent noted problems of chronic fatigue or energy decline and heavy drinking.

All of these health states or responses are more prevalent in the lives of men from deprived families, when compared to the nondeprived, and the difference remains with adjustments for class origin (Table 9). Most significant is the level of energy deficiency and heavy drinking among the sons of deprived families, an outcome perhaps symptomatic of the stress which comes from a life course that sorely tested or threatened defenses and inner resources, a life course that brought to mind enduring insecurities and limitations and painful memories of a childhood in which important adults were not strong or present when needed. Achievement pressures seem to have produced situations of this type in the adolescent experience of deprived men, and they also warrant consideration as a prime source of emotional distress among those who managed to do very well in their occupational life despite limitations of formal education and self-assurance. Though health problems are more often acknowledged by the least successful men, and especially those from deprived homes, energy decline, heavy drinking, and the use of therapy are most prevalent in the lives of men who moved upward from Depression hardship to work life achievement. Such hardship did not hamper work life accomplish-

Table 9

Reported Health States of Berkeley Men (1969 - 1970) by Adult
Achievement and Family Deprivation, in Percentages
Adjusted for Class Origin in Multiple Classification Analysis

Percentages[c] of Men on Health Reports by Adult
Achievement and Deprivation

Reported health states	Achievement level		Family deprivation		Low achievement		High achievement	
			Non-dep.	De-prived	Non-dep.	De-prived	Non-dep.	De-prived
	Low (N=24)	High (N=35)	(N=31)	(N=28)	(N=16)	(N=8)	(N=15)	(N=20)
Men who reported (%):								
Some health problem or impairment	56	52	41	64	50	76	33	58
Chronic fatigue or energy decline	29	32	20	46	21	36	17	50
Heavy or problem[a] drinking	24	30	26	44	29	27	21	49
Therapy[b]	35	55	50	53	47	0	51	68

[a] Heavy drinking refers to daily consumption of alcoholic beverages, usually two or more drinks. The problem drinker is a person who claimed that drinking is or could become a problem.

[b] This includes psychiatric hospitalization, individual psychotherapy, group therapy, counseling, (marital, pastoral), Alcoholics Anonymous, Synanon.

[c] In evaluating differences between subgroups, we favor comparisons of percentage differences rather than a test of the difference between proportions. The latter is heavily influenced by subgroup size and the subgroups in this table are both variable and small in size.

ments among the college entrants but its psychic toll continues to blight a sense of well-being.

For these offspring of hard times, the mid-life *experience of disparity* may have less to do with desire and reality than with haunting memories of a childhood and adolescence that ill-equipped them for living a life with self-assurance and purpose, compassion and trust. We suspect that they share some of the memories and concerns of a young professional who lost his father through severe emotional depression after the family business collapsed (Paul and Paul, 1975): ". . . you know, he fell apart in my life when I needed him to be strong. When I was a young kid trying to cope with the problems of adolescence, I had to be strong for him" (p. 142).[11] From time to time, the hurt "pops up"; "I've still got a lot about me that has to do with sort of a little boy in me . . . it feels incompetent, helpless, insecure. I keep that little kid inside. He can't get out . . . He still hollers . . ." (p. 290).

Life Review

In looking back on life experience from the beginnings of middle age, the Berkeley men are most inclined to regard adolescence as the very worst period, followed at a distance by childhood and early adulthood (Table 10). Not surprisingly, we find this judgment primarily among the men who grew up in a deprived home, particularly if they achieved a successful work life. As documented by our analysis, the Depression's legacy of impaired life chances and development is manifested in an adolescent world of generalized prosperity and wartime mobilization, in a life stage more removed from the economic collapse than childhood but one marked developmentally and historically by the intersection of past and future, of life history and possibilities. Drastic family losses in the Great Depression may have fashioned a childhood that seemed out of control, unpredictable, and threatening to boys who remained largely dependent on parental nurturance, but it is in their wartime adolescence that such experience confronted the identity and mastery demands of the larger society. Adolescence in the Berkeley cohort bears the Depression's imprint through deficient lives, relationships, and options.

According to available evidence, men from deprived families typically look back on the Depression as more consequential in their lives than the experience of World War II, and yet they consistently refer to wartime adolescence as the worst period of all: "My entire adolescence was a period of painful and frustrating disorientation." This statement, by a small businessman from the deprived middle class, was coupled with bitter memories of family deprivations that made life miserable as a teenager; thinking poor, feeling inferior, and rejected by peers, a lack of parental interest and affection, confusion as to what was expected. "I don't know for sure if the Depression or the general emotional makeup of my family is responsible, but I am left with no respect for our society, its authority figures and establishments. I am bitterly disillusioned about people and their motives. . . . I feel that with loving guidance that I might have evolved into a far more useful personality."

The best years of life, for the cohort as a whole, are those of career building in work and family—from the age of 30 to mid-life; and this assessment is even more characteristic of men who experienced hard times as children. In retrospect, this phase of life seems "best of all" to most of the successful men, as one might expect, but it also represents a high point in the lives of deprived men who have not done as well in their careers. It seems that any adult course fared better in life review than

Table 10   The Best and Worst Years of Men by Family Deprivation and
Achievement Level, in Percentages Adjusted for Class Origin

Self-Reports in Middle-Age (1969–70) by Deprivation
and Achievement Level[a]

Best and worst years	Family deprivation		Deprivation by achievement level			
			Low		High	
	Non-deprived	*De-prived*	*Non-deprived*	*De-prived*	*Non-deprived*	*De-prived*
Best Years						
Childhood	—	—	—	—	—	—
Adolescence	12	4	16	13	8	0
20–30 yrs.	31	22	56	18	11	24
30 yrs. +	57	74	28	69	81	76
	100 (29)	100 (27)	100 (13)	100 (9)	100(16)	100 (18)
Worst Years						
Childhood	28	19	33	25	24	16
Adolescence	31	52	25	31	35	62
20–30 yrs.	26	20	8	25	41	18
30 yrs. +	15	9	34	19	—	5
	100 (28)	100 (27)	100 (12)	100 (9)	100 (16)	100 (18)

[a]Test factor standardization is applied to remove percentage differences associated with social class.

memories of Depression hardship through the adolescent years. The men
were of course too young in 1932–1933 to remember much about family
misfortunes at the time or to recall what their parents were like before the
Depression. What they do remember of Depression life in the family
generally extends back to the latter half of the 1930s, and yet it is the
aftermath of this early experience in a troubled adolescence that is so
profoundly part of their life as they know it. Whether understood or not,
the Depression experience established a frame of reference which continues to influence their perception of good and bad times.

This emotional course is not unique to the Berkeley cohort; consistent
with social comparison theory, the very same pattern was observed
among the older men from Oakland who experienced at first-hand the
deprivation of family losses. From the vantage point of middle age, their
peak years of life satisfaction occurred in adulthood, especially since the
age of 30 (Elder, 1974: 259); by contrast, the nondeprived were more
inclined to regard childhood and adolescence as favorably as adulthood.
In both cohorts, then, work life advancement increased the perceived
standing of adulthood relative to early life stages, though maturity had

special significance even to the economically deprived whose adult experience offered little consolation for a troubled past.

As shaped by the Great Depression, this past entailed persistent handicaps for the Berkeley men in life chances and well-being; from adolescent personality to higher education and adult health, the adverse effects of Depression hardship are more pronounced in the life course of these men than in the lives of older men from the Oakland cohort. But even with this comparative disadvantage, we find considerable evidence to support claims of life improvement among the Berkeley men with deprived family histories; that the adult years brought greater fulfillment and satisfaction than either adolescence or childhood. Though a good many of these Depression offspring lost out in formal education, when compared to the attainments of nondeprived men, most were able to surmount this handicap through accomplishments in work, a pattern also observed in the Oakland cohort. Developmental gains in competence and health were observed among the sons of deprived families between adolescence and adult responsibilities, and the years after age 30 are also noteworthy in this respect. Such change is most striking among those who achieved success in their work life, and yet, paradoxically, symptoms of distress (heavy drinking, energy decline, therapy) were most often reported by these men at mid-life. If muted by the passage of time and a rewarding career, the Depression's legacy of impairment remains a source of life problems at middle age for men who were born at the end of the twenties in Berkeley, California.

OVERVIEW

Over the past decade, sociological developments in age stratification have underscored the significance of historical considerations in the study of life chances for health, happiness, and valued accomplishments in society. The emerging framework is that of social science, as C. W. Mills (1959:149) once defined it, ". . . the study of biography, of history, and of the problems of their intersection within the social structure." Life prospects are influenced at birth by family position within the class structure, by genetic transmission, and by the historical context of one's birth cohort. Differential life opportunities are associated with membership in birth cohorts that vary according to size, composition, and historical experience; and with age and class position at the point of historical change. Unequal age entails variations in developmental stage and social roles, which implies variations in the life outcomes of historical events. Such variations are also likely by class position within specific cohorts to the extent that it structures exposure to change and adaptive resources.

This perspective informed the present investigation of historical change in life experience, a longitudinal analysis of Depression hardship in one cohort of men (birth dates, 1928–29) who were born in the city of Berkeley. We designed the study to permit selected comparisons with the effects of such change in the lives of older men (birth dates, 1920–1921) from Oakland, California, as reported in *Children of the Great Depression*. This comparative framework enabled us to place the Berkeley men in historical context through tests of a life-stage hypothesis; Depression hardship entailed more adverse consequences in the life course and psychological health of the Berkeley men, owing to their younger developmental age and family dependence during the worst phase of the economic crisis. A second hypothesis focused on class differences in family resources and child support; we expected family deprivation to be most strongly associated with negative outcomes among the Berkeley men from working-class families. Lastly, we proposed a hypothesis based on the assumption that developmental change occurs throughout the life course; that negative outcomes of family deprivation will be manifested primarily in the early life course of the Berkeley men, in an educational disadvantage and impaired psychological functioning. Only the first and third hypotheses were supported by the analysis.

The Berkeley archival data are based on eighty-three men from the well-known Guidance Study at the Institute of Human Development, University of California. All of the men were involved in an extensive program of data collection through their adolescence during World War II, and they also provided life-history information at mid-life. Most of the men participated in two adult follow-ups (approximate ages 30 and 40) which included lengthy interviews, questionnaires, and psychological assessments. Whether in the middle or working class at birth, a large number of men encountered severe economic deprivation through the family, whereas others benefited from the good fortune of their fathers. Using cost-of-living estimates and socioeconomic data, we identified the relatively nondeprived by an economic loss of 34 percent or less between 1929 and the low year (1932–1934); heavier losses placed families in the deprived category. As defined, economic deprivation was more common in the working class than among families of higher status in 1929 (57 percent vs. 44 percent). Hardship thus refers to a decremental change in family status, unlike its usual association with chronic poverty.

Some cautionary points on cohort comparison warrant special emphasis before a general review of findings. This paper presents a limited test of the life-stage hypothesis, since it reports outcomes from the Berkeley cohort and only compares them with *published* results of corresponding research on the Oakland cohort. Identical psychological indicators for both cohorts would be needed for a direct assessment of Depres-

sion hardship and health states. Equally important are the differing prop-
erties of the two cohorts (other than life stage) and their implications for
the interpretations we have drawn—differences in social composition,
locale, etc. Though such variations may offer plausible alternative accounts of the results obtained, relevant evidence at hand does not alter the
emphasis we have placed on differential life stage and timing as the key
variable between the cohorts. Small class variations between the cohorts
(the Oakland sample includes a larger proportion of working-class
families) do not present a problem, since the effects of Depression hardship are examined within class strata in each cohort. As a final point,
sample characteristics (small, nonrepresentative, selected from a particular locale) and the problems inherent in long-term longitudinal studies
(repeated measurements, attrition) discourage generalization to other
samples of the birth cohorts represented in the study. Our interpretation
of the interaction between life stage and Depression hardship is necessarily limited to the Berkeley and Oakland samples. We believe the results of
this study and of *Children of the Great Depression* support the life-stage
hypothesis, but wholly convincing documentation must await further research

Cohort comparisons suggest that family deprivation produced greater
disadvantage for the life course and health of the Berkeley men up to
middle age, when compared to deprivational effects in the Oakland
cohort; an effect most pronounced during the early years of adolescence
and formal education. The beginning of hard times and family strain occurred when the Berkeley men were of preschool age, and yet we observed no evidence of this stress until they reached adolescence during
the more prosperous years of World War II. From a background of insecurity and privation, the sons of hard-pressed families were often exposed
to persistent hardship during adolescence as well as achievement pressures. It is the combination of these circumstances at a time of generalized
prosperity that appears to account for their psychological inadequacy
relative to the nondeprived, especially in the middle class. Unlike the
Oakland cohort, family deprivation is associated with lower adolescent
aspirations and school performance among the Berkeley men, with impaired self-esteem, vulnerability to the evaluations of others, indecision,
and passivity—with actions that generally enhanced their difficulties.

Through economic and developmental constraints, Depression hardship restricted life prospects by curtailing higher education among the
Berkeley men, regardless of class origin, and it did so to a greater extent
than in the Oakland cohort. However, deprived men in both cohorts
generally succeeded in minimizing this handicap through the course of
their work life to middle age. Owing perhaps to the maturity demands of
work, military service, and marriage, this achievement is correlated with

developmental gains among the Berkeley men. The years between age 30 and 40 brought greater satisfaction and well-being to men from deprived families in general, owing partly to their accomplishments, and they were more likely than the nondeprived to claim that life had improved since the troubled years of adolescence. But the benefits of work life achievement did not completely eliminate the health risk of family hardship by middle age—the emotional pain and detachment, confusion, and insecurity. The healthiest Berkeley men are among those who combined the support of a nondeprived family with the rewards of adult achievement; at the other extreme we find men whose work life bears some resemblance to family misfortune in the Great Depression; that is, the sons of deprived parents who were relatively unsuccessful in their work life.

Comparison of the Berkeley and Oakland cohorts thus identifies both similarities and differences in the life outcomes of Depression hardship. Similarities include the concentration of developmental handicaps during the early years of adolescence and formal education, the effectiveness of work life experience in countering educàtional limitations, and the perception that life has become more satisfying since adolescence. Differences center on the relatively young age of the Berkeley men when hard times occurred and on their more prolonged exposure to such conditions; from adolescent development to higher education and health at mid-life, family deprivation entailed more adverse outcomes for these men than for their older counterparts in the Oakland cohort. It is among the Berkeley offspring of deprived families that we see the greatest discontinuity between childhood and adult experience, and their significant contributions to psychological well-being in middle age. The legacy of family deprivation remains a problem at mid-life even among the most successful men.

FOOTNOTES

*This research is part of a larger project which is supported by Grant MH25834, National Institute of Mental Health (Glen H. Elder, Jr., principal investigator). We are grateful for this support and also wish to acknowledge with appreciation the material and collegial support of the Boys Town Research Center. The computational assistance of David Ross and suggestions by our colleagues were most valuable in the course of this work.

1. Lipset and Bendix's *Social Mobility in Industrial Society* (1959) represents a pioneering study in this tradition, and Kerckhoff's recent article (1976) provides an excellent overview of the major developments since that publication. Over the past decade Mel Kohn has directed one of the most outstanding programs of research on the psychological effects of social position. See *Class and Conformity* (1969) and his most recent article, "Occupational Structure and Alienation" (1976), for a partial list of publications from the program.

2. *Aging and Society* (1972), authored by Riley, Johnson, and Foner, is the single most important contribution to this development. For a review of developments since then, see Elder, "Age Differentiation and the Life Course" (1975). An example of a comparative cohort approach to social mobility is provided by Stephan Thernstrom's *The Other Bosto-*

nians (1973). The studies listed in Note 1 are by no means oblivious to historical change in the life opportunity associated with particular class positions, but historical considerations are not paramount and the analytic framework of this work differs markedly from that advocated by the sociology of age.

3. Relevant to this assertion is Lois Murphy's research on coping and resilience among young children (1974) and Miller and Swanson's conclusions (1960) that children from the lower strata are more apt than middle-class children to employ a primitive, global, reality-distorting means of defending self against conflict; the latter tend to use more differentiated and socially adaptive defenses that require greater cognitive skill (see also Weinstock, 1967).

4. Socieoeconomic change over the first half of the 40s is reported in a California State Chamber of Commerce report on individual incomes (1947). Kidner (1946) provides an historical analysis of business cycles in California and the State's recovery from the Great Depression

5. One might also argue that the timing of military service among youth with deprived backgrounds (before school leaving) accounts in part for their lower educational attainment, when compared to the nondeprived. Sharp and Krasnesor (1968) found such an effect in a nationwide cohort of 1958 college graduates, mainly among enlisted men. More importantly, they note that military service before college graduation proved to be beneficial to men who were *undecided* about their civilian career. This benefit appears most relevant to deprived men in our cohort, given their family history, and may be coupled with constraints that lowered their chances for completing college.

6. This *Q* set (adapted from an adult version of the California *Q* Sort, Block, 1958) is not that developed by Jack Block and his team of skilled judges (Block, 1971), but instead represents the judgment of a skilled clinician at the Institute who reviewed all case materials on each subject. The 100 items in the *Q* set were sorted according to a forced, normal distribution of nine categories, with lower scores representing traits that were judged to be least characteristic of the subject. The *Q* sort approach is well suited to longitudinal analysis, since judgments take into account the relative salience of each item within a person's ordering of all other traits and thus avoid problems associated with shifts in frame of reference by time period. We assume that the clinician's ratings characterize the Berkeley *S*s in adolescence, even though she had access to information on childhood as well. The principal rationale for using this *Q* set instead of Block's is that it is available on a much larger number of cases. Less than 30 boys in our sample had ratings in Block's set, a subgroup which is too small to permit the desired analysis. Within this subgroup, our items correlate satisfactorily with corresponding items in Block's data set. For the adult years of the Berkeley men, the number of cases with Block's ratings at age 30 is large enough to be used in an assessment of adult health.

7. Owing to sample limitations, statistical examination of deprivation by mother's aspirations required inclusion of all boys in the cohort (not simply those from middle-class families where the main psychological effects were observed). Mean scores adjusted for class origin were calculated for each of four cells (high and low aspirations by nondeprived and deprived status). In deprived families ambitious mothers tended to have sons with significantly higher aspirations than other mothers ($p < .05$), but their sons also ranked higher than any other subgroup on low self-esteem and vulnerability to the judgments of others (Thin-skinned, $p < .05$). Mother's aspirations did not have this effect under nondeprived circumstances. Beyond this outcome, the price of achievement pressure is underscored by the adolescents who were least likely to be characterized by other modes of pathogenic behavior, boys in nondeprived families whose mothers did not emphasize high goals. It is these youth who represent the most positive contrast to the health disability of boys from deprived families on withdrawal from adversity, lack of personal meaning, and sense of victimization ($p < .01$). They also share with other nondeprived youth a lower ranking on self-defeating behavior

and reluctance to commit self, when compared to the economically deprived. Across all of these results, the ambitions of mothers seem to reflect their needs, disappointments, and hopes as much or more than their son's interests.

8. The average path coefficient for the effect of persistent hardship on the three characteristics is .40. This compares to an average coefficient of .07 for the direct effect of family deprivation.

9. As indicated by beta coefficients with class origin controlled, deprived men were more likely than the nondeprived to enter the labor force at an early age ($-.24$), to complete their education early ($-.50$), and to marry significantly later (.76). They also tended to have more employers between 1955 and mid-life (.45), started a stable line of work at a later age (.21), spent more of their work life in manual jobs (.27), and were more likely to experience a break or two in work life up to age 40 (.29). The deprivational groups were similar in size; eight men in each category.

10. Their developmental gains are especially noteworthy when compared to the persistent disabilities of deprived men who followed a course of low achievement. Using the Wilcoxon test, we find no similarity between the adolescent and 40-year scores (rank ordered) of deprived achievers on low self-esteem, withdrawal from adversity, self-defeating behavior, and reluctance to commit self to a course of action ($p=.04$). This compares to an average probability of .65 for low achievers with a deprived family background.

11. Loss of father in this man's life generally corresponds with mid-life descriptions of "relation to father" among deprived men who achieved success in their work life. These men were more likely than any other group to report very little closeness with father ($p=.05$), but they were also more likely to claim that the relationship had become closer over the year (46 percent vs. 30 percent or less). Judging from this evidence, paternal significance and support are largely absent from the childhood memories of these men.

REFERENCES

Allingham, John (1967), "Class regression: An aspect of the social stratification process," *American Sociological Review* 32 (June):442–449.

Baltes, Paul B., and Warner Schaie (1973), *Life-Span Developmental Psychology: Personality and Socialization.* New York: Academic Press.

Block, Jack (1958), *The Q Sort Method in Personality Assessment and Psychiatric Research.* Springfield, Ill.: Charles C. Thomas.

—— (1971), *Lives Through Time.* Berkeley, California: Bancroft.

Brim, Orville G. (1976), "Theories of the male mid-life crisis," *The Counseling Psychologist* 6 (No. 1):2–9.

California Medical Association (1937), *California Medical-Economic Survey.* San Francisco.

California State Chamber of Commerce (1947), *Individual Incomes of Civilian Residents of California by Counties,* 1939–1946, Research Department.

Douglas, J. W. B. (1964), *The Home and the School.* London: MacGibbon and Kee.

Elder, Glen H., Jr. (1968), *Adolescent Socialization and Personality Development.* Chicago: Rand McNally.

—— (1974), *Children of the Great Depression.* Chicago: University of Chicago Press.

——(1975), "Age differentiation and the life course," Alex Inkeles (Ed.), *Annual Review of Sociology* 1:165–190.

Erikson, Erik H. (1968), *Identity: Youth and Crisis.* New York: W. W. Norton.

Furstenberg, Frank F., Jr. (1976), *Unplanned Parenthood: The Social Consequences of Teenage Childbearing.* New York: Free Press.

Haan, Norma, and David Day (1974),"A longitudinal study of change and sameness in personality development: Adolescence to later adulthood," *International Journal of Aging and Human Development* 5:11-39.

Harris, P. M. G. (1969), "The social origins of American leaders: The demographic foundation," *Perspectives in American History* 3:159-346.

Inbar, Michael (1976), *The Vulnerable Age Phenomenon*. New York: Russell Sage.

Inkeles, Alex (1955), "Social change and social character: The role of parental mediation," *Journal of Social Issues* 11 (No. 2):12-23.

Jordan, Bill (1974), *Poor Parents: Social Policy and the "Cycle of Deprivation."* London: Routledge and Kegan Paul.

Kerckhoff, Alan C. (1976), "The status attainment process: Socialization or allocation?" *Social Forces* 55 (December):368-381.

Kidner, Frank L. (1946), *California Business Cycles*. Berkeley: University of California Press.

Kohn, Melvin L. (1969), *Class and Conformity: A Study in Values*. Homewood: Dorsey Press.

—— (1976), "Occupational structure and alienation," *American Journal of Sociology* 82 (July):111-130.

Levinson, Daniel J., Charlotte M. Darrow, Edward B. Klein, Maria H. Levinson, and Braxton McKee (1976), "Periods in the adult development of men: Ages 18-45," *The Counseling Psychologist* 6 (No. 1):21-25.

Lipset, Seymour Martin, and Reinhard Bendix (1959), *Social Mobility in Industrial Society*. Berkeley: University of California Press.

Livson, Norman, and Harvey Peskin (1967), "Prediction of adult psychological health in a longitudinal study," *Journal of Abnormal Psychology* 72 (No. 6):509-518.

Macfarlane, Jean Walker (1938), "Studies in child guidance: I. Methodology of data collection and organization," *Monographs of the Society for Research in Child Development*, Volume 11 (No. 6).

—— (1963), "From infancy to adulthood," *Childhood Education* 39:336-342.

——(1964), "Perspectives on personality consistency and change from the guidance study," *Vita Humana* 7:115-126.

Manor, Stella (1963), "Geographic changes in U.S. employment from 1950 to 1960." *Monthly Labor Review* (January):1-10.

Mechling, Jay E. (1971), "A role-learning model for the study of historical change in parent behavior: With a test of the model on the behavior of American parents in the Great Depression," Unpublished Dissertation, University of Pennsylvania.

Meyer, John W. (1976), "The effects of education as an institution," Unpublished (August).

Miller, Daniel R., and Guy W. Swanson (1960), *Inner Conflict and Defense*. New York: Holt.

Mills, C. Wright (1959), *The Sociological Imagination*. New York: Oxford University Press.

Murphy, Lois B. (1974),"Coping, vulnerability, and resilience in childhood," Chapter 5 in George V. Coelho, David A. Hamburg, and John E. Adams (Eds.), *Coping and Adaptation*. New York: Basic Books.

Nisbet, Robert (1965), *Emile Durkheim*. Englewood Cliffs: Prentice-Hall.

Offer, Daniel, and Judith B. Offer (1975), *From Teenage to Young Manhood: A Psychological Study*. New York: Basic Books.

Paul, Norman L., and Betty Byfield Paul (1975), *A Marital Puzzle*. New York: W. W. Norton.

Robins, Lee N. (1966), *Deviant Children Grown Up*. Baltimore: Williams and Wilkins.

Riley, Matilda White, Marilyn Johnson, and Anne Foner (1972), *Aging and Society: A Sociology of Age Stratification*, Volume 3. New York: Russell Sage.

Rosenberg, Morris (1965), *Society and the Adolescent Self-Image*. Princeton: Princeton University Press.

Sacks, Howard L. (1975), *Socialization and Status Change in the Development of Self*. Unpublished Ph.D. dissertation, University of North Carolina.

Sanford, Nevitt (1966), *Self and Society*. New York: Atherton Press.

Sharp, Laure, and Rebecca Krasnesor (1968), "College students and military service: The experience of an earlier cohort," *Sociology of Education* 41:380-400.

Smelser, Neil J., and Gabriel Almond (1974), *Public Higher Education in California*. Berkeley and Los Angeles: University of California Press.

Smelser, William T. (1963), "Adolescent and adult occupational choice as a function of family socio-economic history," *Sociometry* 26:393-409.

Smith, M. Brewster (1968), "Competence and socialization," Chapter 7, in John A. Clausen (Ed.), *Socialization and Society*. Boston: Little, Brown and Co.

Thernstrom, Stephan (1973), *The Other Bostonians: Poverty and Progress in the American Metropolis, 1880-1970*. Cambridge: Harvard University Press.

Vaillant, George E. (1975), "Natural history of male psychological health: III. Empirical dimensions of mental health," *Archives of General Psychiatry* 32 (April):420-426.

———(1974), "Natural history of male psychological health: II. Some antecendents of healthy adult adjustment," *Archives of General Psychiatry* 31 (July):15-22.

———, and Charles C. McArthur (1972), "Natural history of male psychological health: I. The adult life cycle from 18-50," *Seminars in Psychiatry* 4 (November):415-427.

Weinstock, Allen (1967), "Longitudinal study of social class and defense preferences," *Journal of Consulting Psychology* 31:539-541.

LONG-RANGE INFLUENCES ON ADULT MENTAL HEALTH: THE MIDTOWN MANHATTAN LONGITUDINAL STUDY, 1954 – 1974*

Anita Kassen Fischer, COLUMBIA UNIVERSITY

Janos Marton, COLUMBIA UNIVERSITY

E. Joel Millman, COLUMBIA UNIVERSITY

Leo Srole, COLUMBIA UNIVERSITY

To the poet's insight that "the child is father to the man" and the playwright's observation that "what is past is prologue," supporting evidence has been offered by investigators of individual personality development. They have illustrated, through research and in clinical practice, that the adult both suffers and benefits from the permeating experiences of early, formative years.

The present chapter is a sociopsychiatric epidemiological exploration of the estimated effects of a selected series of childhood and midstream-adult experiences and developments on subsequent mental health across a substantial arc of the life cycle. Our target interests encompass not only

Research in Community and Mental Health, Vol. 1, pp 305 –333.

psychopathology but the entire psychological range of mental health differences, and reach beyond the individual to scan a large, living-at-home, general population.

Specifically, we have conducted our research within the circumscribed framework of the Midtown Manhattan Longitudinal Study, which was implemented in the two stages or "waves" that we call Midtown I (1954) and Midtown II (1974).

The present chapter is a preliminary report of analyses currently under way that articulate data drawn from both waves. Both stages have already been described in a series of publications. However, it may serve the reader here to briefly recapitulate the central features of each wave in turn.

Midtown I was an investigation of the cross-sectional type that can be summarily characterized along the following seven dimensions:

1. Its 1,660 interviewed subjects were a sixteen per 1000 probability sample representative of the entire resident Midtown population universe of 110,000 adults (99 percent whites) between the ages of 20 and 59.

2. The two-hour (on average) prestructured interview included an inventory of 120 possible symptoms of mental disturbance. Twenty-eight of these covered the pre-adult period, with the rest having a recent time reference. Most of the latter symptom items had, in previous research, satisfied the requirements of criterion validity, in the sense that they had been significantly more prevalent among patient than nonpatient groups.

3. The respondent's replies to all symptom items, plus his/her spontaneous comments and elaborations, together with the interviewer's systematically recorded observations of the respondent made during the interview session, were independently assessed and classified by two Study psychiatrists under the supervision of Dr. Thomas Rennie, the 1954 Study's senior psychiatrist and first director.

4. The psychiatrists placed respondents on a six-class symptom range that reflected Rennie's conception of mental health as "an inclusive continuum of gradient degrees and weights of symptom formation, ranging from the extremes of the symptom free ("Asymptomatic Well") to the Incapacitated, and accompanied by four intermediate grades of symptom severity (Mild, Moderate, Marked and Severe), *with impairment in one or more areas of social role functioning* as his arbitrary benchmark of morbidity" (Srole, 1975, p. 353). The Impaired encompassed the Marked, Severe, and Incapacitated categories, which accounted for 13.2, 7.5, and 2.7 percent respectively, of the interviewed sample.

5. The primary goal was to test the Study's most fundamental postulate: "Sociocultural conditions, in both their normative and deviant forms, operating in intrafamily and extrafamily settings, during childhood and adulthood, have measurable consequences reflected in the mental health differences to be observed in a population" (Srole et al., 1975, p. 119). Accordingly, the interview instrument included a large array of questions designed to tap life-domains that were believed to be consequential for adult mental health.

6. Taking the latter as its dependent variable to be accounted for as an emergent

from life experiences, Midtown I was the first cross-sectional investigation in psychiatric epidemiology to make a sharp distinction between two sets of situational-experiential factors contributing to that emergent:

    a. The independent, antecedent variables, defined by the criterion that each could potentially influence the course of individual mental health development, but could hardly have been influenced by it in return. Examples are age, sex, and parental socioeconomic status, which largely defined the respondents' place in the social space of their childhood, one that was beyond their power to alter.

    b. The reciprocal social variables, defined by the criterion that each can be influenced by the individual's mental health, as well as potentially contribute to it. Examples are marital status and the adult's self-acquired socioeconomic status.

    7. The most important etiological finding of Midtown I was this: With the independent variable of *parental* SES (during respondent's childhood) sorted into six classes, adult respondents of poverty-level parentage had in their ranks almost five times as many Impaired people per 100 Asymptomatics as had respondents of wealthy or affluent parents (Srole et al., 1975).

This finding presented Midtown II with one of its major hypotheses, which can be stated in the form of two propositions:

    1. Families' diverse positions in the community's socioeconomic sun permeate their inner life processes and extramural interactions, thereby creating drastically different milieu settings for offspring to grow into and out of.

    2. These differences penetrate childrens' developing psyches during their most impressionable, formative years.

Thus, we could postulate that, according to their SES position, parents and the family life setting within which they socialize and indoctrinate the child play a crucial part in the development of the child's vulnerabilities and resistances to mental health risk factors throughout the entire span of the life cycle. Part of the data to be presented in this chapter will address some of the issues surrounding the impacts of early life experiences on adult mental health.

METHODS

Midtown II of 1974, which had neither been provided for nor foreseen in the interviews of 1954, can next be briefly outlined as follows:

    1. The feasibility of conducting follow-up interviews twenty years later was established after a major Trace Operation had located 1,124 of our original 1,660 respondents.

    2. Among those located, 858 were alive and 266 were deceased. Reinterviewed in 1974 were 695 persons (81 percent of the located alive respondents). Some 72 percent

of the reinterviewees were found residing in New York City or contiguous counties; 26 percent were dispersed across the rest of the U.S.A.; and 2 percent had their home base abroad.

3. Among the total unlocated at the close of field work (N = 536), an actuarially estimated 100 were presumed to be dead. Most of these were, of course, from the ranks of the oldest men and women. Another 129 of the unlocated were women known to have been unmarried or formerly married in 1954. They were beyond the reach of our trace modalities, most likely because they had changed not only addresses but surnames as well, by marriage.

4. We have systematically compared our 695 panel reinterviewees with the original sample of 1,660 on a large number of demographic and behavioral characteristics. Based on these comparisons, we can infer that the reinterviewed panel is representative of the surviving portion of the 1954 sample with several relatively small, precisely known deviations[1] (Fischer and Biel, forthcoming).

5. Compared to 1954, the 1974 interviews, of three-hour average duration, covered a far larger landscape of somatic, intrapsychic, and social assets as well as liabilites, satisfactions as well as dissatisfactions. Our explicit interest here was to take into account the respondent's strengths in facing and surmounting adversities.

Also, major emphasis was placed on retrospective documentation of major life changes, both gains and losses, that had come about in the long interregnum since 1954.

Thus, the time framework was expanded to encompass four segments or points of the individual's life span:

    a. The pre-adult period through age 19 (largely recovered retrospectively in 1954).

    b. Characteristics at the Midtown I baseline year.

    c. Developments since 1954.

    d. Characteristics at the Midtown II terminal year.

6. Most important, however, was our replication of eighty-three adult symptom questions that had been asked in 1954. This was a first step toward achieving necessary comparability in 1974 with the 1954 baseline global mental health measure. The second step, namely the psychiatrists' six-fold classification of degrees of symptom formation and social impairment, was impossible to replicate after twenty years for a number of reasons, e.g., the unavailability of the same psychiatrists. Instead, a statistical procedure was utilized to derive an equivalent measure of mental health that would simulate the psychiatrists' judgmental ratings of 1954 (Singer, 1976a).

Specifically, by applying stepwise multiple regression techniques to the panel's 1954 symptom information, twenty-two of the eighty-three replicated items were identified that together yielded a score range highly predictive (multiple correlation of .83) of the psychiatrists' merged judgmental ratings. This score range was then cut into six categories in such fashion as to almost precisely reproduce the panel's distribution on the psychiatrists' original six-category classification scheme.

This computer-simulated six-fold categorization of 1954 mental health status (MH54) is a statistically acceptable surrogate for the psychiatrists' subjective classificatory ratings (PR54) of a far larger base of symptomatic and behavioral information.

7. The identical methods were applied to the information from the replicated

twenty-two symptom items in 1974, yielding a computer-simulated six-fold classification of the reinterviewees that we label SIM74. Thus, SIM54 had PR54 as its reference model, and SIM74 in turn is strictly standardized to SIM54 as reference model (Singer, 1976a). However, to ease matters for the reader, we shall hereafter refer to mental health status in 1974 by the acronym MH74, with MH54 as its twenty-years earlier counterpart.

FINDINGS

The analytic tasks we have chosen for this chapter center on two questions:

1. What predictors of our panel's 1954 mental health status (MH54) can be uncovered in a selected series of childhood experiential domains?
2. What predictors of our panel's 1974 mental health status (MH74) can be elicited in a larger series of antecedents that comprehend not only the childhood domains but socioemotional well-being in 1954 (using MH54 in combination with several other measures of individual functioning), and two circumscribed indicators of mental health developments that occurred subsequent to 1954 and prior to 1974? (The Appendix describes the antecedent variables included in the set of potential predictors. It also presents further technical aspects of the analyses.)

Figure 1 is a graphic representation of the hypothesized order of three sets of dimensions of the childhood period as they may have been imprinted on respondents' mental health in 1954.

The chapter's Appendix lists the item contents of all antecedent variables selected as potential predictors of the dependent variable. Here we would enter a particular comment on parental socioeconomic status (P-SES).[2] As already mentioned above, the latter is significantly correlated with MH54. In longitudinal perspective, we can begin to discern how

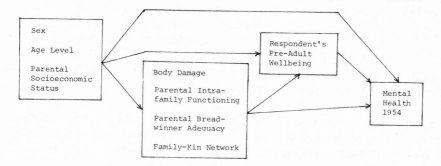

Figure 1   Model of antecedents of 1954 mental health status.

Parental SES influences MH54 (and MH74) conjointly with the following dimensions of the childhood experience:

1. Body damage, i.e., a body defect at birth that required medical attention, or a heart condition during the childhood-adolescence years, both assumed to handicap childhood functioning.

2. Parental Breadwinner Adequacy (P-BA) is based on questions probing such facets as chronic shortage of money for necessities, instability in the area of father's work including unemployment, and mother having been required to work.

3. Parental Intra-Family Functioning (P-IF) covered respondent's retrospective evaluations of father's and mother's physical and emotional sides, and of their behaviors in the parent-child dyad.

4. The index of the Family-Kin Network (F-KN) refers to the completeness of the family unit relative to the ideal of having both parents, one or more siblings, and extended kin in, or accessible to, the home.

5. Respondent's Pre-Adult Well-being during childhood is conceived as a postualated consequence of the above four contexts of the childhood setting, and also an antecedent, reactive domain potentially influencing adult mental health. Under this rubric we cover functioning on three subdomains, namely *(a)* the somatic, *(b)* the interpersonal, and *(c)* the intrapsychic.

Our immediate task is to discern the linkages to MH54 of the above domains plus, of course, respondent's gender and age level. But before we report the values of the zero-order correlations and multiple regression coefficients, we might consider in what range of magnitude we can realistically expect them to fall. The eight childhood domains together add up to only a fragment of the total world of daily, intimate experiences that encompassed the individual's universe from birth through adolescence. Therefore, each of the separate domains can reasonably be expected to have only a small discrete influence on our dependent variable of MH54. We have accordingly set as our criterion of significant influence a Pearson or beta coefficient of $\pm$ 0.100 or more, a value that explains at least one percent of the variance in a dependent variable.

Table 1 reports the Pearson and standardized multiple regression coefficients of the eight childhood domains with our panel's MH54. The betas estimate the influence of each independent variable upon MH54, independently of the other antecedent variables. Five of the eight domains present significant Pearson correlations, with Parental Socioeconomic Status and Respondent Pre-Adult Well-being as the strongest of these five. The beta values tell us that Body Damage but not Parental Breadwinner Adequacy continues to exert a discrete influence on MH54 when all the other domains of childhood are controlled.

Table 1

Zero-order Correlations and Standardized Multiple-Regression
Coefficients (Betas) for Antecedents of MH54

Antecedent variables	r	Beta
A. Demographic variables		
1. Sex	0.03	0.02
2. Age level	0.13+	0.16+
3. Parental socioeconomic status	-0.16+	-0.15+
B. Contexts of childhood functioning		
1. Body damage	0.12+	0.10+
2. Parental breadwinner adequacy	0.11+	0.06
3. Parental intrafamily functioning	0.08	0.08
4. Family-Kin network	0.05	-0.005
C. Respondent Pre-Adult Well-being	0.23+	0.23+

+ Exceeds the criterion of ± 0.100.

Parental Socioeconomic Status and Age Level also continue to exert significant influence on MH54 when the other childhood domains are controlled. Respondent Pre-Adult Well-being, substantively more akin to mental health in 1954, continues with an undiminished beta of 0.23 when all effects of the other seven antecedent variables are controlled. Taken together, the multiple correlation of all eight of the childhood domains with MH54 is 0.35, explaining 12 percent of the variance in 1954 mental health.

We move next to isolate predictors of MH74 from a matrix of antecedents that include the above eight childhood domains and five other antecedent variables, two operating in the 1954 baseline year and three that subsequently emerged in the period before 1974.

A factor analysis was performed on five dimensions of respondent functioning in 1954, namely *(a)* MH54, *(b)* affective symptoms, *(c)* quantitative extra-family social network density, *(d)* qualitative sense of extra-family social integration (as indexed by the nine-item Srole anomia scale), and *(e)* excess intake (of coffee, alcoholic beverages, tobacco, and/or food). Two factor structures emerged which we designate MH54A and MH54B. (See Appendix, p. 509ff).

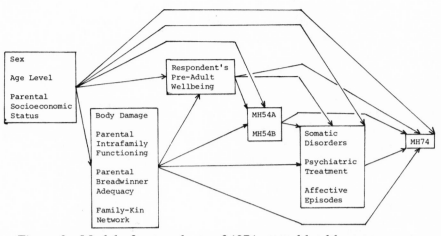

Figure 2   Model of antecedents of 1974 mental health status.

The three post-1954 developments include the following:

  1. Troublesome Somatic Illnesses, including the life-threatening ones of heart attack, stroke, and cancer.
  2. Unusual Affective Episodes (Depressive and/or Manic), each lasting a week of more.
  3. Psychiatric Treatment in a hospital and/or clinic and/or private office.

Figure 2 and Table 2 are counterparts of Figure 1 and Table 1 above, except that they also include as potential predictors of MH74 the above five 1954-and-after variables.

We now observe on the level of zero-order correlations that childhood variables which were significantly linked to MH54 are also linked, with somewhat diminished strength, to MH74, Body Damage being the sole new dropout. Three of the 1954 and post-1954 factors register strong correlations of 0.38, 0.33 and 0.31, with Affective Episodes and Psychiatric Treatment presenting lesser Pearson coefficients of −0.21 and 0.14.

When all thirteen predictors of Table 2 are entered into multiple regression equations which control each for the other 12, the betas of all eight childhood factors fall to near zero. Although there is also a drop in the betas of all five of the 1954 and post-1954 variables, all five manifest significant independent impacts on MH74. The strongest impacts of all are traced to the two enriched MH54 factored indices.

The multiple correlation of all thirteen predictors is 0.56, accounting for a substantial 31 percent of the total variance in MH74.

Table 2

Zero-order Correlations and Standardized Multiple-Regression
Coefficients (Betas) for Antecedents of MH74

Antecedent variables	r	Beta
A. Demographic variables		
1. Sex	0.06	0.003
2. Age level	0.12+	0.05
3. Parental socioeconomic status	-0.13+	-0.04
B. Contexts of childhood functioning		
1. Body damage	0.06	-0.02
2. Parental breadwinner adequacy	0.12+	0.06
3. Parental intra family functioning	0.12+	0.06
4. Family-Kin network	0.07	0.02
C. Respondent Pre-Adult Well-being	0.15+	0.02
D. The 1954 Baseline Predictors		
1. MH54A	0.38+	0.28+
2. MH54B	0.33+	0.22+
E. The Post-1954 Developments		
1. Somatic Illness	0.31+	0.20+
2. Unusual Manic and/or Depressive Episodes	-0.21+	-0.15+
3. Psychiatric Treatment	0.14+	0.11+

+ Exceeds the criterion of $\pm$ 0.100.

DISCUSSION

Before proceeding to interpret the tables presented above, we offer the caveat that the data yielded are exploratory and provisional, facing further analytic probing and elaboration as we move along in our larger analysis of stability and change in mental health over time.

Particularly important is that a number of other variables, some antecedent to MH54, and others antecedent to MH74 (because they intervened between Midtown I and Midtown II) will be entered into regression equations together with those antecedent factors which have now emerged with significant values in Tables 1 and 2 above. Such further screening may change beta magnitudes now appearing in those tables. At the completion of that screening program, we should be able to arrange our data bank's entire pool of life conditions that are antecedent to our dependent variables in a rank order of relative impact, net of the effects of other antecedents, on adult mental health. Such a ranking should suggest *(a)* the relative etiological significance of major dimensions of the intrafamily and extrafamily environments, and *(b)* programmatic priorities for mental health promotive and preventive efforts in the community.

Returning to Tables 1 and 2, our major effort has been to focus on a single life outcome, adult mental health, measured on the same population by a comparable metric, at two appreciably removed points of time in the life span of its members. Time (and its corollary, human aging) is here the key variable. And the new question that can now be raised is this: Fixing on this time variable, how do the components in our present series of antecedent factors change in their relationship to the dependent variable, adult mental health, across the life cycle? The question can be phrased in somewhat different terms: What is the relative durability of the influences on later human well-being of different life conditions that operate at several earlier stages of individual development?

To approach an answer, we have hypothetically defined four kinds, or patterns, of sequences in the impacts of a given pre-adult life condition on mental health at several later points of time.

1. The pre-adult life circumstances may continue to exhibit more or less the same magnitude of effect at a later age as at a younger one—which might be called a *pattern of durability*. We had expected only our early body damage component to fit this pattern. In fact, with MH54, body damage's zero-order and beta coefficients are both at a significant level. But by MH74, both coefficients have fallen toward zero, confounding our expectation.[3]

2. The pre-adult life condition may have a slow, "snowballing" effect on mental health over time, i.e., it may exert an early significant influence and later exhibit an even larger effect, or what might be called a *cumulative pattern*. We had expected only parental SES to fit this pattern. In fact, with MH54, both the zero-order and beta coefficients are of significant magnitudes. By MH74, its zero-order value is approximately the same as twenty years earlier, suggesting a durable, rather than a cumulative pattern. However, its beta, net of the other twelve antecedents in Table 2, had fallen far below our .10 criterion. We shall be trying to identify other post-1954 variables which may have diminished the discrete influence of parental SES on MH74.

The expectation stated above had originally been prompted by our image that the poverty level of parental SES, in particular, would "snowball" on mental health over time. This localized possibility we have not yet isolated analytically, and therefore we must postpone judgment until a later date.

3. The pre-adult life circumstance may have a *"sleeper" effect,* i.e., it initially may be innocent of perceptible impact, but by prolongation turn up decades later with a seemingly sudden and powerful punch. The established case of cigarette smoking in relation to lung cancer is, for example, a somatic analog.

Completely unforeseeable suicides and acute breakdowns in functioning are often terminal manifestations of an early life trauma that had seemed to have been successfully surmounted, but no instances of such a sequence in sufficient numbers are as yet discernible in the data currently analyzed.

The nearest approximation to a sleeper effect is to be found in the Parental Intra-Family Functioning domain. In Table 1, neither the Pearson nor the beta coefficients meet our criterion of significance. In Table 2, the Pearson r does achieve significance, but the beta does not.

4. The pre-adult life condition may describe a *subsiding* pattern of impact on mental health over time (i.e., strong early and weak later pattern). The previously discussed early body damage component is a clear expression of this pattern of attenuating influence.

Pre-adult well-being (like parental SES), partially fits this pattern; that is, although its zero-order correlations with mental health in 1954 and 1974 are both high, its beta coefficient falls precipitously from .26 in 1954 to .02 in 1974.

We can restate the above data in somewhat different terms. In the Longitudinal Study's preceding articles (Srole, 1975; Singer, 1976a), we reported that MH54 and MH74 stand in a zero-order relationship to each other of 0.45. The former (MH54A, pp. 11, 28), in an enlarged version, is represented in Table 2, and its presence is visible there among the eight pre-1954 factors. Specifically, whatever the magnitude of their Pearson coefficients (four are at a significant level), the betas of all eight portray values little above zero. This suggests that an interesting process may be operating. The impacts of the four childhood variables that appear in Table 1 with both zero-order and beta coefficients at significant levels account for an appreciable part of the variance in MH54. However, after MH54 has "soaked up" their impacts, they have little or no residual influence on MH74, when MH54 in particular is controlled. Thus far in our analysis, it is the latter which exerts the dominant influence on mental health status in 1974, independently of other potent life circumstances. It appears, then, that response styles to life experiences in the earliest years have the greatest leverage for magnifying vulnerability and resistance to the exigencies and crises of the adult years.[4]

If this important finding stands up under further analytic scrutiny with additional variables to be tested, it will tend to add support to the position of those who have emphasized that the earlier in the life cycle preventive efforts are applied, the more effective they are likely to be. In that event, policymakers in the helping professions would have longitudinal epidemiological evidence pointing to (1) an expansion of resources for preventive and promotive mental health programs, and (2) a shift in service, training, and research priorities from adult to adolescent and child psychiatry.

From this venture into longitudinal terrain, we might next indicate several further exploratory directions on our analysis horizon. In this report we have primarily focused on selected life conditions and their changing effects on subsequent mental health in our adult panel as a whole. One of our next tasks is to approach the same kind of issues from a different angle, namely by sorting our panel into three sequences of change in individual mental health between 1954 and 1974.

1. Those who improved in mental health status, comprising about one-third of the panel.

2. Those whose MH54 and MH74 standings are identical, representing a two-fifths plurality of our respondents.

3. Those whose mental health slipped during the twenty years, accounting for about one-fourth of our study subjects.

With this classification as our dependent variable, we shall systematically search our extensive data bank for life circumstances differentially associated with, and explanatory of, these three sequential patterns of individual mental health change.

Included in the 1974 interviews for this particular purpose are an array of coverages of such realms as behavioral signs of characterological strengths (e.g., resiliency) and deficits (e.g., rigidity), the current availability or absence of social resources (e.g., a supportive kin network), and the net weight of post-1954 life events representing gains (e.g., achievements) and losses (e.g., "hard knocks") bearing on one's "fitness" within his/her self-to-others social fabric. Here we shall be probing our three types of mental health changers for their distinctive approaches to, interactions with, and mental health outputs from, encounters with their changing social arenas. We hope to statistically synthesize a series of composite case history profiles for each of our three mental health change types.

It is also our plan to focus on a new finding presented in a predecessor paper, namely that the historical generation one is born into (which we call the "birth cohort" variable) has important mental health consequences. Briefly put, among the panel's four ten-year-span birth cohorts (born ± 1900, ± 1910, ± 1920, and ± 1930) we have found, with chronological age controlled, that the later in the twentieth century the cohort was born, the higher is its mental health Well rate and the substantially smaller is its Impaired rate. We intend to delineate the converging, historically linked, individual and contextual factors that have impinged upon and turned the course of this newly discovered inter-generation trend (Srole, 1977).

In both the present analysis and those proposed as next steps, we shall be concerned with sex differences in relation to the long-range effects of early experiences upon mental health status, changes in mental health, and with sex-linked differences in the birth cohorts and subsequent mental health.

Midtown I was an exploratory epidemiological investigation of the cross-sectional kind. Midtown II adds to it the fourth dimension of time and brings us to a new frontier, namely social and individual life history processes that contribute to a population's mental health gains and losses.

We emphasize "process" because it replaces the etiologically ambiguous statics of a single point-of-time study design with the etiologically suggestive, dynamic progression of action-interaction-reaction patterns discernible only in the longitudinal perspective.

In a sense, one of the important functions of this report has been to formulate the new kinds of conceptual issues and empirical questions which surface when investigators breach the operational wall that has turned back researchers from exploring the longitudinal vistas of psychiatric epidemiology.

APPENDIX

The general purpose of this appendix is to provide technical information which may be helpful, in whole or in part, to the reader's understanding of the statistics presented in the body of this report. The appendix is organized into four sections:

I. The items included in
   A. Indices of pre-1954 variables.
   B. Indices of 1954 and post-1954 functioning.
II. The construction of factored indices.
III. The complete multiple regression analysis of 1954 psychiatric symptom level (psychiatrists' ratings).
IV. The complete multiple regression analysis of 1974 psychiatric symptom level (MH74).

SECTION I. *Items*
   A. *Indices of pre-1954 variables*
      1. The composition of the *Parental Socioeconomic Status* is discussed in Footnote 2, p. 332.

2. *Family-Kin Networks Index* includes the following 1954 interview items:

"When you were growing up (6–18 years old), were there any other relatives (uncles, aunts, grandparents, etc.) who lived in your home with you?"

"When you were growing up (6–18 years old), were there any other relatives you were close with? How many families were you close with?"

"Did you always live with both your real parents up to the time you were 16 years old?"

Number of brothers and/or sisters the respondent reported.

Scores on this index range from 2 (most complete family-kin network) to 16 (least complete family-kin network), with a mean of 7.316 and a standard deviation of 2.519.

3. The *Parental Somatic and Role Functioning Combined Index* includes the following 1954 interview items:

Respondents reported whether or not their father or their mother had any of the following ten disorders: arthritis, asthma, bladder trouble, colitis, diabetes, hay fever, high blood pressure, sciatica or neuralgia, stomach ulcer, or skin condition. These reports were summed to form an index of Parental Psychosomatic Conditions, to which was added the Parental Role Functioning Index:

"When you were growing up (ages 6–18) were either of your parents (parent substitutes) in poor health?"

"Were either of your parents (parent substitutes) the worrying type?"

Respondents reported whether or not their father or their mother "had a nervous breakdown."

Respondents reported whether or not their father or their mother "had heart conditions."

"Mother wants to run her children's lives. When you were growing up, did you ever feel that way too?"

"My parents are always proud of their children. When you were growing up, did you ever feel that way too?"

"Mother does not understand me. When you were growing up, did you ever feel that way too?"

"My parents often don't practice what they preach. When you were growing up, did you ever feel that way too?"

"Father wants to run his children's lives. When you were growing up, did you ever feel that way too?"

"All in all, in your opinion, what one person do you take after most in character (personality, temperament, etc.)?" This item was scored to indicate if a respondent reported having taken after *only the opposite* sex parent.

Scores on this index range from 7 to 18, with low scores indicating high levels of parental adequacy, and high scores indicating low levels of parental adequacy (unfavorable). The index's mean is 11.943, with a standard deviation of 1.965.

4. The *Index of Parental Adequacy as Breadwinners* includes the following 1954 interview items:

Respondents were asked to identify "the chief problems or troubles that your parents (or parent substitute) had to face while you were growing up (ages 6–18)." This item was scored to indicate if a respondent reported that "unemployment, work, and/or financial" problems were "chief problems" for his parents.

"During the years you were growing up (ages 6–18), did your parents (those who brought you up) ever have a hard time making ends meet?"

"During those years you were growing up (ages 6–18), did your mother (or parent substitute) work outside the home?"[5]

In addition to these three 1954 interview items, a 1974 interview item is also included in this index, viz.:

"When you were 13–17 years old, were your parents considered by others as wealthy, comfortably fixed, getting by, barely getting by, or poor?"

Scores on this index range from 2 to 16, with the former indicating the highest level of parental adequacy as breadwinners (favorable) and the latter indicating the lowest level of parental adequacy. The index's mean is 6.584, with a standard deviation of 2.795.

5. The *Body Damage Index* was constructed by assigning a 1 to respondents who reported any of the following in 1954:

"As far as you know were you born with any physical condition that needed correction?"

"Before the age of 20, did you ever have a heart condition?"

"Did you ever have epilepsy?"

Eighty-six respondents received a 1 on this index, whereas the remaining 609 respondents received a 0.

6. Although Respondent Pre-Adult Well-being is considered to be a global index, indices of the three separate domains which compose it were constructed:
   a. *Intrapsychic Malfunctioning* is the sum of each respondent's Childhood Fear Score and his/her Childhood Neurotic Score. (The composition of these are discussed in Langner, 1963.)
   b. The *Index of Social Malfunctioning in Childhood* includes the following 1954 interview items:

"I am happy only when I am at home. When you were growing up, did you ever feel that way too?"

"Some children like school; others don't. As a child, how did you feel about going to school? Would you say you liked school: very much, liked it all right, disliked it, or hated it?"

"Now as to when you were a teenager, say 13–18 years old, in those years, did you usually have dates with girls (boys) more often or less often than most other boys (girls) your age?"

Also included is the following 1974 interview item:

"When you were about 13–17 years old, did you learn to depend mainly on yourself to get things done or did you depend mainly on others to help you get things done?"

Scores on this index range from 0 (least malfunctioning) to 4 (most malfunctioning), with a mean of 1.578 and a standard deviation of 0.760.
   c. The Index of *Somatic Malfunctioning in Childhood* was computed by aggregating two subindices. First, respondents' re-

ports of having had the following disorders before the age of 20 were summed: arthritis, asthma, bladder trouble, colitis, diabetes, hay fever, high blood pressure, sciatica or neuralgia, stomach ulcer, and/or skin condition. Scores on this index range from 0 (fewest childhood somatic disorders) to 3 (most childhood somatic disorders), with a mean of 0.261 and a standard deviation of 0.545.

Second, two 1954 interview items and one 1974 interview item were combined. The 1954 items were:

"Now, about your health in early childhood–that is, in the first six years of life: As far as you can remember or have been told, was your health in early childhood good, fair, or poor?"

"As a child, did you catch cold very often?"

From the 1974 interview, it was determined whether or not a respondent had a "serious illness as a child or teenager."

The mean of this subindex was 1.066, with a standard deviation of 0.952. It ranged from 0 (most favorable) to 3 (least favorable).

The index of Somatic Malfunctioning in Childhood constructed by summing these two subindices ranged from 0 (most favorable) to 6 (least favorable), with a mean of 1.328 and a standard deviation of 1.192.

B. *Items included in indices of 1954 and post-1954 variables.*

1. The respondents' *general health in 1954* is measured by the following 1954 interview item: "About your health now, would you say it is: excellent, good, fair, or poor?" Scores on this index range from 1 (excellent) to 4 (poor), with a mean of 1.768 and a standard deviation of 0.783.

2. The *Affective Symptoms Index* includes the following 1954 interview items:

"Do you feel you have had your share of good luck in life?"

"On the whole, life gives you pleasure. Do you agree or disagree?"

"Nothing ever turns out for me the way I want it to."

"Of course we all have our emotional ups and downs, and laymen as well as doctors know that these can sometimes have effects on our health. What about yourself? in general, would you say that most of the time you are in high spirits, good spirits, low spirits, or, very low spirits?" (For scoring purposes, high and good spirits were combined, as were low and very low spirits.)

Affective Symptoms Index scores range from 0 (no symptoms) to 4 (most symptoms), with a mean of 0.340 and a standard deviation of 0.739.

> 3. *Excess Intake* is indexed by counting respondents' reports in 1954 of "often" drinking more coffee, smoking more cigarettes, eating more food, and/or drinking more alcoholic beverages "than is good for you." Scores on this index range from 0 (no excess intakes) to 4 (most excess intakes), with a mean of 1.088 and a standard deviation of 0.956.
>
> 4. The index of *1954 Anomia* included the following nine items:

"Most public officials (people in public office) are not really interested in the problems of the average man."

"These days a person doesn't really know whom he can count on."

"Most people don't really care what happens to the next fellow."

"Nowadays, a person has to live pretty much for today and let tomorrow take care of itself."

"In spite of what people say, the lot (situation, condition) of the average man is getting worse, not better."

"It's hardly fair to bring a child into the world with the way things look for the future."

"Next to health, money is the most important thing in life."

"You sometimes can't help wondering whether anything is worthwhile."

"To make money there are no right and wrong ways any more, only easy and hard ways."

1954 *Anomia* ranged from 0 (most favorable) to 9 (least favorable), with a mean of 2.555 and a standard deviation of 2.105.

> 5. *Social Network Density* is indexed by summing the standardized scores for respondents' reports in 1954 of how many friends, relatives, and neighbors they have, plus how many organizations they are active in. Index scores range from -5.109 (most restricted social networks) to 9.626 (least restricted social networks), with a mean of -0.020 and a standard deviation of 2.434.

6. The construction and composition of the Indices of *Psychiatric Symptom Level* in 1954 (MH54) and 1974 (MH74) has been reported elsewhere (cf. Srole, 1975; Singer et al., 1976a).

7. *Post-1954, Pre-1974 Somatic Events* are measured by combining two sets of variables:

Respondents' reports in 1974 of having had a heart attack, a stroke, and/or cancer after 1954.

Respondents' reports in 1974 of having had other serious health conditions after 1954.

Scores on this index range from 0 (no somatic disorders) to 5, with a mean of 1.212 and a standard deviation of 1.002.

8. *Unusual Affective Episodes (Depressive and/or Manic) Index* includes the following 1974 interview items:

"Have there been times when you changed for a whole week or more from your usual self to unusually high spirits, i.e., everything in you seemed to be working at top speed and you felt on top of the world?"

"Have there (also) been times when you changed for a whole week or more to unusually low spirits, i.e., you felt utterly miserable and everything seemed too much of an effort for you?"

Scores on this index range from 2 (both types of episodes occurred) to 4 (neither type of episode occurred), with a mean of 3.571 and a standard deviation of 0.655.

9. *Psychiatric Treatment Index* assigns a 1 to respondents who answered any of the following 1974 items in the affirmative for the period following the 1954 interview, and a 0 to the others:

"People sometimes go to a hospital or nursing home for an emotional or nervous condition. Of course, these too are medical problems treated by doctors and nurses. Have you ever been in a hospital or nursing home for such an emotional or nervous condition?"

"Have you ever gone to a hospital clinic or non-hospital clinic for an emotional or nervous condition? How old were you when you went to such a clinic for the first time?"

"To get help for an emotional problem or nervous condition people also go to other kinds of professionals outside of a hospital or clinic. For such personal problems have you ever gone to a private psychiatrist, psychologist, counselor, clergyman, social worker, group therapist, or other similar kind of professional?"

Scores on this index ranged from 0 (no psychiatric treatment) to 1 (psychiatric treatment), with a mean of 0.209 and a standard deviation of 0.407.

SECTION II. *Construction of factored indices.*

In formulating models of mental health in 1954 and 1974, the investigators recognized that measures of social, emotional, and physical well-being at any point in time are reciprocal: i.e., contemporaneous and simultaneously causal for each other. Therefore, we conceived of respondent well-being (social, physical, and emotional) at a point in time as an unobservable variable, with several indicators available to us. To index *Pre-Adult Well-being* we had available to us indices of three domains of childhood functioning: social, somatic, and intrapsychic. (The composition of these indices is discussed above, pp. 320–321.) Additionally, several sets of indicators were available to measure *Adult Well-being in 1954:* an indicator of General Health, two indicators of social well-being (Anomia and Social Network Density), two indicators of emotional well-being (Affective Symptoms and Excess Intake) and (MH54). The composition of these indices is discussed above, (pp. 321–322).

To convert these indicators into indices of respondent well-being in pre-adulthood and in 1954, we relied on the demonstration of Hauser and Goldberger (1971) that the path analytic treatment of the relationship of indicators to "unobservable variables" is equivalent to "a factor-analysis model" in which "the unobservables z^* and y^* represent oblique factors, and the absence of direct paths from z^* to the y's and from y^* to the z's represents certain zero factor loadings" (p. 90).

1. To measure *Respondent Pre-Adult Well-being,* we therefore first factor analyzed our indices of the three domains of Pre-Adult Well-being: somatic, social, and intrapsychic. One factor was extracted, using a principal component solution with nine iterations. Therefore, the factor scores could be computed without a rotation. Social Malfunctioning had a factor score coefficient of 0.308, Somatic Malfunctioning, 0.107, and Intrapsychic Malfunctioning 0.326. These coefficients were used to compute the index of Respondent Pre-Adult Well-being, as follows:

    Respondent Pre-Adult Well-being = 0.307 × Social Malfunctioning + 0.106 × Somatic Malfunctioning + 0.326 × Intrapsychic Malfunctioning.

Scores on this index ranged from 1.487 (least malfunctioning in pre-adulthood) to 2.279 (most malfunctioning in pre-adulthood), with a mean of 0.118 and a standard deviation of 0.732.

2. 1954 *Adult Mental Health (Expanded)* was measured by first factor analyzing for four indicators of adult well-being in 1954. A principal components solution with seventy-five iterations yielded two factors, one explaining 79.5 percent of the shared variance in the five variables and the other explaining 20.5 percent of the shared variance in the five variables. An oblique rotation with seven iterations was then performed. The two factors yielded by this procedure intercorrelated 0.158. (This correlation is controlled for in subsequent multiple-regression analyses of mental health in 1954 and 1974 by treating the two factored indices of 1954 functioning as reciprocally causal.) The factor score coefficients of each variable on each of the two factors were used to compute factored indices corresponding to each of the two factors. The two factored indices were designated "MH54A" and "MH54B" to indicate that they can be thought of as expanded 1954 indices, i.e., mental health in 1954 was incorporated into a group of concurrent measures to describe a broader domain of adult well-being in 1954 than is covered by MH54 alone.

The equations for the factored indices computed from the five 1954 adult functioning variables are as follows:

MH54A = 0.358 × MH54 + 0.339 × Affective Symptoms + (−0.975) × Excess Intake + 0.235 × Anomia + (−0.223) × Social Network Density

MH54B = 0.672 × MH54 + (−0.050) × Affective Symptoms + 0.217 × Excess Intake + (−0.066) × Anomia + 0.134 × Social Network Density

Scores on MH54A range from −1.345 (most favorable) to 5.589 (least favorable) with a mean of 1.670 and a standard deviation of 1.117. Scores on MH54B range from −0.487 (most favorable) to 4.264 (least favorable), with a mean of 1.537 and a standard deviation of 0.785.

Note that the sign of Social Network Density is negative on the first factored index because it is scored in the opposite direction from MH54. In general, the higher a respondent scores on MH54, the more constricted is his social network ($r = -0.18$). However, the sign of Social Network Density is positive on the second factored index. Respondents who score highly on this second factored index do not have constricted social networks, although they do have high MH54 scores.

The two factored indices also correlate differently with many other variables in the model of MH74 (see Table 3). In general, high scorers on

Table 3

Zero-order Correlations Among Variables in the Models of MH54 and MH74

	Variables	(2)	(3)	(4)	(5)	(6)	(7)	(8)	(9)	(10)	(11)	(12)	(13)	(14)	(15)	(16)	Mean	S.D.	n
(1)	Sex[1]	0.96	.029	-.057	.031	.084	-.077	.012	.105	.016	.004	.033	.122	.033	.094	.063	1.577	0.494	695
(2)	Age in 1974	--	-.054	-.061	.230	-.016	-.038	-.147	.141	.079	.073	-.160	.177	.128	.151	.117	58.811	10.548	694
(3)	Parental SES	--	--	.070	-.220	.106	-.330	.006	-.289	-.011	.015	.182	-.066	-.156	-.144	-.134	3.678	1.615	695
(4)	Body Damage	--	--	--	-.044	.074	-.009	.143	.056	.074	-.108	.081	.107	.121	.104	.057	2.121	0.331	695
(5)	Family-Kin Network	--	--	--	--	-.143	.134	-.024	.109	-.001	-.011	-.101	.045	.052	.067	.067	7.316	2.519	694
(6)	Parental Intra-family Functioning	--	--	--	--	--	-.022	.046	.004	.138	-.010	.059	.071	.079	.100	.105	11.943	1.965	581
(7)	Parental Adequacy as Breadwinners	--	--	--	--	--	--	.070	.133	.018	-.008	-.012	-.011	.111	.088	.115	6.584	2.795	692
(8)	Respondent Pre-Adult Well-being	--	--	--	--	--	--	--	.095	.262	-.137	.183	.041	.232	.238	.149	3.259	1.058	544
(9)	MH54A	--	--	--	--	--	--	--	--	.141	-.042	-.027	.192	.589	.635	.380	1.670	1.117	619
(10)	MH54B	--	--	--	--	--	--	--	--	--	-.105	.109	.131	.578	.826	.332	1.537	0.785	619
(11)	Affective Episodes	--	--	--	--	--	--	--	--	--	--	-.122	-.099	-.144	-.103	-.214	3.571	0.655	678
(12)	Psychiatric Treatment	--	--	--	--	--	--	--	--	--	--	--	.035	.065	.069	.137	0.209	0.406	685
(13)	Somatic Events	--	--	--	--	--	--	--	--	--	--	--	--	.186	.216	.312	1.212	1.002	678
(14)	PR	--	--	--	--	--	--	--	--	--	--	--	--	--	.780	.406	2.324	1.075	695
(15)	MH54[2] SIM54	--	--	--	--	--	--	--	--	--	--	--	--	--	--	.455	2.333	1.085	695
(16)	MH74	--	--	--	--	--	--	--	--	--	--	--	--	--	--	--	2.249	1.072	695

1 "Male" coded "1", "Female" coded "2".
2 SIM54

MH54A were older (r with Age Level = 0.14), more likely to be women (r with Sex = 0.10), and more likely to be from low SES families (r with P-SES = 0.29) than were low scorers on MH54A. High scorers on MH54A tended to have come from broken and/or isolated homes (r with Family Kin Network = 0.11). Such respondents were much more likely to have had high levels of Pre-Adult Well-being (r = 0.26) than did respondents who had high MH54A scores (r = 0.10). Respondents who scored highly on MH54B were more likely to procure psychiatric treatment (r = 0.11), and/or to have had an Affective Episode (r = 0.10) than were respondents who received a low MH54B score.

SECTION III. *Multiple regression analysis of 1954 Mental Health.*

In addition to the model discussed in the text (p. 309), two models have been developed which specify in greater detail the relationship between the predictor variables and adult mental health in 1954 and 1974. These models differentiate among variables within and between blocks and distinguish effects of antecedent and intervening blocks of variables (cf. Figs. 1 and 2).

Multiple-regression analyses were computed using the SPSS program with hierarchical inclusion of blocks of variables (see Nie et al., 1975, p. 344). The demographic variables of Sex, Age Level, and Parental Socioeconomic Status were treated as one block, the four measures of the contextual domains of Childhood Functioning as a second block, and the factored index of Respondent Pre-Adult Well-being as a third block, with MH as the dependent variable.

Three sets of multiple regressions were computed. The first set sought to decompose the zero-order correlations between remote influences on 1954 mental health by controlling for intervening variables.[6] The standard regression coefficients (subsequently referred to as betas) yielded by this procedure are presented in the second column of Table 4, labeled Beta I, C, (viz., betas controlling for Intervening and Concurrent variables).

Virtually all of the influence of Parental Socioeconomic Status upon MH54 is attributed to the direct linkage between Parental Socioeconomic Status and MH54 (r = −0.16, beta = −0.15). This suggests that the objective availability of economic resources to parents or parental substitutes is *per se* an important influence upon subsequent adult functioning.

Of the examined influences on MH54, Pre-Adult Well-being has the largest influence (beta = 0.23), followed by Age Level (beta = 0.16) and Parental Socioeconomic Status (beta = −0.15). It should be noted, however, that the relationship between Age Level and MH54 is virtually entirely accounted for by the linkage between Age Level and General

Table 4

Multiple-Regression Analysis of 1954 Mental Health*

Antecedent variable	Beta$_{A,C}$	Beta$_{I,C}$	Beta$_{A,I,C}$
A. Demographic Variables			
1. Sex	0.026	0.023	0.023
2. Age Level	0.117+	0.163+	0.163+
3. Parental Socio-economic Status	-0.150+	-0.146+	-0.146+
B. Contexts of Childhood Functioning			
1. Body Damage	0.135+	0.089	0.104+
2. Parental Intra-family Functioning	0.085	0.073	0.077
3. Parental Breadwinner Adequacy	0.075	0.091†	0.058
4. Family-Kin Network	-0.003	0.059	-0.005
C. Respondent Pre-Adult Well-being	0.234+	0.232+	0.232+

R^2 = 0.124

* The headings of the three columns of coefficients should be read as follows:

Beta$_{A,C}$	=	Beta controlling for antecedent or concurrent variables.
Beta$_{I,C}$	=	Beta controlling for antecedent variables concurrent with or intervening between an antecedent variable and MH54.
Beta$_{A,I,C}$	=	Beta controlling for all other antecedent variables (prior, concurrent and intervening).

+   Exceeds the criterion of ±0.100.
†   F = 4.0.

Health (partial correlation between MH54 and Age Level controlling for General Health = 0.05). Respondents in poorer general health in 1954 tended to have higher levels of psychiatric symptoms ($r = 0.42$). The large influence of Pre-Adult Well-being on MH54 suggests that the respondents tended to continue to function at the same level in adulthood (1954) as they did in pre-adulthood.

The second set of multiple regressions were computed in an effort to estimate the relationships between antecedent variables and MH54 controlling for differential levels of these antecedent variables. For example, we were interested in seeing what the influence of Parental Adequacy as Breadwinners would be upon MH54 when Parental Socioeconomic Status and other variables concurrent with or antecedent to Parental Adequacy as Breadwinners were controlled for. The betas produced by this analysis are shown in the first column of Table 4, labeled Beta A, C, (viz., betas controlling for Antecedent and Concurrent variables). Again, Pre-Adult Well-being is the strongest influence upon MH54 (beta = 0.23), followed by Parental Socioeconomic Status (beta = 0.23), followed by Parental Socioeconomic Status (beta = -0.15), Body Damage (beta = 0.14), and Age (beta = 0.12).

Parental Adequacy as Breadwinners has neither a significant Beta A, C, nor a significant Beta I, C, although its zero-order correlation with MH54 is 0.11. This suggests that its role in influencing MH54 is entirely an intermediary one, i.e., intervening between the predictor variables antecedent to it and following it in the model of MH54. All other predictor variables having significant zero-order correlations with MH54 also have both significant Beta A, Cs and significant Beta I, Cs.

The model in Figure 1 (p. 309) explains 12.36 percent of the total variance in MH54 (as estimated by the square of the multiple correlation of all model variables with MH54).

A third multiple-regression analysis was performed to determine the net influence of each variable upon MH54, independent of all other influences. The betas yielded by this procedure are presented in the third column of Table 4, labeled Beta A, I, C, (viz. betas controlling for variables antecedent to, concurrent with, and intervening between an antecedent variable and MH54). These betas are discussed in the text (pp. 310ff). In summary, the three multiple regression analyses of MH54 show that, regardless of which other of the predictor variables are controlled, Parental Socioeconomic Status is the most powerful predictor in our model of MH54.

SECTION IV. *Multiple-regression analysis of 1974 Mental Health.*

Our model of 1974 mental health is presented in Figure 2 (cf. p. 312). In planning this analysis we had two primary interests: first, to examine how the antecedents of 1954 mental health would relate to 1974 mental health; and second, to determine how the 1954 baseline year variables and post-1954 developments would relate to 1974 mental health.

Again, three sets of multiple regressions were computed. The first set attempted to decompose the zero-order correlations between remote influences of 1974 mental health and MH74 by controlling for intervening variables.

All of the 1954 well-being variables (MH54A and B) and post-1954 variables predict MH74, even when their linkages with variables intervening between them and MH74 are removed. Respondents whose well-being in the baseline year was impaired (high MH54A and/or MH54B) had high levels of psychiatric symptoms in 1974, independent of the occurrence of Somatic Disorders, Affective Episodes, or Psychiatric Treatment. Respondents who had Somatic Disorders and/or Affective Episodes and/or Psychiatric Treatment also had higher 1974 levels of psychiatric symptoms, regardless of the occurrence of the other two types of post-1954 developments.

That these linkages of 1954 well-being indices and post-1954 indices to MH74 are not explicable on the basis of antecedent variables in the model of MH74 is shown in the betas presented in the first column of Table 5, labeled Beta A, C (betas controlling for antecedent and concurrent variables). Regardless of their previous level of Pre-Adult Well-being, Childhood Functioning Contexts, or Demographic Background, respondents who had impaired functioning in 1954 (high MH54A and/or B) and/or Somatic Disorders, Affective Episodes, and Psychiatric Treatment had significantly higher levels of psychiatric symptoms in 1974.

None of the pre-1954 variables predict MH74 independent of their linkages with variables intervening between them and MH74 in the model of 1974 mental health (viz., there are no significant Beta I, Cs for those variables). Age Level, Parental Socioeconomic Status, and Pre-Adult Well-being do correlate significantly with MH74 independently of their linkages with variables that precede them in the model (i.e., they have significant Beta A, Cs with MH74). The linkages of Parental Socioeconomic Status and Pre-Adult Well-being are mediated primarily by their associations with the 1954 functioning variables, resulting in nonsignificant Beta I, Cs.

The third set of Betas presented in Table 5 (betas controlling for all other predictor variables, labeled Beta A, I, Cs) is presented and discussed in the text (pp. 312ff).

The model in Fig. 2 explains 31.46 percent of the total variance in MH74 (as estimated by the square of the multiple correlation of all model variables with MH74).

Table 5

Multiple-Regression Analysis of 1974 Mental Health*

Antecedent Variable	Beta A,C	Beta I,C	Beta A,I,C
A. Demographic Variables			
1. Sex	0.057	-0.002	-0.003
2. Age Level	0.105+	0.053	0.053
3. Parental Socio-economic Status	-0.130+	-0.038	-0.038
B. Contexts of Childhood Functioning			
1. Body Damage	0.069	-0.024	-0.020
2. Parental Intra-family Functioning	0.115+	0.059	0.061
3. Parental Breadwinner Adequacy	0.086	0.070	0.063
4. Family-Kin Network	0.023	0.032	0.017
C. Respondent Pre-Adult Well-being	0.171+	0.013	0.020
D. Baseline Adult Functioning (in 1954)			
1. MH54A	0.274+	0.303+	0.278+
2. MH54B	0.256+	0.237+	0.223+
E. Post-1954 Developments			
1. Somatic Illnesses	0.193+	0.291+	0.196+
2. Affective Episodes	-0.151+	-0.172+	-0.148+
3. Psychiatric Treatment	0.103	0.105	0.107+

R^2 = 0.315

* Headings of columns of coefficients are the same as in Table 4 (q.v.).
+ Exceeds the criterion of ±0.100.

In conclusion, our three multiple regression analyses of MH74 demonstrate two findings: (i) MH54 is the most powerful predictor of MH74, regardless of which other predictor variables are controlled; and, (ii) events occurring between 1954 and 1974, represented by the three predictor variables of Affective Episodes, Somatic Illnesses, and Psychiatric Treatment, have an impact on MH74 independent of the other predictor variables in our model, including MH54. It should be remembered, however, that since P-SES was shown to be the most powerful predictor of MH54, its influence on MH74 is contained in the relationship between MH54 and MH74. In other words, since respondents from economically disadvantaged families of origin were the most likely to receive unfavorable MH54 ratings, they were also the most likely to receive unfavorable MH74 ratings.

FOOTNOTES

*This report is the fourth in a continuing series of research reports from the Midtown Manhattan Longitudinal Study, and carries the identity number RS/4. The Midtown investigation has been conducted under NIMH Grant Number 13369, and is sponsored jointly by the New York State Psychiatric Institute and the Columbia University Department of Psychiatry, Leo Srole, Principal Investigator. Preparatory funding is acknowledged from the Foundations Fund for Research in Psychiatry and the National Clearinghouse for Smoking and Health. The Longitudinal Study draws its baseline data from the investigation launched on July 1, 1952, under NIMH Grant Number M515 to the late Dr. Thomas A. C. Rennie, Professor of Psychiatry, Cornell University Medical College.

We want to acknowledge the constructive suggestions of Dr. Dolores Kreisman, Associate Research Schientist, New York State Psychiatric Institute, and Dr. Michael Freund, our colleague on the Midtown Longitudinal Study staff.

Anita Kassen Fischer, Research Associate, Department of Psychiatry, Columbia University College of Physicians and Surgeons and Codirector, Midtown Manhattan Longitudinal Study.

Janos Marton, Staff Associate, Department of Psychiatry, Columbia University College of Physicians and Surgeons.

E. Joel Millman, Staff Associate, Department of Psychiatry, Columbia University College of Physicians and Surgeons.

Leo Srole, Chief of Psychiatric Research (Social Sciences), New York State Psychiatric Institute, Professor of Social Sciences, Department of Psychiatry, Columbia University College of Physicians and Surgeons and Director, Midtown Manhattan Longitudinal Study.

1. Where they differ most from the original sample of 1,660 is to be expected in a panel study of such long duration, namely in the oldest age group (19 percent in 1974 vs. 27 percent in 1954), the lower SES (25 percent vs. 33 percent) higher SES (43 percent vs. 34 percent) and among the younger women (21 percent vs. 27 percent).

2. The Parental Socioeconomic Status variable is a composite constructed by study staff from respondents' separate reports in 1954 of (a) father's years of schooling and (b) father's kind of work performed when respondent was age 18, classified into an occupational rank order.

3. Parenthetically, a number of hypotheses can now be proposed, that might account for such change in the magnitude of the effect of a presumably irreversible somatic defect. However, such proposals would be somewhat premature until further detailed statistical analysis is performed.

4. Our conceptualization is close to that expressed by Norman Garmezy, James Anthony, and Cynthia James in their separate studies of risk factors and invulnerability in the childhood years (Richard Flaste, *New York Times,* July 22, 1977).

5. This item was included in the Index of Parental Breadwinner Adequacy because the "need to earn money" was the predominant reason reported by respondents with working mothers.

6. Three sample regression equations for this analysis are:

1. PR = function of (respondent Pre-Adult Well-being)

2. PR = function of (Parental Somatic Conditions and Role Functioning controlling for the concurrent variables of Parental Adequacy as Breadwinners, Family-Kin Network Completeness, and Body Damage, and the intervening variable of Respondent Pre-Adult Well-being)

3. PR = function of (Parental Socioeconomic Status controlling for the demographic variables of Sex and Age, and the intervening variables of Parental Adequacy as Breadwinners, Parental Somatic Conditions and Role Functioning, Body Damage, Family-Kin Network Composition, and Respondent Pre-Adult Well-being).

REFERENCES

Fischer, Anita K., and Renee Biel (forthcoming), "First steps in a follow-up study: Tracing and selecting the panel."

Flaste, Richard (1977), "The 'invulnerable children'. . .", *New York Times,* July 22, p. B4.

Hauser, Robert M., and Arthur S. Goldberger (1971), "The treatment of unobservable variables in path analysis," pp. 81–117 in H. L. Costner (Ed.), *Sociological Methodology.* San Francisco: Jossey-Bass.

Langner, Thomas S., and Stanley Michael (1963), *Life Stress & Mental Health.* (Midtown I) Glencoe: The Free Press.

Nie, Norman H., C. Hadlai Hull, Jean G. Jenkins, Karin Steinbrenner, and Dale H. Brent (1975, *Statistical Package for the Social Sciences.* New York: McGraw-Hill.

Singer, Eleanor, Steven Martin Cohen, Robin Garfinkel, and Leo Srole (1976a), "Replicating psychiatric ratings through multiple regression analysis: The Midtown Manhattan Restudy (Midtown II)," *Journal of Health and Social Behavior* 17: 376–387.

———, Robin Garkinkel, Steven Martin Cohen, and Leo Srole (1976b), "Mortality and mental health: Evidence from the Midtown Manhattan Restudy (Midtown II)," *Social Science and Medicine* 10: 517–525.

Srole, Leo (1975), "Measurement and classification in socio-psychiatric epidemiology: Midtown Manhattan Study (1954) and Midtown Manhattan Restudy (1974) (Midtown II)," *Journal of Health and Social Behavior* 16: 347–364.

——— (1977), "Long term trends in urban mental health: Old theories and new evidence from the Midtown Manhattan Restudy (Midtown II)," Special Lecture to the American Psychiatric Association, Toronto, Canada, May 2, 1977.

———, Thomas S. Langner, Stanley T. Michael, Price Kirkpatrick, Marvin K. Opler, Thomas A. C. Rennie (1975, 1977), *Mental Health in the Metropolis (Midtown I),* revised and enlarged edition, Leo Srole and Anita K. Fischer (Eds.). New York: New York University Press, 1978.

PART IV

COMMUNITY SERVICES
AND MENTAL HEALTH

MONITORING COMMUNITY MENTAL HEALTH SERVICES: A CASE IN POINT*

August B. Hollingshead, YALE UNIVERSITY

In recent years health and welfare agencies have been faced with increasing demands for their services by the populations of communities. As the cries for help have grown louder and more insistent, funds for the support of agencies and services have tended to lag behind the professed needs of the general public. The gap between demands for service and the funds to pay for them stimulated the project I am going to discuss in this paper.

The site of the research is the community of New Haven, Connecticut. This research grew out of an expressed need by the Community Council of Greater New Haven, Inc., for factual information on the use of health and welfare agencies. In general, the Community Council received from

Research in Community and Mental Health, Vol. 1, pp 337–355.

Copyright © 1979 by JAI Press, Inc.
All rights of reproduction in any form reserved.
ISBN 0-89232-063-X

each of its member agencies only gross information on the services rendered to clients on which to base its decisions regarding the allocation of dollars for services in the different agencies. As a consequence, programs and budgets presented to the Community Council were backed by unequal amounts of factual information and subjective interpretations, often verbalized with feeling by agency representatives.

Briefly, the project had two objectives: (1) the development of an information system to determine who uses social services; and (2) a test of its feasibility in a number of health and welfare agencies. The research was based on the assumption that service transactions in an agency could be recorded as they occurred from hour to hour, day to day, and week to week. The long-range purpose of the research was to provide a factual base for decision-making by the community.

The application of electronic data-processing techniques was essential if we were to record the masses of discrete items that would be generated in the course of answering the deceptively simple question of who does what for whom. The management of this problem was centered on the use of an identity card similar to those so widely used in credit transactions in our society. Machinery was available for making the cards, recording specified items on them, and storing the information on tape. The use of the computer would enable us to analyze the information we would gather in the participating agencies.

An identity card was designed specifically for this project. We called this item the personal service card. Information for the personal service card was elicited from a client by a designated person in each participating agency. The information the project required was written on a single face sheet which was then transmitted to the research office. Completion of the face sheet was the only writing required by the project from the participating agencies. The research office made the personal service card, embossing on it sociobiographical items relevant to a client and the head of the household. It was then mailed to the client by first class mail or handed to him/her personally by a designated worker in the agency in which the client was receiving service.

The personal service card is interchangeable from agency to agency. A letter of instruction was enclosed with each personal service card informing the client that he should present it to the agency in which he was receiving service each time he visited the agency so that the service he received could be recorded. The letter also listed the agencies that were participating in the information system.

Each time a service was rendered by a participating agency, the information embossed on the personal service card plus the date, the agency rendering the service, and the type of service rendered to the client by the agency were imprinted mechanically by the agency on a standard card similar in size to an IBM card. The imprinted form was then sent to the research office, where it was scanned optically and the items were transmitted electronically to an IBM card. The data punched into the IBM card were transferred for storage and statistical analysis by the computer.

Invitations to participate in the project were extended to selected agencies on an individual basis. The executive secretary of the Community Council made the first contact, usually with the executive responsible for the agency operation. Shortly afterwards, we made arrangements for a conference during which the project was explained and an invitation to participate in the information system was extended to the agency. Each executive assured us that the agency would be willing to explore the possibilities of participating in the project. However, this was only the first step. It was followed by a series of negotiations between the staff from the Community Council and the research project and each agency. These negotiations extended from five to nine months. In addition, the Community Council appointed an advisory committee to work with the research staff and agency representatives.

Before we could begin to gather information, we had to have formal clearance from each agency as to its willingness to participate in the project. Several problems came into focus during this phase of the research: The issue of confidentiality was raised by some agencies. Informed consent was another area of concern to a number of people. Was participation in the project to be voluntary on the part of the clients? How were the data from the project to be used? By whom? As each question was raised, we attempted to work out satisfactory answers. A series of meetings was held by the research staff, members of the advisory committee, and concerned citizens. The issues of confidentiality, informed consent, and voluntary participation were resolved by changes in our procedures for processing data and by persuasion. Confidentiality was assured by the decision not to retain any identifying data on individuals in the research office. We recorded data in the central files only by number, geographic area of residence, and the sociobiographical characteristics of an individual and a household.

The question of how the data were to be used and by whom was answered by stating emphatically that only statistical tables would be available to the Community Council, the agencies, and the general public. Since no identifying data as to names and addresses were to be recorded in the central files, only the client and the agency where he was receiving service knew whether he was or was not in the information system. No problems were encountered with this issue after data collection began.

From the beginning we had envisaged participation in the information system as being voluntary on the part of individuals. We believed that each participant should be free to choose whether he would or would not enter the information system only after the nature and purpose of the research were explained to him by a representative of the agency where he sought service. In sum, we believed that informed consent and voluntary participation were linked one to the other. We made these points in our conversations with agencies, board members, and concerned citizens. Good relations among the research staff, the Community Council, the agencies, the clients, and the general public were of prime importance to the successful development of the research plans.

An early procedural step was the necessity for the research staff to develop a thorough understanding of each agency and how it works. We soon learned that we had to adapt our data-gathering techniques to the ongoing administrative activities in each agency. Another important step was the education of the agency's staff about the project. Agency personnel knew that as individuals they were expected to cooperate with the project, but if a staff member refused to participate there were no negative sanctions that would be brought to bear by the research office. The executive of the agency might exert pressure on a noncooperating staff member, but this was a matter for decision within the agency.

Agencies selected for a field trial of the information system were: (1) members of the Community Council, and (2) providers of direct services to their clients. We defined direct services as those activities and/or procedures that are provided an individual for problems within himself or his family. Thirteen agencies were selected for a field test of the planned information system. The thirteen agencies covered the spectrum of personal services provided to clients in the community: Some were public agencies; some were small in size with few clients; some were large. Four were mental health agencies. Briefly, these four agencies were:

First, a child guidance clinic. The child guidance clinic provides diagnostic and treatment services on an outpatient basis for emotionally disturbed children up to 16 years of age and their parents and offers mental health consultation services to schools and other agencies. It is a private voluntary agency supported largely by funds from the Community Council.

Second, the community mental health center. The mental health center is a cooperative venture of the state Department of Mental Health and of the School of Medicine, Yale University. Psychiatric services include inpatient, outpatient, day hospital, and emergency treatment. Psychiatric consultation is available to agencies, schools, and organizations.

Third, a youth center. The youth center is a statewide facility for psychiatric inpatient and day-care treatment for boys and girls between the ages of 6 and 15 referred by a psychiatrist, child guidance clinic, or juvenile court, with the certification of a psychiatrist. Only clients resident in the greater New Haven community were included in our study.

Fourth, an aftercare clinic. The aftercare clinic serves adults only. Outpatient care is available as follow-up for mental patients who have had previous treatment elsewhere. Most of these clients had been hospitalized in the state mental hospital whose catchment area covers the New Haven community.

Three of the four mental health agencies participated in the data-collection phase of the research. We were not able to implement our plans in the mental health center because of a series of administrative and organizational changes in this agency. Therefore, the remainder of this paper will focus on the data we gathered in the child guidance clinic, the youth center, and the aftercare clinic.

Before we collected any data, the decision was made to limit invitations to enter the system to newly admitted clients. When a client was already a patient, to have asked him or a responsible surrogate, i.e., the mother of a child, to enter the system would have added a new dimension to the agency-client relationship. By limiting invitations to enter the system to new clients, the burden of explanation was eased for the agency. We believe this procedure gave rise to a much large percentage of acceptance of the invitation to enter the system than might have otherwise been experienced.

It was essential to the primary purpose of the project to determine whether or not clients would be willing to participate in the information system. We assumed that clients would be willing to participate, if the project were explained to them by personnel in each agency. However, we emphasized to the agency that, if a client declined to participate, this decision would have no effect on the service the agency was administering to him or her. Before any data were collected, we discussed with each agency the importance of the inclusion of all new cases. After the initiation of data collection, we audited the admission slips in each agency on a continuous basis to make sure that each client was given the opportunity to enter the information system. We found that in the three agencies under discussion there was systematic coverage of new cases. Overall, the acceptance rate for each agency was: child guidance clinic, 92 percent; youth center, 90 percent; aftercare clinic, 96 percent.

The question of who does what for whom has three essential referents: *who? whom?* and *what?* We will now turn to the presentation of the data gathered in three mental health agencies on each dimension of this question.

The *who* dimension refers to the child guidance clinic, the youth center, and the aftercare clinic. The *whom* refers to the clients who received services in these agencies. To repeat a point I mentioned earlier, the project was focused on sociobiographical characteristics of clients, not individuals. The sociobiographical items included in our data net were:

sex, race, age, marital status, and addresses of the clients; in addition, we included the number of persons in the household and the following items on the head of the household: sex, race, age, marital status, occupation, and education. Each of these items adds to our information regarding the characteristics of clients enrolled in the different agencies. They also tell us something about the interdependencies between an agency and its clients within the social structure of the community.

Referrals Into the System

Before we turn to our presentation of the data on selected sociobiographical characteristics of the clients in the three agencies, we raise the question of how the clients came to the agency. We answer it by pointing out that the first question we asked the client on the application for a personal service card was who referred him to the agency in which he was seeking help. The answer was recorded by the intake interviewer.

Two basic characteristics that have noticeable effects on the roles individuals play in our society are race and sex. Therefore, the data were processed in relation to these sociobiographical characteristics. The category "black" is composed primarily of Afro-Americans, but it also includes five Puerto Rican males, one Puerto Rican female, and one Oriental female. The various sources of referrals are summarized by race and sex for each agency in Table 1.

The figures in Table 1 reveal that the public schools are the largest single source of referrals in both the child guidance clinic and the youth center. The state mental hospital is the primary source of referrals to the aftercare clinic. The family plays a larger part in referrals to the child guidance clinic than to the youth center or the aftercare clinic. Public agencies of one kind or another, such as welfare or the juvenile court, make more referrals of black clients to the child guidance clinic than to the youth center. It is of interest to note that the public agencies refer proportionately more white males and females to the youth center than to the child guidance clinic. Private physicians, not psychiatrists, refer approximately one out of five patients to the child guidance clinic. Private psychiatrists refer few patients to the child guidance clinic. None was named as the source of referral to the youth center or the aftercare clinic. However, the child study center, which is privately operated by Yale University, is the source of a goodly proportion of referrals to the youth center.

To summarize briefly, our data on referrals indicate that each of the three mental health agencies tends to draw upon different segments of the community's helping agencies for its referrals.

Table 1

Distribution of Clients in Each Mental Health Agency
by Source of Referral, Race, and Sex

A. Child Guidance Clinic

Source of Referral	Race and Sex of Clients in Percent			
	WM*	WF	BM	BF
Public school	35	32	51	47
Private physician	21	22	––	6
Family	14	16	18	21
Public agency	8	9	16	15
Friend/neighbor	6	6	6	2
General hospital/clinic	4	4	6	4
Clergy/private social worker	3	1	1	3
Private family agency	3	4	––	––
Private psychologist	3	2	––	1
Private psychiatrist	2	2	2	––
Mental health center	1	1	––	1
Number of clients	486	432	111	126

B. Youth Center

Source of Referral	Race and Sex of Clients in Percent			
	WM	WF	BM	BF
Public school	36	21	16	23
Public agency	24	29	10	8
Child study center	17	13	21	31
Child guidance clinic	11	8	32	15
Family	6	21	10	15
Private physician	6	8	––	––
Aftercare clinic	––	––	10	8
Number of clients	36	25	19	13

C. Aftercare Clinic

Source of Referral	Race and Sex of Clients in Percent			
	WM	WF	BM	BF
State mental hospital	79	64	100	81
Mental health center	9	10	––	6
Family/self	6	7	––	6

Table 1 (cont.)

Race and Sex of Clients in Percent

	WM	WF	BM	BF
Friend/neighbor	2	10	--	--
General hospital	4	--	--	6
Private family agency	--	4	--	--
Child guidance clinic	--	2	--	--
Private physician	--	3	--	--
Number of clients	47	60	8	16

* WM (White Male)   WF (White Female)   BM (Black Male)   BF (Black Female)

Age

Along with race and sex, age is also an important sociobiographical factor. It is of particular interest here because each agency is age oriented. The expressed purpose of the child guidance clinic and the youth center is to serve emotionally disturbed children and the parents or parental surrogates of these children. The aftercare clinic is concerned primarily with service to adults who have been released from the state mental hospital. Examination of the data in Table 2 shows that clients in the child guidance clinic cluster into two age groups: children and adults. Since this agency defines both a troubled child and his parents as clients, no distinction is made between "patient" and "parent." Both presumably receive suitable treatment for the problem that brought them to the clinic. The same observation is appropriate to the youth center. Moreover, there are more adults being serviced than children. This is particularly noticeable among white and black females in the child guidance clinic and the youth center. The clients in the aftercare clinic are predominantly adults; more are female than male among both the whites and blacks.

Class Position

The class structure of American communities has been of prime interest to me for many years. Therefore, we were concerned with locating the client's position in the class structure of the community. Class position is measured by the use of Hollingshead's *Two Factor Index of Social Position*.[1] This index utilizes occupation and education of the head of the household to estimate an individual's position in the class structure. Each factor—occupation and education—is scaled on a 7-point scale and given a factor weight. The weighted scores are grouped and summarized as class position. The highest class in the social structure is denoted as class

Table 2

Age Distribution of Clients by Agency, Race, and Sex

A. Child Guidance Clinic

Age of Clients	Race and Sex of Clients in Percent			
	WM	WF	BM	BF
5 – 9	16	7	16	4
10 – 15	33	17	49	22
30 – 44	36	65	15	56
45+	15	19	20	18
Number of clients	486	432	111	126

B. Youth Center

Age of Clients	Race and Sex of Clients in Percent			
	WM	WF	BM	BF
5 – 9	8	––	11	––
10 – 19	43	17	52	7
30 – 44	26	54	16	79
45+	23	29	21	14
Number of clients	36	24	19	14

C. Aftercare Clinic

Age of Clients	Race and Sex of Clients in Percent			
	WM	WF	BM	BF
20 – 24	11	7	––	13
25 – 44	62	45	50	75
45+	28	48	50	12
Number of clients	47	60	8	16

I and the lowest as class V. It was estimated that the general population of the community was stratified as follows: class I, 3 percent; class II, 9 percent; class III, 20 percent; class IV, 50 percent; and class V, 18 percent.[2]

The class position of the clients in the three agencies under discussion is shown in Table 3. In the child guidance clinic there are proportionately more whites from the three higher classes than blacks. The blacks are

Table 3

Social Class Distribution of Clients by Agency, Race, and Sex

A. Child Guidance Clinic

Social Class of Clients	Race and Sex of Clients in Percent			
	WM	WF	BM	BF
I – II	10	11	4	2
III	18	16	5	9
IV	46	49	30	32
V	26	25	61	56
Number of clients	486	432	111	126

B. Youth Center

Social Class of Clients	Race and Sex of Clients in Percent			
	WM	WF	BM	BF
I – II	14	17	––	––
III	6	2	5	3
IV	33	17	37	26
V	47	63	58	71
Number of clients	36	24	19	14

C. Aftercare Clinic

Social Class of Clients	Race and Sex of Clients in Percent			
	WM	WF	BM	BF
I – II	––	2	––	––
III	9	7	––	6
IV	36	35	25	19
V	55	57	75	75
Number of clients	47	60	8	16

heavily concentrated in class V. However, there are proportionately more clients from class V than there are class V persons in the social structure of the community.

The clients enrolled in the youth center come primarily from the two lowest classes, with the largest proportion coming from class V. There are relatively few clients from class III, whereas classes I and II are overrepresented by whites. No higher-class blacks are enrolled in the youth center.

The aftercare clinic cares primarily for low-class persons. Higher-class whites and blacks are conspicuous by their absence. In sum, the clients of each agency come mostly from the two lowest classes in the community's social structure.

Residence

We were interested in determining which areas of the community contributed clients to the several agencies. For present purposes, residential

Table 4

Distribution of Clients by Area of Residence, Agency, Race, and Sex

A. Child Guidance Clinic

Area of Residence	Race and Sex of Client in Percent			
	WM	WF	BM	BF
C.A.P.	22	23	87	86
Other, New Haven	13	16	6	10
Suburbs	65	61	7	5
Number of clients	486	432	111	126

B. Youth Center

Area of Residence	Race and Sex of Client in Percent			
	WM	WF	BM	BF
C.A.P.	17	17	74	69
Other, New Haven	3	12	––	––
Suburbs	81	71	––	––
Number of clients	36	24	19	14

C. Aftercare Clinic

Area of Residence	Race and Sex of Client in Percent			
	WM	WF	BM	BF
C.A.P.	34	35	88	100
Other, New Haven	11	18	12	––
Suburbs	54	47	––	––
Number of clients	47	60	8	16

areas are summarized into three categories: (1) Community Action Plan areas; (2) other areas in the city of New Haven; and (3) the suburban towns. The C.A.P. areas are "slums," "gray areas," or areas in the process of decay in the city of New Haven. They are the target of urban renewal. The other areas of the city are all essentially "good" or "better" neighborhoods. The suburban towns range from "good" to "exclusive" neighborhoods. Blacks and Puerto Ricans are concentrated in the C.A.P. areas, but there are some blacks and Puerto Ricans in other areas of the city and the suburban towns.

The clients enrolled in the three mental health agencies were differentially distributed in the three residential categories. White clients in the child guidance clinic come predominantly from the suburban towns. The black clients, by way of contrast, reside primarily in the C.A.P. areas of New Haven. The same generalization is applicable to the clients of the youth center, but a higher proportion of the blacks come from the suburban towns. The same pattern holds for the clients in the aftercare clinic: The largest percentage of whites live in the suburban towns, but about a third dwell in the C.A.P. areas of the city of New Haven. The blacks in the aftercare clinic are most heavily concentrated in the C.A.P. areas; no blacks treated in the aftercare clinic live in the suburban towns.

Delivery of Services

In the preceding sections we have focused on the *who* (the agencies) and the *whom* (the clients) of who does what for whom. We now turn to the third part of our basic question, the *what* (the record of services rendered to clients). Here we put it all together. To repeat a point I made earlier, clients were willing to enter the information system when the intake person at the agency explained its purpose. Some nine out of ten clients furnished the items essential for the personal service card. If the client carries the personal service card when he visits the agency and presents it to the staff person and if the staff person places the card in the recorder and records the type of service rendered to the client on each visit, then we can answer the three-part question of who does what for whom. This is a simple procedure, but it assumes the cooperation of the patient and the agency and a knowledge of what was done for the patient on a particular visit by the person responsible for imprinting the record card.

Information on the delivery of services to clients varied among the three agencies. The aftercare clinic provided the research office with data on the services administered to 89 percent of the clients to whom we issued a personal service card. The child guidance clinic recorded the delivery of services to only 71 percent of the clients for whom the re-

Table 5

Number of Contracts During Which Services Were
Rendered, Race, and Sex of Client

A. Child Guidance Clinic

Type of Service	Race and Sex of Client in Percent			
	WM	WF	BM	BF
Individual psychotherapy	92	92	98	96
Family therapy	6	5	1	3
Group psychotherapy	2	3	1	1
Number of visits	959	1,003	145	155

B. Youth Center

Type of Service	Race and Sex of Client in Percent			
	WM	WF	BM	BF
Individual day treatment	43	34	45	70
Individual home interview	35	30	48	12
Individual aftercare	9	8	1	3
Family day treatment	8	18	2	12
Family home interview	3	5	1	2
Visit to family	2	3	2	1
Individual diagnostic	1	3	1	1
Number of visits	1,102	441	651	489

C. Aftercare Clinic

Type of Service	Race and Sex of Client in Percent			
	WM	WF	BM	BF
Individual intake	42	14	75	27
Individual, acute therapy	33	29	——	41
Individual disability	18	47	——	22
Group, acute therapy	13	9	12	10
Medication	4	1	13	——
Number of visits	55	335	8	41

search office issued personal service cards. The record of the youth center was better than the other two, with 99 percent of the clients to whom personal service cards were issued having services recorded. The recorded services rendered to clients by each agency are summarized in Table 5.

The child guidance clinic's services are categorized primarily as individual psychotherapy. Group psychotherapy and family therapy are given to only a small proportion of the clients.

The youth center describes the services it provides its clients in different terms. Some four-fifths of its activities are listed as either individual interviews in the home or individual day treatment in the center. A smaller percentage is focused on the day treatment of family members who come to the center. Visits to the family by the staff of the center are only a small proportion of its services. Individual aftercare is also limited in volume.

The aftercare clinic presents a third pattern of activities. Individual intake interviews and acute therapy to formerly hospitalized clients encompass the largest part of its services. It is interesting to note that 47 percent of the visits of white females were concerned with efforts to establish disability. It is presumed this is for purposes of gaining some kind of official support from a third party—social security, the state, or insurance company. Black females are also well represented in the group who are seeking to establish some kind of disability status. Only a small proportion of the clients are reported to have received medication.

We shall now examine *the amount* of services recorded for those clients whose cases were opened and closed during the two years we were collecting data in each agency. However, we hasten to point out that the aftercare clinic did not close cases; its director stated that their clients drifted back sooner or later and to close a case only added to the clinic's work load. The child guidance center closed 703 cases and the youth center closed fifty-eight. The number of services recorded for clients in these agencies by race and sex is presented in Table 6.

The figures in Table 6 reveal that approximately 90 percent of the clients cared for by the child guidance clinic are seen fewer than five times. What is of particular interest is that two of the four services recorded for the individuals involved opening and closing the case. This leaves only two visits in which the client was seen for therapy. The question I raise here is this: How effective are one or two periods of psychotherapy? The answer lies with professional personnel who work in this area, but the number of visits recorded indicates to me that the clinic's activities are broader than they are deep.

Clients in the youth center have a much higher percentage of services

Table 6

Number of Services Recorded for Clients from Opening to
Closing a Case by Agency, Race, and Sex of Client

A. Child Guidance Clinic

Number of Services Recorded	Race and Sex of Client in Percent			
	WM	WF	BM	BF
2 – 4	90	87	93	97
5 – 9	6	7	6	3
10 – 14	1	3	––	––
15 – 19	2	2	––	––
20+	1	2	2	––
Number of clients	309	267	63	64

B. Youth Center

Number of Services Recorded	Race and Sex of Client in Percent			
	WM	WF	BM	BF
2 – 4	43	57	20	––
5 – 9	10	14	40	100
10 – 14	19	7	––	––
15 – 19	14	7	––	––
20+	14	14	40	––
Number of clients	30	19	5	4

C. Aftercare Clinic*

* The aftercare clinic did not close the cases of its clients.

recorded beyond four visits than those in the child guidance clinic. Some
57 percent of the white males, 43 percent of the white females, 80 percent
of the black males, and all the black females had more than four visits
recorded for them. However, the number of black males is only five and
the number of black females is only four.

Referrals on Closing a Case

We now turn again to the idea we discussed in relation to Table 1,
namely, referrals. In our earlier discussion we were concerned with referrals into the system. Here we confine our remarks to referrals from one

Table 7

Agencies to Which Clients Were Referred by the
Child Guidance Clinic at Closing of Case, by
Race and Sex of Client

Agency Referred to	Race and Sex of Client in Percent			
	WM	WF	BM	BF
No referral	67	67	77	77
Public school	5	3	3	5
Public agency	19	20	15	12
Private psychiatrist	4	6	2	—
General hospital	4	3	—	—
Mental health center	1	1	3	6
Number of clients	309	267	63	64

agency to another when a case is closed. Before we began to gather data
from the agencies participating in the feasibility study, we compiled a list
of possible sources of referral into agencies when cases were opened and
referrals out of agencies when cases were closed. We were able to delineate 255 agencies which might be a source of help to an individual or
family. These agencies were coded numerically so that we could record
how a client reached an agency as well as what agency, if any, a client was
referred to for further help when his case was closed.

I have pointed out that the aftercare clinic did not close cases. Although
the youth center closed fifty-eight cases, it made no referrals. The child
guidance clinic made referrals. However, some two out of three cases of
white clients in the child guidance clinic were closed without a referral.
The proportion of no referrals was well beyond three out of four blacks.
When there was a referral, reference was made, in large part, to schools
or nonhealth agencies of one kind or another, such as City Welfare. We
believe it is of interest to note that proportionately more closed cases
were referred to private psychiatrists than were referred to the child guidance clinic by private psychiatrists when the cases were opened.

Summary and Conclusions

In this paper I have focused attention upon two principal themes: the
larger research project and some findings relative to three mental health
agencies. To recapitulate, the project grew out of the expressed need by
the Community Council for factual information upon which it could base

decisions for the allocation of dollars to health and welfare agencies. The Community Council was interested also in gathering empirical data on the use of agencies by the population of the community for planning purposes. To meet these needs an information system was designed to answer the question of who does what for whom. This system was built around the use of automatic data-processing procedures. The designed system's feasibility was field tested in twelve agencies. Three of these were mental health agencies: a child guidance clinic, a youth center, and an adult aftercare clinic.

Selected empirical findings for each of these agencies were presented. We found that some 93 percent of the newly admitted clients were willing to participate in the information system. Sociobiographically, the clients were divided into two racial groups—whites and blacks. Whites predominate in the population of the community and as clients in the three agencies. Their age distribution in each clinic is controlled by the clinic's intake policy. Both children and adults are enrolled for care by the child guidance clinic and the youth center. The aftercare clinic limits intake to adults. Clients reach these clinics from diverse sources: The public schools are the major source of referrals to the child guidance clinic and to the youth center, while the state mental hospital for the area is the primary source of referrals to the aftercare clinic. White clients in the child guidance clinic reside for the most part in the suburban towns. This is also the principal residential pattern for clients enrolled by the youth center. The clients in the aftercare clinic, both white and black, are concentrated in the slum and gray areas of the city of New Haven.

There is an unequal distribution of clients in the class structure. Speaking broadly, the clients, whether white or black, are identified disproportionately with the lowest class. The strongest relationship between class position and being a client in a mental health agency is found among blacks.

The services the agencies recorded are highly correlated with the agency's own definition of what it does for its clients. The child guidance clinic specializes in individual psychotherapy; the youth center in personal conferences with the young person and a parent or parents; the aftercare clinic focuses its attention, in large part, on intake interviews and brief therapy for acute episodes of emotional disturbance.

The intensity of services rendered, or more appropriately, the lack of it, is revealed in the cases that were followed from intake to formal closing. In the vast majority of cases serviced by the child guidance clinic, the clients had only four entries in their records, and two of them involved opening and closing the case. The youth center recorded more services rendered to clients whose cases were closed than did the child guidance clinic, but the general pattern was traced by relatively few services having been delivered. Although the aftercare clinic did not close cases, the number of services rendered to clients was very limited; the mean number of visits was three for both whites and blacks.

Strong commitment from the administration and governing boards of agencies is vital or an information system will become snarled at the staff level. Interpersonal relations between the executive of an agency and the governing board of the agency are influential in the determination of how smoothly an agency functions. Likewise the interpersonal relations that prevail between an agency executive and the staff may determine the margin of success or failure of a program. Schisms between factions in an agency lead to stalemate. A stable organization within an agency is essential to success. In the three mental health agencies where the information system was tested, there was a strong executive who remained in charge throughout the test period. The community mental health center was a relatively new agency with a large staff—psychiatric nurses, clinical psychologists, and psychiatrists. When the project was being planned, there was a change in directors. The original director made the commitment to participate in the information system. The second director was a stranger to the community. Differences between the psychiatric nurses, clinical psychologists, and psychiatrists gave rise to meetings and petitions protesting participation in the proposed program. After several months of negotiation between project personnel and agency personnel, the decision was reached to drop the community mental health center from the trial run of the information system.

Although this project was initiated by the Community Council, we were not able to go beyond the trial phase of the program. During the planning phase of the project, conflict developed between the Community Council and the seven neighborhood organizations in New Haven City. In the ensuing struggle for control over the allocation of funds to the older agencies and the newer neighborhood organizations, the Community Council was dissolved. The Executive Secretary of the Community Council resigned; the executive secretary of the United Fund was forced to resign. A new organization—the United Way—was created. During the turmoil the decision was reached to drop the information system. As a consequence, we do not know who does what for whom in the various agencies extant in the community. The project has demonstrated that it is feasible to install an information system in mental health agencies that is acceptable to the vast majority of clients if the agency is committed to the program, but such a system is unlikely to survive in a context of inter or intra-agency conflict.

FOOTNOTES

*This research was supported by Grant #MH-10576, National Institute of Mental Health, Applied Research Grants Program.

1. Hollingshead, A. B. (1957), *Two Factor Index of Social Position,* New Haven, privately printed (mimeograph), pp. 1–11.

2. ———, and F. C. Redlich (1958), *Social Class and Mental Illness,* pp. 198–199, 387–397. New York: Wiley.

FAMILY SYMPTOM TOLERANCE AND REHOSPITALIZATION EXPERIENCES OF PSYCHIATRIC PATIENTS*

James R. Greenley, UNIVERSITY OF

WISCONSIN – MADISON

Attempts to locate factors related to the rehospitalization of psychiatric patients are increasingly important as the deinstitutionalization of psychiatric care becomes more widespread and community treatment programs are initiated. Yet the search for an adequate understanding of rehospitalization still continues. In a recent review of relevant studies, Rosenblatt and Mayer (1974) conclude that the only consistent predictor of rehospitalization is the number of previous psychiatric hospitalizations.

For most factors found related to rehospitalization in any study, there are other studies finding these same factors unrelated to rehospitalization. Measurement and research design differences may lead studies to varied conclusions. To some extent divergence among studies may be due to

Research in Community and Mental Health, Vol. 1, pp 357–386.
Copyright © 1979 by JAI Press, Inc.
All rights of reproduction in any form reserved.
ISBN 0-89232-063-X

research differences in the types of patients, the types of psychiatric problems, the types of treatment facilities, and the nature of the families or communities patients are discharged to. The diversity of this research and the complexity of the rehospitalization process itself have led to few consistent findings. However, a number of studies involving families of rehospitalized patients do come to a similar conclusion, i.e., psychiatric symptoms are the major cause of rehospitalization. Freeman and Simmons (1963:205–206) conclude from their follow-up study of functional psychotics that both relatives' retrospective reports and hospital records indicate symptomatic behavior to be the cause of rehospitalization. Angrist et al. (1968), Davis et al. (1974), Dinitz et al. (1961), and Myers and Bean (1968:90) come to similar conclusions from cross-sectional or retrospective data. Prospective studies reported by Freeman and Simmons (1963), Ellsworth et al. (1968), Michaux et al. (1969:138–140), and Myers and Bean (1968) all indicate that family assessments of their ex-patient's symptomatic behaviors are positively related to subsequent rehospitalization. The conclusion often drawn from these studies may be paraphrased as follows: *Rehospitalization occurs when the ex-patient exhibits sufficient symptomatic behaviors that the family can no longer tolerate the ex-patient.* This finding is sometimes reported as if obvious and a not very interesting confirmation of the "medical model": Patients are hospitalized when they become symptomatic, released when their condition is cured or controlled, and rehospitalized when the symptoms reappear. The implication is that rehospitalization is due to the disease process (cf. Freeman and Simmons, 1963:206).

Professional evaluations of these disease processes, however, have not been consistently good predictors of rehospitalization (Rosenblatt and Mayer, 1974; Ellsworth et al., 1968). Diagnoses, professionally assessed level of psychiatric impairment, and type of treatment are often not found related to rehospitalization rates (Stein et al., 1975; Bogdanow, 1976). If psychopathology alone is the key factor in rehospitalization, then experts in assessing this psychopathology, e.g., psychiatrists and psychologists, might be thought to be better at predicting rehospitalization than are inexperienced family members of patients reporting on symptoms. Yet this is not the case.

One explanation for these seemingly incongruous findings is that families are in a better position than professionals generally are to assess their patient's psychopathology in the community. Family members see the patients in relevant home and community settings rather than in the hospital or clinic. Family members are also in close contact with ex-patients over longer periods of time and thus have more accurate information on which to base their judgements (Ellsworth et al., 1968).

Another possible explanation is revealed upon closer inspection of the common conclusion from these family studies, namely that rehospitalization occurs when symptoms are exhibited that the family cannot tolerate. The focus has generally been on the importance of symptoms to the neglect of the latter phrase, "that the family cannot tolerate." Family tolerance for symptomatic behavior may be the key to understanding rehospitalization.

Family Tolerance

Tolerance implies the sufferance of conduct with which one is not in accord. A tolerant family is forbearing or able to put up with a situation. Freeman and Simmons (1963:6) defined tolerance in their study of released psychiatric inpatients as *"the continued acceptance of the former patient by his family members, even when he fails to perform in instrumental roles."*

Freeman and Simmons (1963) suggested that differential family tolerance of patient role performance might explain rehospitalization. They argued that patients who did not adequately perform in instrumental social roles would be rehospitalized by families who expected them to perform these social roles and that patients whose families had lower initial expectations concerning role performance would be able to remain longer in the community in the absence of adequate role performance. The basic assumption was that rehospitalization would occur because families who were intolerant of deviance would sanction their inadequately performing ex-patient by rehospitalizing him. Freeman and Simmons (1963:133) found, contrary to their initial theory, that neither familial expectations nor inadequate role performance were substantially related to rehospitalization. The family performance tolerance hypothesis was not supported (see also Angrist et al., 1968:89).

This paper presents a revised family tolerance hypothesis based on a different conceptualization of the role of tolerance in rehospitalization. As one psychiatrist put it, the key to understanding why patients are rehospitalized lies not in patient behavior but in the amount of their own anxiety the family can tolerate. It is assumed here that some families more than others need to feel in control and cannot live with uncertainty and unpredictability (cf. Freeman and Simmons, 1963:199). They are afraid of being out of control of the patient or situation and cannot or will not tolerate the associated anxiety. Their anxiety is dealt with through rehospitalization of their ex-patient.

In this conceptualization of the role of family tolerance in rehospitalization, the patient's behavior may or may not play a role. Symptomatic behavior might be rather marked and the family might not feel out of control and anxious. Symptomatic behavior might be rather minimal and the family might experience considerable fear and anxiety. Families may even feel as much or more anxious when they simply expect the patient to behave symptomatically as when the behavior occurs. Family interaction patterns, family structure and sociodemographic characteristics, and personalities of family members may conceivably contribute to these fears and anxieties as much or more than the patient's behavior. Because often bizarre and unpredictable psychiatric symptoms are probably more likely than instrumental role behaviors to leave a family feeling out of control and anxious, it is suggested that family tolerance of symptomatic behavior, not family tolerance of role performance, is the key factor in psychiatric rehospitalization. It is hypothesized that the less tolerance families have for symptomatic behavior, the more likely they will be to rehospitalize their ex-patient. Families are hypothesized to vary on the extent to which they fear symptomatic behavior and feel that they are able to cope with it. When ex-patients exhibit or are expected to exhibit symptomatic behavior, families with more fear of these symptoms and families more afraid they will not be able to cope with these symptoms, i.e., families with less tolerance of symptomatic behavior, will more readily rehospitalize their ex-patient.

If differential levels of family tolerance of their patient's symptomatic behaviors are significant factors in rehospitalization, then for any given level of psychopathological behavior, families who are more fearful of or less confident of their ability to cope with this behavior should move to rehospitalize their ex-patient sooner. This paper represents data relevant to this hypothesis.

Rehospitalization Experiences

Studies of rehospitalization typically contrast patients who remain in the community for a given period, such as one year, with those rehospitalized in that period. While such studies tend to polarize the groups into "successes" and "failures," the successes are simply those who stay in the community longer than the failures. With a follow-up period of one year, a patient may stay in the community eleven months and be a failure and his "successful" counterpart may have been rehospitalized after thirteen months. Thus, these studies are crudely measuring and studying time until rehospitalization. Understanding time until rehospitalization is important because community tenure of ex-patients reflects on the quality and efficacy of inpatient care, and may provide clues to how treatment, discharge decisions, or community placement may be best managed.

An implicit assumption often made in these studies of who is rehospitalized earlier is that patients rehospitalized early are likely to be patients rehospitalized often, i.e., "revolving door" patients. While patients never rehospitalized will by definition never become part of an early readmitted patient cohort, patients readmitted soon after release do not necessarily have to be those readmitted several times subsequently. A patient may be rehospitalized once shortly after release and not be rehospitalized again. In this study, no assumption will be made that those rehospitalized earlier are representative of multiple readmission patients. Rather, those patients experiencing multiple rehospitalizations will be studied as a special group, for they certainly present a unique and disproportionately heavy burden on the mental health delivery system.

This study will therefore examine the family symptom tolerance hypothesis with reference to (1) early rehospitalization and (2) multiple rehospitalizations. If early rehospitalization is a good indicator of a potential revolving door patient career, then similar findings should appear with respect to both these dependent variables.

METHOD

Longitudinal data were gathered on patients admitted to a large New England state mental hospital in 1969. During this hospitalization each patient was interviewed twice, his psychiatrist was interviewed twice, his "closest relative" was interviewed, and the hospitalization records were examined. These data were all gathered during approximately the first three weeks of the patient's hospitalization. About four years after the patient's release, a follow-up interview was obtained from the patient's "closest relative," as defined by the patient. This longitudinal design allows the use of prospective data gathered during the patient's 1969 hospitalization to predict his rehospitalization experiences.

The study patients were a subset of 125 consecutive admissions to a large New England state mental hospital from May to September, 1969. These admissions, selected for a study of length of hospitalization (Greenley, 1972), were all 21 to 65 years old and not primarily suffering from drug addiction, alcoholism, or senility.

A full set of interview and record data was sought on only those eighty-one patients who remained in the hospital for twenty-one days, a limitation dictated by the design of the earlier study. Of these eighty-one, seventy agreed to participate in the study, and of these seventy, fifty-eight both had an identifiable relative in the area and gave permission for this family member to be contacted for an interview. From this target population of fifty-eight family members, fifty-three, or 91 percent, were interviewed.

An average of three years and seven months after a patient's discharge, follow-up interviews were sought for the fifty-three originally interviewed family members. Among these cases twelve patients had died or moved beyond the New England or New York metropolitan area and follow-up information on these cases was not sought. For the remaining forty-one cases, five family members (12 percent) refused a follow-up interview, five family members could not be located or identified, or the patient was living in isolation (12 percent), and 31 family members (76 percent) were reinterviewed.

Examination of the data shows no significant differences between the thirty-one completed follow-up cases and the twenty-two cases not reinterviewed on a wide variety of sociodemographic attitudinal, or expectation variables. Only two significant differences were found. Significantly more nonrespondent cases (95 percent) than respondent cases (32 percent) had been previously psychiatrically hospitalized four or more times. Also significantly fewer nonrespondent patients (19 percent) than respondent patients (69 percent) expressed a wish to stay in the hospital longer when initially interviewed in 1969.

The patients in the respondent sample are 61 percent female, 29 percent Black, and 32 percent presently married. Most were working or lower class (Classes IV and V according to the Hollingshead Two-factor Index). Two-thirds of these patients were diagnosed as functional psychotics, almost all schizophrenic. Prior to their 1969 hospitalization, only seven had never had a psychiatric hospitalization, five had been psychiatrically hospitalized once, and five had five or more mental hospitalizations. Of those previously psychiatrically hospitalized, the average time since they last left the hospital was eleven months.

Rehospitalization Measures

Two measures of rehospitalization experiences are reported here: (1) time until rehospitalization and (2) number of rehospitalizations during the follow-up period. Responses by the patient's "closest relative" in the follow-up interviews were the data from which the time until the rehospitalization variable was constructed. Time until rehospitalization was defined as the number of days from the release from the original 1969 hospitalization until the next subsequent psychiatric rehospitalization. Release was defined as having left the hospital to live outside it, regardless of the patient's formal status, e.g., conditional or unconditional release. No patient was rehospitalized in less than two weeks. The large variance in this variable, due to 39 percent of the sample being rehospitalized in the first year and 39 percent never having been rehospitalized, suggests that even misreporting of readmission data by as much as several months would not seriously affect our conclusions. Patients never rehospitalized were given a score reflecting the length of time from their release until the follow-up interview.

This variable focuses on the length of time a patient remains out of the hospital following release and is thus conceptually similar to common rehospitalization measures which dichotomize patients into those rehospitalized and not rehospitalized in a given period, such as six months or one year. This measure is more sensitive to differences among patients, because, unlike some studies which dichotomize, it does not necessitate treating similarly patients rehospitalized, for example, after two weeks and after eleven months or after one and one-half years or never.

The second hospitalization variable is the number of psychiatric hospitalizations the patient's family member reported the patient to have had during the follow-up period. For all analyses, the number of reported rehospitalizations was adjusted by dividing it by the number of months at risk, i.e., the number of months the patient was living in the community. This adjustment was desirable to avoid patients being given artifically low number-of-rehospitalizations scores because they had been hospitalized for long periods during the follow-up interval. While the variable used here is therefore the average number of rehospitalizations per month the patient spent in the community, it will be referred to simply as the number of rehospitalizations.

Family members may have less difficulty recalling the number of their patient's readmissions than many other factors, although remembering the exact number may have been difficult if more than several had occurred. The large variation in this variable makes it less probable that faulty family recall or reporting of rehospitalizations substantially distorts the data. About one-third of the sample were never rehospitalized and about one-third were rehospitalized an average of over five times each.

Family Tolerance

As conceptualized here, family intolerance is closely related to family anxieties and feelings of being in control. Family intolerance is not seen as a rehospitalization response triggered at a given level of patient symptomatic behavior.[1] Therefore indicators of family tolerance used in this study do not ask about specific behaviors but rather about family fears and feelings of being out of control. Family tolerance was measured in the interview with families prior to the patient's release from the 1969 study hospitalization. Two indicators of family tolerance are used; the exact wording of each item is listed below with an indication of the response categories provided.

"Do you ever fear what [the patient] might do to himself (herself) or to others when he (she) comes home?" Six response categories from very frequently to never.

"Are you afraid that you will not be able to control his (her) behavior when he (she) is at home?" Six response categories from very frequently to never.

Family member responses to those questions varied substantially. In response to the question concerning fears of what the patient might do to himself or others, 26 percent responded "very frequently," 42 percent responded "never," and the remainder gave an intermediate response. When asked whether they are ever afraid they would not be able to control the patient, 26 percent of family respondents said "very frequently," 42 percent answered "never," and the rest gave an intermediate response. These two items were correlated with $r = .85$ but were not combined because they refer to different family fears.

Family members' responses to these questions might reasonably be thought to reflect the patient's past behavior, treatment history, and expected future behaviors. A wide range of other measures in these areas were obtained through hospital records and the interviews with patients, their psychiatrists, and their family members. These measures will be described as findings relating to them are presented.

Analysis

Pearsonian correlations and partial correlations are presented in this paper. Findings are considered substantively meaningful if they are unlikely to have occurred by chance more than five percent of the time ($p < .05$). This standard may cause us to ignore potentially consequential findings due to the small number of cases in this study. However, this is preferable to reporting as meaningful relationships often likely to occur by chance.

Due to the small sample size and deviations from normal distributions which may occur in it, we were aware of the possibility that certain correlations may have been relatively high due to only a few extreme outlying cases. In such cases, levels of significance could be improperly inferred, because they are calculated making the rigorous assumptions of these parametric methods. Therefore, the entire analysis was replicated with two nonparametric measures of association, Gamma and Kendall's Tau. The parametric and nonparametric analyses, including significance tests on Kendall's S, fully support the parametric analysis. Minor differences which did appear are reported in the tables.

FINDINGS

Time Until Rehospitalization

Following discharge from the hospital, 39 percent of the follow-up sample were psychiatrically rehospitalized within one year, with almost all of these rehospitalizations occurring within the first six months. Another 22 percent were rehospitalized more than one year from discharge but before the follow-up, and 39 percent were never psychiatrically rehospitalized during the approximately four year follow-up period.

Families who had fears concerning what the patient would do to himself or others after coming home and families who were afraid they could not

Table 1

Rehospitalization Experiences Related to Family
Attitudes and Expectations[a]

Family Tolerance, Expectations and Attitudes	Rehospitalization Experiences	
	Days until rehos-pitalization	Number of admissions
Family Tolerance		
Family fears patient	-.42*	.31[c]
Family afraid they will not be able to control patient	-.51*	.28[c]
Expected Problems for the Family[d]		
"It will be like having a ten-year-old child around."	-.46*	.39*
Financial burden will be high	-.25	.37*[b]
Expected Ex-Patient Role Performance[d]		
Employment-household role performance good	.20	-.34
Instrumental task performance good	.07	-.33
Social role performance high	.18	-.24
Expected Symptoms[d]		
Symptoms high	-.35*	.35*
Family Attitudes[d]		
Family members do not like the patient	-.39*	.45*
Family members do not want the patient to return home	-.41*	.31[c]

[a] Coefficents are zero-order Pearsonian correlation coefficients; *p < .05; N = 31
[b] Relationship not significant when examined with nonparametric statistics.
[c] Relationship is statistically significant when examined with nonparametric statistics.
[d] These variables are described in footnote 3.

control the ex-patient's behavior in the home were both significantly more likely to have patients who were hospitalized earlier (see Table 1). A cross-tabulation of time until rehospitalization and family fears of being able to control their patient is presented in Table 2. Both correlations and cross-tabulations show that families who fear what their patient will do and are afraid they will not be able to control his behavior have patients who are rehospitalized substantially sooner.

A variety of sociodemographic and psychiatric factors were examined to see if they might be causing time until rehospitalization and these family tolerance measures to be spuriously associated. Rehospitalization is not significantly related to any sociodemographic variable examined in this study, including sex, age, race, religion, marital status, education, and occupation. Several indicators of psychiatric impairment were examined and none were significantly related to rehospitalization.[2] No particular diagnostic group, including whether the patient was diagnosed as psychotic or not (see Table 3), was significantly different in terms of rehospitalization. There is a strong tendency, consistent with other studies, for rehospitalization to occur sooner for those individuals having had more prior psychiatric hospitalizations (cf. Rosenblatt and Mayer, 1974). No other "impairment" rating, whether made by the patient's psychiatrist or a family member (including the prehospitalization psychiatric symptom measure), was significantly related to rehospitaliza-

Table 2

Family Expectations of Being Unable to Control
Their Patient's Behavior and Time Until Rehospitalization

Patient Rehospitalized In:	Family Fears of Being Unable to Control Patient[a]					
	Most afraid		Intermediately afraid		Least afraid	
	%	N	%	N	%	N
Under 1 year	50	(4)	62	(5)	15	(2)
1 to 3 years	37	(3)	25	(2)	8	(1)
Over 3 years or never	13	(1)	13	(1)	77	(10)
	100%(8)		100%(8)		100%(13)	

[a] Family expectations of being unable to control their patient's behavior were measured on an ordered six-point scale from 1 (most afraid) to 6 (least afraid). The intermediately afraid category includes all families scoring 2 through 5 on this scale. N = 29. Insufficient data existed for two cases.

tion. This includes variables concerned with prognosis and chronicity (see Table 3). In addition, a twenty-one-item symptom scale completed by family members concerning the patient's symptoms prior to the 1969 study hospitalization was constructed. This index of psychiatric symptoms was also not significantly related to time until rehospitalization. Finally, time until rehospitalization was not found related to family member reports that prior to the 1969 hospitalization the patient damaged

Table 3

Rehospitalization Experiences and
Psychiatric Factors[a]

	Rehospitalization Experiences	
	Time until rehospitalization	Number of readmissions
Psychiatric Factors		
Diagnosis (psychotic)	.07	.04
Number of prior hospitalizations	-.33	.27
Poor prognosis (psychiatrist's rating)	-.10	-.02
High impairment during hospitalization (psychiatrist's rating)	-.24	.31
Chronically ill (psychiatrist's rating)	-.26	.21
Harmful if released (psychiatrist's rating)	-.14	.02
High impairment during hospitalization (family member rating)	-.21	.27
High impairment before hospitalization (family member rating)	.02	.04
Psychiatric symptoms high before hospitalization (family member rating)	-.26	.24
Damaged or wrecked things before (family member report)[b]	.00	.01
Hit or hurt others before (family member report)[b]	-.06	.11
Attempted suicide before (family member report)[b]	-.05	-.08

[a] Coefficients are zero-order Pearsonian correlation coefficients; N = 31; no coefficients are statistically significant with $p < .05$.

[b] This item is included in the summary symptom index.

or wrecked things, hit or hurt others, or attempted suicide (see Table 3). Thus, no sociodemographic factor or measure of psychiatric impairment at or before the 1969 study hospitalization is a significant predictor of time until rehospitalization.

Several other family expectations and attitudes assessed at the initial interview were significantly related to time until rehospitalization.[3] When families expected that having the patient home would be "like having a 10-year-old child around," patients were significantly more likely to be rehospitalized earlier (see Table 1). Significantly earlier rehospitalization occurred for patients whose families expected more symptoms. Also families whose members did not like the patient and families whose members did not want the patient home were significantly more likely to have patients who were rehospitalized earlier (see Table 1). The following family expectations concerning what life would be like with the patient home were not found significantly related to time until rehospitalization: (1) there would be problems socializing with friends of family members, (2) there would be problems of family members participating in organizational activities, (3) there would be more family friction (fights, quarrels, nagging, etc.), (4) and there would be more work to do around the house. A measure of family stigma due to having a member in a mental hospital was also not related to time until rehospitalization.

Because of the interest of Freeman and Simmons (1963) and Angrist et al. (1968) in the effects of family role performance expectations on post-release adjustment, measures of expected employment-household role performance, instrumental task performance, and social role performance were constructed. None of these were significantly related to time until rehospitalization (see Table 1). This is further indication that family role performance expectations are not substantially related to rehospitalization rates.

The relationships between time until rehospitalization and the family tolerance measures were examined controlling for each of the other possibly confounding variables one at a time. As shown in Table 4, this analysis indicates that family fears of being unable to control their ex-patient remain significantly related to rehospitalization even when any of the test variables or variables not included in Table 4, such as number of prior hospitalizations, are statistically controlled. These test variables, however, are not significantly related to rehospitalization after controlling for the family fears variable.

Family fears of being unable to control their ex-patient's behavior are significantly correlated with the patient's prior psychiatric symptomatology. Yet the family fears of being unable to control their ex-patient's behavior remain significantly correlated with rehospitalization, controlling for the patient's prior symptomatology or any other prehospitaliza-

Table 4

Time Until Rehospitalization and Family Fears
of Not Being Able to Control Patients[a]

Test variables[b]	Correlation of test variables with family fears of uncontrollability (zero-order correlation)	Correlations of time until rehospitalization and each test variable controlled by family fears of not being able to control patient	Correlation of time until rehospitalization and family fears of not being able to control patient controlled by each test variable
Family Expectations and Attitudes			
It will be like having a 10-year-old child around.	-.54*	-.25	-.35*
Expected psychiatric symptoms.	.45*	-.15	-.42*
Family members do not like patient.	-.48	-.20	-.40*
No family member wants patient to return home.	-.60*	-.08	-.39*
Prior 1969-Hospitalization Behavior			
Psychiatric symptomatology (family rating)	.41*	-.06	-.46*

a $N = 31$; * $p < .05$

b All variables which are significantly related to family fear of not being able to control patient and time of rehospitalization with one exception. Family fears patient is not included because it is conceptually redundant and correlated with family fears of patient uncontrollability with $r = .85$.

tion behaviors, including specific measures of alcohol consumption and destructive, assaultive, and suicidal behaviors (see Table 4). Thus, the single best predictor of earlier rehospitalization in our data is the presence of fears on the part of the patient's family that they will not be able to control his behavior when he comes home.

Correlates of family fears of being unable to control the patient were further examined as a means of identifying the possible source of some of these fears. These family expectations of being unable to control their patient's behavior were significantly correlated ($r = .44$) with reported past attempts by the patient to "hit or hurt" someone but were not significantly correlated with prior suicide attempts ($r = -.02$). As shown in Table 3, early rehospitalization itself was not significantly correlated with prior attempts of the patient to "hit or hurt" someone ($r = -.06$) or with past suicide attempts ($r = -.05$). This suggests that our understanding of this finding must go beyond fears of physical harm.

Another source of these family fears appeared to be the bizarre and difficult to interpret behaviors of patients, such as the patient talking to himself, appearing nervous, and thinking that other people are talking about him. These latter three symptoms were correlated with family expectations that the patient might hurt himself or others (r's, respectively, .54, .41, and .61) and with family fears of not being able to control the patient on his return home (r's, respectively, .36, .33, and .46). Also these two family fears variables were correlated .61 and .45, respectively, with the pre-1969 hospitalization symptom index. With one exception, no other psychiatrist or family psychiatric status measure was related significantly to either family fears variable; a psychotic diagnosis was significantly more common ($r = .37$) among patients whose families feared the patient might hurt himself or others upon return home. (The reader will recall that none of these psychiatric status variables, either from before or during the 1969 study hospitalization, are significantly related to early rehospitalization.) Thus, family fears may be generated out of a variety of experiences with psychiatric symptomatology.

Examination of specific cases suggests that family fears occur in a wide variety of situations often having more to do with the family than the patient. For example, one family might be quite afraid following their patient's initial incoherent episodes, while another family who had experienced their patient's assaultive behavior over some years would be less apprehensive, possibly because they had learned to deal with it. Families, for a variety of reasons, appear to be differentially tolerant of their patient's symptomatic or other behavior.

The following two cases are of family members who have substantial apprehension of how events will go upon the patient's return home, in the absence of past assaultive, destructive, or suicidal attempts by the patient.

Patient A. This 28-year-old white male had been hospitalized three times with a diagnosis of schizophrenia before his 1969 study hospitalization. At that time he had bizarre delusions, active hallucinations, and talked incoherently about his life. His deceased mother, and his father, who had been an Ivy League educated corporate lawyer, left him a substantial trust fund income. He lived with his younger brother, who was a student in a local university. His brother described his typical symptoms as appearing in a daze, staying by himself, and "living in his own world" with little understanding of what was going on around him. He had never been destructive, assaultive, or suicidal, yet his brother indicated being afraid they couldn't control his behavior following release. During his hospitalization of several weeks, he appeared considerably improved and stabilized. He was rehospitalized forty-three days following his release.

Patient B. This 40-year-old black patient was hospitalized for the first time with a diagnosis of transient situational reaction following a permanent disabling brain hemorrhage suffered by her husband which left her alone to raise six children. She had been increasingly worried, depressed, argumentative, forgetful, and confused, although she had never been destructive, assaultive, or suicidal and none of her family expected any of these behaviors in the future. Her 21-year-old married daughter had initiated the hospitalization to get her mother help and was visiting her regularly. The daughter was caring for the children during the hospitalization and wanted the mother and her children to come live with her following discharge. Yet the daughter was overtly fearful that she would not be able to control the patient's behavior following her release. The patient was hospitalized slightly over three weeks and was rehospitalized twenty-seven days after her discharge.

These are examples of cases in which family fears, which we find so consistently related to rehospitalization, appear not to be related to overtly dangerous patient behavior but rather to an apprehensiveness surrounding the uncertainty or unfamiliarity with which family members experience serious psychiatric symptomatology. These case descriptions lend strength to the interpretation of the quantitative data as supporting the family symptom tolerance hypothesis.

Number of Readmissions

The average respondent was initially discharged 3.6 years before the follow-up and reported 1.93 readmissions during this period. Eleven patients were never rehospitalized, ten were rehospitalized once, three were rehospitalized twice, and six were rehospitalized three or more times. These latter six were rehospitalized an average of seven times each and are most clearly "revolving door" patients. The family symptom tolerance hypothesis is investigated here as an explanation for this variation in number of readmissions.

As shown in Table 1, number of rehospitalizations is not significantly correlated with either of our family tolerance indicators, i.e., family fears that the patient will harm someone ($r = .31$) or family fears of being unable to control the patient's behavior ($r = .28$). While these correlations are not trivial in magnitude and would be significant were the sample size somewhat larger, these correlations are decidedly smaller than the correlations of several other variables with number of readmissions. Also correlations between family tolerance indicators and number of rehospitalizations are substantially reduced when statistical controls are applied for other variables discussed below. Family tolerance as measured here is not a strong predictor of number of readmissions.

A variety of other factors were therefore investigated as possible predictors of number of rehospitalizations. No sociodemographic characteristics are significantly correlated with number of readmissions. As shown in Table 3, no psychiatric factors were strong predictors of number of readmissions. The more frequently rehospitalized patients tend to have experienced more prior hospitalizations, and as might be expected, tend to be rated as more impaired psychiatrically during their hospitalization and to have exhibited more symptoms prior to their 1969 study hospitalization. However, none of these relationships were statistically significant at the .05 level.

As shown in Table 1, family expectations or attitudes significantly related to number of readmissions include: having the patient home would be like having a ten-year-old child around, the patient would create a financial burden for the family, the family members do not like the patient. However, nonparametric statistics did not reveal the expectation that the patient would create a financial burden was significantly or even strongly related to number of readmissions, and thus its importance must be discounted.

When higher levels of psychiatric symptomatology, as measured by the symptom index, are expected by the family, significantly greater numbers of subsequent readmissions occur (see Table 1). Family expectations of three individual symptoms included in the symptom index are significantly related to number of admissions: ex-patient will appear in a daze ($r = .47$), ex-patient will attempt suicide ($r = .57$), and ex-patient will drink too much alcoholic beverages ($r = .50$). Reports that prior to the 1969 study hospitalization the patient appeared in a daze and drank too much alchoholic beverages are also significantly related to number of rehospitalizations (correlations are .42 and .43, respectively). As indicated in Table 3, the index of prior symptomatology is not significantly related to number of rehospitalizations. The expectations of symptoms are related more strongly to number of rehospitalizations than are reports of past symptoms. Past symptoms, with the exceptions noted above, are not generally related to number of rehospitalizations.

Although the expected social role performance measure is not significantly associated with number of subsequent hospitalizations, two single item indicators in this area are: the expected number of close friends the ex-patient will have ($r = -.35$) and the expected time before the patient will go visit friends ($r = .38$). Therefore, expected friendship ties appear related to frequency of rehospitalizations.

Because these expectation variables are often highly intercorrelated, all become insignificantly related to number of rehospitalizations, controlling for one or more of these other expectation variables. This suggests that they are best seen as a complex of family expectation factors related to number of rehospitalizations. Patients readmitted more often tend to have families with negative attitudes toward them, and are expected to have few friends outside the family, be like having a child around the house, and to exhibit certain severe psychiatric symptoms. This suggests that frequently readmitted patients have families who expect them to be dependent and at the same time do not like the patient.

Careful examination of individual cases was undertaken to help understand these findings. This analysis suggests that those patients with multiple readmissions tend to have one of two distinct types of relationships with their families. We will call them ambivalent-inconsistent and ineffective-rejecting. The basic dislike or rejection of the patient is central to both types, although the process is very different.

The ambivalent-inconsistent type consists of families who have negative and rejecting feelings about patients, but have countervailing feelings, such as guilt, loneliness, fear, or family obligation, which keep them from simply disowning their patient. Case C is an example of ambivalence in a family.

Case C. This patient was a 22-year-old white male hospitalized for the first time with a diagnosis of drug-induced psychosis due to marijuana use. He was a recent college graduate with increasing fears of being drafted into the Army. He had been living with his mother, a 53-year-old divorced high school teacher with a graduate degree. They lived comfortably in a fashionable residential area and had close ties to a Protestant church. The patient had increasingly secluded himself in his bedroom, expressing bizarre thoughts when he emerged for occasional meals. His mother had arranged for him to see a psychiatrist on an outpatient basis. Later he felt witches were in his aunt's car so he broke the windows to get them out; shortly thereafter the police found him on a cold night running nude in a park and initiated his first hospitalization. His mother was very ashamed, especially that their pastor came to know of the hospitalization, and she felt that the hospitalization was such a disgrace that the patient ought to turn in his Eagle Scout medal. She blamed herself, tracing the cause back to her divorce. She was sometimes lonely without him, having recently lost her elderly mother, her only other close relative. However, she did not miss him too much, recognizing that he sometimes caused her trouble, blamed her for things, and was generally critical of her. Before he was initially hospitalized, she thought of sending him to school in a distant state. She did not see any other place he might go live after his release. This patient was rehospitalized four times during the follow-up period.

In this case, the patient's mother was inconsistent as well as ambivalent toward the patient. At times, as when the patient was most symptomatic at home, she wanted to get him out of the house. When he was in the hospital and the immediate pressures of life with him were removed, her loneliness and guilt led her to want him back home again. In this way, the ambivalence plus the inconsistency may be seen leading to multiple admissions resembling the revolving door pattern.

The next case represents an inconsistent-ambivalent *situation* where certain persons in a patient's life reject and are likely to initiate hospitalization while others are much more tolerant. In this case, the patient's mother had ample tolerance but police, shopkeepers, and other family members had previously initiated hospitalization.

Case D. This 31-year-old white male patient lived alone with his mother, a 56-year-old working-class widow. He had been psychiatrically hospitalized three times before with a schizophrenic diagnosis. Before his last hospitalization, he began to seclude himself more and to stay up all night in the kitchen preaching and talking weirdly. He went to make a purchase in a bakery and ended up slapping the baker. The police were called and initiated his hospitalization. His mother was outspokenly lonely at his being away, but recognized that the hospitalization would "do him good." Although she did not expect him to do anything either outside the house or within it when he was home, except "lay around," she loved him dearly and wanted him home where she could be sure he was well fed and taken care of. She felt there was no other possible place her son could go live. The other members of her family did not like the patient and would have nothing to do with him. This patient was rehospitalized sixteen times during the follow-up period.

The ineffective-rejecting type, like the inconsistent-ambivalent type, is also characterized by negative feelings on the part of the family toward the patient. Cases E and F represent this pattern.

Case E. This is a 43-year-old black male hospitalized with a schizophrenic diagnosis. He had been living with his 74-year-old widowed mother, a retired waitress. She feared him immensely, having been beaten by him hard enough several months previously to require an eight-day hospitalization. The patient had also beaten his sister and had set fire to his mattress more than once. The family wanted him "put away permanently" but had learned from experience with jails and mental hospitals that he would before long be back at their doorstep. His mother had her house locks changed to keep him out, although she really expected him to show up and move in, with her being unable to stop it. The only way they knew to handle the patient was to call the police from pay-phones down the street so as not anger him. They would do so when he did something especially frightening, and the police, who knew the patient to be mentally ill, would proceed to have him committed to the state hospital. This patient was rehospitalized seven times during the follow-up period.

Case F. This 26-year-old black male only marginally lived with his parents and three younger siblings. He generally would "bum off" friends or sleep in the park. Occasionally he would sleep on the floor at his parents and would daily come and ask his mother for a meal, which she would give him if he would go before his father came home from his work as a barber. His parents adamantly did not like him or want him around. His teen-age brother had driven him from the house with a baseball bat on occasion. The family felt in no physical danger, for the patient had never made any threats or done anyone harm, but they did feel he had stolen small things from the house. The patient generally appeared very nervous, felt life was hopeless, stayed by himself for long periods, talked without making sense, talked to himself, and drank too much, but was not suicidal. On his previous six psychiatric hospitalizations he had a schizophrenic diagnosis. He had previously been apprehended by the police and had been committed and jailed for stealing, drunkenness, and indecent exposure. He had also sought psychiatric admission himself, and had been refused once by a local emergency room physician who thought he simply wanted "to go there for a free meal." His older sister and her husband initiated the study hospitalization a few days before his mother went on an out-of-town trip because they feared "he would have no place to go and nothing to eat for a week." His mother had unsuccessfully worked with the local family service agency to get him "indefinitely committed," which the family felt was the proper solution. This patient was rehospitalized five times during the follow-up period.

In each of these cases, the family or community would like to but is unable to rid itself completely of its disruptive member. They each put up with the patient in their own way, resorting to the psychiatric hospital to cope with what they perceive as unmanageable situations.

These case descriptions suggest multiple rehospitalizations may be the result of a family-patient relationship characterized by both a feeling on the part of the family that the patient is dependent on them and a dislike of the patient by the family. Neither negative attitude nor perception of the patient's dependency may itself be sufficient to produce multiple rehospitalizations. The quantitative data were reinspected for evidence of such a pattern. In Table 5, the relationship between numbers of hospitalizations and two relevant variables, i.e., whether the family liked the patient

Table 5

Family Attitudes and Number of Rehospitalizations

Number of rehospitalizations	Family Attitudes[a] Patient like a child[b] and family dislikes patient[c]			
	Neither attitude present	Patient like a child only	Family dislikes patient only	Both attitudes present
0	69 (9)	0	0	25 (2)
1	23 (3)	100 (3)	50 (1)	0
2	8 (1)	0	50 (1)	0
3 or more	0	0	0	75 (6)
	100%	100%	100%	100%

[a] Five cases are missing data on one of these variables. Column percents given with non-zero N's in parenthesis.

[b] Considered present if family answered 1 or 2, on a five-point scale where one equals strong agreement, that they expected having the patient home would be like having a 10-year-old child around.

[c] Considered present if family answered 3, 4, or 5 on a five-point scale, where five indicated strong disagreement, that they like the patient.

and whether they expected his being home would be like having a 10-year-old child around, are presented. Where the family both disliked the patient and expected having him home would be like having a 10-year-old child around, 75 percent of the cases had three or more rehospitalizations. In no case where only one of these conditions was met were three or more rehospitalizations experienced. These quantitative data tend, therefore, to support hypotheses generated from inspection of individual cases.

The data presented here show that certain family expectations and attitudes may be useful predictors of the frequency of rehospitalization during a specified follow-up period. The particular constellation of family expectations and attitudes suggests more rehospitalizations would occur among patients whose families did not like them, thought they would be like having a 10-year-old child around the home, lack friends outside the home, and exhibit certain generally more severe psychiatric symptoms. This pattern suggested that patients with numerous readmissions, "revolving door" patients, might more likely have an unstable hostile-dependent relationship with their families. Inspection of particular cases suggested two types of such relationships, which we tentatively named ambivalent-inconsistent and ineffective-rejecting.

Multiple Readmissions and Early Rehospitalization

The correlates of time until rehospitalization and number of rehospitalizations are different in this study, suggesting that those patients readmitted early may be substantially distinct from those rehospitalized often. As noted previously, time until rehospitalization is correlated with number of rehospitalizations with $r = -.57$, indicating that those patients rehospitalized more often tend also to be rehospitalized earlier. This relationship reflects in large part the fact that those patients never rehospitalized were by definition not rehospitalized early.

The data were inspected, eliminating this artifact, to assess to what extent those patients rehospitalized early were indeed different from those rehospitalized often. Eleven patients were rehospitalized within one year of their release, but four of these had only that one readmission during the follow-up period. Of those patients having three or more rehospitalizations during the follow-up period, all six were rehospitalized the first time within six months of their release. Thus, not all patients readmitted early experienced multiple readmissions, but those readmitted multiple times all were readmitted relatively soon after release.

As the correlational data suggest, these groups differ strikingly on whether their family says they like the patient or not. Of those rehospitalized within one year of release, those four patients rehospitalized only once averaged 1.5 on a five-point scale where a score of one indicated the family "definitely liked" the patient and a score of 5 indicated the family definitely did not like the patient. Those six patients rehospitalized three or more times averaged 4.3 on this same scale. (This difference is statistically significant with $p < .01$ using the Mann-Whitney test.) The difference between those rehospitalized many times and those rehospitalized only once was that the multiple readmission group had families who expressed dislike for them.

DISCUSSION

The major finding of this study is that family symptom tolerance as measured here is related to earlier rehospitalization. Follow-up studies such as those by Freeman and Simmons (1963) explored a different tolerance hypothesis with negative results. I believe many researchers became disillusioned with the concept of tolerance and looked elsewhere to understand recidivism. The results of this research convince me that many researchers may have given up on tolerance hypotheses too soon and that there is much important and fruitful work to be done on family tolerance and other family expectations and processes as these relate to psychiatric rehospitalization.

Family fears of what the patient would do to himself and others upon returning home and feelings that the family could not control the patient upon his return were found to be critical factors in early rehospitalization. An analysis of individual cases along with the other quantitative data helped confirm our interpretation of these findings. These family fears are seen as expressions of family intolerance for aberrant behavior.

The level of tolerance of any family was seen as linked to family resources, structure, attitudes, and experience with their patient's illness. The small sample size in this study prohibited an adequate assessment of those variables most closely related to family symptom tolerance. Spouses of patients, it is speculated, experience less fear of controlling the ex-patient and thus do not as readily rehospitalize them, with the result that married patients tend to have longer community tenure. Family members who work or otherwise spend considerable periods away from the patient may be more shielded from their ex-patient's anxiety-provoking behavior. Such family members may also have more sources of support and gratification themselves outside of their relationship with the ex-patient and thus be better able to tolerate him (cf. Vaughn and Leff, 1976). These and other hypotheses may best be investigated in future studies.

An alternative explanation which is admittedly simpler was explored and rejected, i.e., rehospitalization occurs because of assaultive, destructive, or suicidal behaviors which families realistically fear. As we reported above, neither past evidence of these behaviors nor post-release reports of such behavior were significantly or even substantially related to rehospitalization experiences. Thus, other data and individual cases were explored in route to the explanation proposed. Psychotic-like behavior seems an even more common source of family uneasiness than overtly dangerous behavior; some families can and some families cannot tolerate their anxiety and fear generated by the patient's expected or exhibited "crazy" behavior, such as talking to oneself, prolonged self-imposed isolation, seeing visions, paranoid thoughts, dazed expressions, muteness, compulsive ritual behavior, and even extreme anxiety. Rehospitalization is seen as most commonly occurring when the limits of this family tolerance are exceeded.

This explanation undeniably implies that rehospitalization occurs when behavior we would call symptomatic appears and that rehospitalization would be generally more common the more symptomatic the behavior.

Even more so it suggests that families who hospitalize a member would report symptoms and experience these symptoms, from their point of reference, as severe. This, of course, would account for why rehospitalization is usually attributed by families to symptomatic behavior. Yet as other families who do not rehospitalize their member may be experiencing similar levels of symptomatic behavior, the variation in rehospitalization behaviors may be more appropriately attributed to differences in family tolerance for bizarre behaviors.

The tolerance hypothesis explored by Freeman and Simmons, it will be recalled, was not supported by their research or this study. They argued that family expectations reflect levels of tolerance for performance of instrumental and social roles; rehospitalization was expected to occur when ex-patients failed to meet family performance expectations. The family symptom tolerance hypothesis suggested here is in some ways simpler and fits well with available data from this and other studies.

Successful programs to prevent psychiatric hospitalization can be interpreted in ways supportive of this symptom tolerance hypothesis. Both the research programs by Stein et al. (1975) and the earlier work by Pasamanick et al. (1967) were structured such that a random portion of patients judged as appropriate to be admitted to psychiatric hospitals were ushered back into the community. As Mechanic (1968) observes with regard to the Pasamanick study, this must have been a strong message to families that their member's behaviors were not serious or severe enough to warrant hospitalization. The communication was: A person like this does not need to be hospitalized. Family members may have learned that using the hospital to cope with their patient's behavior was not effective and that other means of coping were going to have to be tried. Family members may also have felt, given their experience, that they were being too intolerant of their patient. This may have been consistently reinforced as psychiatric professionals in both studies repeatedly saw their patient and consistently informed the family that the patient did not need to be hospitalized. Thus, these programs may have had success in part because they taught families new and more lenient standards of tolerance for their patient's behaviors.

Multiple readmissions were not substantially associated with low family symptom tolerance as measured here. This suggests that it is misleading to investigate early rehospitalizations, as is done in the common success vs. failure study, and interpret the resultant findings as useful in understanding "revolving door" patient careers.

Why are family fears of not being able to control their patients' behavior strongly related to early rehospitalization but not to multiple rehospitalizations? Probably because these family fears are not stable over time. These fears may reasonably be thought to vary by the length of family experience of their patients' symptoms, variation in patient behaviors, family contact with mental health professionals, and changes in family situations and attitudes. Family members may expect more severe and bizarre behavior from their patient than is exhibited, thus reducing their fears and associated anxieties. Families may be more anxious in expectation of their patient's symptomatic behavior than they are when the behavior is eventually exhibited. Thus, for a number of reasons, family fears may vary markedly over the course of a patient's career.

A key question for psychiatric professionals is certainly how repeated hospitalizations are generated. One possibility is that negative family attitudes toward patients may be pathogenic. Alteration of these family attitudes may be beneficial. Certainly psychiatric professionals often try to make families more accepting of their patient on return. Yet actual exposure of strong negative feelings by families is rare in my experience, in part because inpatient professionals find it more comfortable to assume the family has a basic positive attitude toward the patient and means well. Families with negative feelings contribute by presenting a positive socially acceptable picture of themselves at most times or, in the case of strong negative attitudes toward the patient, families simply easily avoid the half-hearted attempts of the average state hospital staff to involve the family (Greenley, 1970). Thus, much less may be done to confront these negative attitudes than could be.

Leff (1976) reviews several longitudinal studies showing that hostile family attitudes toward patients are key factors in rehospitalization. Hostile family attitudes plus a high emotional involvement of the family with the patient were more commonly present in families of rehospitalized patients (Brown et al., 1972; Vaughn and Leff, 1976). Freeman and Simmons (1963) and Angrist et al. (1968) may have ignored the importance of hostile family attitudes because they found large proportions of their patients' families willing to take the patient back into the home. It is probable, however, that negative family attitudes and willingness to take the patient back into the home are not mutually exclusive. In fact, the presence of both may be necessary for the hospitalization-release-rehospitalization cycle to repeat itself.

In addition to negative family attitudes toward the patient, patients with multiple rehospitalizations were significantly more likely to have families who expected having them around would be like having a 10-year-old child in the home. These families also expected frequently rehospitalized patients to have few friends outside the family and to exhibit certain symptoms more frequently. We interpret this as a family expectation that the patient would be highly dependent on them. This expectation of dependency coupled with hostility is seen as the key to understanding multiple readmissions.

These quantitative data were consistent with our analysis of individual cases which suggested that revolving door patients had certain hostile-dependent relationships with their families. Two types were outlined and suggested for possible future study: ambivalent-inconsistent and ineffective-rejecting. To the extent that these family-patient relationships bring about the admission-release-readmission cycle, intervening in them may be a useful strategy. Stein and his colleagues have in fact conceptualized certain multiple-admission patient careers as being due to such pathologically dependent relationships (Stein et al., 1975). In their highly regarded programs designed to keep patients out of the hospital, one unique intervention is to break this dependency relationship by physically separating the patient and family (finding the patient a place outside the home to live) and minimizing family-patient contact. In addition, they provide substantial support and teaching of coping skills to the patient to help the patient get along in the community without the family. While separating patient from family may seem a strong and even offensive intervention to some, the data they have collected suggest it is effective. Dr. Stein and his colleagues tend to describe their program and its success predominantly in terms of the professional support and coping skills aspects of their anti-institutional programs. Our data suggest that breaking a family-patient interaction pattern may be at least as critical an intervention.

Strengths and Limitations of the Research

The small sample size in this study makes it impossible using a multivariate analysis to examine simultaneously a broad range of variables as these are related to post-release outcomes. The analysis is limited to zero- and first-order partial correlations. Similar to most other follow-up studies, we must be cautious in generalizing from this study due to the unique characteristics of our sample: New England state mental hospital patients, hospitalized for at least three weeks, who had identifiable relatives. Also, unlike samples studied by Freeman and Simmons (1963) and Pasamanick et al. (1967), our sample included nonpsychotics

A series of similarities in the samples and observed relationships between this study and other follow-up studies help reassure us that this research is not simply a description of an aberrant sample exhibiting unusual processes. In a one-year period, 39 percent of our sample were rehospitalized. Rehospitalization data from other studies conducted at about the same time show that our study sample is not unusual in this regard (Weinstein et al., 1973; Lamb and Goertzel, 1971), although differences may be expected due to varied patient populations, treatment systems, and years in which studies were conducted (see also Myers and Bean, 1968; Heckel et al., 1973; Freeman and Simmons, 1963).

Like most, but not all, previous studies, sociodemographic variables were not useful predictors of rehospitalization in this research (Freeman and Simmons, 1963; Michaux et al., 1969; Pasamanick et al., 1967). Many other variables in this study are related to rehospitalization in a manner similar to that reported in other studies. For instance, only one psychiatric factor, number of previous psychiatric hospitalizations, approaches statistical significance in its relationship to rehospitalization. In a review of 118 studies of rehospitalization, Rosenblatt and Mayer (1974:697) conclude "only one variable . . . consistently predicted to rehospitalization of mental patients: the number of previous admissions" (see also Ellsworth et al., 1968).

Compared to previous samples, family members in this sample were more likely to express negative and rejecting feelings toward the patient. In this study, 40 percent of informants and other family members definitely did not want the patient to return to live in their household; Freeman and Simmons (1963:89) report only 5 percent of their family sample was similarly oriented (see also Clausen and Yarrow, 1955). As negative feelings toward the patient must be difficult for many family members to express, the form of a particular question, how it is asked, and whether the patient is living with the family when it is asked, may have substantial impact on the feelings revealed. It may be as likely that the more negative family attitudes expressed in this study were due to methodological differences in the research as substantive differences in the samples.

SUMMARY

Different correlates were found for two types of rehospitalization experiences: early rehospitalization and multiple rehospitalizations. Early rehospitalization was significantly correlated with low family symptom tolerance as measured by family fears that they could not control the patient's behavior upon return home. Indicators of family symptom tolerance were not useful predictors of multiple rehospitalization. Repeatedly readmitted patients were more likely to have families who reported they did not like the patient. This finding, in conjuction with other data, suggests these "revolving door" patients have some form of hostile-dependent relationship with their families. These findings suggest that further research may fruitfully examine family attitudes and expectations as factors related to postrelease treatment experiences of psychiatric patients.

FOOTNOTES

* This research was supported in part by the Graduate School Research Fund of the University of Wisconsin. The author wishes to thank David Mechanic, Leonard Stein, Charles Kleymeyer, and Philip Leaf for helpful comments on earlier drafts of this paper.

1. Using this latter view, Freeman and Simmons (1963:134–135) asked families if they would contact the hospital if their patient behaved in a variety of symptomatic ways. Rehospitalization was not related to whether or not the family member said they would or would not contact the hospital.

2. The variables described in this paragraph and presented in Table 3 were based on interviews with psychiatrists and family members plus hospital records gathered at the time ,of the initial 1969 study hospitalization. Psychiatric hospital records were used to obtain diagnosis at time of discharge and number of prior psychiatric hospitalizations which took place in any facility. Psychiatrists were interviewed while the patient was in the hospital and asked, "How psychiatrically impaired is this patient now?" The psychiatrist's response on a 6-point scale from "very seriously impaired" to "no visible impairment" is used as a measure of psychiatric impairment. As a measure of prognosis, the patient's psychiatrist was asked, "What is his (her) prognosis?" and was given a four-category response continuum from "very good" to "poor." Chronicity was measured by asking the patient's psychiatrist, "Patients are often described as chronic cases, acute cases, or somewhere in between. How chronic do you think this patient's psychiatric problems are?" Five response categories were given, ranging from "definitely chronic" to "definitely not chronic." Finally, psychiatrists were asked whether the patient would be a harm to himself or others if released and were given five ordered response categories from "definitely harmful' to "definitely not harmful." Families were also asked about the degree to which their patient was "sick" before the study hospitalization and presently (after approximately three weeks of hospitalization), and six ordered response categories were supplied for each of these questions.

Family members were asked at the initial interview, on a 5-point scale from "very frequently" to "never," how often their patient had exhibited any one of twenty-one symptoms prior to his hospitalization. Ordered response categories were numbered and added into an index with Cronbach's Alpha = .74. In addition to the index, individual symptom items were used in the analysis. This measure is thus a measure of symptoms as observed and reported by a family member. Studies of the reliability and validity of this type of family rating of ex-patient behaviors and symptoms indicate they can be as adequate and useful as ratings made by mental health professionals (cf. Ellsworth et al., 1968:19–20). Items in this scale include "talks without making sense," "appears nervous," "hears voices," and "tries to commit suicide." A few items may be confounded with instrumental role performance, e.g., "cannot dress or take care of himself," or with social role performance, e.g., "stays by himself" and "gets in arguments with neighbors." Nevertheless, because of the previous work done on this scale and for comparability with other data, we chose to use the same items as Freeman and Simmons (1963) did.

3. Variables discussed in this and the subsequent paragraph are described here. Family

expectations were measured in several areas using a series of questions concerning what the family expected would happen when the patient returned home. The questions concerning posthospital behaviors of their patient/member were asked of family members while the patient was in the hospital. The items were adopted from those used by Freeman and Simmons (1963:252–253) and Myers and Bean (1968:175ff). Family members were asked to respond whether or not (or to what degree) they thought certain things would happen. Additive indices were constructed from these responses and each is described here by its name, number of items, content of items, and Cronbach's Alpha.

Expect problems with friends of family: five items concerning whether the family expected that when the patient returned home, friends of the family would be bothered by him, it would be more difficult to be with close friends, the family would get together with friends less often, the family would go out with friends less often, and entertaining at home would be more tense and embarrassing. Alpha = .77.

Expect problems of family members in organizational activities: two items concerning the expectation of family members that they would have difficulties attending meetings of organizations or religous services. Alpha = .78.

Expect family friction: four items concerning expected tenseness, fights and quarrels, criticizing and nagging, and a generally less easy-going and pleasant home life. Alpha = .81.

Expected family financial burden: three items concerning expected postrelease difficulty of family members working outside the home, general financial burden, and having to give up things for financial reasons. Alpha = .62.

Expected employment-household role performance: Families identified major roles appropriate for their patient following discharge, i.e., work, school, or housework. A score of 3 was given if the family expected after one year that the ex-patient would work "full time," carry a "full load" of school work, or "be doing the housework that other housewives do." A score of 1 was given if no performance was expected, and a score of 2 was given if partial performance was expected. This measure is not an additive index.

Expected instrumental task performance: four items concerning how long after release the expatient would be expected to begin helping with household chores, dressing and taking care of himself, managing the family finances, and helping with the family shopping. Alpha = .65.

Expected social role performance: four items concerning participation in social activities were combined through the addition of standardized scores to achieve equal weighting. The items involved the expected number of the ex-patient's close friends, how often he was expected to get together with friends and relatives, how often he was expected to attend parties and other social functions, and how many organized groups (clubs, lodges, unions, etc.) he was expected to belong to. Alpha = .39.

Expected symptoms: twenty-one items, each representing observable symptomatic behavior (the same twenty-one items used in the measure of pre-1969 hospitalization psychiatric symptoms). Each item was scored by the family as being expected very frequently, frequently, occasionally, rarely, or never; these responses were scored 5 through 1 respectively and summed. Alpha = .83.

Expected family stigma: five items used by Freeman and Simmons (1963:220) concerning experiences families could expect because one of the family was in a mental hospital. These include avoidance of relatives and friends due to shame and embarrassment, loss of co-worker's respect, and avoidance of others when the ex-patient was around. These were each scored on a 5-point scale from agree to disagree and summed. Alpha = .79.

In addition to these indices, four single-item indicators of family expectations or attitudes are used. The exact wording of each item is listed below with an indication of the response categories provided.

Family member expectation regarding life when the patient returns home. "It will be like having a 10-year-old child around." Five response categories from "strongly agree" to "strongly disagree." Adopted from Freeman and Simmons (1963:253).

Family member expectation regarding life when the patient returns home. "There will be more work to do around the house." Five response categories from "strongly agree" to "strongly disagree."

"Do other members of your family like him (her)?" Five response categories from "definitely yes" to "definitely no."

"Do other persons in your home want him (her) to come live with you?" Three response categories from "definitely all do" to "none want him (h·r)."

REFERENCES

Angrist, S., D. Dinitz, and B. Pasamanick (1968), *Women After Treatment; A Study of Former Mental Patients and Their Normal Neighbors.* New York: Appleton-Century-Crofts.

Bogdanow, W. C. (1976), "Predicting Rehospitalization Among Mental Patients" Ph.D. Dissertation, Sociology Department, University of Wisconsin–Madison.

Brown, G. W., J. L. T. Birley, and J. K. Wing (1972), "Influences of family life on the course of schizophrenic disorders: A replication," *British Journal of Psychiatry* 121: 241–258.

Clausen, J. A., and M. R. Yarrow (1955), "Further observations and some implications," *Journal of Social Issues* 11(4): 61–64.

Davis, A. E., S. Dinitz, and B. Pasamanick (1974), *Schizophrenics in the New Custodial Community 5 Years After the Experiment.* Columbus, Ohio: Ohio State University Press.

Dinitz, Simon, Mark Lefton, Shirely Angrist, and Benjamin Pasamanick (1961), "Psychiatric and social attributes as predictors of case outsome in mental hospitalization," *Social Problems* 8 (Spring):322–328.

Ellsworth, Robert B., Leslie Foster, Barry Childers, Gilbert Arthur, and Duane Krocker (1968), "Hospital and community adjustment as perceived by psychiatric patients, there families, and staff," *Journal of Consulting and Clinical Psychology Monograph* 32, 5, Part 2 (October): 1–41.

Freeman, H. E., and O. G. Simmons (1963), *The Mental Patient Comes Home.* New York: Wiley.

Greenley, James R. (1970), "Exit from a Mental Hospital." Unpublished Ph.D. dissertation, Yale University.

——— (1972), "The psychiatric patient's family and length of hospitalization," *Journal of Health and Social Behavior* 13 (March): 25–37.

Heckel, R., C. Perry, and P. Reeves, Jr. (1973), *The Discharged Mental Patient: A 5-Year Statistical Survey*. Columbia South Carolina: University of South Carolina Press.

Lamb, H., and V. Goertzel (1971), "Discharged mental patients—are they really in the community," *Archives of General Psychiatry* 24(1): 29–34.

—— (1972), "The demise of the state hospital—a premature obituary?" *Archives of General Psychiatry* 26(6): 489–495.

Leff, Julian P. (1976), "Shizophrenia and sensitivity to the family environment," *Schizophrenia Bulletin* 2(4): 566–574.

Mechanic, David (1968), *Mental Health and Social Policy*. Englewood Cliffs, New Jersey: Prentice Hall.

Michaux, William W., Martin M. Katz, Albert A. Kurland, and Kathleen H. Gansereit (1969), *The First Year Out: Mental Patients After Hospitalization*. Baltimore: Johns Hopkins Press.

Myers, Jerome K., and Lee L. Bean (1968), *A Decade Later: A Follow-up of Social Class and Mental Illness*. New York: Wiley.

Pasamanick, B., F. Scarpitti, and S. Dinitz (1967), *Schizophrenics in the Community: An Experimental Study in the Prevention of Hospitalization*. New York: Appleton-Century-Crofts.

Rosenblatt, Aaron, and John E. Mayer (1974), "The recidivism of mental patients: A review of past studies," *American Journal of Orthopsychiatry* 44 (October):697–706.

Stein, Leonard I., Mary Ann Test, and Arnold J. Marx (1975), "Alternatives to the hospital—A controlled study," *American Journal of Psychiatry* 132(#5), 517–522.

Vaughn, C. E., and Leff, J. P. (1976), "The influence of family and social factors on the course of psychiatric illness: A comparison of schizophrenia and depressed neurotic patients," *British Journal of Psychiatry* 129: 125–137.

Weinstein, A., D. Dipasquale, and F. Winsor (1973), "Relationships between length of stay in and out of New York State mental hospitals," *American Journal of Psychiatry* 130 (8): 904–909.

ADVANCES IN SPECIAL EDUCATION

Series Editor: Barbara K. Keogh, Special Education Research Program, University of California, Los Angeles.

Volume 1.   Spring 1979   Cloth   Institutions: $25.00
ISBN NUMBER: 0-89232-077-X   Individuals: $12.50

TOPICS COVERED:
Attention, Physiological Substrates, Behavioral Indices, Selective Attention, Cognition, Memory, Language, Motivation, Social Competence, Cross Cultural Psychology, Socialization, Behaviorism, Psychodynamics, Perception, Piagetian Theory.

PARTIAL LIST OF CONTRIBUTORS:
Stephen Porgess, University of Illinois; **Antoinette Krupski**, University of California, Los Angeles, **Daniel Hallahan**, University of Virginia; **Margaret S. Faust**, Scripps College; **William L. Faust**, Pomona College, **Joseph Torgesen**, Florida State University; **Gerald Mahoney**, University of California, Los Angeles **Diane Ruble**, Princeton University; **Norma D. Feshbach**, University of California, Los Angeles, **Douglass Price-Williams**, University of California, Los Angeles; **Ronald Gallimore**, University of California, Los Angeles; **Kenyon S. Chan**, University of California, Los Angeles; **Harry Wachs**, Catholic University; **Hans Furth**, Catholic University, **Donald Macmillan**, University of California, Riverside; **Jules Abrams**, Hahnemann Medical College; **Frank R. Vellutino**, Albany Medical College and State University of New York, Albany; **Melinda Tanzman**, State University of New York, Albany; **Robert V. Kail**, University of Pittsburgh; **Gayle Morrison**, University of California, Riverside.

A 10 percent discount will be granted on all institutional standing orders placed directly with the publisher. Standing orders will be filled automatically upon publication and will continue until cancelled. Please indicate which volume Standing Order is to begin with.

∕∧i   JAI PRESS INC.
P.O. Box 1285
165 West Putnam Avenue
Greenwich, Connecticut 06830

(203) 661-7602   Cable Address: JAIPUBL.

OTHER SERIES OF INTEREST FROM JAI PRESS INC.

Consulting Editor for Sociology: Rita J. Simon, Director, Program in Law and Society, University of Illinois

COMPARATIVE STUDIES IN SOCIOLOGY
Series Editor: Richard F. Tomasson, University of New Mexico

POLITICAL POWER AND SOCIAL THEORY
Series Editor: Maurice Zeitlin, University of California — Los Angeles

RESEARCH IN COMMUNITY AND MENTAL HEALTH
Series Editor: Roberta G. Simmons, University of Minnesota

RESEARCH IN LAW AND SOCIOLOGY
Series Editor: Rita J. Simon, Director, Program in Law and Society, University of Illinois

RESEARCH IN RACE AND ETHNIC RELATIONS
Series Editors: Cora B. Marrett, University of Wisconsin, and Cheryl Leggon, University of Illinois, Chicago Circle

RESEARCH IN SOCIAL MOVEMENTS, CONFLICTS AND CHANGE
Series Editor: Louis Kriesberg, Syracuse University

RESEARCH IN SOCIAL MOVEMENTS, CONFLICTS AND CHANGE
Series Editor: Louis Kriesberg, Syracuse University

RESEARCH IN SOCIAL PROBLEMS AND PUBLIC POLICY
Series Editor: Michael Lewis, University of Massachusetts

RESEARCH IN SOCIAL STRATIFICATION AND MOBILITY
Series Editor: Donald J. Treiman, University of California — Los Angeles

RESEARCH IN SOCIOLOGY OF EDUCATION AND SOCIALIZATION
Series Editor: Alan C. Kerckhoff, Duke University

RESEARCH IN SOCIOLOGY OF KNOWLEDGE, SCIENCES AND ART
Series Editors: Robert Alun Jones, University of Illinois, and Henrika Kuklick, University of Pennsylvania

OTHER SERIES OF INTEREST FROM JAI PRESS INC.

Consulting Editor for Sociology: Rita J. Simon, Director, Program in Law and Society, University of Illinois

RESEARCH IN THE INTERWEAVE OF SOCIAL ROLES: WOMEN AND MEN
Series Editor: Helena Z. Lopata, Center for the Comparative Study of Social Roles, Loyola Unive sity of Chicago

RESEARCH IN THE SOCIOLOGY OF HEALTH CARE
Series Editor: Julius A. Roth, University of California—Davis

RESEARCH IN THE SOCIOLOGY OF WORK
Series Editors: Ida Harper Simpson, Duke University, and Richard Lee Simpson, University of North Carolina, Chapel Hill

STUDIES IN SYMBOLIC INTERACTION
Series Editor: Norman K. Denzin, University of Illinois

ALL VOLUMES IN THESE ANNUAL SERIES ARE AVAILABLE AT INSTITUTIONAL AND INDIVIDUAL SUBSCRIPTION RATES

PLEASE ASK FOR DETAILED BROCHURES ON EACH SERIES

A 10 percent discount will be granted on all institutional standing orders placed directly with the publisher. Standing orders will be filled automatically upon publication and will continue until cancelled. Please indicate which volume Standing Order is to begin with.

◢Ai   JAI PRESS INC.
P.O. Box 1285
165 West Putnam Avenue
Greenwich, Connecticut 06830

(203) 661-7602   Cable Address: JAIPUBL.